THE WEEKEND GARDEN GUIDE

THE WEEKEND GARDEN GUIDE

Work-Saving Ways to a Beautiful Backyard

◆ SUSAN A. ROTH ◆

Photography by the Author

Rodale Press, Emmaus, Pennsylvania

Printed in the United States of America
on acid-free paper ∞

Editor in Chief: William Gottlieb

Senior Managing Editor: Margaret Lydic Balitas

Senior Editor: Barbara W. Ellis

Editor: Ellen Phillips

Copy Editor: Sally Roth

Research Associate: Heidi A. Stonehill

Editorial assistance: Stacy Brobst and Deborah Maher

Cover and interior design: Linda Jacopetti

Illustrations: Elayne Sears

On the Front Cover:
A swing invites gardeners to sit in the shade and enjoy the garden around them. The purple flowers and straplike foliage of Siberian iris (*Iris sibirica*) provide an exciting contrast to the massive, bold-textured clumps of 'Krossa Regal' hosta. Both the iris and hosta require little more than a semi-shady site. Garden Design: Conni Cross.

On the Back Cover:
Top: The weekend garden can be as showy in the autumn as it is in spring and summer. In this border, asters and 'Autumn Joy' sedum provide late-season color. Garden Design: Barbara Damrosch.

Bottom: Wild blue indigo (*Baptisia australis*) is one of the most beautiful low-maintenance perennials, with spikes of blue pealike flowers, blue-green foliage, and decorative charcoal-gray pods.

If you have any questions or comments concerning this book, please write:

Rodale Press
Book Reader Service
33 East Minor Street
Emmaus, PA 18098

**Library of Congress
Cataloging-in-Publication Data**

Roth, Susan A.
The weekend garden guide : work-saving ways to a beautiful backyard / Susan A. Roth.
  p.   cm.
Includes bibliographical references and index.
ISBN 0-87857-933-8 (hardcover)
1. Gardening.   I Title.
SB453.R739   1991
635—dc20   90-9060
                               CIP

**Distributed in the book trade
by St. Martin's Press**

  4 6 8 10 9 7 5   hardcover

This book is dedicated to my husband and weekend gardening partner, Mark Schneider, who's been my helpmate and laborer in most of my gardening endeavors.

Whenever acquaintances ask who's the gardener in the family, Mark inevitably answers, "Susan is the expert. She tells me where to dig the hole and I just dig it!" Even though I am supposedly the expert, my husband jumps into most of my schemes with as much enthusiasm as I—and comes up with a few of his own overly ambitious projects as well. It is Mark who gets planting fever before the snow's left the ground and who hungers after an unusual tree or shrub that has caught his fancy at a nursery or in a catalog. And though he is always accusing me of purchasing plants that I have no garden space for, it was Mark who bought practically every plant of distinction at the Rhododendron Society's plant sale last fall. He filled up our car's backseat with dwarf rhododendrons and then carefully fitted two tremendous royal azaleas (*Rhododendron schlippenbachii*) into the trunk, rigging the lid so it wouldn't chop off their heads. And then it was Mark, of course, who immediately unloaded the car upon getting home and demanded to know where to dig the holes!

I also wish to dedicate this book to my mother, Virginia Austin Roth, and grandmother, Martha Allio Roth (1893–1989), both avid flower gardeners and garden club members. Not only did my mother teach me about flowers, I am certain that I inherited my mother's and grandmother's love of gardening in my genes.

CONTENTS

ACKNOWLEDGMENTS

I wish to thank the following people, without whom this book, its photographs, and its stories would have been exceedingly dry, for their generous offerings and assistance: Jeff and Liz Ball, Keith Barnes, Kathryn Belville, Donna Bickley, Virginia Blakelock, Andrew and Mitsuko Collver, Dick and Pam Dalhaus, Barbara Damrosch, Neil Diboll, Marcia Eames-Sheavley, Louis Edmonds, Joe Elmer, Barbara Emerson, Judy Glattstein, Diann Goldstone, Marjorie Harris, Suzanne Helburn, Carole Johnson, Julie Johnson, Dick Lighty, Ngaere Macray, Michael McConkey, Amy Melenbacher, Nicole Novak, Carole Otteson, Marvin Pritts, Howard Purcell, Claudia and John Scholz, Marla Thomas, Chris Woods, Amy Wright, and Kathy Zar-Peppler. And to the neighbors and other folks I've good-naturedly poked fun at, I would like to beg your forgiveness!

Special thanks go to Conni and Jim Cross for generously opening their garden to me and my camera, and for giving me the opportunity to earn their respect and friendship, an attainment that I do not take lightly.

I wish to thank my father, Rex Roth, for supporting my education and my dreams and ambitions. Much appreciation goes to my stepdaughters, Johanna and Elizabeth Schneider, for their help in weeding and mulching and for their company on many a photography foray. Finally, I wish to thank my remarkable editor, Ellen Phillips, who encouraged me every step of the way, and gave me the courage to continue with what seemed like a monumental task.

Thank you one and all.

INTRODUCTION

Welcome to the Weekend Garden

This book is the fruition of almost 20 years of weekend gardening experience—experience gained from gardening at six different homes, in three different hardiness zones. Twenty years, I might add, of never, ever having the amount of time I'd have liked to spend in the garden. My past and present gardens have had to lend themselves to being tended in whatever time graduate school, followed by a demanding career and weekend stepchildren, allowed. That usually boiled down to several hours on the weekends and ten minutes here and there during the week. My gardens looked beautiful through several major career moves between each garden, and even a change in husbands between gardens number two and three.

Mark, husband number two, is my gardening companion and helpmate, working alongside me in the garden. Working—Mark and I actually call it playing these days because we get so much enjoyment from it—in the garden is one of the best ways to relieve tension brought on by a stressful job and demanding personal life. It is therapeutic and just plain enjoyable to work the soil, grow something delicious or beautiful, and observe the change of the seasons in your garden—as long as you don't dig up more than you can tend. This book ought to help you avoid that pitfall.

Demands of career and family have meant that I am a true weekend gardener in every sense of the expression. I've experienced it all: For several years I lived in an apartment in New York City during the work week and commuted to my home and garden on Long Island each weekend. After that became tiresome, Mark and I purchased a home closer to the city. I gladly gave up my apartment, but spent almost two hours commuting each way between home and office via car, train, subway, foot, and elevator. By the time Mark had fed me after I staggered off the Long Island Railroad each night, darkness had engulfed the garden.

The most I managed from Monday through Friday was a twilight inspection tour, still wearing my heels and business suit. (That's when I realized the beauty and practicality of white and pastel flowers, which linger ghostlike in the last rays of the sun and shimmer on into the moonlight.) If a weekend were rainy or—even worse—necessitated our leaving town to visit relatives, I might not see or tend my garden for two weeks! Still, in four years of weekend gardening we transformed that boring third of an acre into a garden showplace that was a major selling point when it came time to move.

Over the years I've made the inevitable mistakes, and learned enough from them that our latest yard and garden—I think of this as the epitome of our landscaping and gardening endeavors—though extensive, can be cared for with whatever free hours we have on the weekends. Since I no longer commute to the city, but work as an editor and writer from an office in my home, most people think that I while away the hours every day tending this half acre. But I don't. "Working at home," as I found out, didn't translate into less time on the train and more time enjoying home and garden, but simply translated into more hours at the desk and word processor. Admittedly, I often take a lunchtime stroll outside to survey the grounds or cut some herbs or roses, and I may pull a weed or two on the way to and from the mailbox, but our major efforts are still concentrated on Saturday and Sunday mornings from March into November, whenever we can call our time our own.

By choosing easy-care, disease-resistant plants, designing the gardens, lawn, and landscape with a view toward low maintenance, improving the soil before planting, mulching heavily, and using a variety of quality tools and techniques, we've achieved the epitome of a spectacular low-maintenance landscape. Our property contains several rock gardens, two perennial borders, a woodland garden, an ornamental grass garden, a bulb garden, an herb garden, shrub beds, roses, and much more that's difficult to categorize! We've reduced the demanding lawn space to a small-scale design element and replaced weedy patches with expanses of bulbs and groundcovers. Blooms begin in early spring with masses of crocus, scilla, and narcissus, and continue until frost with late-season perennials and flowering shrubs. The gardens involve much less drudgery and a lot more pleasure than anyone can imagine.

I'd like *The Weekend Garden Guide* to be a gift to all those busy and harassed gardeners and homeowners who want to find more pleasure in their yards and gardens, but who have minimal time to spend. The idea behind this book is to share the ways I've discovered to maximize the pleasurable aspects of yard- and garden-tending and minimize the really hard work, while creating something beautiful in the process. This isn't to say that gardening won't sometimes be a lot of work—but for most of us the physical work is part of the pleasure. Creating a weekend garden may involve an investment of time and money in the beginning—but it will pay off in the long run with a reduced amount of work and a healthier, more beautiful landscape. You'll learn to get the most out of your time and property so that you aren't taking on more than you can handle.

Follow the recommendations for low-maintenance plants—groundcovers, shrubs, trees, flowers, vegetables, and fruits—and you'll reduce your garden chores dramatically. You'll grow plants that flourish with little care and won't have to constantly pamper and prune to keep them presentable. And I won't leave you in the lurch by recommending some fantastic-sounding plants that can't be found anywhere—mail-order sources are given for the hundreds of low-maintenance landscape and garden plants described here. To be sure you don't make some regrettable and costly mistakes, lists of plants to avoid appear in pertinent places in the book. These plants might be perennials that demand staking, trees that produce year-long litter, or groundcovers that will invade the lawn and can never be gotten rid of.

Whatever your reasons for being a weekend gardener—whether it is because you commute or work long hours, spend hours taxiing children to and from ballet lessons or Little League, garden at a second home, or simply that the demands of life in the 1990s leave you little time for leisure—I hope this book speaks to you. And most of all, I hope that whatever you put into practice from *The Weekend Garden Guide* will enable you to say that you're spending part of your weekend "playing in the garden" rather than working in it.

THE WORK-SAVING WEEKEND GARDEN

Have Your Garden and Relax in It, Too

The time you spend tending your garden ought to bring pleasure and satisfaction, not provoke anxiety because there just isn't enough time to plant the petunias, tie up the tomatoes, and prune the privet before sunset. If you're racing the clock to complete the necessary gardening tasks, you might as well be gunning it on the freeway to beat the traffic home when it comes to the amount of healthful relaxation you're feeling. When the demands of your garden and the time you have to devote to it aren't in agreement, that spells trouble.

But, despite some claims to the contrary, you *can* have your garden and relax in it too. You needn't be a slave to even a large, extensively planted property if the landscape is carefully designed and planted with a selection of trouble-free plants. When planned—or renovated—with ease of care a primary goal,

a yard and garden can be a knockout while practically taking care of itself. And that's a promise!

Gardening can be work; there's no question about it. But most gardeners find the physical activity of gardening to be a relaxing source of old-fashioned, tension-relieving exercise as long as the tasks aren't overly strenuous or time-consuming. Gardening can be the perfect antidote to civilization in the 1990s! When you plan a low-maintenance garden, you'll have enough weekend left for some old-fashioned relaxation with a book and hammock after the garden work is done. And because a beautiful garden deserves to be admired—especially by its creator—after the garden tending, some garden admiring ought to follow, such as sitting or strolling outside, alone or with friends and family. With a well-planned low-maintenance garden, there'll be time enough to spend some restful hours soaking up its beauty and letting it lift your spirit.

A Tale of Two Gardens

When your time is limited, one additional pressure you can surely do without is to feel like a slave to your yard and garden. How you design the garden spaces, the selection of plants you include in your garden and landscape, and the techniques you use to care for them can make the difference between a garden that practically cares for itself and one that nags at you like a fussy child.

The Wrong Kind of Weekend Gardening

One of my former neighbors used to spend almost every daylight hour each Saturday and Sunday, spring through fall, working in his yard. You might call him a weekend gardener, except that he seemed to derive so little pleasure from his efforts. Bill scowled continually as he watched our comings and goings, peering over his glasses, which had slipped to the tip of his sweaty nose, as he shoved the mower, wielded the hedge shears, or whacked at the edges of the lawn to keep the grass from growing over the curb. The yard looked remarkably neat and tidy but offered nothing special or eye-catching in the way of plantings, and his work never seemed to end. The source of all Bill's misery lay in the design of the landscape and in the choice of plants—it was a high-maintenance landscape.

Bill's front lawn was small, but it was difficult to care for. It sloped steeply to the street—making mowing the grass a precarious adventure—and in the center stood a 25-foot-tall weeping cherry, which was beautiful but made mowing the slope even more tortuous. The cherry's roots broke through the surface of the lawn, forming gnarled lumps that unsettled Bill's mower, and its weeping limbs grew toward the ground, swatting him in the face as he mowed beneath the wide-spreading crown. Several times a year he vowed to cut the tree down, but we and other neighbors prevailed upon him to leave the tree in place. Once when he sounded really serious, I swore I'd tie myself to the tree next time I saw him brandishing the chain saw. So, instead of removing the cherry, Bill gave the tree a crew cut by evenly cutting the graceful dangling branches off at head height—better than cutting it down, the neighbors agreed, but a sadly unattractive solution.

Japanese hollies and cotoneasters lined the front walk that led from the driveway to the porch. Once upon a time they had seemed like cute, innocent, little edging shrubs, but even way back then they were the wrong choice for that location. Their natural tendency was to grow tall, and, despite regular pruning, they had become overgrown and threatened to close off the path. To keep them in bounds, Bill had been cutting the shrubs back with hedge shears; but this common practice actually encourages shrubs to grow larger. The shrubs had long ago lost their individuality and identity as they grew together, their branches intermingling: holly with cotoneaster, cotoneaster with holly. Bill's shearing had eventually transformed them into a loaflike patchwork hedge. Not only did the shrubs look comical, they demanded pruning several times a year to keep them confined to the loaf.

When we bought our house, an unattractive, high-maintenance hedge confined the walkway leading to the porch. I opened up the area by removing the overgrown plants and created an inviting, low-maintenance shade garden of dwarf rhododendrons underplanted with spring-flowering bulbs, maidenhair ferns, and pastel impatiens.

The backyard consisted of a large lawn, bordered in part by a raised stone wall and given privacy from neighbors by a tall hemlock screen on one side and trees and shrubs on the other sides. Several perennial beds, a rose bed, and an apple tree decorated the yard, which also contained a flagstone patio. Since the hemlock screen bordered my yard, I was never quite sure what Bill was doing back there, but he *did* work. Sundrops had taken over the perennial garden, which had become so shaded that little else would grow, and the invasive plant required continual surgery to prevent it from overgrowing the other struggling plants in the garden. Come fall, Bill carted bag after bag of leaves to the road.

A Better Kind of Weekend Gardening

When my husband Mark and I moved in next door to Bill, the front yard of our pie-shaped property consisted of lawn, overgrown foundation evergreens, and a sycamore tree and a bright-pink-flowered crabapple, both with low-hanging branches and gnarled surface roots that menaced the lawn mower— and the lawn mowee. Though our lawn didn't slope, many of our problems were identical to those in Bill's yard.

A brick path led from the driveway to the breezeway and kitchen door. This path was confined by a formally pruned low boxwood hedge. The north side of the house was further cast into darkness by Bill's hemlock screen, and the lawn there was sparse and compacted since a child's swing set had once stood there. The other side yard, with a southerly exposure, was bordered by a privet hedge, and its narrow sloping lawn baked in the sun into weedy ugliness.

The major part of the property was in the back, giving us a large area for creative gardening. It had once been professionally landscaped, but now the shrub borders were crowded and out of shape. An attractive, large bluestone patio began two steps down from the breezeway, but a hedge of ugly, squared-off azaleas hemmed it in, making the space seem cramped and cut off from the rest of the yard. A huge crabapple dominated the side of the lawn, and more overgrown foundation evergreens bordered the back of the house. A mature 'Bloodgood' Japanese maple, a dead mimosa, and assorted shrubbery stood in front of a falling-down fence that surrounded the yard. In the corner of the pie, behind the crabapple, stood a small woods, but underbrush and weeds—and old tin cans and discarded toys—marred its beauty.

We had moved in the dead of winter, so weekend gardening didn't begin in earnest that year until late winter. The first thing we did was transplant that offending azalea hedge to the side of the yard behind the crabapple, an area where nothing was planted. We were amazed that the cramped hedge consisted of 15 separate, rather large—if flat-topped—plants. When we untangled their branches and spaced them out along the fence, they quickly attained a more graceful, natural shape and became a flowering privacy screen that camouflaged the unsightly split-rail fence. And the patio, which was raised a

step above the lawn, seemed more spacious without a rigid border, acting as a viewing platform for the rest of the garden.

However, the patio jutted out alarmingly into the lawn, distracting from the shape and lines of the garden, and since it was raised a foot or so above the ground level, it was also an obstacle to traffic. We fixed that one weekend by installing a curved herb garden along one side. The herb bed transcribed a gentle arc that swung from the corner of the patio to the end of the back wall of the garage. The arc left a narrow but graceful sweep of lawn that directed visitors around the patio and promised an interesting garden just out of sight. Stepping stones through the herb garden also created a visual and practical link from the patio to the lawn and side yard. I bordered the garden with a mowing strip—an edging low enough to accommodate the mower's wheels. I made my mowing strip out of brick to match the trim around the bluestone of the patio.

When we made the herb garden, we stripped the sod off the bed and consigned it to the bottom of our new compost pile. The pile fit nicely into a corner of the yard and was partly hidden by existing shrubbery and the shade of the hemlocks. We planted a few more shrubs to create a curving line from the back of the yard around to the side, completing the necessary screening so the compost was out of view but in a convenient location. This screened space also offered a place to stack firewood and pile brush and shrub trimmings.

The herb garden was so easy to create and so successful that later that summer we dug up three or four times as much lawn in front of the foundation shrubs at the back of the house and planted a perennial border. The perennial garden began at the front

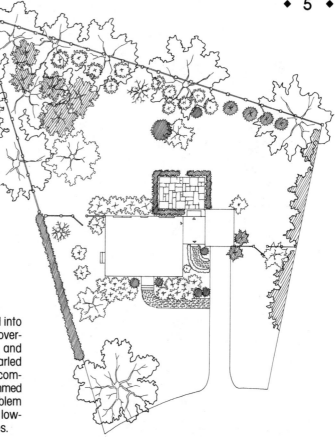

Susan and Mark's Yard Before: When we moved into our house, the front yard consisted of lawn, over-grown foundation evergreens, a sycamore tree, and a crabapple with low-hanging branches and gnarled surface roots. The back and side yards had com-pacted soil, scraggly shrubs, and a lovely patio hemmed in by an azalea hedge. We transformed our problem property into an easy-care yard brimming with low-maintenance flowers, shrubs, herbs, and edibles.

edge of the patio and curved back toward the house, serving to visually anchor the patio and repeat the curve of the herb garden on the other side. I edged the perennial bed with a matching brick mowing strip. The following summer, Mark and I tucked a shorter but much deeper perennial border into the curves of the existing shrub border along the back fence. He was delighted with the changing display of flowers and with having about half the original amount of lawn to mow.

We made mowing much easier in the front under the crabapple by creating a wide bed of pachysandra beneath the tree—an example Bill stubbornly refused to follow. And we eliminated mowing entirely in the sun-baked sloping side yard by turning the whole area over to vegetables and berries. We dealt with the slope by building terraces of raised beds for vegetables, cut flowers, strawberries, and blueberries. A heavy layer of mulch spread around the raised beds covered the paths and required no maintenance.

The little brick path leading from the driveway to the breezeway turned out to be one of my favorite spots in the garden. It had started out as my most hated spot because it felt so dark and cramped. But after ripping out the boxwood hedge, I began to see the possibilities for a dandy shade garden. I planted several 'Windbeam' rhododendrons, which bear pale, translucent pink flowers in early spring, to give the spot more privacy

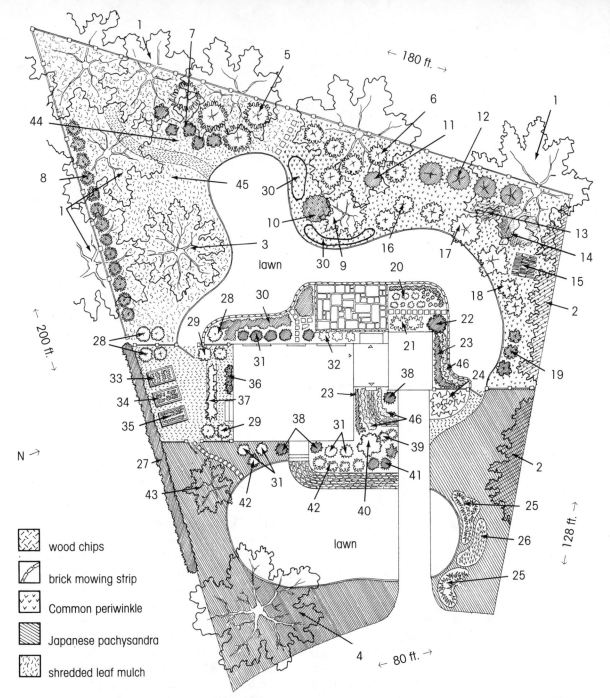

Susan and Mark's Yard after Four Years. (1) existing shade trees, (2) eastern hemlock, (3) Japanese flowering crabapple, (4) sycamore, (5) 'Roseum Elegans' catawba rhododendron, (6) existing azaleas, (7) flame azalea, (8) transplanted azaleas, (9) Japanese maple, (10) mugho pine, (11) common juniper, (12) eastern red cedar, (13) brush pile, (14) compost heap, (15) woodpile, (16) pinxterbloom azalea, (17) linden viburnum, (18) koreanspice viburnum, (19) 'PJM' rhododendron, (20) herb garden, (21) Meyer lilac, (22) flowering quince, (23) ferns,(24) hostas, (25) daylilies and daffodils, (26) Siberian iris, (27) border privet, (28) blueberry, (29) red currant, (30) perennials, (31) Japanese holly, (32) 'Gumpo White' azalea, (33) strawberries, (34) vegetables, (35) cut flowers, (36) tomatoes, (37) raspberries, (38) English yew, (39) 'Windbeam' azalea, (40) mountain laurel, (41) creeping juniper, (42) 'Gumpo Pink' azalea, (43) Sargent crabapple, (44) sweet woodruff, (45) wildflowers and ferns, (46) impatiens and bulbs

Legend:
- wood chips
- brick mowing strip
- Common periwinkle
- Japanese pachysandra
- shredded leaf mulch

N →

← 180 ft. →

← 200 ft. →

← 128 ft. →

← 80 ft. →

from the street. Along the curved walkway itself I created a display of ferns and flowers with textures and colors that delighted me endlessly as I sat close at hand on the breezeway, where we often ate breakfast and dinner. Early spring bulbs began the season and were followed by delicate maidenhair ferns, which I accompanied with mounds of pastel impatiens that brightened the dark corner for months and months.

I echoed this same theme along the side of the garage, extending the brick edging from the herb garden right around the corner and creating a planting border along the garage wall. Here I combined ferns, hostas, and masses of impatiens, fulfilling the promise of something interesting around the bend made by the curve of the back lawn and the stepping stones leading through the herb garden. We renovated the straggly lawn by sowing a shade-tolerant grass mixture.

Our last major project, during the fourth growing season we lived in that house, was to begin planting the wooded corner. My vision was a woodland garden, complete with pretty wildflowers, ferns, groundcover plants, and native American azaleas. We had been gradually weeding the area, cutting out the brambles and saplings, and pulling out the celandine poppies, pretty but weedy wildflowers that seemed to pop up everywhere we looked. We had bagged no leaves since the first year we moved in, but mowed them up into a fine mulch that we spread on the woodland floor.

I'd venture to say that Mark and I were spending about a quarter of the time in the garden that our neighbor Bill was, and we spent the majority of that time installing new garden areas, needing only a short time each week to maintain what we had. Bill spent 90 percent of his time on maintenance

—pruning, mowing, edging, and weeding— and he seemed to derive little pleasure or satisfaction in the process! Bill could have been saved from his yard and garden chores by the advice in this book. I probably should have dedicated it to him, but I hope he at least reads it . . . if he has time.

Evaluating Your Garden's Maintenance Needs

If you want to avoid Bill's fate, you can begin by giving the maintenance needs of your yard and garden a critical examination. Take a stroll around your property and think about how much time you actually spend tending the various areas. Which plants require the most maintenance? Are there areas that please you visually and don't need much care? Are there certain garden features you wouldn't be happy without, even though they require high maintenance? Do you have high-maintenance garden areas that you might happily scale down in size, or improve with a low-maintenance design or gardening technique? Do you hate weeding? Mowing the lawn? Planting out annual and vegetable seedlings each year? Do you grow more tomatoes and squash than you can possibly eat or give away? Later in this book, you'll find solutions to most of the problems you encounter as you think critically about the maintenance requirements of your yard and garden.

The first step is to decide which areas demand the most work—it's okay to define "work" as any garden chore you hate doing.

We each seem to have our own opinions when it comes to that! My husband simply abhors mowing the lawn; in fact, he hates it so much he becomes irritable even thinking about it! But my artist friend Amy Wright proudly announces that she loves mowing her lawn! Amy may enjoy being a bit contrary, but she truly finds the mowing good exercise and enjoys getting out in the sun and fresh air as a break from the drawing board. Some of us find weeding tedious, but my mother derives such satisfaction in hand-pulling weeds that she has been known to venture into the neighbors' gardens when they aren't home to pull the weeds disgracing their flower beds. I've never seen her use a tool for weeding—she likes the hand-to-hand combat.

Take a walk around your property and consider all the garden chores you usually do, or ought to do. List all the time-consuming chores and high-maintenance areas you can think of. Study your list and then put checks next to the areas that you want to keep even if they demand extensive maintenance. Put question marks next to high-maintenance areas that you enjoy looking at but that take too much work; later in the book you will probably discover techniques that will save you time when caring for these areas. Aim to eliminate the garden spots on your list that are left unmarked, and replace them with a low-maintenance solution or a garden that may require maintenance time but will also provide you with more gardening pleasure.

Setting Gardening Goals

Now that you've evaluated the maintenance needs of your property, think about your gardening and landscaping goals—how you'd like to use the gardens in your property. Do

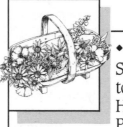

Solutions to Common High-Maintenance Problems

Here are brief solutions to the most common high-maintenance problems posed by home landscapes. These solutions are discussed in more detail later in the book; the index can help you locate the information you need quickly.

Problem: Formal hedges require time-consuming shearing several times a year or they look unsightly.
Solution: Transform formal hedges into informally pruned hedges, which have a natural shape and require much less attention. The makeover may take several years of corrective pruning.

Problem: Large lawn requires too much time to care for.
Solution: Replace some or all of the lawn with a low-growing groundcover, or install a patio or deck.

Problem: Lawn growing on a steep slope is difficult, even dangerous, to mow.
Solution: Landscape the area with groundcovers and groups of shrubs.

Problem: Lawn grows poorly beneath trees and in other shady areas.
Solution: Turn the spot into a decorative shade garden with ferns, groundcovers, wildflowers, and other suitable perennials and shrubs.

Problem: Lawn grass encroaches into flower beds and under shrubbery.
Solution: Install an edging or mowing strip around beds and borders to keep the grass in its proper place.

Problem: Large flower beds of annuals take too much time planting, weeding, and deadheading.
Solution: Plant a border of flowering perennials instead, or choose low-maintenance annuals that require less care and mulch heavily to conserve moisture and keep down weeds.

Problem: Weeds keep growing between bricks or flagstones of walk and patio.
Solution: Remove soil or sand from between the bricks and replace with mortar, or plant an attractive fine-textured groundcover between the bricks to crowd out the weeds.

Problem: Large vegetable garden requires too much work.
Solution: Scale down the size of the garden and plant it closely in beds, which will shade out weeds, rather than rows. Mulch heavily to prevent weeds from invading young vegetable plants.

Problem: Fruit trees require too much pruning and pest control.
Solution: Grow low-maintenance berry bushes instead of high-maintenance fruit trees. Choose fruit plants that require the least pruning or can double as landscape plants.

Problem: Numerous trees and shrubs growing in the lawn make mowing tedious.
Solution: Surround trunks with tree rings or plant a bed of groundcover to surround and visually link the trees and shrubs together into an attractive unit.

Problem: Shrub borders and beds are weedy.
Solution: Lay down a thick layer of organic mulch to prevent weeds from germinating beneath shrubs and to improve the health of the plants.

Problem: Shrubs are too large and are obscuring windows and crowding walkways.
Solution: Drastically prune the shrubs by thinning and cutting back the branches. Follow these measures with proper annual thinning techniques to keep the shrubs in bounds. It may be best to replace overgrown shrubs with shrubs that grow no larger than the place you have for them.

Problem: Trees drop many seedpods that later geminate into annoying weeds.
Solution: Landscape the area beneath problem trees with groundcovers, shrubs, and heavy mulch, which will prevent many seedlings from germinating. Or remove and replace the problem tree with a seedless variety.

Susan and Mark's

High-Maintenance Problems

Two years ago, this was Mark's and my list of high-maintenance areas and problems for our latest home—a neglected, hilly half-acre of partially wooded property.

• Front lawn on slope—difficult to mow ☑

• Strip of weedy lawn between street and white pine privacy screen—difficult access, serves no purpose

• Weedy, thin lawn beneath trees in side yard—too shady for grass, soil compacted

• Back lawn in valley—must carry mower down steps to reach

• Overgrown junipers along driveway—need continual pruning to keep from scratching cars, looks bad ☑

• Unsightly back hillside—full of weeds, needs landscape solution

• Unsightly corner of side yard—full of weedy shrubs, needs landscape solution

• Dogwood trees marred by disease ☑

• Sheared yew hedge between driveway and backyard—too much work, but does provide screening ☐

• Mimosa tree—spreads numerous seedlings, disease-ridden

• Climbing rose—needs winter protection, tying, pruning, insect and disease treatment ☑

• Neighbor's boat and tool shed too obvious

Key:
☑ Indicates areas that need an immediate solution.
☐ Indicates areas that require high maintenance but that you may still want to retain.

you want to garden primarily to grow pesticide-free food for your family? Or are you interested in cultivating flowers? Maybe both? Do you collect certain kinds of plants, or do you want to beautify your home's landscape while increasing its value? You might want a larger patio off the sliding doors in the back for entertaining, or crave a swimming pool for cooling off on beastly summer days. If you're like most gardeners and homeowners, your goals are many and varied. Make another list of your *general* gardening

goals and the landscape problems you wish to correct. Some of these goals will be for personal gardening satisfaction, and others may be necessary to fix eyesores and improve the appearance of your property.

Once you've listed these general gardening and landscaping goals, consider the particular garden and landscape features you'd like to have, such as a formal herb garden, a wildflower garden, a strawberry patch. You don't have to walk around your property to create this list—it can be a sort

Susan and Mark's Landscaping Goals

Two years ago, this was our list of gardening goals for our new home.

- Redo overgrown foundation planting
- Beautify weedy back hillside
- Get rid of lawn in valley in back of property
- Remove overgrown shrubs from rock walls in front of house
- Remove overgrown junipers along driveway
- Get rid of inaccessible, weedy strip of lawn between street and privacy shrub border
- Get rid of thin lawn beneath trees near woods
- Get rid of weedy shrubs under trees along side yard fence
- Beautify front door landing/stoop with container plants
- Beautify kitchen door landing/stoop with container plants
- Create privacy in winter from neighbors at rear of property
- Camouflage the view of the neighbor's tool shed
- Camouflage the view from over the fence of the neighbor's big boat with blue cover

of armchair gardener's list, a wish list, so to speak.

Making Choices

Now that you have your wish list and your list of goals, you can begin some real planning and may have to make some hard decisions. The first task is to decide which solutions and goals are realistic and which are not. This decision making may come easily if you're a gardening team of one, or might be accomplished with more difficulty if, like my husband and me, you're a gardening couple.

What it usually boils down to is that one person plays the dreamer while the other takes the hard line—these roles may alternate from person to person, depending upon who starts the dreaming first. For instance, I frequently stare at the lawn in the valley at the back of our property (which was once an actual stream bed) and conjure up scenes of naturalistic garden settings. I imagine what the site would look like with a black-bottomed swimming pool landscaped to resemble a real pond fed by a babbling brook and planted with ferns and wildflowers.

Whenever I wistfully describe my vision to Mark, he reminds me that there are two kids fast approaching college. Whenever he looks at that same lawn, which he detests mowing, and starts imagining a Japanese garden with cloud-pruned pines and a dry stream bed of glistening river stones, I challenge him with the details of how we couldn't possibly cart all those stones down there and shift around all that dirt, and so on. Consequently, the lawn in the valley remains lawn, and once a week during the growing season he and I carry the mower down and back up the stairs that meander down the

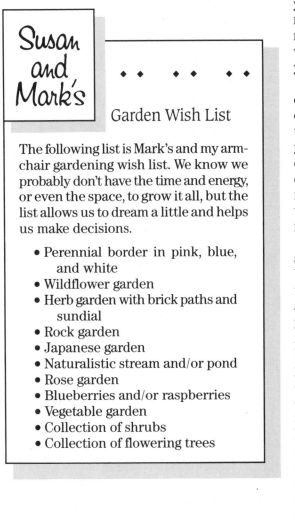

Susan and Mark's

Garden Wish List

The following list is Mark's and my arm-chair gardening wish list. We know we probably don't have the time and energy, or even the space, to grow it all, but the list allows us to dream a little and helps us make decisions.

- Perennial border in pink, blue, and white
- Wildflower garden
- Herb garden with brick paths and sundial
- Rock garden
- Japanese garden
- Naturalistic stream and/or pond
- Rose garden
- Blueberries and/or raspberries
- Vegetable garden
- Collection of shrubs
- Collection of flowering trees

hillside. A more realistic and affordable low-maintenance solution may someday occur to us. Meanwhile, we curse the previous owners. They reportedly flattened out the original contours of the valley floor with fill brought from the construction site next door, then planted the blasted lawn.

If you're a single gardener, not to worry. You can carry on quite a dialogue with yourself. The two sides of your personality may slug it out with each other in a kind of mental argument, the dreamer side arguing with the sterner, more realistic side, until you reach a decision.

But don't let the more realistic gardener or personality get away with totally writing off all the seemingly unrealistic ambitions—this book may offer you solutions to creating your dream garden by making some happy compromises and employing labor-saving gardening techniques. Leave your most desired, most unrealistic gardening goals on your wish list for further consideration, perhaps flagged with question marks.

For instance, your wish list might include a perennial border dream-garden in the Victorian cottage garden style like those of the famous British garden designer Gertrude Jekyll. The garden's floriferousness would—in your vision—take the breath away; your realistic side tells you that caring for such a border would probably take a lot more than your breath away! But a weekend gardener can care for a very satisfying perennial border about 50 feet long and 3 to 4 feet wide if it's designed for low maintenance. You don't have to spend every weekend planting, dividing, staking, weeding, watering, and deadheading a large bed or border if you plan it right and choose among the specially selected, easy-care perennials described in chapter 3. Your border may not look like those on an English estate, but it will burst with flowers and color for a long season.

After you've hashed out your dreams, the next step is to come up with a revised wish list—let's call it the realistic wish list—and rewrite it in order of priority. The *order* of your goals becomes important here in helping you determine the size and effort to put into any particular garden area. Because you have only a limited amount of time to spend tending the garden, you'll want to invest the most effort in maintaining those areas that hold the most importance to you, and devote the least effort to the areas that interest you least. Is that perennial border uppermost in your mind? Maybe an herb garden tops the list; perhaps even a lush, large lawn is a primary goal. But whatever your desires, list them in order of preference from most to least desired. If you're gardening by committee, here's where some more compromises may have to be reached—you might try taking turns choosing candidates for the list.

You might also consider why you want a particular type of garden, and determine which features are necessary to satisfy you and which you might eliminate without too much regret. For instance, I reconsidered my decorative herb garden, which I considered placing in that ill-fated valley. (The geometric designs of the beds would have looked very appealing when viewed from the patio above.) Though I muse over romantic herb garden designs, I really didn't need a large garden with paths brimming with numerous herbs; besides, the valley was probably too shady, and I also worried that the formal design of the herb garden would not look in keeping with the more naturalistic designs in the rest of the property.

I realized that I actually only wanted to grow some culinary herbs such as basil, dill, coriander, parsley, and rosemary. So I scaled down my wish to a small culinary herb garden, which I later decided to grow in decorative pots on the stoop by the kitchen door—a spot that received plentiful sun and also cried out for some ornamentation. Likewise, the vegetables I really wanted to grow turned out on reflection to be no more than some

Susan and Mark's Realistic Wish List

When we revised our wish list, we evaluated our goals and numbered them in order of importance. This is what our new wish list looks like.

1. Perennial border
2. Shade garden
3. Rock garden
4. Woodland garden
5. Shrub borders for growing shrub collection
6. Roses for cutting
7. Culinary herb garden
8. Salad garden
9. Berry garden

interesting salad greens, ones I couldn't purchase at the local farm stand. My wish for a vegetable garden got scaled down to a more manageable salad garden of fancy lettuces and salad greens such as chicory, radicchio, spinach, and curly endive. I put these in a dooryard garden just beside the back stoop where I had ripped out an overgrown yew.

Now take your realistic wish list and see how it matches up with your list of landscaping and gardening goals. Try to see if you can cross-match the lists, rather like taking a test in grammar school where the questions are in a column on the left and the answers are out of order on the right. In this

Mix-and-Match
Solutions

My "quiz" ended up looking like this:

Landscaping and Gardening Goals

Redo overgrown foundation planting
Beautify weedy back hillside
Get rid of lawn in valley in back of
    property
Remove overgrown shrubs from rock
    walls in front of house
Remove overgrown junipers along
    driveway
Get rid of inaccessible, weedy strip of
    lawn between street and privacy
    shrub border
Get rid of thin lawn beneath trees
    near woods
Get rid of weedy shrubs under trees
    along side yard fence
Beautify large front door landing/stoop
    with container plants
Beautify kitchen door landing/stoop
    with container plants
Create privacy in winter from neigh-
    bors at rear of property
Camouflage the view of the neighbor's
    tool shed
Camouflage the view from over the
    fence of the neighbor's big boat
    with blue cover

Realistic Wish List

Perennial border

Shade garden

Rock garden

Woodland garden

Shrub borders for growing shrub
    collection

Roses for cutting

Culinary herb garden

Salad garden

Berry garden

"test," you'll be trying to match goals and problems with solutions. Put the realistic wish list on the right and the landscaping and gardening goals list on the left. If you're lucky, you'll be able to solve most of your goals with your wishes. But unlike in school, it's okay to have more than one line match-ing a wish with a problem or goal. If you have a goal that lacks a match, then you'll have to come up with some creative solutions. You fail the test if you can't come up with an answer to each goal from the wish list in the right column. You get a gold star if you can match them all up!

Easy Weekend Gardening Solutions

Successful weekend gardeners don't necessarily grow fewer shrubs, flowers, and edibles than other gardeners; nor are their properties smaller. They do, however, seem to have a knack for growing plants that can care for themselves. Choosing the right plant for the right place makes a crucial difference in how well a plant performs. And organizing your garden space so that high-maintenance areas are concentrated together can reduce garden chores considerably.

Take It Slowly

Don't attempt too much at once. Renovate your yard slowly. That's the most valuable, cautionary word of advice you can follow, and it comes from someone who ought to know (me). Be realistic about what you attempt to accomplish each season. If you are overly ambitious and attempt to renovate your entire property all at once, as we unwisely began to do at our present house, you'll probably never get anything completed. Make a long-range plan and space out your projects over several years, if necessary. The work will wait—it (unfortunately) won't go away!

If you attempt too much all at once, you may be creating worse problems. Mark and I attacked our newly acquired neglected half acre with a vengeance. We hired a professional tree-care company to yank out most of the offending overgrown shrubs along the foundation and driveway. They also cut down the dying, diseased, and unwanted trees, such as the mimosa, and turned them into wood chips for us to use as mulch. Then Mark and I spent weekend after weekend pulling weeds, which grew thickly almost everywhere! The hillsides in back were somewhat wooded, but weeds, unwanted brush, brambles, and poison ivy blanketed the ground. We yanked weeds out by the roots, trying not to disturb the soil too much, which would just bring more weed seeds to the surface where they would happily germinate. We cut away volunteer saplings and brambles and piled them in a corner for future chipping. From the front of the house, we wheeled wood chips down the hill, across the lawn in the valley, and over to the newly-weeded hillside, where we used the chips to prevent erosion and discourage new weeds from popping up.

Needless to say, all this active weed, tree, and shrub removal left us with a lot of clear ground—ground that begged to be landscaped! By the time we had gotten rid of most of the offending plants, it was too late in the season to do much planting. And we simply didn't have the time, energy, or budget to replant all the cleared areas! Weeds started reappearing in places where we hadn't spread mulch. We even wondered whether we had made matters worse by our ill-fated enthusiasm.

Choose Plants Adapted to Your Climate and Site

A seemingly obvious—but all too often overlooked—key to an easy-care landscape is to begin with plants that are suited to your climate and to the particular exposure, soil, moisture, and other conditions in which you're planning to grow them. When plants are happily situated, they'll grow better and cause fewer problems. For example, Japanese andromeda (*Pieris japonica*) prefers partial shade and rich, acid soil. When grown in ideal soil and light conditions, it is an easy-care shrub that can take care of itself. Grow the shrub in too much sun, and you're sending an open invitation to a lacebug picnic. The small pests flock to the leaf undersides and suck out the chlorophyll, making the evergreen foliage unsightly and reducing the plant's vigor.

Many plants can be damaged when grown near the limits of their cold or heat tolerance. Heavenly bamboo (*Nandina domestica*), for instance, is a pretty shrub that is borderline hardy in USDA Plant Hardiness Zone 6; cold winters can kill it to the ground. When this happens, you wait and wait for the late-leafing plant to finally begin growth in spring, wondering whether it has totally died or not. When new shoots emerge from the plant's base, you have to prune away the deadwood, a maintenance chore you would be better off without. In climates where a particular plant, such as heavenly bamboo, suffers an uncertain fate, it makes sense to choose another plant better suited to the climate.

It also follows that landscape and garden plants will fare much better—and so will you—where the natural rainfall patterns suit their moisture needs. This premise is no more obvious than in the desert Southwest, where annual rainfall averages only several inches a year and falls usually only during winter and during tremendous but brief thunderstorms in late summer. It seems insane to try to grow lawns, Japanese maples, and other moisture-loving plants in such an alien climate, but many transplanted Northeasterners have done just that. At great expense to their water bill and the water table, I might add!

Go Native— With an Exotic Touch

Many back-to-nature advocates preach planting native American plants in our gardens, on the theory that these plants ought to be best adapted to the growing conditions we have to offer. That theory has a lot of truth to it, but only goes so far. Plants native to other continents can and do grow just fine in American gardens where the climate and growing conditions mimic those back home. Some of our most common landscape plants had their origins in other continents: Norway maple, Japanese maple, forsythia, bridal-wreath spirea, and pachysandra, to name just a few. And these grow just fine outside of their homeland when given proper care in a garden setting.

Going native in the garden should be considered an ecological approach, not necessarily a purist endeavor in which you cultivate only native plants and avoid those from other lands. If you place more emphasis on creating a garden ecosystem that groups together plants with similar needs in a naturalistic design, you'll be gardening with ecological sensitivity. You won't be wasting water or changing the environment to cultivate your garden, but adapting your garden to suit the environment. Using solely native plants in your designs is much less important to the garden's success than matching plant to site.

Introduced azaleas and rhododendrons are good examples of exotics that make good playmates with native American plants. Many different species of azalea and rhododendron grow as understory plants in mountainous regions of both Asia and North America, where the soil is moist, loose, acid, and humusy, sunlight is filtered, and rainfall is plentiful. These exotic azalea and rhododendron species will flourish as long as their native conditions are duplicated. Many Asian species were used in hybridizing the modern-day azalea and rhododendron cultivars so popular in this country. And the Asian species and hybrids look right at home in a naturalistic garden.

Plants grow naturally in many different habitats—deserts, swamps, bogs, woods, meadows, and rocky screes. Perennial borders, foundation plantings, and open lawns hardly duplicate such natural settings and many times offer plants conditions far from their own ideal. The trend toward going native ought really to emphasize duplicating natural settings, and not necessarily the native plants, if we are to have true low-maintenance gardens. Chapter 6 describes how to landscape your property in a naturalistic style that mimics many natural plant habitats.

Scale Down

One way to have everything on your wish list is to keep the high-maintenance areas small-scale. Try not to think so big. Instead of planting an orchard, plant a row of low-maintenance blueberries. Rather than planting a large formal garden of herbs, which would require a lot of preparation and tending, compromise as I did by confining the particular herbs you really want to ornamental clay planters. Brimming with various colors and textures of foliage and flowers—including silvery gray rosemary, emerald green parsley, burgundy-colored purple basil, and yellow-green dill—my planters provided a decorative country look on the back stoop and were right at hand when I was cooking. Though container-grown plants are not usually considered low-maintenance

because they dry out so fast, mine were close at hand and easy to water.

This solution pleased me enormously and required practically no care. I simply filled the planters with potting soil, popped in the transplants, and presto—an instant herb garden. No digging and other soil preparation, and no weeding because the herbs grew thickly and the potting soil was pasteurized. I watered them whenever I watered my houseplants. Maybe someday I will have the formal herb garden of my dreams, but by then the other areas of my property will be planted and filled in to the point where they will practically care for themselves.

Landscape a Mini-Oasis

Another way to scale down the scope of your gardening is to reduce the amount of your property that you actively cultivate. This technique, described aptly in *Plants for Dry Climates* by Mary Rose Duffield and Warren Johnson, works beautifully in arid climates, but is adaptable to any region. Typically one area of the desert garden, often an entry courtyard, is set up with automatic watering or drip irrigation so that tropical-type plants that need regular water can be easily grown. The garden is kept small-scale to conserve water and reduce maintenance, and may be enclosed by a wall or fence to further enhance the visual separation from the rest of the landscape. Other areas of the property rely on desert plants, which require no supplemental watering, to complete the landscape.

Many landscapes in arid climates also rely on walls to enclose the backyard, marking off the area of the property to be used for outdoor living. The area inside may be landscaped in many styles, relying on more or less water, but the wall forms a clear transition between the part of the property that is yard and garden and the remainder, which is left natural. Walls are often low enough to see the natural landscape beyond, creating a mini-oasis in the midst of the natural desert.

Gardeners in other climates might well borrow some wisdom from our fellow gardeners in desert climates. Even if water conservation isn't an issue in your area, locating plantings that need intensive attention together in a convenient spot makes caring for them easier. And framing areas for outdoor living with a low wall or fence, then letting the rest of the property grow wild, can make a lot of sense, too. How wild you want to let it become is another matter–to prevent a forest from growing, you may want to mow the "wild area" once a year. And, of course, your neighbors may not see eye to eye with you on the wild part of your yard– you may have to compromise by fencing off your "meadow garden" rather than your lawn.

Dick and Pam Dalhaus, a couple whose garden I stopped to admire when driving along a back road in New Hampshire, built their own country-style house complete with cottage-style garden on several acres of farmland. (A photo of their garden appears on page 120.) Though they probably never heard of the term, their low-maintenance garden is a perfect mini-oasis. All the outdoor living spaces and gardens, located on the front and side of their house, are enclosed within picket fences. The area inside the fences is intensively gardened, while the outside is left as rough pasture and woods.

Sliding doors lead from the house to a patio in the fenced yard, which is bordered by flower beds. Farther from the house, low raised beds brim with vegetables and more flowers. The front garden, separated from the side garden by another picket fence, boasts a colonial herb garden laid out in tidy beds.

Rather than wasting time tending a large lawn, the Dalhauses left the area outside the fence as pasture, and their horses graze there. Woods border the pasture. To keep woody plants from invading the pasture and turning it into woodland, Dick mows it once or twice a year.

Low-Maintenance Alternatives to Conventional Landscaping Styles

The traditional way most homes in the United States are landscaped demands high upkeep. Large lawn areas, evergreen foundation shrubs, and neatly trimmed hedges require regular maintenance and provide very little visual interest. The lawn, long a symbol of suburban affluence, must be watered, fertilized, zapped with chemicals, and, last but not least, regularly mowed to attain its full glory.

Traditionalists will be glad to know that by choosing low-maintenance landscape plants and replacing lawn areas with groundcovers and shrub borders, they can reduce the amount of maintenance required, while retaining a traditional formal appearance. You'll find plenty of ideas to guide you in the rest of this book.

Bucking Conformity

Unless you are a rigid conformist, you might consider other ways to landscape your home.

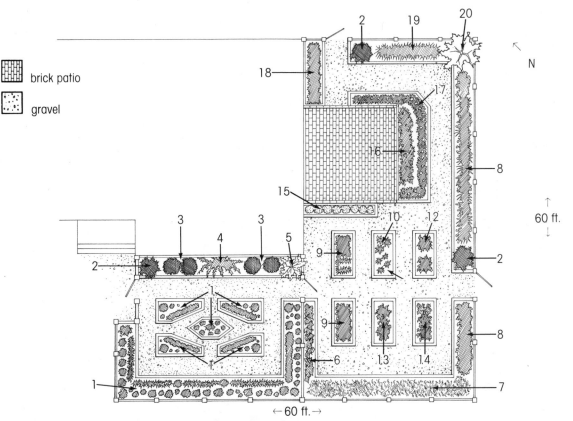

brick patio

gravel

N

60 ft.

← 60 ft. →

Plot Plan of Dick and Pam Dalhaus's Garden. (1) herbs, (2) burning bush, (3) red barberry, (4) ferns, (5) variegated red-twig dogwood, (6) rhubarb, (7) asparagus, (8) perennials, (9) assorted vegetables, (10) eggplant, (11) peppers, (12) tomatoes, (13) summer squash, (14) cucumbers, (15) sweet alyssum, (16) beans, (17) marigolds, (18) daisies and violets, (19) lavender and periwinkle, (20) dwarf cherry

Naturalistic landscape styles and plant choices require less work and often provide more beauty than the traditional manicured appearance. The front lawn can be reduced in size or totally eliminated and replaced with groundcovers; you'll find a host of low-maintenance choices described in the next chapter. You also might consider planting a meadow garden of flowers and grasses instead of all or part of the lawn in the front or backyard.

A shady site might be transformed into a woodland garden by planting native or adaptable shrubs, ferns, and wildflowers. Ornamental grass gardens seem to be all the rage these days and have even been termed the new American landscape. Ornamental grasses offer a striking array of foliage, flower, and seedhead colors and textures, and range in height from 1 to 10 feet. Designing an attractive grass garden can be as challenging as designing a perennial border, but the result requires a lot less regular maintenance.

All these alternative landscape designs are described in detail in chapter 6, where you'll find low-maintenance landscape designs to borrow for your own property.

Throughout this chapter I've presented some of the garden and landscape features that require the most maintenance. Solving

Enclosed by a picket fence, the Dalhaus's garden is the epitome of low maintenance and livability. Raised beds of vegetables and colorful flowers enhance the outdoor living space, while gravel paths give the garden structure and accessibility.

the challenges posed by these problem sites isn't always easy. Often, replacing high-maintenance traditional landscaping with naturalistic plantings will create a beautiful, low-maintenance garden setting. Transforming landscape problems into landscape solutions, however, may require an initial investment of time and money, but the early investment pays off in reduced maintenance several years down the line.

CHAPTER

2

DESIGNING EASIER YARDS AND LAWNS

Great Ways to Reduce Yard Chores

Maintaining the typical suburban yard, such as that of my neighbor Bill, provides little satisfaction: It's just another monotonous chore. The drudgery involved in keeping an expansive lawn acceptably emerald green, the hedges and shrubs neatly pruned, and the fallen leaves all raked and bagged for collection gets old pretty fast. An easier, more enjoyable lawn and garden comes from employing a low-maintenance landscape design and planting it with easy-care groundcovers, shrubs that don't need pruning, and low-maintenance trees. And, best of all, your new, easier lawn and yard is likely to be more appealing and colorful than your old one!

Planning a Low-Maintenance Yard

One of the most maintenance-free yards I've seen doesn't have a blade of grass in it except

as an occasional weedy invader. It is a small, modest property owned by the Nelsons, an older couple who are both schoolteachers. When they are at home, which isn't all that often, their RV sits prominently in the driveway. The couple spends the summers and school vacations touring the country, and their yard has to take care of itself, which it does beautifully.

Tall, high-branched black locusts (*Robinia pseudoacacia*) lightly shade the front yard. When these trees, which are native to the area, drop their foliage in fall, the leaflets are so small and dry up so quickly that they need only a quick raking. Several kinds of low groundcovers blanket the ground beneath the trees, reaching from the street right up to the low, spreading yews bordering the house. These groundcovers—purple-foliaged bugleweed (*Ajuga reptans*), green-and-white variegated wintercreeper (*Euonymus fortunei* 'Gracilis'), and dark green pachysandra (*Pachysandra terminalis*)—are each

Without any grass to mow, the Nelsons' low-maintenance landscape leaves its owners free to travel in the summer with no worries about returning to an unkempt lawn. Featuring an assortment of groundcovers, well-sited shrubs, and a stone path and patio, the property needs very little attention from its owners and is sparklingly attractive.

planted in large sweeps that form an attractively colored and textured carpet. The wintercreeper, a vining plant, also climbs unaggressively up the bottoms of several of the tree trunks. A walk leads through the groundcovers from the driveway to the front door.

The house sits on a corner lot with a varied terrain. The house and front yard, and part of the backyard, rest on level ground that nestles up against a fairly steep hillside. The hillside curves around from the rear to the corner of the property, leveling off where it meets the street. Several shade trees grow on the hillside. Beneath them, the Nelsons have mass-planted groups of white and red azaleas and rhododendrons.

Azaleas, which are indigenous to hilly, wooded areas and prefer humusy, moist, but well-drained soil, are perfectly adapted to the site. The owners have allowed the azaleas to grow unhindered into their natural loosely spreading shapes, which look lovely without being pruned. A thick mulch of wood chips beneath the azaleas' boughs keeps out weeds while a new planting of periwinkle (*Vinca minor*) gets established. The mulch and groundcover mimic the forest floor environment that is essential to the shrubs' happiness.

A dark gray pea-gravel path leads from the street along the base of the hillside to a large patio leading off the kitchen door and running along the back of the house. Like the front yard, the backyard contains no grass. The patio, made of flagstones, is situated in an open area covered with the same pea gravel that forms the path, providing a maintenance-free open area that can be walked on. The patio is shaded by several dogwoods and tall trees growing on the hillside, contains a table and chairs, and is large enough for socializing.

Edging strips play an important role in this garden. The gravel in the path and around the patio is kept in place by a steel edging inset in the ground. The edging rises about ½ inch above the gravel. This forms a shallow trough to hold the pebbles in place. The edging strip also prevents the wood-chip mulch under the azaleas from washing into the gravel. Black plastic (which the Nelsons punched with an ice pick for drainage) is laid beneath the gravel and keeps weeds from growing through it. The Nelsons' yard is practically maintenance-free.

This type of yard isn't for everyone, however. When the grandchildren come to visit, they have no place to ride their tricycles except in the street. The gravel surface looks naturalistic but provides too much resistance for small-wheeled toys.

The Nelsons have just sold their house. A family with two toddlers is moving in and is planning to alter the landscape a bit. The lack of lawn poses a real problem for small residents. Grass is the only living cover that can withstand the kind of abuse that frolicking children can inflict, and the new family needs some grass for a safe play area. They are planning to remove the gravel in the backyard and plant a small lawn around the patio, yet their property will still be exceptionally easy to care for.

The Nelsons' low-maintenance landscape didn't just happen—it was carefully thought out and installed. During the initial stages, the owners undoubtedly spent a significant amount of time and energy planting the shrubs and groundcovers, then weeding and mulching the young plantings until they filled in enough to discourage weeds. Though this was a lot of work, the owners were smart—the time they initially invested reaped benefits in the form of reduced labor for many years afterward—and they knew enough to be guided by the major principles in designing an easy-care yard.

Rethinking Lawn Areas

Lawn maintenance consumes more time than just about any other garden chore. Lawns must be mowed, weeded, watered, fertilized, limed, dethatched, reseeded, edged, and raked free of fallen leaves and debris. If this list doesn't seem daunting enough, consider the fact that all of these chores must be performed at crucial times in the lawn's seasonal cycle.

If the maintenance isn't carried out exactly when needed, the lawn suffers

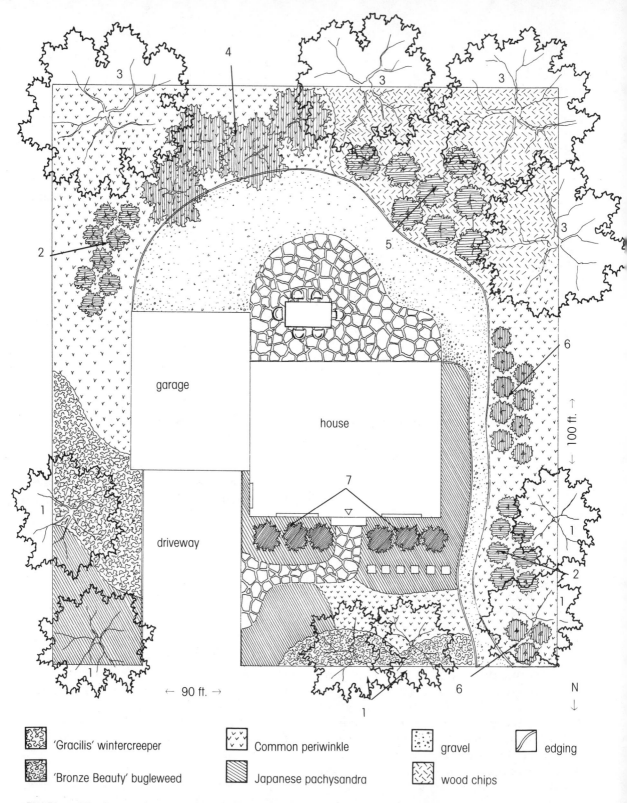

Plot Plan of the Nelson Yard. (1) black locust, (2) 'Stewartsonian' azalea, (3) sugar maple, (4) flowering dogwood, (5) 'Nova Zembla' catawba rhododendron, (6) 'Rose Greeley' azalea, (7) 'Repandens' English yew

Legend:

- 'Gracilis' wintercreeper
- 'Bronze Beauty' bugleweed
- Common periwinkle
- Japanese pachysandra
- gravel
- wood chips
- edging

← 90 ft. →

100 ft.

N

◆ ◆ ◆ ◆ ◆ ◆

Guidelines for Designing an Easy-Care Yard

Follow these tips to make your yard care easy and manageable.

• Reduce lawn areas and replace with groundcovers or other low-maintenance garden choices, such as mulched shrub borders or a meadow garden.

• Use large areas of decking or pavement to reduce lawn areas in the backyard and to provide maintenance-free recreational areas.

• Use shade trees that have minimum fall cleanup needs, or plant them in a setting where leaves can be left on the ground.

• Choose shrubs that, when they mature, will have sizes and shapes that fit into your landscape design, so routine pruning will be unnecessary.

• Choose landscape and garden plants well-adapted to the climate and site.

• Choose plants that are disease- and insect-resistant.

• Use a mulch to reduce weeding and watering chores.

• Use edging to separate different garden areas from each other so lawn, groundcover, and mulching materials will stay in place.

• Install weed-barrier materials beneath mulch, paving, or gravel to prevent weed growth.

• Keep scattered plantings and unconnected lawn areas to a minimum.

dramatically—left unraked, wet leaves smother the grass and encourage mildew; allowed to grow too long before mowing, the grass goes into shock when it is finally mown; fertilized too late, the turf grows rapidly when it should be dormant and may then be zapped by heat and drought; mown too short, the grass withers in the sun and encourages unsightly weeds. And even when maintenance is on schedule, a weak or unsuitable kind of grass, an outbreak of moles or grubs, or an undisciplined dog can turn your lawn into a disaster area.

One of the most satisfactory steps I've taken everywhere I've gardened is to reduce the amount of space taken up by lawn. In various situations, I've replaced lawn with flower and herb gardens, shrubbery borders, and expanses of decorative groundcovers. Wherever lawn was too difficult to mow, out it went!

This doesn't mean that lawn is all bad. Far from it! A well-kept expanse of lawn delights the eye and sets off shrub borders and flowers to perfection. Green lawn plays a neutral but nevertheless very important role in making a landscape work visually. It is a peacemaker. It is restful. It integrates. The green color and fine texture help counteract bolder textures of foliage and bright masses of flowers and keep the whole garden show from looking too busy or being overpowering.

The expanse of fine-textured green simply can't be duplicated by any other landscape plant. No other groundcover is as good a peacekeeper as lawn grass. Evergreen groundcovers such as pachysandra, periwinkle (*Vinca minor*), and wintercreeper (*Euonymus fortunei*) have a bolder texture that can become overpowering in some situations if planted in quantity. The texture can compete with other landscape plants rather than complement them. Many groundcovers aren't as neutral as grass, and they command more attention. When groundcovers are planted as extensively as grass, the effect often becomes too busy.

If there was a flaw in the Nelsons' low-maintenance yard, it was that the foliage textures of the different groundcovers vied visually with each other. This was heightened by overusing variegated wintercreeper, a visually stimulating plant even in small quantities. Even a bit of carefully placed lawn can counteract this effect by providing a neutral breathing space between vying elements.

The shape of a lawn also plays a crucial role in a garden's design. Whether curving, square-cornered, elongated, or absolutely round, the contours of a lawn add visual interest to a design and direct the eye, while separating one area from another. And lawns don't block views.

Lawns should—and do—play an important role in most landscape designs. The shape and size ought to be planned and planted to enhance the overall garden. Don't make the mistake of assuming that lawn is the automatic answer to filling up leftover yard space. Do just the reverse—plan the lawn shape and then plant around it!

Most landscapes require some lawn space for visual impact, for playing and lounging, and for its cooling effect—an effect that is literal as well as visual, because as water evaporates from the lawn it actually cools the air. For purely aesthetic reasons, lawns shouldn't be eliminated entirely in most traditional landscapes. Lawn grass offers a beautiful, bright green, fine-textured carpet that creates a foil for the rest of the garden. And, relatively speaking, grass is an inexpensive choice compared to the alternatives:

mass plantings of groundcover plants or installing extensive decking or a brick or stone patio.

It's best to remove grass entirely in the following situations.

• Where surface tree roots interfere with mowing
• Where low-hanging tree or shrub branches interfere with the mower or necessitate stooping
• Where the ground slopes so much that maneuvering the mower is difficult
• Where many specimen trees and shrubs grow in the lawn, requiring extra time to trim around the trunks
• Under or bordering a fence
• Where shade or poor soil causes the grass to struggle for health
• Where access is difficult
• Where the soil or climate is unfavorable, such as in an arid or desert location

Rethinking Lawn on a Slope

Mark and I like to take long walks in the evenings to unwind. When walking we discuss our day's activities, make plans, and also spy on any yard or garden we find of interest. One house we occasionally walk by always caused us to speculate about how the owners could possibly mow the lawn. The house—a 1930s type of two-story stucco—was situated atop a very steep hill. Lawn covered the entire hill.

Near the house the ground sloped gently, but closer to the street it dropped off precipitously. A stucco wall was cut into the face of the hill along the street. We couldn't imagine how the steep part of the lawn above the wall got mown. It must have sloped at a 90-degree angle.

One evening we found out. A young—and very strong, I might add—man was struggling with his power mower. He had mowed all the lawn except the slope, and was proceeding to conquer that. His solution was to tie a rope to the handles of the mower and lower the machine to the top edge of the wall. He then pulled it back, hand over hand. We tried not to stare. In our wildest dreams we had never imagined this mowing solution! I concluded, given the stamina needed to carry out this mowing chore, that a less direct solution might have been in order.

Slopes like this can be regraded by terracing them with landscape timbers or retaining walls. Then the level areas can be planted with a flower garden, shrub border, or whatever delights you. This can be an expensive solution, however, and one that is often too difficult for a do-it-yourselfer if the slope is very steep.

A simpler choice might be to remove the lawn on a steep slope and plant the area with shrubs, groundcovers, or both; plants that bind the soil with creeping roots are best where the grade is steep. Plants that trail, weep, or arch look stunning cascading down a slope. In this situation, I'd use a variegated English ivy—it's less aggressive and prettier than all-green ivy—and let it drape over the wall. At the top, the ivy will need trimming to keep it from overgrowing the lawn.

Low, spreading shrubs such as cotoneasters, 'Hidcote' hypericum, or junipers also look attractive and provide a low-maintenance solution to slopes. If your slope is held by a wall, think about plants to tie it to your yard. Perennials such as edging candytuft (*Iberis sempervirens*), snow-in-summer (*Cerastium tomentosum*), and basket-of-gold (*Aurinia saxatilis*, formerly *Alyssum saxatile*) will tumble over the edge of a wall, bringing bright spots of bold color to soften the structure.

It's important to prevent erosion on slopes until your groundcover establishes itself. Rather than stripping away the sod, which could be a tricky chore on a steep slope, you might want to kill it instead, leaving the dead plants in place. You can kill grass without herbicides by smothering it with a sheet of black plastic weighted down with rocks, or with a thick layer of wood chips. The grass should die after three to four weeks, especially if the plastic-covered area bakes in the sun. Remove the plastic and plant the groundcover directly through the dead grass, or pull back the wood chips where you want to make a planting hole. The grass roots will hold the soil until they decay, long enough for the groundcover to establish itself and carry on the erosion control.

When we moved into our present house, a weedy strip of lawn about 8 feet wide grew along the street in front of a tall screen of pines and rhododendrons. This was terribly inconvenient to mow and served no practical purpose. We easily smothered the grass and weeds under 8 inches of wood chips, and a few months later planted masses of shrub roses and groundcovers there without having to improve the soil at all.

Groundcover plants—actually any type of plant installed on a slope—should be planted in pockets leveled out of the slope so water gets a chance to soak in around their roots. It's important to apply a thick mulch to the newly planted area to keep out weeds, slow erosion, and retain moisture until the plants can cover the ground. Even if you've planted directly in dead grass, you might wish to add a thin layer of wood chips or other good-looking mulch as a coverup; shredded bark holds well on a slope without washing away.

Rethinking Lawn in Shade

Why try to grow a lawn where a lawn simply doesn't want to grow? In shady areas on the north side of a building or under trees, grass often struggles to survive. But the same sites that are bad for grass are good places to plant a shade-loving groundcover or create a garden of shrubs, perennials, or wildflowers that grow best in shade. I did this in one corner of the side yard of my house, by planting dwarf rhododendrons, ferns, hostas, creeping phlox (*Phlox stolonifera*), foamflower (*Tiarella cordifolia*), and dwarf Chinese astilbes (*Astilbe chinensis* 'Pumila'), among others, and couldn't be happier with the result. It's pretty all year long and requires very little care. (See "A Shady Flower Garden" on page 83 for more information on shade gardening.)

Making a Smaller Lawn

Reducing the size of the lawn, rather than totally eliminating it, often makes sense in a landscape, especially if the property is large. Remember to think of the lawn as playing an important landscape design role, not as occupying whatever space remains after installing the perennial and shrub borders, and you can't go wrong. Make the lawn only the size required to visually hold your landscape together, and only as large an area as you have time to care for.

How to Remove Lawn Grass

There are right and wrong ways to remove unwanted lawn area from your yard so you can turn it into a planting area for flowers, groundcovers, or shrubs. The right way relies on using a garden spade to strip the grass away from the soil without actually digging into the ground. By stripping off the sod, you eliminate most of the grass and weed roots, so the grass won't come back to haunt you. The wrong ways include power tilling the lawn or digging it under with a shovel or spade. Both of these methods return grass and weed roots to your planting bed, where the grass and perennial weeds will be sure to resprout, creating a weed problem in your new garden. Power tilling and deep digging can also harm tree roots, causing even more trouble in shady spots under trees.

Begin by using a clothesline or garden hose to mark the contours of the lawn that will remain. After you're satisfied with the shape, apply garden lime as a marker along the line and remove the rope or hose. Then, using a spade or an edger, cut down into the sod all the way around the contour, being careful to make curves rounded and straight sides razor sharp. In moist soil, it takes little effort to angle the spade just under the grass roots, pushing firmly with your foot. As you steadily slice off the sod, it will curl up, and you can roll it off in sections. The sod pieces may surprise you with their weight, so cut them into man-

• The best way to get rid of grass is to strip off the sod before turning over the soil. This technique will keep the grass from returning as a weed.

1. Mark the shape of the new bed with garden lime, then cut through the sod along the outline with a spade.

2. Use your foot to push the spade just under the grass roots, removing as little soil as possible.

3. Roll the sod up in strips of manageable size. You can compost the pieces or plant them elsewhere.

ageable pieces that are easy to lift.

Once you've removed the sod, you can turn over the soil and incorporate organic matter such as compost, well-rotted manure, and/or peat moss. The better you prepare the area now, the healthier your new garden will be. Once it is permanently planted with perennials, groundcovers, and shrubs, the soil is more difficult to improve.

If the sod you removed is healthy and weed-free, you can use it to repair sparse or weedy patches elsewhere in your lawn, or transplant it to prepared soil where you'd like to have a lawn. But sod also has less-obvious uses. It makes a wonderful addition to your compost heap, adding both organic matter and beneficial soil microorganisms. Mark and I used sod once to begin a compost heap that, when combined with leaves, garden debris, and kitchen scraps, produced delicious-looking, crumbly brown compost that we used in our garden for several years. A word of warning, though: Don't compost sod if it has rhizomatous weedy grasses; if the pile doesn't heat up enough to kill the rhizomes, they'll spread wherever you put the compost.

We also used sod to form the basis of a berm for a rock garden. We turned the sod root-side up and piled it directly on top of the soil to create a miniature mountain with several peaks and valleys. Then we buried the "mountain" in a mixture of soil, manure, and peat moss. Finally, I placed rocks so they jutted out of the "mountain." This became a sensational little landscape, fertile enough to grow dwarf conifers and miniature rhododendrons and azaleas.

Replace the rest of the lawn with a low groundcover, one that grows no more than about 6 to 8 inches tall, if you want the open feeling of a lawn. You can also get creative and replace lawn areas with more exciting plantings, such as a perennial flower border, a shrub bed, a meadow, or, in shady areas, a wildflower garden. In arid climates, stones or pebbles can make attractive naturalistic mulches for covering ground that, in a climate more conducive to grass, might otherwise be lawn.

In the backyard, another alternative is to replace lawn areas with an attractive *hardscape*—as nonplant areas of the landscape, such as a deck or brick patio, are called by landscape designers. In townhouse gardens or courtyard gardens, the hardscape can completely cover any areas not devoted to beds and borders.

Islands in the Lawn

Mark the contours of your proposed reduced lawn shape with a clothesline or garden hose and study the size and shape to see how it balances with the rest of the garden before you make any decisions. Create the contours of the remaining lawn so they transcribe visually appealing lines—a small semicircle of lawn can be inviting when bordered by groundcovers, flowers, and shrubs and is less difficult to mow than an area with irregular edges.

The usual choice is to bring in the edges of the lawn, planting the perimeter, but this may create a more closed-in feeling, especially with shrubs planted around the edges. An alternative is to create islands within the lawn and plant these with whatever you wish. If trees already grow in the lawn, it makes sense to arrange the islands around them.

For an open feeling, plant the bed with low flowers and/or evergreen groundcovers. For a more wooded look, include flowering shrubs within the island and blanket the ground with mulch or groundcovers.

When you create several island beds, the remaining grass acts as an alluring path or corridor meandering through the beds. With wide paths and an open planting, the feeling will be spacious and more formal; with narrower paths and taller plantings, the feeling will be of a woodland.

Another alternative is to turn part of the lawn into a field of colorful flowers. A meadow garden is less work than a lawn, but it isn't as easy and carefree as is often implied in magazine articles. Don't be taken in by those pretty pictures! The meadow can't be started by simply scattering wildflower seeds on the lawn! Like any garden, it takes some tending. (See chapter 6 for information on how to grow a meadow garden.)

Go for Groundcovers

Lawns can be totally replaced or reduced in size in many landscapes by mass-planting groundcovers. When planted in quantity, in great sweeps and beneath shrubs and trees, a groundcover unifies the entire landscape. The uniform groundcover adds texture and interest without overpowering the more dominant plants and serves as a backdrop for the changing flowers and foliage in the garden.

The term groundcover applies to many kinds of plants. Most groundcovers are herbaceous (nonwoody) plants. Some, such as periwinkle (*Vinca minor*), are evergreen, while others, such as leadwort (*Cerato-stigma plumbaginoides*), are deciduous and lose their foliage in winter. Some ground-

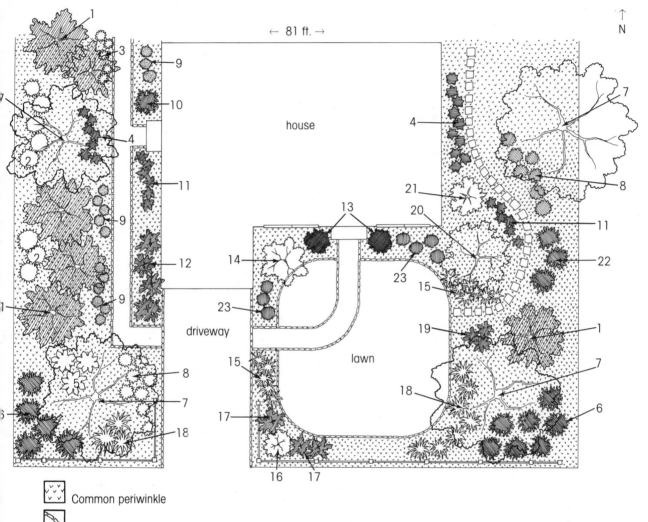

← 81 ft. →

↑
N

house

driveway

lawn

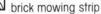

Common periwinkle

brick mowing strip

Plot Plan of a Low-Maintenance Front Yard. (1) kousa dogwood, (2) cinnamon fern, (3) lady's-mantle, (4) bishop's hat, (5) 'Elegans' Siebold hosta, (6) 'Delaware Valley White' azalea, (7) 'Shademaster' thornless honeylocust, (8) 'Deutschland' astilbe, (9) fringed bleeding-heart, (10) 'PJM' rhododendron, (11) 'Blue Cadet' hosta, (12) 'Dorothy Wycoff' Japanese pieris, (13) 'Compacta' inkberry, (14) Japanese snowbell, (15) 'Stella d'Oro' daylilies and glory-of-the-snow, (16) 'Palibin' Meyer lilac, (17) Bumald spirea, (18) daylilies and daffodils, (19) 'Frances Williams' Siebold hosta, (20) 'Bloodgood' Japanese maple, (21) 'Snow Queen' oakleaf hydrangea, (22) 'Dora Amateis' rhododendron, (23) 'Crimson Pygmy' Japanese barberry.

Where a high-maintenance lawn would dominate a traditional landscape, periwinkle (*Vinca minor*) forms an undemanding evergreen carpet in this low-maintenance front yard. The circular shape of the small (650 sq. ft.) lawn makes mowing easy, and a brick mowing strip keeps the lawn from invading the planting beds. When left to grow in their natural shapes, none of the shrubs in this yard needs routine pruning.

covers, such as sweet woodruff (*Galium odoratum*), die back to the ground, disappearing after the growing season. There are also attractive woody groundcovers, including deciduous plants like rock cotoneaster (*Cotoneaster horizontalis*), which are leafless in winter but provide an interesting branch structure all year, and others, such as creeping juniper (*Juniperus horizontalis*), that are evergreen. Groundcovers also cover a range of heights, from an inch or less as in woolly thyme (*Thymus pseudolanuginosus*) to several feet as in gardener's-garters (*Phalaris arundinacea* var. *picta*).

Groundcover plants share the ability to spread horizontally and blanket the ground. They are often vining or creeping plants, or plants that spread rapidly by underground roots or stems. Though turf grasses meet the definition of a groundcover, usually the term groundcover is used to mean alternatives to turf grass. In this book, whenever I say groundcover, I mean all those other, more interesting ground-covering plants; when I mean lawn grass, that's what I'll say.

Groundcovers that don't need some controlling won't really cover the ground well or compete with weedy invaders. You must reach a happy compromise when choosing a groundcover for your low-maintenance landscape by reminding yourself that nothing's perfect. The best groundcovers spread rapidly and shade out weeds (without becoming totally uncontrollable), or they wouldn't be desirable groundcovers. These groundcovers need discipline to stay put. You might have to beat them back from time to time and show them who's boss, but the occasional reprimand takes much less time than dealing with the lawn.

Planting groundcovers in place of lawn offers many advantages.

- Once filled in, the groundcover crowds out most weeds.
- Fallen tree leaves usually require little or no removal since they sift to the ground through the groundcover and act as a natural mulch.
- Once established, the groundcover requires only occasional maintenance, if any.
- Trees and shrubs grown in a bed of groundcover (or mulch) are healthier than those grown in open lawn.
- Mowing a lawn where trees and shrubs are planted in an island of groundcover is easier than mowing around trees and shrubs situated in open lawn, because bumpy roots and dangling branches don't become obstacles to the mower. You also won't risk injuring trunks with the mower.
- Most groundcovers are attractive landscape plants in their own right; they can add beautiful foliage, flowers, and texture to a landscape.

The "Big Three" Groundcovers

Three plants—pachysandra (*Pachysandra terminalis*), English ivy (*Hedera helix*), and periwinkle (*Vinca minor* and *Vinca major*)—are by far the most common groundcovers. Taken together, they are probably planted more often than all the other groundcover possibilities combined. Many landscapers and garden writers malign these plants, claim-

ing they're ubiquitous and boring. But the reason they're so popular is that they work. Relatively inexpensive compared to most other groundcover choices, these evergreen plants fill in quickly and provide an attractive low carpet of dark green foliage throughout the year. Many more colorful groundcovers tempt plant lovers, but few groundcovers are affordable enough to be purchased in the quantities needed to replace huge areas of lawn. And many "more interesting" groundcovers lose their leaves in winter, leaving you looking at bare earth for a large part of the year. Other groundcovers make fine clumps or specimens, but because their foliage and flowers attract so much attention, they would look too busy to make good candidates for mass-planting as a neutral landscape element.

Of the three, periwinkle, with its tidy leaves and dainty blue flowers, is by far my favorite, and if it weren't so common I'm sure gardeners would kill for it. I like to use periwinkle to blanket the ground in large sweeps and trail over walls, with more attention-getting plants growing up through it. Pachysandra, with its whorls of green foliage and short spires of creamy white flowers, and English ivy, with its dark green, three-pointed leaves, can be used this way, too. Pachysandra, however, grows much taller than periwinkle, reaching 8 to 10 inches, and English ivy can be an aggressive pest if not regularly trimmed, but both establish themselves more quickly than periwinkle.

Popular Pachysandra

I read somewhere that pachysandra is the most popular plant in the United States. That's some reputation! And though a few gardening friends of mine hate the plant—

probably because it is so frequently seen—they can't argue against the fact that it is a great problem solver. Pachysandra will grow in part sun or deep shade, in moist or dry conditions, and even in the dense shade and terribly thin soil beneath a Norway maple, where little else will grow. Once filled in, which it does quickly, it practically defies weeds.

Tree leaves falling on pachysandra don't need raking unless they form a layer heavy enough to smother the plants, because during winter pachysandra foliage curls up when the weather is really cold and uncurls when it's warmer. This movement serves to sift the fallen leaves to the ground beneath the groundcover, where they can decompose.

A native of Japan, *Pachysandra terminalis* has glossy, dark green, evergreen leaves with jagged edges arranged in whorls around the stem. (Its American cousin, Alleghany pachysandra [*Pachysandra procumbens*] is semi-evergreen to deciduous and tends to grow in clumps rather than form a uniform mass.) Three uncommon cultivars of the common Japanese pachysandra might beguile even those who detest the plant. A variegated cultivar called 'Silveredge' will brighten any shady spot. Its gray-green foliage has creamy white variegations on the edges, making it glow softly in the shade where dark green foliage would be further cast into gloom. 'Silveredge' grows less vigorously and less tall than the species, so don't plant them together. The cultivar 'Green Carpet' grows lower, featuring leaves that are darker green and wider than the species; and 'Kingwood' has deeply serrated foliage, with a lovely fine texture.

Elegant English Ivy

English ivy features dark, almost black-green, star-shaped foliage densely packed along ground-hugging vines. In some cultivars the veins are lighter green and show up prettily against the contrasting leaf background. English ivy can scale buildings and tree trunks. Where it grows high, the vines may suddenly change into a bushy form; this adult form produces rounded leaves, flowers, and berries.

Though English ivy is rugged and attractive, it has several drawbacks. Being a vine, English ivy tends to leave the ground and climb walls and trees, as well as wind its way into shrubs, where it becomes a problem to contend with. A little climbing ivy on a tree trunk looks pretty, but once it starts dangling from the branches, its weight can topple a tree. It can also shade the tree's foliage, cutting off photosynthesis and in effect starving the tree. Some people (about 10 percent of the population) get a poison-ivy-like rash when they handle English ivy.

English ivy spreads even faster than pachysandra. In fact, it spreads much too enthusiastically to be used in small, tidy gardens, unless you are prepared to clip it back regularly. But in large gardens beneath trees that cast dense shade, such as maples or beeches, English ivy makes a good low-maintenance choice compared to a lawn, which would just struggle in the shade. Keep the ivy in bounds where it starts creeping onto the lawn or sidewalk by trimming it with a power mower. And restrain it from scaling too high up tree trunks by cutting back the vines once a year.

The variegated and needle-leaf cultivars of English ivy grow less aggressively than the species and make beautiful, well-behaved groundcovers. Use white- or golden-edged types to liven up shady corners, especially where the vines can trail over a wall or wind up a sturdy tree trunk. Needle-leaf cultivars display well espaliered against a wall or fence, but keep in mind that the vine's sticky suction cups can damage the surface.

Fancy-leaf forms of ivy aren't the easiest plants to come by. My friend Conni Cross, a talented garden designer, planted a lovely patch of white-and-green ivy under a stand of birch trees near her front door. "You should have some of this. It would look great trailing over your rock walls," she kept telling me.

"But where do I get it?" I would say. I was truly bewildered about where to buy variegated ivy. It seemed like a rare find, indeed. (Garden centers rarely offer these fancy forms of ivy, though there's plenty of the standard green kind available in flats.)

I had blatantly admired Conni's ivy so many times that I thought the hint was embarrassingly obvious—but she never offered to give me a cutting. And she seemed to be carefully guarding her source. My questions about where she had bought it always brought the same answer: "Oh, I can't remember."

I considered asking my usually generous friend for some cuttings but decided against that plan, because it seemed gauche. I was conceiving a plan to steal some of the coveted ivy and stuff it in my jeans pocket when Conni's back was turned, when she unexpectedly let me in on the secret, which she didn't realize was a secret: "Of course if you can't find it at the nursery, buy houseplants." Variegated- and fancy-leaf cultivars of ivy, it seems, are sold mostly as houseplants. It was that simple. I was that dumb. Note, however, that the variegated cultivars aren't usually as cold-hardy as the all-green ivies. All-green cultivars can be grown in USDA Plant Hardiness Zone 4, while the variegated cultivars are usually hardy only to Zone 7 when grown outdoors.

I made a beeline for the greenhouse on my way home and triumphantly purchased two enormous hanging baskets of variegated ivy. The gray-green leaves were marked with a wide creamy white edge. I carefully arranged the plants to trail over an eye-level rock retaining wall, locating them in the curve of the wall that caught my eye as I opened the gate to the backyard. The ivy looks as pretty as Conni promised! And it will spread.

Pretty, Practical Periwinkle

Periwinkle, also known as vinca and myrtle, is the daintiest-looking of the "big three" groundcovers, but don't let its appearance fool you. It is tough and it can spread, sometimes where you don't want it. It grows in sun or shade but prefers semi-shade, and it tolerates moist or dry soil. The oval foliage remains shiny and dark green all year. In spring, star-shaped, lavender-blue flowers bloom for about a month during the time daffodils flower, making a beautiful blue and yellow combination. The slender trailing stems root as they march along and will drape effectively over a wall, but they don't climb.

Several cultivars are available. 'Alba' has white flowers and grows slowly compared to the traditional blue-flowered form. 'Bowles' has larger, darker blue flowers and creeps less, forming denser tufts than the typical vining form. 'Atropurpurea' features reddish purple flowers, which are unusual but, in my opinion, muddy-looking and far less attractive than the species. A blue-flowered variegated cultivar, 'Aureo-Variegata', has gold-edged leaves, and 'Flore Pleno' produces double blue flowers.

In Zones 9 and 10, greater periwinkle (*Vinca major*) flourishes. Resembling a hefty cousin of *Vinca minor*, it has larger leaves, bigger blue flowers, and grows several feet tall before its trailing stems flop over. A lovely variegated cultivar has creamy leaf margins that sparkle throughout the year.

Beyond the Big Three

Expanses of a single type of groundcover repeated throughout a landscape unify the setting by replacing large areas of lawn and acting as a beautiful living mulch beneath trees and shrubs. This style of design creates a traditional, elegant setting in the front of a home. If your aim is to have a tidy-looking, easy-care landscape, then one of the big three groundcovers—pachysandra, English ivy, or periwinkle—would probably work well in your landscape. However, don't feel that you're locked into one of the big three—several other less common groundcovers might suit your needs and be better choices in sunny locations. For mass plantings that will be viewed all year, be sure you choose plants that are evergreen or that offer an attractive woody branch structure for winter interest if they are deciduous.

Probably one of the hardiest evergreen vines is wintercreeper (*Euonymus fortunei*). The vines thrive in moist soil in full sun to partial shade and send out rootlets from the nodes, making a thick carpet. Wintercreeper comes in a dandy array of cultivars, offering a variety of leaf shapes, from tiny to half-dollar-size ovals; leaves may be variegated or take on beautiful winter colors.

Purple wintercreeper (*Euonymus fortunei* var. *coloratus*) makes an elegant groundcover on a bank or hillside, or as a broad expanse beneath high-branched trees. The dark green foliage has deep reddish purple undersides; in fall and winter, the entire leaf takes on this rich hue. The best green cultivar of wintercreeper is 'Acutus', which is similar to purple wintercreeper but doesn't change color. Variegated cultivars include 'Emerald and Gold', with golden leaf edges, and 'Gracilis', with bright white markings that take on a burgundy hint in winter.

'Longwood' has dainty oval leaves from ¼ to ½ inch long, and it grows more slowly than the other types.

Flowers and fruits seldom form, so wintercreeper won't become weedy, though it may need occasional clipping to restrain the vines from outgrowing their allotted space and to stop them from climbing up walls and tree trunks. Euonymus scale insects, noticeable as white flecks on stems and leaf undersides, can attack wintercreeper with a vengeance. If this pest presents problems in your area, you probably shouldn't plant the vine. Spraying several times a year with horticultural oil will help keep the pest in check, however, if you want to go to this much trouble.

In USDA Plant Hardiness Zone 5 and south, several different grassy-looking plants in the lily family, collectively called lilyturf, make effective, easy-care mass plantings in light shade, and do well in full sun as long as they are assured of getting plenty of moisture. Mondo grass (*Ophiopogon japonicus*) forms 8- to 10-inch-tall, dense clumps of ⅛-inch-wide, dark green leaves. Spikes of white flowers bloom in late summer, but remain mostly hidden among the foliage. The plants spread steadily by sending out underground runners that produce new plants. A mature planting forms a uniform green sea with a coarse linear texture. Dwarf mondo grass (*Ophiopogon japonicus* 'Nana') grows only 2 to 3 inches tall and tends to form clumps rather than spreading so readily.

Taller and more broadleaved than mondo grass, members of the genus *Liriope* may form large clumps or spread into dense stands by underground runners. Creeping lilyturf (*Liriope spicata*) works best for mass-planting because it spreads so well. Leaves measure about ½ inch across and fall softly to form mounds about 9 inches high. The pale lilac or white flowers remain close to the foliage. Growing into ever larger individual clumps of cascading foliage, big blue lilyturf (*Liriope muscari*) produces showy spikes of purple, lavender, or white flowers in late summer. Both species offer variegated forms with gold- or white-striped foliage, which are quite pretty in the shade.

Liriope and mondo grass are both evergreen, but can look pretty bedraggled come spring, especially at the northern limits of their hardiness range. (*Liriope muscari* is hardy to Zone 6; *L. spicata* to Zone 5; and *Ophiopogon* to Zone 7.) Julie and David Johnson, avid gardeners in Georgia, cut back their lilyturf as far as they can in spring, just before the last frost date or when they see signs of new growth. (A power mower set high will do a fine job of this.) "Georgia gardeners who cut back the liriope get much healthier plants," claims Julie. After cutting back, the planting begins filling in, producing abundant new leaves as the warmer weather progresses, and it will eventually produce nice flowers later in the season. "We have also had good luck transplanting lilyturf to other locations after frost, and we have divided a number of 1- to 2-year-old-plants by using a sharp knife and letting the plants dry out for a few hours before replanting."

In sites with full sun and even in dry or poor soil, groundcover junipers can save your landscape. Tough and durable, groundcover junipers feature fine- to coarse-textured evergreen needles in a variety of shades of green, including gray-green, blue-green, and grass green. Some even take on rusty or silvery shades in winter. Junipers provide a uniform cover throughout the year and look great when used on banks and slopes, or in broad borders along a driveway or street. Because they are dense and woody, junipers cannot be combined with bulbs or perennials. But their rough texture looks especially good with wooden homes that have rustic or contemporary designs.

Be very certain when shopping for junipers that you are purchasing a cultivar destined to stay low to the ground, not one of the vase-shaped types that are programmed to mature into 10-foot-tall shrubs. Groundcover junipers vary from ground-hugging plants to low shrubs that send out layers of branches to a height of about 2 to 2½ feet.

My favorite juniper for use as a groundcover is Japanese garden juniper (*Juniperus procumbens* 'Nana'). It has very tiny, bluish green needles and forms soft mounds as it creeps along close to the soil. Sargent juniper (*J. chinensis* 'Sargentii') retains its bright green color throughout the winter, a trait few others can boast. Beautiful steel blue foliage and slow growth characterize 'Blue Star' juniper (*J. squamata* 'Blue Star'). Admired for its rough-textured, soft blue foliage that takes on a silvery plum color for winter, 'Bar Harbor' juniper (*J. horizontalis* 'Bar Harbor') grows rapidly. 'Blue Rug' juniper (*J. horizontalis* 'Blue Rug') retains its blue color all year round. These are but a few of the choice groundcover junipers available for mass-planting. Your nursery will have others.

A trendy low shrub for mass-planting as a groundcover these days is 'Hidcote' Aaron's-beard (*Hypericum calycinum* 'Hidcote'). A semi-evergreen that grows about 1½ to 2 feet high, the shrub spreads into a dense stand by underground runners. Large, oval, blue-green leaves are arranged opposite each other along the graceful arching stems, creating a lovely pattern. For most of the summer, huge, bright yellow flowers adorn the length of the stems.

In mild climates, the foliage may be evergreen, but in northern climates it may be winterkilled. This is actually a point in the shrub's favor, for the dried foliage and stems turn a beautiful rusty gold color that adds great interest to the winter landscape. Simply cut the shrub to the ground in spring and the new growth will fill the planting back in; since flowers form on new growth, the annual cutting actually promotes dramatic flowering.

Another woody plant that adapts itself to covering the ground is rock-spray cotoneaster (*Cotoneaster horizontalis*). With its fine-textured foliage, perky flowers, and showy red berries, it's a plant for all seasons —even winter. After the foliage drops, the red berries remain to emphasize the unusual fishbone pattern of the twiggy branches. This and other species of cotoneaster are effective as a mass planting in a sunny area. However, if fallen tree leaves get blown into the branches, they can be difficult to remove. Cotoneaster is susceptible to most of the diseases that strike rose-family members.

Counting the Cost

If you're landscaping on a tight budget, you may be dismayed at the cost of groundcovers. The big three cost the least, but when you start counting the large number needed to create a mass planting, even the cost of these may seem shockingly high. If you're willing to purchase 500 to 1,000 rooted cuttings of a single type of plant, many wholesale nurseries will sell to retail customers and ship plants to them by UPS. *American Nurseryman* magazine (American Publishing Company, 111 N. Canal St. #545, Chicago, IL 60606) lists wholesale nurseries.

When renovating a landscape and transforming large patches of lawn into groundcover, I am in favor of simply getting the bare ground inexpensively covered as fast as possible with one of the big three groundcovers, preferably periwinkle, and then highlighting it with clumps and clusters of taller, showier, deciduous or herbaceous groundcovers such as daylilies and large hostas. These will grow right through the primary groundcover, which acts as a unifying theme in the landscape, and eventually spread into sizable stands. This treatment solves a landscape problem without breaking your budget or leaving you with bare ground in winter.

A Tapestry of Groundcovers

A wealth of groundcovers awaits anyone adventuresome enough to move beyond a mass planting of the big three and their alternatives. Rather than planting a green groundcover backdrop, another option is to combine several less aggressive groundcovers to create a tapestry of various forms, textures, and colors. (Don't mix aggressive and nonaggressive plants, or the vigorous growers will overcome the others unless you intervene.)

Virginia Blakelock, who's been gardening in Ohio for more than 20 years, delights in her garden's groundcovers. "One of my most pleasant gardening experiences was the serendipitous discovery of a marvelous groundcover combination: sweet woodruff (*Galium odoratum*) interplanted with European wild ginger (*Asarum europaeum*)," says Virginia. "The contrasting leaf textures look attractive all season, and the *Galium* in bloom with the shiny *Asarum* leaves looks delightful . . . Nearby is a patch of leadwort

(*Ceratostigma plumbaginoides*), which is happily merging with the *Galium/Asarum* combo to provide another thread to the tapestry. The plumbago is at its best in late summer with its brightest-of-blue flowers and in the fall when its leaves turn a rich mahogany color before dropping. All of this thrives in the shade of a maple, surface roots and all!"

"Another wonderful discovery for me—I'm always looking for shade-happy groundcovers—is dwarf Chinese astilbe (*Astilbe chinensis* 'Pumila'), the mat-forming spreading astilbe with dusty rose blooms. This is terrific interplanted with hostas and the Japanese painted fern (*Athyrium nipponicum* 'Pictum'), which has elegant silver markings," Virginia continues. "I've tried every groundcover imaginable. These are my favorites."

When I asked my friend Donna Bickley—whose Maryland property contains lawn only in the paths between her garden beds—if she grew groundcovers, she exclaimed, "Do I grow groundcovers? I am the Groundcover Queen!" Donna explained that instead of lawn, she likes to grow a sea of different groundcovers. And she plants groundcovers under all of her perennials. "Only occasionally do I have to pull out some groundcover a few inches away from a new small plant," she explains. In new plantings, Donna covers the ground thickly with mulch to keep out weeds and then brings in the groundcovers, letting them intermingle as they see fit. "I like a blending of groundcovers and kind of let nature take its course."

Donna has observed that, when left to their own devices, English ivy wins the groundcover competition no holds barred, overgrowing periwinkle, ajuga (*Ajuga reptans*), and all her species of sedum (*Sedum* spp.). Ajuga grows faster than creeping phlox

(*Phlox stolonifera*), but sedum and periwinkle both overpower the ajuga in her garden. As for pachysandra, she claims hers isn't very vigorous, and the wildflower bloodroot (*Sanguinaria canadensis*) and daffodils come up through it with no problem.

Probably Donna's favorite groundcover is *Ajuga reptans*, sometimes called bugleweed, which grows about 6 inches tall when in bloom. She has several cultivars of this semi-evergreen creeper, which forms rosettes of heavily veined leaves. 'Bronze Beauty' is her favorite because its purplish leaves contrast so delightfully with the green foliage of the rest of the garden. It produces indigo blue flowers in early spring. She observes that the plant self-sows and many of the seedlings have green leaves, although they still retain the beautiful blue flowers. In the backyard, Donna grows *A. reptans* 'Alba', a green-leaved cultivar with white flowers, and 'Silver Beauty', with green and white foliage and white flowers.

Ajugas flourish in semi-shade, but don't like full shade. They'll grow in full sun, but only if kept moist. Donna has observed that ajugas won't die if too dry, but they'll wilt. She says they require little maintenance and intermingle well with other plants. You may need to pull some ajuga out if it encroaches on a precious plant that can't take care of itself—but ajuga is shallow-rooted and easy to hand-pull.

Another favorite is three-toothed cinquefoil (*Potentilla tridentata*), which displays strawberry-like leaves and white strawberry-like blooms. It is well behaved and noninvasive. Donna likes to plant this near *Lamium maculatum* 'White Nancy', a green-and-white variegated creeper in the mint family that spreads fast but won't overpower it. The lovely white flowers of 'White Nancy' stand

(continued on page 43)

Get More Groundcovers for Your Money

Given the high price of most groundcovers, you'd think they were difficult to propagate. Actually, just the opposite is true or they wouldn't be groundcovers! Most readily increase as they grow and spread. You can take advantage of this natural propensity and divide many groundcovers, transplanting offshoots to new garden sites, or you can start new plants from old ones by rooting cuttings or by layering stems.

How to Divide Vining and Creeping Plants

Use this method to divide periwinkle, English ivy, Virginia creeper, wintercreeper, foamflower, creeping phlox, wintergreen, partridgeberry, and ajuga.

1. First, cut through the runner, completely separating the young plantlets from any connection to the original plant. Leave the plantlets in place.

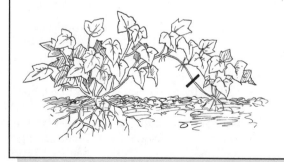

2. Wait a week or so—the young plants will be growing a better root system—then dig them up and replant.

How to Divide Mat-Forming Plants

Spreaders that form mats of tangled stems and roots, so that it's difficult to tell where individual plants end and others begin, can be easily divided almost anytime. Use this method to propagate moss phlox, sweet woodruff, snow-in-summer, baby's tears, Irish moss, and woolly thyme.

1. Chop the mats into pieces with a spade.
2. Transplant or space out the resulting smaller pieces, nestling the roots into the soil. Plants will fill in quickly.

How to Divide Clump-Forming Groundcovers

Groundcovers that grow by forming ever-larger clumps can be divided the same way as flowering perennials. Use this method for hosta, astilbe, painted fern, crested iris, daylily, hay-scented fern, blue fescue, bergenia, and fringed bleeding-heart.

1. Dig up the main clump in early spring and pull or cut apart the individual crowns from the large clump, retaining as many roots as possible.

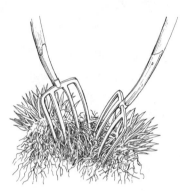

2. Space the divisions out to enlarge the bed, or transplant them to other areas.

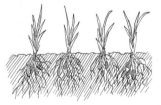

How to Make Cuttings

Many groundcovers can be most easily increased—and increased in large numbers—from stem cuttings. Most plants can be rooted from cuttings taken when the new growth has elongated but not hardened in late spring or early summer. Use this method for periwinkle, English ivy, pachysandra, lamium, leadwort, sedum, and *Forsythia* 'Arnold Dwarf'.

1. Using a sharp knife, clippers, or scissors, take 4- to 6-inch-long cuttings from the tip growth; remove foliage from the lower 2 inches of stem to reduce water loss. Plants that are more difficult to root (those that don't readily produce roots from runners, for instance) may root better if the lower end of the cutting is dipped in rooting powder.

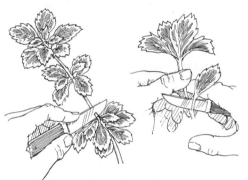

2. Insert the cuttings into flats or small pots of moist rooting medium—a mixture of half peat and half sand, vermiculite, or perlite works well.
3. Keep the cuttings enclosed in a plastic bag, such as a dry cleaner bag, to increase the humidity around the rootless plants. Use popsicle sticks, half-straws, twigs, or some other prop to hold the plastic up off the leaves. Don't ever allow them to dry out, but on the other hand, don't overwater, either. Store the cuttings in bright but indirect light until roots form.

(continued)

Get More Groundcovers for Your Money—*(Continued)*

4. After the cuttings begin to root, gradually open the plastic to let in drier air and move the flat or pots to brighter light.
5. Once the cuttings are well-rooted, transplant to the garden, where they'll be off and running in no time.

How to Layer

Some woody groundcover plants, such as cotoneaster and juniper, may naturally send out roots where their branches touch the soil. These and woody or semi-woody plants that do not readily form such roots can be encouraged to do so by a technique called layering. It may take a year for the layered stem to root and grow enough to be separated from the main plant, so don't count on this method for propagating large numbers of groundcovers.

1. Start layers very early in spring or in fall. To layer, bend a flexible branch and pin it to the ground with a piece

of wire coat hanger or similar sturdy device.

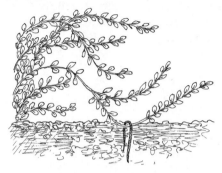

2. Bury the part of the stem in contact with the ground under an inch or two of soil.

3. Check after a year to see if the stem has rooted. When it has, sever the stem between the rooted part and the parent plant.
4. After another month, dig up the new plant and transplant it to a new location.

above the foliage in very visible clusters. Donna finds this lamium performs well in shady and semi-shady spots and makes no demands.

Donna planted Persian catmint (*Nepeta mussinii*) in front of the bench in her fragrance garden. "It really covers the ground quickly in full sun and requires little care," she notes. "If you cut it back after the first bloom in May or June, Persian catmint will rebloom, and the silvery gray leaves look attractive all year."

Donna grows lungworts in her blue garden, both for their spotted foliage and their interesting flowers. *Pulmonaria saccharata* 'Mrs. Moon', admired for its silvery white spotted leaves and early-spring flowers that open pink and age to blue, is a cousin of 'Sissinghurst White', which has more heavily spotted leaves and white flowers. *P. angustifolia* 'Azurea', with spotted leaves, and *P. angustifolia* 'Johnson's Blue,' with all-green leaves, don't spread as fast as *P. saccharata*, Donna notes.

In her California garden, Diann Goldstone, a technical service manager for a Silicon Valley company, completed the renovation of her garden with groundcovers playing a major role. "When we bought the house, the yard was terribly overgrown and the only blooming plants were naturalized nasturtiums," says Diann. The yard is now a glorious display of perennials and bulbs blooming in beds of groundcovers. Diann chose three low groundcovers especially suited to her Zone 9 California climate: isotoma (*Laurentia fluviatilis*), sometimes called bluestar creeper, for its neat foliage and mist of tiny pale blue flowers that bloom in spring and summer; baby's-tears (*Soleirolia soleirolii*) for its mosslike growth habit and rapid spread in moist, shady spots; and sun-loving lamb's-ears (*Stachys byzantina*) for

its bold-textured mats of woolly gray foliage. "I have these interplanted with various tulips, daffodils, hyacinths, and gladiolus (which I don't have to dig up in this climate), iris, liatris, blanket flower, purple coneflower, black-eyed Susans, and geraniums," Diann explains. "All my roses have isotoma as a groundcover, and I plan to add tulips and daffodils to the planting this fall."

All of these expert gardeners chose groundcovers for their beauty, using them to weave a pattern of foliage and dainty flowers on the garden floor or as a backdrop for showier specimens. There's a wealth of delightful low-maintenance groundcovers to choose from if you want to plant a changing tapestry, a living mulch beneath flowers, shrubs, and trees, or even a mass planting where you want to cut down on lawn. Browse through the lists in this chapter and the encyclopedia section near the end of the book for detailed information.

Naughty Groundcovers— Be Forewarned

It's surprising how many of the same plants are listed both in books on groundcovers and in books on weeds! Ironically, the very qualities that make groundcovers so desirable can make them a menace. Groundcovers are meant to spread—but some of the best spreaders can do their job too well! Be very cautious when buying an unknown groundcover because you may find yourself introducing a pest to your garden—even the weedy species are often offered in catalogs.

Curbing Unruly Groundcovers

When a groundcover is properly situated in the soil and light conditions it prefers, it spreads most agreeably. However, even the best groundcovers, such as sweet woodruff

Avoid These Invasive Groundcovers

The following groundcovers are difficult to keep in bounds and often turn into hard-to-eradicate weeds in lawns or gardens.

Aegopodium podagraria (goutweed, bishop's weed)
Arundinaria pumila (dwarf bamboo)
Coronilla varia (crown vetch)
Dichondra micrantha (dichondra)
Duchesnea indica (mock strawberry, Indian strawberry)
Glechoma hederacea (ground ivy)
Hedera helix (English ivy)
Lonicera japonica 'Halliana' (Hall's Japanese honeysuckle)
Lysimachia nummularia (moneywort, creeping Jennie)
Parthenocissus quinquefolia (Virginia creeper)
Phalaris arundinacea var. *picta* (ribbon grass)
Polygonum cuspidatum (Japanese knotweed, Mexican bamboo)
Prunella vulgaris (self-heal, heal-all)
Ranunculus repens (creeping buttercup)
Veronica incana (wooly speedwell)
V. repens (creeping speedwell)
Viola spp. (violets)

*Indicates plant may be useful in the landscape if controlled by edging or pruning or if planted where its rapid spread is welcome and will not threaten other plants.

(*Galium odoratum*), often have to be controlled. And the worst, such as Hall's honeysuckle (*Lonicera japonica* 'Halliana'), are almost impossible to stop, becoming out-and-out pests—homeowners should just avoid them. (There are plenty of other attractive groundcovers to choose from!) Others can be easily controlled when they wander where they aren't wanted, as long as you are vigilant.

Most groundcovers that spread by stolons or underground stems can be controlled in gardens by installing edging. An edging strip, such as landscape timbers or inconspicuous vinyl lawn borders sunk in the ground, will keep your groundcovers from trying to find out if the grass is really greener on the other side.

Vining types of groundcover won't be arrested by an edging—they'll step right over it. With the less aggressive kinds, an occasional clipping around their borders controls their spreading—others may need more frequent attention. We have successfully kept periwinkle and English ivy in place at the edge of a lawn by mowing their tips with the power mower as the vines poke into the lawn area. Just be sure that each time you mow the lawn you aren't giving the groundcover the benefit of the doubt and allowing it to creep ever so slightly inward. It helps to have an edging strip as a guideline for mowing, even if it won't stop the vines, so you know where the edge of lawn and the beginning of the groundcover are supposed to be. And the edging keeps lawn grass from moving in with the groundcover.

Shrubby groundcovers, such as junipers and cotoneasters, can spread by sending out long horizontal branches that root where they touch the ground; these usually grow slowly enough not to pose a weed problem. If shrubby groundcovers start encroaching on spots where they aren't wanted, yearly pruning with hand shears may be required.

Top Groundcovers for Shady Areas

Shade plants don't have to be boring, as you can see from this list. You can select plants with complementary colors and textures to create a wonderful tapestry in shade.

Aegopodium podagraria 'Variegatum' (variegated goutweed, bishop's weed), Zone 3

Ajuga reptans (bugleweed, carpet bugleweed), Zone 5

Akebia quinata (five-leaf akebia, chocolate vine), Zone 4

Arenaria verna (moss sandwort), Zone 2

Asarum spp. (wild gingers), Zones 4–6, depending on species

Bergenia spp. (bergenias), Zone 3

Convallaria majalis (lily-of-the-valley), Zone 4

Dichondra micrantha (dichondra), Zone 9

Epimedium spp. (epimediums, barrenworts), Zone 3

Euonymus fortunei (wintercreeper), Zone 5

Galium odoratum (sweet woodruff), Zone 4

Gaultheria procumbens (wintergreen), Zone 4

Hedera helix (English ivy), Zone 5

Hosta spp. (hostas, plantain lilies), Zone 4

Hypericum calycinum (Aaron's beard, creeping St.-John's-wort), Zone 6

Lamium maculatum (spotted deadnettle), Zone 4

Leucothoe spp. (fetterbushes), Zones 5–6, depending on species

Liriope spp. (lilyturfs), Zones 4–6, depending on species

Mahonia repens (Oregon grape-holly), Zone 5

Mitchella repens (partridgeberry), Zone 4

Ophiopogon japonicus (mondo grass), Zone 7

Pachysandra terminalis (Japanese pachysandra), Zone 5

Parthenocissus quinquefolia (Virginia creeper), Zone 3

Sarcococca hookerana var. *humilis* (sweet box), Zone 6

Sedum spp. (stonecrops), Zones 3–5, depending on species

Tiarella cordifolia (foamflower), Zone 4

Vinca major (greater periwinkle), Zone 8

V. minor (common periwinkle, myrtle), Zone 4

Waldsteinia fragarioides (barren strawberry), Zone 4

*Indicates plant may be invasive if not contained by an edging, pruned, or planted where it can be left to run rampant.

Making Mowing and Lawn Care Easier

Once you've gotten rid of most of your lawn, there are still ways you can make the mowing you have to do easier. The outlines of the lawn should be straight or gently curved. Sharp curves—those that necessitate heading the mower in and then pulling it back out, rather than smoothly gliding through the curve—are a headache and a backache! Straighten out troublesome curves and the mowing will go more smoothly.

Where low-hanging tree or shrub branches scratch your arms or jab your eyes when you try to get at the grass beneath them, get rid of either the limbs or the grass—preferably the grass.

Grass Choices

If you're like me, you really haven't a clue what kind of grass grows in your lawn. The grass—like the wall-to-wall carpet—came with the house and I didn't have much say in the matter. Knowing what kind of grass you have is important, however, in knowing how to care for it. But if you don't know and your lawn is flourishing, then I say, "Who cares?"

If you're struggling to grow a good-looking lawn it just may be that you've got the wrong kind of grass for your situation. There's more to lawns than bluegrass—there are many species of lawn grasses and many cultivars of those species. They differ in climate preference, light and moisture requirements, ability to stand up under wear and tear, disease and insect resistance, even mowing height.

Usually, lawns are made up of a mixture of grass types. Using a mixture means that the grasses that are happiest will flourish and crowd out the less well adapted. It also means that if disease strikes, you are unlikely to lose your entire lawn. And it means that your lawn will green up earlier in spring and stay green later in fall, because of the differing dormant periods of grass species. For all these reasons, most grass seed and sod is sold in mixtures of species and cultivars.

If you're starting a new lawn, take the opportunity to install a well-adapted, disease-resistant, low-maintenance grass mixture. If lawn care isn't high on your priority list, then it pays to plant a low-maintenance lawn. Choose species and cultivars that grow thickly enough to crowd out weeds, require less frequent mowing, and stay green with less fertilizer and water. Then you'll be spending more time relaxing on the lawn than taking care of it.

In general, cool-season grasses are grown in the North. These grow best and are greenest during the cool months of spring and early summer and will brown out in late summer unless kept watered. In the South, warm-season grasses are usually grown. These may turn brown for the winter, but remain green during the hot summer months. Climatic factors such as the degree of humidity, amount of rainfall, and extent of cold and heat, as well as the type and condition of soil, vary throughout the country. These factors influence which types of lawn grass do well where.

According to Dr. Eliot C. Roberts, director of the Lawn Institute, the best grass choices for low-maintenance lawns in the Northeast and Midwest are Kentucky bluegrass (especially the new named cultivars, which are more insect- and disease-resistant) with small amounts of perennial ryegrass and fine fescue (especially hard fescue). In the transition zone between North and South, Dr. Roberts recommends 100 percent turf-type tall fescue for low maintenance, because it's hardier, tolerates summer temperatures better, and requires less care than other popular grasses. In the South, he recommends named Bermudagrass cultivars like 'Cheyenne' and 'Sahara', which have increased insect and disease resistance. In the Southwest, Dr. Roberts suggests buffalograss, which is excellent for dry, arid regions, but recommends bluegrass in the higher elevations. In the Pacific Northwest, he recommends colonial bentgrasses and fine fescues, which perform particularly well in moist, mild climates; as an alternate, he suggests turf-type tall fescues.

Growing Grass in the Shade

Grass needs sun to keep it photosynthesizing and growing—and green! In the shade, grass can struggle for survival, grow thinly, and be susceptible to disease. If you insist on having a lawn in a shady spot rather than growing a groundcover or a shade garden, you will be most successful if you reseed with a shade-tolerant mixture.

In general, fine fescues, St. Augustinegrass, and bentgrass are more shade-tolerant than Kentucky bluegrass, tall fescue, and perennial ryegrass. However, plant breeders have brought us cultivars of most of these species that are exceptionally tolerant of low light. Shade-tolerant Kentucky bluegrass cultivars include 'A-34', 'Benson', 'Bristol', 'Glade', and 'Nugget'. Shade-tolerant tall fescues include 'Alta', 'Falcon', 'Houndog', and 'Rebel'. 'Pennfine', 'Prelude', and 'Repell'

perennial ryegrasses grow well in moderate shade. They are also among the many insect-resistant perennial ryegrass cultivars. 'Biljart', 'Reliant', and 'Scaldis' are shade-tolerant hard fescues.

Modifying your cultural practices a little when caring for shaded lawns helps the grass grow better. Here are some tips to save shady lawns.

- Be sure the area gets good air circulation to discourage fungal diseases, which flourish in the shade.
- Mow the lawn ½ to 1 inch higher than recommended for your mixture, so the grass retains enough leaf for photosynthesizing in low light.
- Increase fertilizer by one-half if the lawn is growing under a tree.
- The shaded lawn *may* need extra water if tree roots compete for water.

Managing Lawn around Tree Trunks and Roots

Have you ever managed to mow right up to a gnarled tree trunk and actually cut off all the grass ringing it? Chances are that if you wanted a neat look you had to go back and hand-trim the hard-to-reach blades. Roots of some trees grow just under the soil surface, forming lumps in the lawn that make mowing a bumpy affair. Where roots actually break through the ground, they can be slashed by the mower, which isn't good for either of them. I've had to face this problem with crabapple, sycamore (London plane), silver maple, and purple-leaf sand cherry trees. Other shallow-rooted trees that may cause you mowing headaches include Norway maple, European larch, sweet gum, dawn redwood, bald cypress, lindens, elms, cottonwoods (poplars), pin oak, white mulberry, Colorado spruce, some ashes, American beech, 'Dale Carlica' weeping beech, white willow, and Pekin willow.

Creating a bed of pachysandra beneath the branches quickly eliminated the problem in my yard. Many other shade-tolerant groundcovers, such as periwinkle (*Vinca minor*), English ivy (*Hedera helix*), dead nettle (*Lamium* spp.), and bugleweed (*Ajuga reptans*), to name only a few, will thrive beneath trees. Remember to choose evergreen plants for areas on view throughout the year, or you'll be looking at bare ground when winter comes.

When planting a groundcover beneath a tree, it looks best to make the bed large enough to visually anchor the tree. I often see hostas planted in a ring around a tree trunk. This looks terribly stiff, rather like a starched collar, and the whole assembly seems top-heavy. When the groundcover extends to the edge of the tree's canopy, or even beyond it, the groundcover bed balances the scale of the tree and appears much more pleasing. And using a large-scale planting rather than lawn beneath a tree is a lot better for the tree's health.

Under deciduous trees, you can also plant drifts of spring-flowering bulbs right in the groundcover. Daffodils, narcissus, Spanish bluebells (*Endymion hispanicus*), and summer snowflake (*Leucojum aestivum*) will naturalize and grow tall enough to rise above low groundcover plants. The foliage of these bulbs will have enough time to mature before the tree leafs out. You can plant other shade-loving perennials, such as the larger hostas, fringed bleeding-heart (*Dicentra eximia*), and astilbes (*Astilbe* spp.), in the groundcover to provide summer flowers.

Tree Rings, Edgings, and Mowing Strips

Fortunately, gardeners have plenty of low-care options for keeping lawns (and groundcovers) in their place and making mowing less time-consuming. Some of the most useful are tree rings, edgings, and mowing strips.

Trunk-Saving Tree Rings

A tree ring is another solution for keeping grass from growing right up to the edge of a trunk. Strip away the sod in a ring about 6 to 8 inches from the trunk. Rather than leaving it bare, fill the tree ring with mulch, gravel, or wood chips, or even decorative bricks set in sand. If you wish, you can extend the tree ring beyond the outer branches of the tree as described for mass-planting groundcovers, keeping the same principles of scale in mind. This reduces competition for water and nutrients and is much healthier for the tree than an underplanting of lawn.

Any of these solutions will help keep weeds out of the ring and make mowing a breeze because the mower wheels can run over the edge of the tree ring and clip off all the grass. You won't have to worry about hand-trimming again. You may need to use an edging tool a couple of times a year to cut away encroaching grass, unless you encircle the tree ring with a lawn border as described below.

Easy-Care Edgings

Most lawn grasses spread by rhizomes, creeping roots that run just below the soil surface. This habit keeps the lawn lush; however, it also means that, seemingly while your back is turned, the grass has crept into the chrysanthemums, slithered into the shrub border, and wandered all over the walkways. Installing a permanent edging between the lawn and other garden areas will dramatically reduce the need to pull unwanted grass from the beds and borders or from between the bricks and paving stones.

The primary idea behind an edging is to keep grass from growing over, under, or between it and reaching forbidden territory on the other side. But edgings also stop plant traffic approaching from the other direction. For instance, the characteristics that earn groundcovers their admirable reputation for blanketing the ground can transform them into pests if they wander where they aren't intended. Periwinkle, ajuga, and sweet woodruff (*Galium odoratum*) are just a few of the many groundcovers that can invade the lawn,

causing an unsightly problem. An edging can stop their underground wanderings and keep the lawn and groundcover neatly in their separate places. And that means less maintenance work for you.

You can choose from a diverse assortment of edging materials and styles. Some are inconspicuous, while others become an obvious and decorative part of the landscape. Your choice depends on the contours of your garden and the effect you wish to create.

Sink the edging at least 4 inches deep to prevent creeping grass roots and roots of most other groundcovers, such as pachysandra, from tunneling under it. If you grow bamboo, you'll need a deeper barrier. Bamboo species that spread aggressively by rhizomes, as opposed to the clump bamboos

A double row of staggered paving bricks set along the edge of a flower bed significantly reduces garden maintenance. The bricks prevent grass from invading the garden, reducing weeding chores, and you can set the lawn mower right on the bricks, so you don't need to hand-trim the lawn edges.

that don't spread, are plants to be feared. These deep-rooted species of bamboo travel by rhizomes that won't be stopped by a 4-inch-deep barrier. Rhizomatous bamboos need an 18-inch-deep barrier, preferably one made from concrete or corrugated steel, to keep them in bounds. Contrary to what one bamboo grower claims in his catalog, bamboo cannot be stopped by a sheet of heavy-duty plastic used as a barrier. The spiky rhizome tips can penetrate plastic and aluminum barriers. And new shoots have been known to emerge from the ground 20 feet away from the main plant.

When installing the edging or lawn border, make sure it's even with the surface of the soil or protrudes only slightly above it so it acts as a mowing strip, allowing you to straddle the edging with the mower wheels and clip all the edges of the grass. If the edging rises more than about ½ inch above the soil surface, the mower blades may collide with it. This mowing problem occurs with many types of decorative edgings that gardeners unwittingly install around their beds. Angled bricks or bricks laid on end rising halfway out of the ground and scalloped cement or terra-cotta edgings may look pretty, but the lawn will look ragged unless it's hand-trimmed after each mowing. Fieldstones and rocks used as borders can provide decorative edgings, but grass gets ensnarled in their irregular borders and must be clipped by hand after mowing. (I ought to know: I used a low rock wall as a border in my present garden and am facing the consequences.) Another edging to reconsider is wood rounds or half-rounds resembling a rustic sunken picket or palisade fence. These look handsome in the right setting but, again, prevent close mowing.

Work-Saving Mowing Strips

Wherever a raised bed, a wall, or a raised edging makes mowing difficult, a mowing strip can solve the problem. A mowing strip is an edging that is low enough and solid enough for the mower's wheels to run along it. Landscape timbers used as an edging double as a mowing strip.

Bricks make a decorative mowing strip in many garden settings if they are set almost flush with the ground. If you want the bricks to double as a lawn-holding edging, they must be set on end or sideways, not flat, or they won't be deep enough to arrest creeping grass roots. A double row of staggered bricks set edgewise into the ground will be deep enough to stop grass roots and wide enough to accommodate the lawn mower wheels. It's best to set bricks into a trench of sand rather than directly into the soil; this keeps the bricks clean and reduces heaving from alternate freezing and thawing in cold climates. Be sure to use paving bricks, which are designed to hold up under continual contact with moisture.

Unfortunately, weeds and grass have many sneaky ways of getting into the spaces between bricks. To reduce a potential weed problem between bricks, stagger them and butt them closely together or lay them over a piece of landscape fabric, which is permeable to water and air but not weed roots.

Choosing and Using Edgings and Mowing Strips

Professional landscapers often use steel edging, the heavy-duty driveway curbing sold at building supply yards, to edge borders. Steel edging is expensive, but very durable and almost inconspicuous once it turns red-brown. It usually comes in sections 10 feet long and 4 inches high and is flexible enough to outline curving borders.

Gardeners can also purchase many types of edging strips at well-stocked garden centers. Corrugated aluminum has been available for some time. It comes in shiny silver or bright green, but, frankly, both look conspicuous and horrible, so avoid them if you can. A more attractive choice is dark brown, black, or dull green vinyl with a tubular top edge. The top edge provides extra durability against nicks from the mower. The best kinds have a flap along the bottom edge to help the edging grip the soil and stay buried. When buried, the tubular edge should rest along the top of the soil. It is inconspicuous when used to edge lawn, since the grass blades camouflage the edge.

It's easy to install steel, aluminum, or vinyl edging. Use a flat garden spade to cut along the edge of your bed, creating a straight-sided trough a little deeper than the width of the edging. Lay the edging flat against the outer side of the trough with the rounded edge protruding just above the soil line. Backfill with soil and firm it in place with your hands or feet.

Mark and I installed about 35 feet of vinyl edging along a new garden border in about half an hour. A little readjustment was necessary in a few places to smooth out a curve and to even out the top, but the job was easily and speedily accomplished. This half-hour's work was an investment of time and energy that saved us from spending countless hours yanking grass out of the flower bed during forthcoming summers. At the end of the border, we ran out of edging and left a 3-foot length of garden unedged. The grass quickly pounced through the opening, making inroads 4 inches into the garden only a year later.

Wood and bricks make more conspicuous edgings that give a permanent structure to the garden throughout the year. Any wood in contact with the soil must be naturally rot-resistant or treated with preservatives, or it won't be long for your garden. Bricks, too, should be weather-resistant; use those graded SW (severe weathering) for projects where bricks will be in contact with the ground.

Landscape timbers can be sunk in the ground to make edgings and mowing strips along walks, beds, and borders. They look attractive and natural, but have one major drawback—they are unbendable. Timbers can be used only to edge straight lines and square corners.

If you want the natural look of wood, but have curving contours to edge, you'll have to forgo the solid look of timbers. Planks thinner than an inch are flexible enough to be bent into gentle curves. If you soak them beforehand in water or saw grooves every few inches into the outer side of the curve, you'll add to their flexibility.

Long strips of wood called bender boards are often available at lumberyards. These are about ⅜-inch thick and 4 inches tall. Their intended use is for making curved forms for poured concrete slabs. Bender boards are usually used in layers for greater durability and a sturdier appearance. Use at least three boards together. To keep bender boards or thicker planks bent in the proper shape, hold them in place with strong stakes. Pound the stakes into the ground on both sides of the wooden edging at 3-foot intervals. Then nail the boards to the stakes with galvanized nails.

The Garden Floor

Landscape designers encourage gardeners to think of their gardens as outdoor rooms, containing a floor, walls, and a ceiling. Looked at this way, it is easy to conclude that green lawn carpets the floor in most suburban yards. I've encouraged you to consider trading in the grass carpet for a floor of low-maintenance groundcovers. Another easy-care alternative to a lawn floor is to install or expand the hard-surface areas, such as decks and patios. If well designed, these areas look attractive and need only an occasional sweeping, weeding, or hosing off. A spacious deck or patio provides a comfortable setting from which you can view your garden, and it expands your living space if you and your family enjoy spending time outdoors. When more of your property is under cover, there is less of it to take care of.

Be careful, though, to keep the patio or deck in scale with the rest of the landscape, or it will dominate the design and your yard may begin to resemble the asphalt jungle rather than a garden. A good rule of thumb is that the hardscape should be no larger than one-third of the yard. However, breaking this rule in a small garden, such as a city garden, and paving or putting decking over all the ground except for the planting borders or island beds, looks wonderful when high walls or a fence enclose the space, creating an easy-care secret garden.

Choose the location for your patio or deck carefully—for maximum comfort and livability, it should be shaded during summer afternoons. Usually, a deck or patio leads directly off the house with access from the kitchen door or from sliding doors or French doors in other rooms. Being physically and visually linked to the house anchors the patio or deck to the landscape. If built in the middle of the lawn, for instance, a patio would seem to float, unconnected to other structural elements. For the best design effect, if you wish to build a large deck or patio away from the house, be sure to link it with a wide walk to a smaller structure alongside the house.

It isn't necessary to ring a patio or deck with plantings to integrate it into the garden. This is usually a terrible mistake, closing in the area and making it seem cramped—exactly what I found when I moved into my previous house. We removed the rigid enclosing hedge, opening up the patio to the lawn on one side, and created planting beds to border the other two sides. I placed a half-barrel directly on the patio at one corner and planted pink petunias—the kind that cascade over the edge—in it to create a transition between the hardscape and the garden.

A large patio begs to be decorated with attractive planters filled with flowers, herbs, or vegetables. You can choose from a broad and tempting array of clay pots, half-barrels, or wooden planters. Arrange them in groups where color is needed. Decks often include built-in planters, whose sides can double as seating areas and railings. A brick patio might also feature built-in planters along one or two sides, or at the corners. But unless you install a drip irrigation system to water it, a container garden, which dries out quickly, becomes a high-maintenance endeavor.

Patio Pointers

Masonry such as bricks, flagstones, concrete patio blocks, or slabs of granite river rocks

Using Pressure-Treated Lumber and Wood Preservatives

Any wood to be used outdoors, especially wood that will be in contact with the soil, should be resistant to rot, decay, and insects. Redwood, cypress, and cedar are the most naturally rot-resistant woods, but they are expensive. The best grades originate from the heartwood and are the most durable and expensive.

Pressure-treated wood stacks up quite well against naturally rot-resistant wood. When a wood preservative is forced under high pressure deep into fir, spruce, or pine, the result is a strong wood that will last longer than redwood or cedar. Pressure-treated wood usually has a greenish cast when purchased. This will weather to an attractive silvery gray, as will redwood and cedar, after three to six months in the sun. All these woods accept stains, so you can change their color readily.

Pressure-treated wood can cost up to 30 percent less than redwood or cedar. It is sold by both the grade and level of chemical retention, measured in pounds per cubic foot. For aboveground use, choose a minimum treatment level of 0.25 pounds per cubic foot; for underground use, choose a minimum of 0.40 pounds per cubic foot. Use marine grade for underwater projects.

Almost all pressure-treated wood is treated with chromated copper arsenate (CCA), a water-soluble chemical that penetrates wood deeply. Creosote and pentachlorophenol (penta) are oil-borne preservatives that are no longer available to homeowners, because they are toxic and can leach from wood, harming people and plants. Copper naphthenate can be purchased and painted onto a wood surface, but surface treatment doesn't penetrate deeply enough to provide long-lasting protection.

Because CCA seeps all the way through lumber during pressure treatment and chemically bonds to the cellulose, there is no danger of it leaching out and harming plants in the garden. The only way to break the chemical bond is to burn the wood, although ingesting or inhaling sawdust can also be dangerous. Ash from pressure-treated wood is highly toxic.

To avoid inadvertently consuming or inhaling the wood dust, follow these safety procedures recommended by the EPA when working with pressure-treated lumber.

• Wear a dust mask when sawing pressure-treated wood.

• Saw pressure-treated wood outdoors if possible.

• Wash thoroughly before eating, drinking, or smoking after sawing pressure-treated wood.

• Wash work clothes separately from regular laundry.

• Compost scraps from pressure-treated wood or deposit in a landfill—do not burn.

• Do not use pressure-treated wood in constructing kitchen counters or cutting boards, beehives, livestock feeders, or food or water storage bins.

are attractive materials for constructing patios and walkways. Base your choice on which type complements the color and architecture of your home as well as on the availability and cost of the materials. Locally quarried stones are usually less expensive than imported stones.

Bricks make an excellent paving that blends with most styles of architecture. Do-it-yourselfers can lay bricks (and flagstones) with professional-looking results. Bricks and flagstone for patios and walks can be mortared or mortarless. Weekend gardeners should know that installing a mortarless patio is easier (and less expensive if you're hiring the work done), but weeds can finagle their way between the pavers, necessitating many hours on hands and knees in the years to come.

There are some advantages to mortarless patios besides cheaper installation, however: In a mortarless system, rain water can seep into the ground beneath the patio to irrigate tree and shrub roots. In cold climates, moisture can be a problem in mortared joints, causing them to freeze and crack, perhaps letting in weeds as well. Be sure to use paving bricks for patios and walkways; these bricks are formulated to withstand constant contact with soil moisture and should not crack if frozen during winter.

Aesthetically, mortared bricks look more romantic and old-fashioned, if the right color of mortar is used. The mortar enhances the brick pattern when it contrasts with the color of the brick. Using old, soft-colored bricks in a herringbone pattern with a buff, gray, or white mortar creates a lovely effect for a country or Victorian-style home. Crisp red bricks butted closely together without mortar in a running bond pattern enhances

contemporary architecture.

Mortared bricks and flagstones are set in wet mortar on a concrete base. The concrete needs a base of gravel and compacted soil. The spaces between the pavers must be filled with mortar after the base is set. Needless to say, this involves a great deal of skilled labor and expensive materials. The patio should be flush with the ground to facilitate mowing and edging, and this means the gravel and sand beds will have to be excavated.

Mortarless pavers are laid in a bed of sand or rockdust sitting on a bed of gravel. To discourage weeds, place sheets of water-permeable landscape fabric (called geotextile mulch) between the sand and the gravel and butt the pavers as closely together as possible. (Do not use plastic as a barrier since it will not drain properly.) Sweep sand or rockdust between the individual pavers after they are all laid. In this system, a rigid edging is needed to keep the bricks or flagstones in place and prevent heaving during winter. Edging may be made from bricks laid on edge in concrete, landscape timbers, or a buried metal edging.

For a beautiful naturalistic effect, you can use large, flat, granite stones, called river rocks, for paving. These can be mortared or laid in sand just as bricks are laid. It may take a bit of trial and error and some ingenuity to get the stones to fit since, being a natural material, they aren't of a uniform shape and size. These stones look superb used around a naturalistic swimming pool or as a patio beside a manmade or natural pond. The disadvantages are minimal: Since the stones are uneven, furniture may rock a bit, and the surface is better suited for strolling than running, so watch your footing.

Paving Plants to the Rescue

Rather than allowing weeds to pop up between the bricks or stones, you can encourage desirable groundcovers to grow there. Leave a bit more space between individual pavers and fill the spaces with a mixture of half sand and half soil. Then plant "paving plants" in the joints. These plants are usually low-growing and can tolerate being stepped on; many paving plants may also be mass-planted in place of grass to produce a low-maintenance lawn.

Be sure to choose plants that are adapted to the exposure of your patio, especially if it's not in full sun. I am encouraging moss to grow between the bricks on my present patio, which is shaded by the house and tall trees most of the day. The moss appeared by itself, but I am giving it a boost by watering the patio during dry spells in summer. Of course I am aware that mossy bricks can be slippery, but so far the moss has confined itself to the spaces between the bricks.

You can also create planting pockets in a patio by removing bricks or rocks and installing an edging to hold the sides in place. Replace the sand and gravel with good soil, and, depending on the size of the patio and the planting pocket, grow a low shrub, tree, or collection of fragrant flowers.

Ways with Walks

Walkways leading from the street or driveway to the doors of your home are essential parts of the hardscape. The front walk, in particular, ought to be at least 4 feet wide so that two people can walk abreast; walks linking less important parts of the landscape can be narrower. All too often, homeowners tend to outline walks with a symmetrical row of shrubs; this closes in the walkway, making it seem claustrophobic and uninviting. (It's also frequently overgrown!) Leave the walk invitingly open, perhaps edged with a sweeping bed of low groundcovers, bulbs, or flowers, but never a hedge or row of plants.

When designing a walk leading through a lawn, be sure to use a mowing strip along its edge so you won't need to trim the border of the grass. Construct brick or flagstone walks the same way as a patio, using a geotextile base to stabilize the structure and to help deter weeds.

I love a path of stepping stones leading through a flower bed or mass of groundcovers. The path invites people to visit the garden, but also provides easy access when the garden needs maintenance. In a naturalistic setting, a path of gravel or wood chips looks suitably informal and is easy to construct. A base of geotextile laid beneath the wood chips or gravel prevents them from mixing into the soil, and also keeps weeds from germinating in the soil beneath the path and poking their way through.

Design garden paths to meander through the property, so that visitors will slow down and enjoy your garden. Invite them to sit in the cool shade beneath a tree by situating a bench along the path. By arranging large shrubs or a small tree at a bend in the path you can camouflage or frame a view, heightening visitors' sense of anticipation about what lies unseen just around the corner.

Deck-Building Pointers

Decks, whether close to the ground or raised, provide a viewing platform for the rest of the garden—a platform that I might add needs

◆ ◆   ◆ ◆   ◆ ◆   ◆ ◆   ◆ ◆   ◆ ◆   ◆ ◆   ◆ ◆

Groundcovers between Pavers

Low-growing, fine-textured ground-covers that will tolerate light foot traffic can be tucked between stepping stones, bricks, and patio blocks. If you plan to grow plants between the masonry, use a mixture of half soil and half sand rather than pure sand as a bed for the stonework. The following plants look decorative and grow well between pavers, and many of them can also be used as a substitute for grass in a lawn.

*Achillea tomentosa (woolly yarrow), Zone 4

Ajuga reptans (carpet bugleweed), Zone 5

Arenaria montana (mountain sandwort), Zone 4

A. verna (Irish moss), Zone 2

Armeria maritima (sea thrift), Zone 4

Aubrieta deltoidea (aubrieta), Zone 4

Campanula carpatica (Carpathian harebell), Zone 3

*Cerastium tomentosum (snow-in-summer), Zone 3

Euonymus fortunei 'Minima' (dwarf wintercreeper), Zone 5

Laurentia fluviatilis (bluestar creeper, isotoma), Zone 7

†Lysimachia nummularia (money-wort, creeping Jenny), Zone 2

†Mentha requienii (Corsican mint), Zone 5

Phlox subulata (moss pink, mountain phlox), Zone 3

Potentilla cinerea (cinquefoil), Zone 3

P. tabernaemontani (*P. verna*) (spring cinquefoil), Zone 3

P. tridentata (three-toothed cinquefoil), Zone 3

Sagina subulata 'Aurea' (Scotch moss), Zone 5

Satureja douglasii (yerba buena), Zone 5

Sedum acre (goldmoss sedum), Zone 3

S. album (stonecrop), Zone 4

†Soleirolia soleirolii (baby's-tears), Zone 8

Thymus pseudolanuginosus (woolly thyme), Zone 5

T. serpyllum (creeping thyme, mother-of-thyme), Zone 5

*Indicates plant may be invasive if not contained by an edging, pruned, or planted where it can be left to run rampant.
†Indicates plant must be mown to stay low.

---

little or no care. So where it looks good, don't hesitate to use decking to replace part of a lawn. Raised decks are especially useful on sloping or hilly ground, where building a brick patio would entail regrading the terrain.

Extending off the house, a deck serves as outdoor living space with a warm, inviting appeal.

Weather-resistant wood, such as redwood, cedar, cypress, and pressure-treated decking make the longest-lasting decks. However, for the sake of economy, wood such as pine, hemlock, spruce, or Douglas fir can be used for the decking top. These won't last as long as the other types of wood, but will provide many years of service. Any wood in direct contact with the ground should be pressure-treated or of a rot-resistant type. The most stable decks are built on piers set in concrete footings.

A handy do-it-yourselfer can erect a deck, but the work requires a lot more skill than bricklaying. Where the ground is uneven or slopes steeply, considerable expertise will be required if you have to work overhead. If your carpentry skills are limited, consider hiring professionals to install your deck. You can still enjoy designing it yourself, or acting as a consultant in the design process, without worrying that it might collapse during a summer party.

Simple deck designs are squares or rectangles, but decks with angles and several levels appear most dramatic and complement contemporary architecture. When designing a deck, consider how the boards will look if laid in various directions. You might want the boards running perpendicular to the house or parallel, depending on the size and shape of the structures. Boards can run diagonally as well, for an exciting look. Where a change of levels occurs in a deck, the direction of the boards often changes. This adds further interest and visually separates the two levels. High decks should have railings for security.

Tree Tactics

Tree seedlings can be a real nuisance to gardeners. Because they get dispersed far and wide—soaring on the wind, planted by squirrels, and transported by birds—tree seeds can germinate almost anywhere in your garden. Sometimes the little seedlings almost carpet the ground beneath a tree, as in the case of a crabapple in my front yard. The major problem with tree seedlings is that they don't stay little for long. If allowed to continue growing, most tree seedlings send down a long root, which grabs the soil and stubbornly refuses to be gotten rid of.

The best way to avoid such weed problems is to grow only seedless trees. But few of us have that option. Most of us live in houses where the trees were planted, or grew naturally, years ago. I do not advocate mass eradication of large trees, no matter how nasty their habits, and have devised methods to deal with the mess some of them can create. But whenever you have the opportunity to plant a tree—whether it's a small ornamental tree or a tall-growing shade tree —you'd be well advised to select a low-maintenance tree. Many improved seedless trees are now available. Cultivars developed especially for the seedless trait include 'Silver Queen' maple (*Acer saccharinum* 'Silver Queen'), 'Autumn Purple' ash (*Fraxinus americana* 'Autumn Purple'), 'Summit' ash (*F. pennsylvanica* 'Summit'), Marshall's seedless ash (*F. pennsylvanica* 'Marshall'), 'Shademaster' thornless honeylocust (*Gleditsia triacanthos* var. *inermis* 'Shademaster'), 'Sunburst' thornless honeylocust (*G. triacanthos* var. *inermis* 'Sunburst'), 'Siouxland' cottonless cottonwood (*Populus deltoides* 'Siouxland'), and hybrid poplar (*P.* × *euramericana*).

Avoid trees that are known for serious disease or insect problems as well as trees that are naturally short-lived, such as poplars and mimosa. Diseases and insects are not always widespread and are often threats only in limited parts of the country (thank goodness), so it is difficult to give general recommendations.

For instance, landscapers in the Northeast no longer plant flowering dogwood (*Cornus florida*) because a serious fungal disease has recently appeared there and threatens to wipe out most of the dogwoods. So far, the disease hasn't appeared in the Southeast, where dogwoods are synonymous with springtime. Before purchasing an important landscape tree, check with your county's Extension agent for home horticulture to see if any local disease or insect problems menace that kind of tree in your area.

Then go for neatness when making your final choices. Ornamental flowering trees, such as crabapples, flowering cherries, magnolias, and dogwoods, will drop petals and sometimes fruit after flowering—but raking up the aftermath is usually worth the effort. The trees to avoid are those that litter the ground with flowers, foliage, seeds, nuts, or bark, and offer little ornamental compensation.

Weeping willows, for instance, are notorious for dropping leaves and entire branchlets (about 3 feet long!) during the growing season. Though they are gloriously graceful and delightful in spring, when their stems and buds color up before just about any other tree's, their mess makes me shudder. For a list of other high-maintenance trees to avoid, see page 68.

Trees with fine-textured foliage often cast a light, dappled shade, the kind that's easy to garden under. And when the foliage changes color and drops in fall, the leaves may not even have to be raked up. Compound leaves made up of small leaflets, such as those of honeylocust (*Gleditsia triacanthos*), black locust (*Robinia pseudoacacia*), and mountain ash (*Sorbus aucuparia*), fall apart and shrivel up. They often simply blow away or get effortlessly chewed up by the lawn mower and are easily disposed of that way.

The ideal lawn tree would be one that is naturally long-lived and free of insects and disease. It would be beautiful year-round, and wouldn't drop seeds that sprout into annoying seedlings or nuts that lurk like the dreaded banana peel or tempt kids to use them as missiles. The tree would cast a light shade and need little fall cleanup.

But if you can't find the ideal tree, or have inherited trees that are less than desirable, there's another solution—stop trying to grow lawn under your trees. Try surrounding your trees with beds of groundcover or situating them in garden areas. Any litter on the ground becomes less obvious in either of these solutions. A heavy mulch on a garden situated beneath a tree discourages tree seedlings from sprouting.

Evergreen trees, particularly needle-leaved evergreens, drop some foliage every year, often in early summer. The oldest needles drop to the ground and may need raking if the tree is situated in a lawn. But again, by designing a planting bed beneath the tree's limbs, the fallen needles act as a natural mulch and need no extra maintenance.

Shrub Solutions

It's almost comical to see how many homes and yards lie concealed behind the overgrown shrubs planted in front of them. The traditional foundation planting of evergreens lined up along the front of the house, with rounded shapes along the length and accents of columnar shrubs marking each corner and framing the door, more often than not begins to dwarf the house in a few years. Once-sunny windows become dim; an open

Usually Pest-Free Trees

In yard conditions, the following trees usually aren't plagued by insects.

Deciduous

Betula nigra (river birch), Zone 4
Carpinus spp. (hornbeams, ironwoods), Zone 5
Celtis australis (Mediterranean hackberry), Zone 6
Cercidiphyllum japonicum (katsura tree), Zone 5
Cornus kousa (Kousa dogwood), Zone 5
C. mas (Cornelian cherry), Zone 5
Elaeagnus angustifolia (Russian olive), Zone 3
Franklinia alatamaha (Franklin tree), Zone 6
Ginkgo biloba (ginkgo, maidenhair tree), Zone 4
Gleditsia triacanthos (honeylocust), Zone 4
Laburnum × *Watereri* (golden-chain tree), Zone 6

Liquidambar styraciflua (sweet gum), Zone 5
Magnolia kobus (Kobus magnolia), Zone 5
M. stellata (star magnolia), Zone 5
Parrotia persica (parrotia), Zone 6
Pistacia chinensis (Chinese pistache), Zone 7
Stewartia spp. (stewartias), Zone 6
Styrax spp. (snowbells), Zone 6
Zelkova serrata (Japanese zelkova), Zone 6

Evergreen

Chamaecyparis spp. (false cypresses), Zones 5–6, depending on species
Juniperus spp. (junipers), Zones 2–6, depending on species
Podocarpus spp. (podocarpus), Zone 8
Sciadopitys verticillata (umbrella pine), Zone 6
Taxus spp. (yews), Zones 4–6, depending on species

view of the lawn and garden vanishes behind foliage.

When Mark and I moved into our present house, the vase-shaped junipers planted 20 years ago along the driveway formed a tunnel barely large enough to admit a car—and then not without scratching the finish. In another part of the property, I unearthed a path of bluestone stepping stones from deep beneath the boughs of several low-spreading junipers, where they lay buried under an inch of decomposed needles and leaves. A Norway spruce (*Picea abies*) planted at the corner of the two-story house towered above the building; its branches blocked the light from both upper and lower windows and lay on the roof. Stories such as these are sadly all too commonplace.

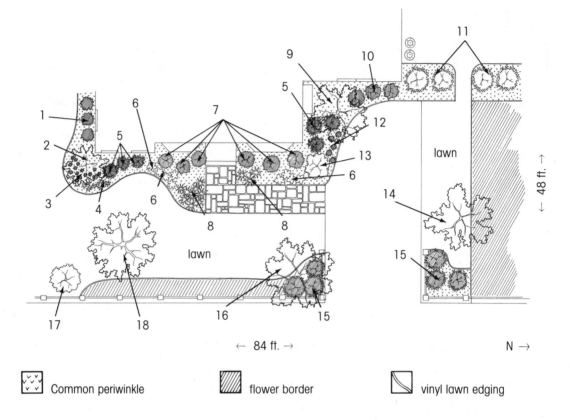

Common periwinkle	flower border	vinyl lawn edging

Plot Plan of a Low-Maintenance Foundation Planting. (1) 'Compacta' Japanese holly, (2) 'Arnold Promise' witchhazel, (3) common snowdrops, (4) crocuses, (5) 'Gumpo White' azalea, (6) 'Gold Edger' hosta, (7) 'Repandens' English yew, (8) 'Stella d'Oro' daylily, (9) 'Bloodgood' Japanese maple, (10) 'Limemound' Bumald spirea, (11) white-flowered Carolina rhododendron, (12) 'Moonbeam' threadleaf coreopsis, (13) 'Compactum' koreanspice viburnum, (14) existing apple, (15) 'Delaware Valley White' azalea, (16) 'Kwanzan' Japanese flowering cherry, (17) existing border forsythia, (18) existing saucer magnolia

You might not be able to avoid coming into possession of such an unfortunate mess—all four of the houses I've owned came complete with overgrown foundation plantings—but you can at least avoid creating such a situation on your own. Shrubs should be the mainstay of weekend gardeners, because they offer so much year-round beauty with so little care—if (and I emphasize *if*) properly selected, situated, and pruned.

A shrub border or hedge can enclose your property, providing privacy and offering flowers, berries, and colorful fall foliage or four-season greenery. Foundation shrubs beautify the front of your home by anchoring it to the surrounding landscape and camouflaging an unsightly foundation. And contrary to popular pruning practices that call for butchering shrubs with hedge shears several times a year, most shrubs ought to be practically carefree, requiring attention only every few years. When properly pruned by thinning the branches with a hand shears, evergreen shrubs grow slowly, look beautiful, and can be kept at the desired height indefinitely.

Taming Foundation Plantings

The primary reason foundation shrubs become so crowded and unsightly is that the wrong shrubs are planted in the first place. Recently friends asked me to take a look at their property with a critical eye and advise them on how to redesign their landscape. The one-story house featured long, low lines and a beautiful stonework facade hidden somewhere behind a row of mountain laurel.

Mountain laurel (*Kalmia latifolia*) is native to this area and creates an enchanting effect in the middle of June, when its pale pink or white blooms light up the woodland. It grows 6 to 15 feet tall and about as wide. In an attempt to keep the three laurel bushes from obscuring the stonework, my friends had been pruning them back every year. As a result, the naturally loose, delightfully gnarled shrubs had become dense balls about 4 feet wide with trunks as thick as fence posts. They never flowered because my friends pruned off the flower buds every year.

(continued on page 64)

I created this easy-care design for my friends the Goldwassers. I wanted to integrate the driveway, which they needed for parking, into the landscape and to replace the overgrown foundation planting with a wide border of dwarf and low-growing shrubs, which require little or no pruning. Installing lawn edging around the lawn greatly reduces weeding and edging chores.

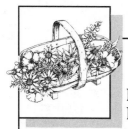

◆ ◆ ◆ ◆ ◆ ◆

Natural Pruning Techniques

There are two basic types of pruning cuts: thinning cuts and heading cuts.

A **thinning cut** is used to direct new growth while allowing a plant to grow into its natural shape. To make a thinning cut, simply cut off a branch where it originates from the main branch or trunk, using hand-pruning shears or loppers. Another way to thin is to shorten a branch by cutting it back to the place where it makes a Y with other side branches or the main stem. By making the cut flush with another branch, the remaining branches continue their growth pattern undisturbed.

Thinning encourages the shrub to produce new growth at a slow pace. Once a shrub has grown to its maximum desirable size, you should be able to keep it that size with stern thinning every year. If you want the shrub to grow larger, you need only thin lightly to direct wayward branches or to remove dead and diseased growth.

When thinning an evergreen such as a juniper or yew, hold the branch you intend to cut in one hand and lift it upward. Reach inside the shrub with the other hand and cut the branch with your clippers where it divides into side branches or where it emerges from the main branch or trunk. Shape by cutting the upper branch layers shortest and leaving the lower layers longer so you have a naturally shingled—or pyramidal—look. By shingling the shrub,

the upper branches do not shade those below, so the lower branches will keep their needles.

Most deciduous shrubs grow by sending up new stems directly from the ground. Every few years, it's a good idea to reinvigorate them by thinning out about a quarter of the stems at ground level—choose the oldest and weakest stems. Make this type of thinning cut with a small pruning saw or loppers, removing the entire stem. You can shape deciduous shrubs by thinning the remaining branches back to side branches. These two thinning cuts allow light to reach the center of the shrub, encouraging thick growth.

If you want a natural-looking garden, emphasize the plants' innate shapes when you prune; don't impose a shape on them. Shrubs in naturalistic arrangements are meant to be appreciated as a mass, not as individual plants.

A proper **heading cut** is made across the branch or stem just above a bud. This type of cut stimulates branching and encourages new growth. Heading cuts can be used to encourage a young shrub or tree to branch; use this type of cut when trying to thicken up growth to obscure a view. **Shearing** is a form of heading cut in which just the tips of many stems are all cut off in one fell swoop with hedge shears. When the shearing cuts are made deep into the shrub, this is called **cutting back hard.** Repeated shearing results in a shrub with a shell of dense twiggy growth and a dead center. Reserve shearing for formal hedges and cutting back hard for formal hedges that have grown too large.

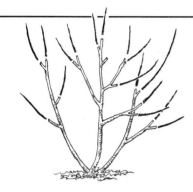

Heading cuts, *left,* leave behind a stub at each branch tip, and these stubs sprout many fast-growing, twiggy side branches, *right.* Heading should be used only to thicken a sparse shrub, not as a routine practice.

To prune an evergreen shrub, lift the branch to be pruned, reach into the shrub, and cut carefully with hand pruners where the branch meets a side branch or the main stem.

Reserve shearing, *left,* for formal hedges, since it promotes fast, twiggy growth that needs repeated attention. Be sure the sheared hedge, *right,* is wider at the bottom than at the top so all the foliage receives full sun; otherwise, you'll have massive leaf drop.

Old deciduous shrubs, *left,* can be rejuvenated by cutting the stems back to the ground, *center,* in late winter. New growth, *right,* will sprout from the stubs, promoting a fuller shape, better flowering, and brighter bark color.

How you prune your shrubs determines how fast they grow, what shapes they ultimately take, and how much effort you must put into their maintenance. Pruning correctly slows growth, preserves the plant's beauty, and saves you time.

At 4 feet, the mountain laurels didn't entirely block the stonework or windows, but the shrubs' shape did nothing to enhance the house, and they no longer bore much resemblance to mountain laurels. My advice: Remove the mountain laurels, transplanting them to a woodland if possible, and plant low shrubs with horizontal branches, such as cotoneasters (*Cotoneaster* spp.), creeping juniper (*Juniperus horizontalis*), or creeping St.-John's-wort (*Hypericum calycinum*). These would emphasize the lines of the house and remain low enough never to require pruning.

The most commonly planted foundation shrubs, I would venture to bet, include: yew (*Taxus* spp.), juniper (*Juniperus* spp.), arborvitae (*Thuja* spp.), false cypress (*Chamaecyparis* spp.), tall-growing rhododendrons (*Rhododendron* cultivars), Japanese holly (*Ilex crenata*), American holly (*Ilex opaca*), podocarpus (*Podocarpus* spp.), common boxwood (*Buxus sempervirens*), hemlock (*Tsuga canadensis*), and photinia (*Photinia* spp.). These shrubs and trees mature at heights of 15 to 100 feet. They're odd choices for landscaping homes whose first-story windows may begin between 2 to 4 feet from the ground!

This poor choice of plant material is often compounded by a poor choice of pruning methods, and prune them you will if you select these tall-growing plants to front your house. The hapless shrubs become rigid boxes, cubes, cones, and balls because many well-meaning homeowners shear them with hedge shears rather than thinning them with hand clippers.

In an attempt to keep foundation plants under control, the homeowner disciplines them with hedge shears several times a year—a time-consuming chore. The worst of it is that no matter how faithfully the shrubs are sheared, they still grow ever larger. The shrub grows two steps forward and the gardener prunes one step backward, resulting in slow but steady enlargement. Eventually, the house disappears behind grotesque geometrical green forms.

When pruned with hand shears by thinning—removing individual branches at their point of origin on another branch—even the typical foundation shrubs can be prevented from outgrowing their allotted space. Shrubs pruned by thinning also retain their inherent naturally graceful shapes. Their interiors are filled with foliage, rather than bare branches with a thin shell of leaves on the outside, which happens when shrubs are sheared.

Weekend gardeners would be better off selecting compact, dwarf, or low-growing foundation shrubs that won't camouflage the house and require little or no pruning. There are many wonderful shrubs to choose from, and many of the commonly planted foundation shrubs have low, spreading, or dwarf cultivars. These improved cultivars are the ones to go for, not the ordinary species. For instance, the English yew (*Taxus baccata*) is a multitrunked tree or shrub that can grow 25 to 60 feet tall. Its cultivar 'Repandens' is a low, broad-spreading shrub that grows no taller than 3½ feet, and twice as wide, in 10 to 20 years.

Room to Grow In

Because newly purchased shrubs are often so small, an all-too-common error is to space them too close to each other and to the house or walkways. Shrubs should be spaced far enough apart so they won't crowd each other once they have matured. This is easier said than done, I admit. New shrubs seem to get swallowed up by the ground once

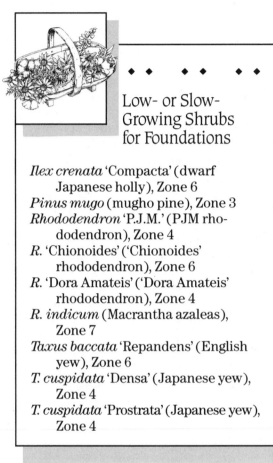

Low- or Slow-Growing Shrubs for Foundations

Ilex crenata 'Compacta' (dwarf Japanese holly), Zone 6

Pinus mugo (mugho pine), Zone 3

Rhododendron 'P.J.M.' (PJM rhododendron), Zone 4

R. 'Chionoides' ('Chionoides' rhododendron), Zone 6

R. 'Dora Amateis' ('Dora Amateis' rhododendron), Zone 4

R. indicum (Macrantha azaleas), Zone 7

Taxus baccata 'Repandens' (English yew), Zone 6

T. cuspidata 'Densa' (Japanese yew), Zone 4

T. cuspidata 'Prostrata' (Japanese yew), Zone 4

ultimately spread 4 feet.

It can look ridiculous to plant small new shrubs as far apart as is really necessary, but do it anyway. In a year or two, you won't know the difference. You can plant groundcovers or flowering annuals or simply apply a thick mulch between the shrubs so the planting looks less sparse to begin with.

It is essential to know a plant's mature height and spread as well as its rate of growth when you plant it. Some dwarf conifers, for instance, grow so slowly that their growth rate during your lifetime is more important than the plant's eventual height, which only your great-grandchildren will see. Dwarf Alberta spruce (*Picea glauca* var. *albertiana* 'Conica'), for instance, grows at a rate of only 1 or 2 inches a year when young. It slows its growth until it eventually forms a cone 10 to 12 feet tall, and as wide at the base, in 40 to 45 years. I'd recommend spacing such slow growers so that they fit comfortably into their landscape space for the next 15 years.

Handsome Hedges

There are two kinds of hedges—formal and informal. Weekend gardeners should avoid formal hedges like the plague. Formal hedges demand a boring, time-consuming shearing at least two or three times a year, and if they aren't pruned on schedule, they begin to look truly ratty. Because they are sheared into flat-sided walls, formal hedges can look pleasingly neat and tidy, but at a high cost in time and labor. And often, they just look boring.

I prefer the appearance of an informal hedge, which looks unpruned. In an informal hedge, the hedge shrubs are planted fairly close together so they fill in as densely as a formal hedge, but their finish is soft-edged. The best way to get this natural

they're planted. Before planting, their balled or containerized roots give the plants false height, rather as if they were wearing high heels. Once planted, they take off their heels and seem to shrink.

Keep telling yourself your new shrubs will grow, and probably grow rapidly! Picture their mature size when you plant them. Bring out a yardstick or tape measure to get a concrete idea of their eventual width. Your goal is for the branches of neighboring shrubs to intermingle somewhat when they are mature. This means spacing the trunks of two shrubs 4 feet apart if they will each

Shrubs for Informal Hedges

The following shrubs make excellent hedges and require little pruning to look good. Many of them offer multi-season interest.

Deciduous

Berberis thunbergii (Japanese barberry), Zone 4

Elaeagnus pungens (silverberry), Zone 7

Euonymus alata (burning bush, winged euonymus), Zone 4

Forsythia × intermedia (forsythia), Zone 5

Ligustrum spp. (privets), Zone 3

Myrica pensylvanica (bayberry); sometimes evergreen, Zone 4

Spiraea × bumalda (Bumald spirea), Zone 4

S. × vanhouttei (bridal-wreath spirea), Zone 3

Viburnum spp. (viburnums), Zones 2–5, depending on species

Weigela florida (weigela), Zone 5

Evergreen

Buxus sempervirens (common boxwood), Zone 6

Gardenia jasminoides (common gardenia, cape jasmine), Zone 8

Ilex crenata (Japanese holly), Zone 6

I. glabra (inkberry), Zone 5

Photinia × fraseri (photinia), Zone 7

Pittosporum tobira (Japanese pittosporum), Zone 8

Podocarpus spp. (podocarpus), Zone 8

Rhododendron hybrids (azaleas and rhododendrons), Zones 5–7, depending on species

Taxus spp. (yews), Zones 4–6, depending on species

---

appearance is by allowing the shrubs to grow unpruned. But if the hedge needs pruning to control its size or to rejuvenate it, thin the branches with hand shears or cut the older stems out at ground level, rather than shearing the hedge with a hedge clipper.

Gardeners value hedges because they provide privacy and mark boundaries in a more friendly manner than a stockade fence or brick wall. And they cost less, too. Infor-

mal hedges can serve the same functions as formal hedges, but in an even friendlier manner.

Evergreen shrubs such as yew (*Taxus* spp.), common boxwood (*Buxus sempervirens*), and Japanese holly (*Ilex crenata*) are commonly sheared into flat-sided formal hedge shrubs. But they also make attractive informal hedges. Once it reaches the desired size, an evergreen hedge should be thinned by hand once a year, in spring, to keep it in bounds. This results in a trim shape, but one with dense fluffy outlines, rather than a rigid flat wall. Unlike a formal sheared hedge, a properly thinned informal hedge will never grow too large for its place. And it looks thicker and greener than a sheared hedge.

Deciduous flowering shrubs make stunning informal hedges. Their cascading branches bend toward the ground, displaying their flowers as graceful garlands. Shrubs such as bridalwreath spirea (*Spiraea × vanhouttei*), forsythia (*Forsythia × intermedia*), and weigela (*Weigela florida*) are ideal choices. I shudder whenever I see a line of forsythia that has been massacred into a straight-sided wall. Deciduous shrubs grown for foliage rather than flowers, such as privet (*Ligustrum* spp.) and burning bush (*Euonymus alata*), are often clipped into formal hedges, but they, too, look great when left with a soft outline—in fact, almost nothing beats the fall display of an informal burning bush hedge, with its red leaves creating a billowing wall of "flame."

Deciduous shrubs in an informal hedge need less pruning than evergreen shrubs. Once every three years or so, remove the oldest branches at ground level to make room for new growth. Don't cut back the length of the branches, but leave them unpruned to grow to their intended height. Because an informal hedge retains the natural branching pattern of the shrubs that form it, the hedge will probably be wider and take up more space than a formal hedge. Make sure you allow enough space, or choose shrubs that remain small.

If you heed the advice in this chapter, you can create a tidy, practically care-free yard. Lawn spaces will be small, and open areas will be carpeted instead with the engaging textures of low-maintenance groundcovers. Leaves will practically rake themselves, and the shrubs won't reprimand you for leaving them unpruned. There will be lots of space—and time—to sit outdoors and relax.

But if you're really in love with gardening, you won't want to stop there. In the following chapters, you'll find out how to be a creative gardener, cultivating special shrubs, flowers, and edibles the easy-care way, in traditional and nontraditional settings.

High-Maintenance Trees to Avoid

According to Kathryn Belville, a professional arborist in Philadelphia, the following problem trees cause headaches in the landscape. They may be highly insect- or disease-prone, weak-wooded and subject to storm damage, inordinately messy, or simply short-lived. Avoid them if you can.

Plant Name	Maintenance Problems	Plant Name	Maintenance Problems

Deciduous Trees

Plant Name	Maintenance Problems	Plant Name	Maintenance Problems
Acer saccharinum **Silver maple** *A. platanoides* **Norway maple**	Silver maple grows fast, so it has soft wood that's highly susceptible to storm damage. Verticillium wilt can kill Norway maple. Norway maple also casts such deep shade almost nothing will grow under it. Both are shallow-rooted, and their numerous seedlings cause weed problems. 'Silver Queen' is a male cultivar of silver maple that produces no seeds.	*Albizia julibrissin* **Mimosa**	Highly susceptible to mimosa wilt, which may kill tree seemingly overnight. Mimosa webworm very disfiguring in some regions. Drops flowers, and seeds cause a weed problem. 'Charlotte' and 'Tyron' are resistant to mimosa wilt.
		Alnus glutinosa **Black alder**	Leafminers, woolly aphids, and tent caterpillars may cause serious disfiguration. Usually short-lived.
Aesculus hippocastanum **Horsechestnut** *A. × carnea* **Red horsechestnut**	Leaf scorch disease disfigures trees in late summer. *Aesculus × carnea* is somewhat less susceptible to leaf scorch and drought injury than *A. hippocastanum*. Both drop leaves, twigs, and buckeyes enclosed in large, spiny shells. *A. hippocastanum* 'Baumannii' has double flowers that do not form nuts.	*Amelanchier* spp. **Serviceberry, shadbush**	Fireblight may kill trees. Mites and scale may weaken the tree, but may be less of a problem in naturalized settings.
		Betula papyrifera and *B. pendula* (*B. alba*) **White birch**	Bronze birch borer can kill trees stressed by drought, especially in the South and Midwest. Leafminers disfigure foliage and reduce tree's vigor. Short-lived because of insect problems. Subject to ice and snow damage. *B. maximowicziana* (monarch birch) is supposedly resistant to bronze birch borers; *B. platyphylla* var. *japonica* 'Whitespire' is known to be resistant.
Ailanthus altissima **Tree of heaven**	Male trees smell bad when in flower. Female trees, if pollinated by nearby male tree, produce seeds that cause a serious weed problem, germinating just about anywhere. Short-lived with soft wood. Litters foliage and twigs.		

Plant Name	Maintenance Problems	Plant Name	Maintenance Problems
Catalpa spp. **Catalpa, Indian bean**	Catalpa worms may defoliate tree. Large, leathery "cigar" seedpods drop over a long period in fall and winter, causing a serious cleanup problem.	*Gleditsia triacanthos* **Honeylocust**	Mimosa webworm can defoliate trees. Long, leathery seedpods pose a major problem. Huge branched thorns are a hazard. *G. triacanthos* var. *inermis* is thornless but not fruitless. The following cultivars are both thornless and fruitless: 'Bujotii', 'Majestic', 'Shademaster', 'Skyline', and 'Sunburst'. Cultivars 'Imperial' and 'Moraine' are thornless, fruitless, and resistant to webworms.
Cercis canadensis **Redbud**	Canker disease is highly destructive, causing trees to be short-lived.		
Cornus florida **Flowering dogwood**	Anthracnose and leafspot disease have become a serious problem in the Northeast, killing weakened trees. Dogwood borers can cause slow decline and death. Usually short-lived.	*Koelreuteria paniculata* **Goldenrain tree**	Weak-wooded and subject to storm damage.
Crataegus laevigata **English hawthorn**	Cedar-apple rust fungus may ruin fruits. Fireblight can kill trees. Aphids and tent caterpillars can weaken and disfigure trees. *C. phaenopyrum* (Washington hawthorn) is less susceptible to pests and diseases.		
Fraxinus americana **White ash** *F. pennsylvanica* **Green ash**	Drops seedpod litter. Seeds cause a serious weed problem. Somewhat prone to storm damage. White ash cultivars: 'Autumn Purple' has good fall color and is seedless; 'Rosehill' is seedless. Green ash cultivars: 'Marshall' or 'Marshall's Seedless' and 'Summit' are seedless.		

(continued)

Plant Name	Maintenance Problems	Plant Name	Maintenance Problems
Deciduous Trees—Continued		*Platanus* × *acerifolia* **London plane tree** *P. occidentalis* **Sycamore, American plane tree**	Sycamore is susceptible to a serious twig blight called anthracnose. London plane tree is resistant to this disease, but suffers from a more serious condition called cankerstain. Both constantly shed leaves, twigs, bark, and fuzzy seedpods. *P. orientalis* resists these diseases but is less cold-hardy.
Malus baccata **Siberian crabapple** *M. floribunda* **Japanese flowering crabapple** *Malus* cultivars **Flowering crabapple**	Apple scab can disfigure or defoliate trees. Mildew may cause premature leaf drop. Fireblight can attack some trees. Tent caterpillars can defoliate trees. Fallen fruits, especially of large-fruited cultivars, can be messy. Fruits may cause a weed seedling problem. Disease-resistant cultivars or hybrids of *M. baccata:* 'Beauty', 'Dolgo', 'Adams', 'Makamik'. *M. floribunda* itself is fairly resistant to fungal diseases, and the fruits are so small they're a minor problem; disease-resistant cultivars include 'Seafoam' and 'Ormiston Roy'. *M. hupehensis* (tea crabapple) is resistant to most diseases.		
		Populus alba **White poplar** *P. deltoides* **Cottonwood** *P. nigra* 'Italica' **Lombardy poplar** *P. tremuloides* **Quaking aspen**	All suffer from serious canker diseases attacking the stems and trunk. Fast-growing and weak-wooded; suffer from storm damage and are short-lived. Roots can clog drainage pipes and disturb pavement. Cottonwood is messy, dropping twigs and leaves, and female flowers release cottony seeds that in quantity can be hazardous and create a weed problem. *P. deltoides* 'Siouxland' is seedless, as is the hybrid poplar *P.* × *euramericana*.
Morus alba **Mulberry**	Purple fruits drop, staining pavement and garden furniture. Birds spread the seeds, causing a widespread seedling weed problem. 'Kingan' and 'Striblingii' are nonfruiting.		
		Quercus rubra **Red oak**	Oak wilt disease can kill trees of this and other species in the red oak group. Large acorns create a litter problem. Oaks in the black and white oak groups do not get wilt disease.
Paulownia tomentosa **Empress tree**	Severe weed seedling problem. Fast-growing and weak-wooded, making it short-lived and subject to storm damage and winter injury.		
		Salix alba var. *tristis* **Golden weeping willow** *S. babylonica* **Babylon weeping willow**	Susceptible to numerous insects and diseases. Weak-wooded, fast-growing, and short-lived. Constantly litter leaves and broken twigs and branches. Roots can invade septic lines and drainage pipes.

Plant Name	Maintenance Problems
Sorbus aucuparia **European mountain ash, rowan**	Fireblight and scab can be serious. Borers can kill trees. Numerous other insect problems, including tent caterpillars and Japanese beetles.
Tilia americana **American linden, basswood**	Several diseases can cause problems, including powdery mildew, leafspot, and verticillium wilt. Mites, aphids, borers, Japanese beetles, and scale can also be troublesome. *Tilia cordata* (littleleaf linden) can become infested by the same insects and diseases, but is usually much less troubled than basswood.
Ulmus americana **American elm** *U. pumila* **Siberian elm**	Dutch elm disease and phloem necrosis kill American elms, especially in the Northeast and Midwest where the fungi are prevalent. Elm leaf beetles cause serious damage to foliage and spread disease. Siberian elm is soft-wooded and subject to storm damage, and it poses a seedling weed problem. Recently developed *U. americana* cultivars 'Homestead' and 'Pioneer' resist Dutch elm disease, as does the Siberian elm. *Zelkova serrata* is often promoted as an American elm substitute; the cultivar 'Green Vase' mimics the vase shape of the elm more than other cultivars.

Plant Name	Maintenance Problems
Evergreen Trees	
Ilex opaca **American holly**	Leafminers can seriously disfigure foliage and reduce tree vigor. Occasional scale problems. Leafspot diseases may mar foliage. Fallen leaves have spines, which makes handling them unpleasant. English holly (*I. aquifolium*) isn't bothered by leafminers.
Juniperus virginiana **Eastern red cedar**	Alternate host for cedar-apple rust, which does little harm to the cedars but can destroy apple crops and hawthorn berries. Mites and bagworms can be serious in some locations.
Larix spp. **Larches**	Larch case-bearer insect can disfigure trees. Twig and cone litter may be annoying.
Pinus nigra **Austrian pine** *P. sylvestris* **Scotch pine** *P. thunbergiana* **Japanese black pine**	Twig blight and beetles are serious in some areas and can kill mature trees.
Thuja occidentalis **Arborvitae**	Mites, bagworms, scale, and leafminers may all be serious. Snow and ice often split off trunks from trees with central leaders.

LOW-MAINTENANCE FLOWER GARDENS

How to Design with Easy Care in Mind

Harry and Maryann are city folks. Neither of them know a petunia from a potato, nor which end of the spade is up. Yet Mark and I are unconcerned about turning over our house and garden to them while we venture forth for a sabbatical in another state. Some of our nongardening friends, who understand how much we love our beautiful gardens, wonder if we are being brave, foolhardy, or just plain stupid to leave our flowers in the hands of neophytes. They continually ask if we are worried that our hard-won yard and flower gardens, which we spent three years carving out of a morass of overgrown junipers, neglected lawn, and poison ivy patches, will be a mess again when we return.

We aren't worried. Flower gardens don't have to be a lot of work. Ours aren't. Despite the fact that our half acre boasts packs of vivid blossoms from early spring through fall, Mark and I actually spend very little time maintaining our gardens, because we designed them for low maintenance. The

shrubs and flower gardens can practically take care of themselves. We know our tenants will expend a minimal amount of unskilled gardening effort, but even a year of total neglect shouldn't harm our flower beds.

The future tenants are almost as concerned about the fate of our gardens as our friends are. But I reassured Maryann and Harry that their garden responsibilities would be minimal by taking them on a tour of the property. I explained what care would be needed and pointed out all the steps we had taken to reduce the time required for boring maintenance chores. I described how the extensive flower beds and borders feature low-maintenance perennials, shrubs, and bulbs that are specially selected to thrive in their sites without any pampering. Drought-tolerant flowers grow in the dry, sandy soil near the front of the property where it's difficult to water with a hose. Shade-loving wildflowers and ferns decorate the border beneath the trees in the side yard, and more formal flowers adorn the curvaceous blue, yellow, and white border in the front yard. All the flowers are low-maintenance types that won't get bugs or diseases and don't require staking or frequent dividing, but will return to delight them next spring and summer with waves of blossoms.

All Maryann and Harry will have to do is pinch off the faded flowers of the spring bulbs, water the flower beds in case of summer or fall drought, and cut the perennials to the ground in winter once the tops have turned dry and brown. We're leaving the beds heavily mulched with a deep layer of shredded leaves to reduce watering and weeding chores, and lawn edging confines each of the planting areas so there will be no need to constantly fight off the grass from invading the flowers.

Creating a Weekend Flower Garden

Because many herbaceous perennials and bulbs live for years and often form ever-larger clumps, a garden relying on a careful selection of these durable flowers makes the perfect low-maintenance flower bed for gardeners short on time. Select those perennials and bulbs that demand little or no care. Avoid those that are floppy and need staking, too invasive for your taste, short-lived, prone to disease and insects, or just plain difficult to grow. And, of course, be sure to match your plant selection to whatever soil and sun conditions the site has to offer. Most perennials and bulbs need full sun—that means at least 6 hours a day—though a shaded or semi-shaded garden is not out of the question if you plan it carefully. By choosing plants from the lists of "Especially Well-Behaved Perennials" and "Easy-Care Bulbs"

as your garden mainstays, and avoiding those on the lists of "Especially Finicky Perennials," "Exuberantly Spreading Perennials," and "Bulbs to Avoid," the work involved in caring for the plants in your perennial border will be minimal. The encyclopedia section near the end of the book provides descriptions and cultural information about flowers and shrubs recommended here.

Adding spring bulbs to the perennial garden involves one terrible risk—that later in the growing season when they have disappeared from sight you will inadvertently slice into the dormant bulbs when dividing a perennial or adding something new to the bed. In fall, you might even—it happens more often than we would like to admit—try to plant more bulbs where bulbs are already located. One way to avoid this potential problem is to plant bulbs in their own designated spaces in the garden—don't mix them in between the perennials—and then when bulb flowers have faded or their foliage begins to look sad, plant shallow-rooted annuals right on top of them. By alternating spring bulbs with summer annuals, you'll get a long display of color *and* have a marker that tells you where the bulbs lie dormant.

Garden Flowers 101

Before getting down to the fun part of designing your low-maintenance flower garden, it helps to understand the basic habits and lifestyles of the plants you will be growing—flowering annuals, biennials, perennials, and bulbs, perhaps accompanied by some evergreen or flowering shrubs. If you're a seasoned gardener already, much of this information will be old hat to you, so forgive me if it sounds too familiar. But beginners, take note: By understanding the different types of plants available to you when planning a flower garden, you'll be better able to create a garden that blossoms from spring through fall and is practically care-free.

Easy-care flower gardens rely primarily on herbaceous perennials, bulbs, and a few flowering shrubs for color, since these plants return year after year. Flowering annuals, especially the more widely grown kinds, usually demand much more attention. But some annuals bloom nonstop without much grooming, and others will self-sow and become a permanent addition to your garden as well—whether you want them to or not!—so even certain annuals deserve a spot in an easy-care flower garden.

Applause for Annuals

Gardeners love flowering annuals because they bloom so prolifically, eliciting rounds of applause for the mountains of color they can be counted on to produce. The essence of an annual is that it germinates from a seed, grows into a mature plant that flowers and then sets seed and finally dies, all in a single growing season. Annuals tend to flower this profusely and form huge amounts of seed because that's their main mission in life, and they get only a brief chance at it. Many annuals die soon after flowering and setting seed: A hormonal trigger set off by seed formation tells the plant the end is near. By removing the fading flowers—a chore called deadheading—you can prevent seed formation, and the annuals will usually just keep on blooming. But deadheading is a time-consuming task in a large annual garden (or even with a few large marigolds) and is just one reason annual gardens can require the care of a horde of gardeners to look their best.

Annuals are native to all kinds of climates, from alpine meadows to low deserts, and individual species have preferred weather conditions within these climates. Some are cool-season annuals, favoring spring and fall conditions, and others are warm-season annuals, thriving in the heat of summer. Because of this variability, horticulturists have classified annuals into three main groups: tender annuals, hardy annuals, and half-hardy annuals. Some seed catalogs code annuals according to these classifications, and this gives you a valuable clue as to how they will perform in your garden.

Most **tender annuals,** including marigolds (*Tagetes* spp.), flowering tobacco (*Nicotiana alata*), zinnias (*Zinnia* spp.), and portulaca (*Portulaca grandiflora*), hail from regions where the summers are hot and winters are mild, even frost-free. The seedlings, and often the seeds, cannot tolerate frost. Cool-season tender annuals may need some shade in the South or Southwest, but may still die out when temperatures soar. Usually, tender annuals need a long growing period before they flower. If you intend to sow their seeds directly in the garden, you must wait until the soil has warmed considerably, which means several weeks after the last frost. So don't expect flowers any time soon—it may be August before blossoms reward your diligence.

If you're bent on starting tender annuals from seed, you're advised to begin indoors in mid- to late winter to get plants large enough to transplant outdoors after frost danger has passed. Otherwise you'll be short-changed on the blooms. I much prefer simply purchasing bedding plants of tender annuals at the garden center in late spring or early summer—it's easier, and the plants are much more healthy than I could grow using a windowsill garden as a seedbed. Usually already in bloom, nursery-grown transplants will fill in quickly and bloom all summer long.

Cold-tolerant **hardy annuals** can withstand light frost in spring and fall. In many climates, their seeds will overwinter in the ground if you sow them in fall, or if they self-sow in your garden, and they'll germinate early enough to provide a good floral show beginning in spring or early summer. You can sow seeds outdoors in spring or fall and don't need to fuss with the bother of trying to get the little beggars to cooperate on your windowsill. Of course, you can purchase young transplants, too. Hardy annuals are often grown in the fall and winter in warm climates.

Bachelor's-button (*Centaurea cyanus*), a delightful blue-flowered hardy annual that defies frost, blooms into the fall long after cold has turned tender annuals to mush. If the seeds are fall-sown, you'll reap flowers quite early in spring. It's also a favorite for naturalizing in meadow gardens (see page 233). Another choice hardy annual is love-in-a-mist (*Nigella damascena*); it forms mounds of needlelike foliage studded with circular lavender-blue, pink, or white flowers, and it readily reseeds. I've observed the daintily flowered sweet alyssum (*Lobularia maritima*) blooming in Arizona in February, where it had reseeded itself and blended prettily into the stony edges of a desert garden. A desert summer, of course, sends this hardy annual into dormancy, but it is ready to make a show again come mild weather. My friend Claudia planted white-flowered sweet alyssum in her rose garden, where it has reseeded itself for five years now, producing a charming carpet of white flowers that softens the thorny stems of her hybrid tea roses.

Neither tender nor hardy, **half-hardy annuals** can tolerate periods of cold in spring and fall, but a frost will do them in. If you sow seeds rather than purchasing bedding plants, it's usually best to sow them outdoors after all danger of frost has passed, although you don't have to wait until the soil has warmed. Seeds of half-hardy annuals will often overwinter if they self-sow or are fall planted, making them choice plants for weekend gardeners who don't want to keep replanting. The flip side is that they'll become a weedy nuisance if you don't want to grow them another season.

My two favorite half-hardy annuals with a proclivity toward self-sowing are both tall: cosmos (*Cosmos bipinnatus*), with its satiny pink, wine-red, or white daisylike flowers, and the lacy spiderflower (*Cleome hasslerana*), which produces large, wispy heads of pale pink, rose, purple, or white blossoms. These can be spring- or fall-sown for early germination and a head start on summer flowers.

I like to tuck another half-hardy annual, edging lobelia (*Lobelia erinus*), between mossy rocks in the front of the border in my pink, blue, and white perennial garden. It spills happily over the rock wall, softening the face of the bed. Lobelia stops producing its electric-blue flowers when the temperature gets too hot, but reblooms, if it has been cut back, when cool weather returns.

Bravos for Biennials

A few favorite garden flowers, such as foxglove (*Digitalis purpurea*), sweet William (*Dianthus barbatus*), and forget-me-not (*Myosotis sylvatica*), are biennial—they live only two years. Other popular biennials include Canterbury bells (*Campanula medium*), honesty (*Lunaria annua*), Iceland poppy (*Papaver nudicaule*), and garden mulleins (*Verbascum* spp.). With a two-season lifespan, biennials get themselves growing during the first season, but don't flower or set seed until the second. Instead of dying back in fall, some biennials (including mullein and foxglove) form a rosette of leaves that hugs the ground all winter. Once they've set seed, they usually die, but some modern hybrids may live on to flower once again the following year, acting like short-lived perennials and defying categorization. I've closely observed an individual foxglove blooming for three growing seasons.

Biennials often self-sow, but you can help them along by scattering the ripe seed where you'd like them to grow. The flower stalks of my foxgloves produce seedpods that I allow to dry on the stem. In mid- to late summer, when they look ripe, I cut off the brown stems and shake the seeds onto the ground. Seedlings appear by fall and over-winter, hidden in the mulch, then take off rapidly in spring to grow tall and produce flowers in summer. Some seeds may not germinate until the spring after seed is set; these seedlings won't flower until the following year.

Praise for Perennials

Perennials offer the weekend gardener an easy and reliable source of flowers, year after year, and with very little effort on the gardener's part. Perennials, more technically termed **herbaceous perennials,** are hardy plants: their tops die down to the ground during winter, but their roots remain alive and send up new growth in spring. Many perennials, including balloon flower (*Platycodon grandiflorus*), bleeding-heart (*Dicentra spectabilis*), and Japanese anemone (*Anemone × hybrida*), die back so thoroughly that not a sign of them lingers in early spring to mark the spot where new shoots will grow. Others, such as snow-in-summer (*Cerastium tomentosum*), perennial candytuft (*Iberis sempervirens*), and lamb's-ears (*Stachys byzantina*), have evergreen foliage.

The pleasure of perennials is that if well situated and cared for, they will return to your garden year after year. Their foliage often peeks out of the ground in early spring, and some, including bleeding-heart and lungwort (*Pulmonaria angustifolia*), undergo such dramatic growth spurts with every warm spring day that you can almost watch them grow. These early spring-blooming perennials provide dependable blossoms before you can even put most annuals in the ground. Also, many perennials spread, their clumps increasing in size each year. Clumps that grow fairly rapidly may need to be dug up and divided every few years to maintain plant vigor. (Dividing perennials provides a ready source of "free" plants for those who want to expand their gardens, but creates a maintenance nuisance for lazy gardeners.) But some perennials grow happily for 10 years or more without needing division—these make ideal plants for weekend gardeners!—and a few perennials, notably peonies (*Paeonia lactiflora*) and poppies (*Papaver orientale*), can live for 50 years without ever being divided. Now those are carefree perennials!

Woody perennials do not die to the ground in winter, though some lose their foliage and become dormant. Their stems and branches are permanent, made of wood that endures. Most woody perennials are large-growing plants—shrubs, trees, and vines. A few smaller woody perennials such as heaths, heathers, and roses find the flower garden a suitable home. So do "subshrubs" like perennial candytuft (*Iberis sempervirens*), which are partially woody. I'll discuss appropriate woody perennials to incorporate in flower gardens later in this chapter.

As with annuals, perennials can be tender or hardy, so be sure to choose plants that will survive the winter in your hardiness zone. In fact, many of our popular "annual" bedding plants are perennials in their native tropics. Impatiens (*Impatiens wallerana*), geraniums (*Pelargonium × hortorum*), and pansies (*Viola × wittrockiana*) are just a few of the tender perennials that are treated as annuals in this country.

Bowled Over by Bulbs

Hardy bulbs deserve equal footing with flowering perennials in a low-maintenance garden. Most will return year after year, blooming reliably with very little care. Early bulbs, such as crocuses (*Crocus* spp.), snowdrops (*Galanthus nivalis*), and glory-of-the-snow (*Chionodoxa luciliae*), brighten the garden in late winter or early spring before most perennials even pop from the ground. Daffodils (*Narcissus* spp.) and grape hyacinths (*Muscari* spp.) extend the flowering season, blooming for weeks well before annuals can even be planted out. Other bulbs, such as lilies (*Lilium* spp.), cannas (*Canna × generalis*), crocosmia (*Crocosmia × crocosmiiflora*), gladioli (*Gladiolus* spp.), and many of the flowering alliums (*Allium* spp.), are summer-bloomers. Still others, such as autumn crocus (*Colchicum autumnale*) and prairie onion (*Allium stellatum*), grace the garden with fall flowers.

Not all plants we think of as bulbs are actually bulbs—some are corms, tubers, or rhizomes. There are technical differences, but suffice it to say that all these "bulbs" are plants that have a specialized underground storage structure. The bulb remains dormant much of the year, usually sending up foliage and flowers for only a few months. Dying bulb foliage can look unattractive, but don't remove it until it's completely yellow or the bulb won't be able to store enough nourishment for next year's growth and bloom. Careful garden design will camouflage—or at least draw attention from—the withering foliage.

Spring-flowering bulbs, such as daffodils and crocus, bloom in late winter or spring. After bloom, their foliage matures and ripens, then dies to the ground by midsummer. For all practical purposes, the plant disappears until the next spring. Summer- or fall-flowering bulbs, such as autumn crocus, may send up spring foliage, which then dies back. When their bloom season arrives, blossoms appear seemingly overnight on naked stalks sent up from the underground bulb. Other bulbs, such as grape hyacinths and sternbergia (*Sternbergia lutea*), send up fall foliage, which overwinters and doesn't die back until late spring or early summer. Such bulbs are often native to regions with extreme summer droughts—they adapt to the inhospitable climate with a long dormancy.

Bulbs, like annuals and perennials, can be tender or hardy. Tender bulbs, such as gladioli, dahlias (*Dahlia pinnata*), tigridias (*Tigridia pavonia*), cannas, and tuberous begonias (*Begonia × tuberhybrida*), live through the winter only where the ground doesn't freeze—or at least freeze as deeply as the bulb is planted. For instance, gladioli, which grow deeply, can overwinter as far north as USDA Plant Hardiness Zone 7 or 8, but shallow-rooted tuberous begonias will survive winter only in Zone 10.

In colder climates, tender bulbs can be grown as annuals, or dug up and stored in a cool, dry place over winter and replanted the next year after danger of frost is past. This is quite a chore for weekend gardeners. I don't recommend growing tender bulbs in cold climates, unless you are willing to tackle the extra work. I can remember more than one occasion on a frigid autumn night when I was digging the tender bulbs out of the flower bed by the light of my camping lantern—a freeze was threatening and I hadn't yet found time to dig up the bothersome bulbs. And then of course I didn't have an appropriate storage area, and many of them perished over the winter.

Hardy bulbs are cold-hardy to different degrees, just like other cold-hardy plants, and are recommended for certain hardiness zones. Most do well in Zones 5 through 8, but some are more or less cold-hardy. In warmer areas, Zones 9 and 10, hardy bulbs such as tulips (*Tulipa* spp.), snowdrops, and daffodils perform poorly, if at all, because they don't experience the chilling necessary to break their winter dormancy. In these areas, hardy bulbs are treated the way tender bulbs are in the North, except that they must be stored in the refrigerator over the winter and replanted in spring. In the Pacific Northwest, where winters are notoriously wet, many bulbs may rot over the winter and so are not reliable there.

Where bulbs find the climate and growing conditions to their liking, many, including daffodils, grape hyacinths, and crocuses, will spread over the years into great clumps and drifts. Depending on the situation, these can be left alone or divided and separated. Other bulbs, notoriously hybrid tulips, seem short-lived in most gardens and need special care if they are to return to your garden year after year.

Raves for Easy-Care Roses

Of the hundreds of flowers you might conceivably plant in your flower garden, none are more beloved or more demanding than modern roses. Their beautiful flowers and sweet perfume inspire poets and lovers—but then again, these woody plants require specialized pruning, heavy fertilization, regular deep watering, and deadheading. They often need winter protection, *and* they are susceptible to a host of disfiguring diseases and insects. You probably should think twice about planting a modern hybrid tea, grandiflora, or floribunda rose in a low-maintenance garden. But tough shrub roses, including smashing new cultivars, and many old-fashioned roses can delight you without demanding constant attention and care.

One of my friends—a new convert to gardening—is replanting her rose garden for the third season because the plants languished over summer and didn't endure through the winter. "I did everything the books said," Marla wailed in frustration. By way of consolation, I gave her two hardy, scarlet-flowering shrub roses—we'll see if she can kill these tough babies.

For any weekend gardener determined to grow roses, as Marla is, I strongly recommend avoiding the temperamental modern roses—their blossoms are heavenly, and many are delightfully fragrant, but unless you can devote time to them, they'll continually disappoint you. Shrub roses, such as the pink-flowered 'Bonica' and 'Simplicity', the Meidiland hybrids, which come in an array of colors and habits, and pink, white, or reddish-purple cultivars of the beautiful rugosa rose (*Rosa rugosa*), on the other hand, are made of sturdier stuff. Plant shrub roses as a flowering hedge, as a background to a flower bed, or along with the perennials in a mixed border. Their blossoms can be enchanting even if they're not as elegant as those of a hybrid tea, and they're practically fuss-free. (See the encyclopedia section near the end of this book for details and descriptions of low-maintenance shrub roses).

Most shrub roses are species or old-time

hybrids. Recently, a number of newly introduced hybrid shrub roses in the Meidiland series—including 'Bonica', 'Ferdy', 'White Meidiland', and 'Scarlet Meidiland'—have been making a splash. Some will spread along the ground to make flowering groundcovers, and others make effective specimens in a flower bed or can be grown as a flowering hedge. 'Simplicity', a beautiful pink rose introduced in 1979, is one of the oldest of the modern shrub roses.

Mark and I have a hedge of 'Simplicity' shrub roses along the front of our property between the road and a screen of rhododendrons and white pines. This 4-foot-deep strip was a weedy mess that barely passed as lawn when we first moved in. We simply piled about 8 inches of wood chips over the grass and weeds, then planted the roses. They—and I—couldn't be happier. Without any pruning on my part, the rosebushes produce a profusion of clear pink, semi-double flowers in late spring that have my neighbors agoggle. The roses bloom throughout the summer until late autumn, though with a little more restraint than that first spring spectacle. I regularly cut a cluster or two to fill a dark blue vase on my desk, and the flowers last there for a week.

One of my favorite shrub roses is the rugosa rose, an exceptionally tough native of Japan that has naturalized in many coastal locations in the United States. This remarkable rose, whose stout, thorny stems can form a shrub 4 to 7 feet tall, produces large, single, purplish-pink blossoms in spring and again sporadically in fall. The dark green leaves have a wonderful pleated texture, as if they had been folded up accordion-fashion and then released. This rugged rose thrives in poor soil and dry conditions. It can also take the seashore's wind and salt. Gleaming red rose hips decorate the shrub in fall. Cultivars with semi-double, white, pale pink, and red flowers are available.

Shrub roses differ from other roses in two important ways. They are not grafted but are grown on their own roots, making them quite cold-hardy. Those shrub roses that bloom repeatedly form new branches and produce more blossoms even if you don't cut off the faded blossoms (deadhead), as is necessary with "modern" roses. This means they require less tending to flower well. You really don't *want* to deadhead shrub roses, because many, especially rugosa rose, form decorative red fruits called hips that are ornamental well into winter.

Because shrub roses bloom profusely, individual flowers need not be as perfect as those of a hybrid tea, which is admired for its tall stems, each bearing a single stunning flower. So if bugs gnaw on the blossoms a little, the damage often goes unnoticed. Though not necessarily "disease-resistant," shrub roses are often called "disease-tolerant" for the very reason that they are tougher and better able to withstand diseases without ill effect. And shrub roses don't need to be perfect to look attractive.

Shrub roses need little pruning. In spring, you might wish to cut out wayward or dead branches to improve the shape or reduce their size. Other than that, leave them alone. And you don't need to provide any special winter protection, though a year-round mulch helps conserve soil moisture.

Easy-care perennials and bulbs will return to grace your garden year after year, and you'll hardly have to lift a tool to take care of them. Add a few flowering shrubs or shrub roses for structure from the lists of

"Shrubs, Vines, and Groundcovers for Mixed Borders." Avoid those plants included in the lists of "Especially Finicky Perennials" and "Exuberantly Spreading Perennials" and you can't go wrong. Be cautious about using annuals from the list of "Annuals That Self-Sow" —include these only if you want volunteers. If you don't want self-sown annuals to pop up willy-nilly, avoid plants from that list or you may find yourself with a weeding chore.

Annuals in the Weekend Flower Garden

Annuals definitely have their place in the weekend flower garden—they're hard to beat for vibrant color and season-long bloom. The keys to letting them work for you, as opposed to having to work endlessly on them, are to choose plants carefully, buy bedding plants rather than starting from seed, focus on plants that self-sow where appropriate, integrate annuals in your flower beds, and do not get carried away. "Don't get carried away" means don't buy more annuals than you have space for, then end up sticking them everywhere and running around all season taking care of them, and don't, *don't,* start an all-annual garden.

An all-annual garden can be an enormous amount of work. First of all, a bed devoted entirely to annuals lies barren for much of the year—at least, it lies bare of *flowers,* but cool-season annual weeds may start sprouting in late winter or early spring before you can plant out the petunias or marigolds. And once you plant the annuals, it may be at least a month before they grow enough to fill in the gaps so that when you look at the garden, you notice the plants before you notice the sea of mulch around them or, worse yet, bare soil or weeds.

If you have an all-annual bed, you need to turn over the plot every year and fluff up the soil by adding organic matter and nutrients for these flowers, which are heavy feeders. And, of course, you can't prepare the soil just anytime you feel like it. It has to be sunny—or at least it can't be raining—and the soil has to have dried out enough since the last rain so that it isn't soggy. A tough order in spring, right? It never seems to fail that the one perfect Sunday when the weather cooperates with your gardening plans coincides with your mother-in-law's monthly visit or with your secretary's retirement party or with your daughter's recital. And if you wait too long to prepare the bed and plant it, you'll be looking at a weed-choked, scruffy patch through most of the summer. The annuals you planned to transplant will be choking themselves in their little containers, their roots spilling from the drainage holes, their stems tall and floppy.

Once you get the annuals in the ground, you still have an intensive maintenance schedule. Young annual seedlings will branch more and grow stronger and bushier if you pinch out their growing points. If you are sowing annual seeds directly in the garden, then you can't mulch until the seedlings have made an appearance—and that appearance will almost certainly be accompanied by a horde of weed seedlings, which you'll have to deal with by hand-pulling or hoeing. Many annuals look and bloom best if they're regularly deadheaded. It's always seemed to me that individual annual flowers don't last but a few days, and you'd better go out there every day or so and get after them. If you don't, the plants will stop producing new growth and will instead display brown, scuzzy-looking dried flowers. Because annuals bloom so prolifically, most are heavy feeders, and they need plenty of water, too.

An easy-care flower garden is just that—easy to care for—but it isn't totally care-free. Thank goodness! The small amount of tending it needs provides a satisfying way to spend a half hour outdoors communing with nature. You will need to divide, stake, and deadhead some of the flowers in your garden, cut back the perennials for the winter, and yank out the dead annuals at season's end. Despite the need for these few tasks, a low-maintenance flower garden takes very little time to care for, especially in midsummer when practically all you have to do is water and admire, perhaps even wishing it required a bit more nurturing.

Designing a Garden for Season-Long Bloom

When I was a very little girl, I lived in Charleston, West Virginia. My mother's flower garden, which (being located in mountainous West Virginia) was spread out over a terraced hillside, was in full view from the dining room window. My father invented a game of "I spy," which my sister and I eagerly played during mealtimes. Whoever spied the first coreopsis flower in bloom each year won. After the coreopsis was spotted, my father would enter another flower in the competition. Through this game, I came to anticipate and observe the ebb and flow of the perennial garden.

In general, perennials, the predominant plants in the weekend flower garden, create less of a show than annuals. Most bloom for only about two weeks a year during a specified season, though some coveted perennials may bloom for as long as 4 to 6 weeks. After flowering, their foliage remains until frost. Fortunately, their leaves and stems can be lovely and contribute to the quiet beauty of a garden, acting as a foil to other flowers. This waxing and waning of bloom can make perennial gardening frustrating, because even with the best-laid plans the garden may occasionally be bare of blossoms. However, in this frustration lies the challenge and art of gardening. Careful planning will orchestrate a garden that cycles from spring through fall with an ever-changing arrangement of flowers to mark the seasons' progress. Anticipating and observing these bloom cycles provides the pleasure and excitement of flower gardening.

If you mix annuals with your flowering perennials, the scenario is remarkably different. Come early spring, all you have to do is pull the protective mulch back from the perennials, clean up leftover litter or leaves that blew into the garden, and plug in your carefully chosen bedding plants when the soil warms. You aren't racing the clock or cursing the weather. An occasional weed may push through the mulch, but it takes just a second to pull it from the soft soil beneath. Because the annuals are used as color accents, there aren't enough of them to make care a major chore. When your mother-in-law comes for dinner, you can show off the garden to her rather than desperately wishing you were out working in it.

I find that annuals' dependably long bloom season really perks up my flower border, which is mostly perennial, and keeps it showy from early summer until frost. I always plant large drifts of impatiens in the foreground of the border, which is semi-shady, and the impatiens ties the everchanging blooms of the perennials together. And—heaven forbid—if an interlude between the bloom periods of the perennials occurs, at least the annuals provide plenty of color.

A Few Favorite Annuals

Impatiens is one of my favorite flowers. I prefer the pastel-colored cultivars, which really glow in the shade. They form spectacular low mounds of dainty blossoms and neat foliage without ever appearing stiff or overwhelming like some annuals. Impatiens are practically care-free—they don't need deadheading, staking, or any other fuss made over them if they are given light shade and enough water. My impatiens self-sow, but because they are tender annuals, the seeds don't germinate until the soil is quite warm in early summer, so I can't rely on them to fill in the garden. The seedlings usually bloom when tiny and if I like the color of the blossoms, which can be a surprise, I transplant the tiny plant to a more desirable location under shrubs or leave it in place if it has sprouted where it adds to the border's color scheme.

Other annuals find their way to my garden, but I usually go for those that require the least care possible. The misty-flowered annuals that can be planted and practically forgotten, such as sweet alyssum (*Lobularia maritima*), spiderflower (*Cleome hasslerana*), and lobelia (*Lobelia erinus*), are favorites. Cleome and annual candytuft (*Iberis umbellata*) will self-sow, returning to the garden year after year in a beautiful and complementary range of white, lavender, mauve, cerise, and purple. I like to use more-troublesome annuals in a cutting garden, where cutting off the flowers for bouquets substitutes for deadheading, and where they are more easily maintained since I plant them along with my vegetables.

Annuals, both natives and exotics, provide instant color in a meadow garden. If they are happy enough to self-sow, they can add color to the meadow for years. (See "Meadow Gardening Practice: Improving on

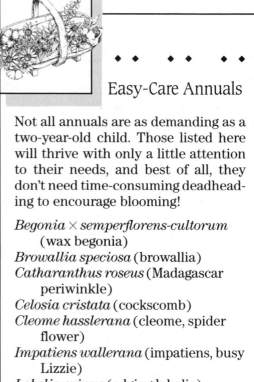

Easy-Care Annuals

Not all annuals are as demanding as a two-year-old child. Those listed here will thrive with only a little attention to their needs, and best of all, they don't need time-consuming deadheading to encourage blooming!

Begonia × *semperflorens-cultorum* (wax begonia)
Browallia speciosa (browallia)
Catharanthus roseus (Madagascar periwinkle)
Celosia cristata (cockscomb)
Cleome hasslerana (cleome, spider flower)
Impatiens wallerana (impatiens, busy Lizzie)
Lobelia erinus (edging lobelia)
Lobularia maritima (sweet alyssum)
Myosotis sylvatica (forget-me-not)
Sanvitalia procumbens (creeping zinnia)
Verbena × *hybrida* (garden verbena)

Mother Nature" on page 228.) Self-sowing annuals—usually the hardy or half-hardy types—planted with perennials contribute to making a charming and care-free cottage garden.

Selecting Easy-Care Garden Flowers

Whether you choose to grow annuals, perennials, bulbs, or roses, you'll work less and have better results if you are careful to match plants to their preferred growing conditions. Simply put, don't expect to grow roses in deep shade or ferns in full sun. Nor should you situate a bog plant in sandy soil or a prairie plant in standing water. Providing the right sun and moisture conditions is probably the single most important factor in influencing whether a plant thrives or fails.

Knowing something about the origins of a plant helps you understand a plant's natural—and preferred—environment. However, if you aren't a naturalist, don't despair. The encyclopedia section near the end of the book will provide you with all the information you need to situate flowers in your garden.

The easiest way to go about gardening is to evaluate your growing conditions and then select plants that will thrive in them. Unfortunately, too many of us do just the opposite. We decide what we want to grow and then go about creating the conditions needed to sustain our selection. This, of course, provides some of the challenge and fulfillment of gardening—if you have time and energy for it. If you don't, stick to growing what is already adapted to your site. Whatever your conditions, you'll probably find more to choose from than you can use.

The lists included in this chapter will help you select flowers for particular sites—such as hot, dry locations, shady sites, or damp and even soggy soils. If you are looking for an annual that will self-sow and grow in a dry site, check each list to see which flowers appear on both. Then read about them in the encyclopedia section near the end of the book.

You can create any style of garden in any type of site as long as you choose plants that match the site conditions. For instance, why not have a cottage garden—usually con-nected with cool, shady England—on the hot, southern side of your house? You can create an undemanding garden as long as you select flowers that prefer direct sun and can thrive with little moisture, then scatter them in a spirited, unstudied design. The same flowers could be arranged into a massed pattern, with large groups of each plant, to create a more formal flower border on the site. Though the flowers are identical, their arrangement and design will make the two gardens look remarkably different.

Successful Gardens for Difficult Sites

Some of the most common problem sites we encounter in our yards are those with too much shade, those that are hot and dry, and those that are always damp. Gardeners tend to despair when confronted with these conditions, and usually end up paving the area or trying (often unsuccessfully) to grow grass there. Instead, why not confront the challenge of growing a flower garden that will actually *thrive* in shade, drought, or damp? If you carefully choose plants that are adapted to these conditions, you'll not only have a colorful, interesting garden, it will also be low-maintenance!

A Shady Flower Garden

Shade under high-branched trees, where only filtered light reaches the ground, or in parts of the yard where direct sun strikes the ground for only a few hours a day, will prevent you from planting the usual types of flower gardens. But as long as the spot isn't in total darkness—and I haven't seen one yet that was—many attractive and unusual flowering and foliage plants will flourish.

It often helps to thin out some of the overhead tree branches to let in a bit more sun. You'll have the greatest choice of plants if the garden receives dappled light rather than being in constant shadow. Cut off the lowest tree branches, then prune off selected upper branches at the tree's trunk or at the junction where major branches fork into side branches to create a more open canopy. You may have to thin out branches every few years as the trees grow larger. But bear in mind that you'll have to look at the tree all year, too, especially in winter when the branch structure is all too apparent, and prune with its appearance in mind.

I've had a lot of experience—maybe too much—gardening in shade. The rear half of our present property is shaded by many tall trees and was a mess when we first moved in. We had a lot of cleanup to do, and were just getting it completed when the Fourth of July sale at our favorite nursery rolled around: Time to begin a perennial garden. However, the spot that cried out for a garden didn't offer much sun. We were determined anyway. We made the new garden in a former weed patch in the fenced corner of the side yard, beneath several scraggly black locusts, a tall wild cherry, and two small ginkgos (they grow very slowly) planted by some long-forgotten former owner.

This area sloped slightly toward the house, so I built the garden bed up in front to level out the site by enriching the soil with compost, peat moss, and manure. This created a level site that was raised about 6 to 8 inches in front. (Any higher and the tree roots might have suffocated.)

We bordered the area and contained the soil with a wall built of native rocks. We had

Plants for Shady Gardens

The lovely plants listed here will brighten up any shady corner. Most prefer filtered shade, but some can do well even in dark shade. Keep in mind that where shade is caused by trees, tree roots may compete with the garden plants for moisture and nutrients, so be sure to provide plenty of both.

Annuals
Begonia × *semperflorens-cultorum* (wax begonia)
Browallia speciosa (browallia)
Coleus × *hybridus* (coleus)
Impatiens wallerana (impatiens, busy Lizzie)
Myosotis sylvatica (forget-me-not)
Nierembergia hippomanica (cupflower)
Torenia fournieri (wishbone flower)
Viola × *wittrockiana* (pansy)

Perennials
Astilbe × *arendsii* (astilbe, false spirea), Zone 4
Chrysogonum virginianum (green-and-gold, golden star), Zone 5
Dicentra eximia (fringed bleeding-heart), Zone 3
D. spectabilis (common bleeding-heart), Zone 2
Digitalis purpurea (common foxglove), Zone 5, actually biennial
Filipendula ulmaria (queen-of-the-meadow), Zone 3

◆ ◆   ◆ ◆   ◆ ◆   ◆ ◆   ◆ ◆   ◆ ◆   ◆ ◆   ◆ ◆   ◆ ◆   ◆ ◆

Hemerocallis cultivars (daylily), Zone 3

Hosta spp. and hybrids (hostas, plantain lilies), Zone 3

Mertensia virginica (Virginia bluebells), Zone 3

Osmunda cinnamomea (cinnamon fern), Zone 3

Penstemon hirsutus (hairy beardtongue), Zone 5

Phlox divaricata (wild blue phlox), Zone 4

P. stolonifera (creeping phlox), Zone 3

Pulmonaria spp. (lungworts), Zone 3

Tiarella cordifolia (foamflower), Zone 4

Uvularia grandiflora (big merrybells), Zone 4

Shrubs

Aucuba japonica (Japanese aucuba), Zone 7

Calycanthus floridus (Carolina allspice), Zone 5

Daphne cneorum (garland flower), Zone 4

Ilex crenata (Japanese holly), Zone 6

Kalmia latifolia (mountain laurel), Zone 5

Kerria japonica 'Variegata' (variegated Japanese kerria), Zone 5

Leucothoe spp. (fetterbushes), Zones 5–6, depending on species

Mahonia spp. (Oregon grape hollies), Zone 5

Nandina domestica (heavenly bamboo), Zone 7

Pittosporum tobira (Japanese pittosporum), Zone 8

Prunus laurocerasus (cherry laurel), Zone 7

Rhododendron spp. and hybrids (rhododendrons and azaleas), Zones 4–7, depending on species

R. mucronulatum (Korean rhododendron), Zone 5

Ribes alpinum (alpine currant), Zone 2

Sarcococca hookerana (sweet box, sarcococca), Zone 6

Skimmia japonica (Japanese skimmia), Zone 7

Groundcovers

Ajuga reptans (ajuga, carpet bugle, bugleweed), Zone 5

Asarum spp. (wild gingers), Zones 4–6, depending on species

Epimedium spp. (bishop's hats), Zone 3

Euonymus fortunei (wintercreeper), Zone 5

Galium odoratum (sweet woodruff), Zone 4

Hedera helix (English ivy), Zone 5

Lamium maculatum (spotted deadnettle), Zone 4

Liriope spp. (lilyturfs), Zones 4–6, depending on species

Pachysandra terminalis (pachysandra, Japanese spurge), Zone 5

Vinca minor (common periwinkle, myrtle), Zone 4

unearthed the rocks from beneath a strip of pachysandra growing in front of the fence. The original homeowners had naively used the rocks to outline the pachysandra, but the pachysandra had advanced both over and under the rocks, which were totally obscured. Using these rocks, we created a low rock wall to run the entire length of the garden, adding a few sweeping curves (one near a massive wild cherry tree near the end of the border), and ended it where lawn and fence met woods. Creating this garden took us two entire weekends—we spent a day stripping off the sod and beginning to improve the soil, and another day constructing the wall and finishing the soil improvement. The next weekend we planted. That was it for the outlay of labor. Three years later, the garden has required no other major effort—it needs just enough nurturing to keep me happy.

Though most of the 29-foot-long border is shaded, the degree of shade varies from deepest at the front end to several hours of sun just beside the woods, with spots of shifting sun in the center. I call the "corner end" the shade garden and the "woods end" the perennial garden, because I grow only shade-loving plants at one end, but can grow some sun-loving perennials and even roses in strategic spots at the other. By making the two areas blend into each other, even though the light conditions are different, the garden appears cohesive rather than a patchwork. To further meld the two areas, I used a pink, blue, purple, and white color scheme throughout and planted repeating masses of pastel pink impatiens in the foreground in both the shade and the perennial sections. These annuals provide a dependable show of color to supplement the perennials as they bloom and fade.

In the rear of the shade garden, I staggered three bright-pink-flowered, compact-growing rhododendrons. Next to these I planted a 'Windbeam' rhododendron—a pale pink cultivar that blooms just after the deeper pink ones pass. The rhododendrons all have pleasing medium-textured foliage that provides evergreen structure to the area all through the year. Beside these rhododendrons, I placed three Korean azaleas (*Rhododendron mucronulatum*), a deciduous species with lavender-pink blossoms that is one of the first shrubs to bloom in spring.

The foreground of the shade garden holds a casual mix of hosta, astilbe, and liriope to provide color after the spring shrubs have flowered. These three bloom dependably in the shade and provide a sequence of bloom from early summer through fall. I like to use white-variegated or blue-green hostas in shade because these colors pop out of the shadows. For the same reason, I used white and pastel pink astilbe and pale pink impatiens, rather than dark pink or red. Ferns found a home between the flowering perennials, and I tucked patches of velvety green moss, which I harvested from other parts of the property, in the foreground between the gaps in the rocks.

The second year, we began including some wildflowers in this garden—ones that Mark and I snatched from the jaws of bulldozers in the woods near my mother's home, where condominiums were scheduled to be erected. These included hepatica, bloodroot, white trillium, wood anemone, jack-in-the-pulpit, wintergreen, partridgeberry, and cinnamon fern. I am happy to report that all are flourishing. (Chapter 6 has more information on planting a wildflower garden.) We purchased wild blue phlox (*Phlox divaricata*), pink-flowered hairy phlox (*Phlox pilosa*), and foamflower (*Tiarella cordifolia*), wildflowers that are at home in such a woodland situation. These are spreading like crazy in the shadiest spots and bloom together with the rhododendron, creating a magical spring scene.

I left the pachysandra along the fence so it could provide some evergreen interest in winter and perhaps fill in under the rhododendrons a little, though I'm concerned about it taking over too much space in the future. Right now, I am happily using the pachysandra as a source of groundcovers for other parts of the property—I rip out the advancing front as the aggressive plants spread and transplant the salvaged pachysandra elsewhere on the property. This has been a happy solution so far, providing enough free transplants to fill in under a group of azaleas by the back door and under new shrubs along the length of the driveway. But once I've filled the pachysandra gaps on the property, we'll have to install an edging strip or the pachysandra will walk all over the more desirable plants in the shade garden. The plot plan of my shade garden is shown on page 91.

A Dry Flower Garden

Where soil is sandy and the sun bakes it hot and dry, a traditional English perennial border will have a tough time. The lupine will fry, the columbine turn crisp, and the campanulas wither and shrivel. After all, England is famous for its misty rains, impenetrable fogs, and moderate climate. So why bother? You'll be defeated before you even begin unless you do what many garden authorities recommend: Remove the poor, infertile soil, and truck in some good topsoil or manure.

You could do this if you have a lot of time, money, and effort to spare. But though the soil would be new, the heat and drought would stay the same. Instead, why not go for the easiest solution and live with your site?

A mixed bed or border composed of perennials and shrubs adapted to dry, infertile sites can be lovely, and will grow with little fuss or bother in the soil your site has to offer. Even in extended dry weather you won't have to worry about watering. The trend toward this type of landscaping—called xeriscaping—has taken hold in many parts of the country, especially in the West, where lack of summer rain and scarcity of ground water is a major issue.

Many plants tolerant of hot, dry conditions are either succulent or have hairy or fuzzy leaves. The hairs, which shade the leaves from intense sun and reduce water loss, are often silvery or gray, creating very striking foliage. One of my favorite themes for a hot, dry site is a "gray garden" composed mainly of silver- and gray-leaved plants. Some of these plants have such fuzzy, felty foliage that it is hard to resist reaching out and stroking the leaves. Lamb's-ears (*Stachys byzantina*), with its feltlike silver leaves, is one such alluring plant. Flowering perennials such as fernleaf yarrow (*Achillea filipendulina*), globe thistle (*Echinops ritro*), and dianthus (*Dianthus* spp.) have gray or blue-gray foliage and lively flowers. Some gray plants, such as the many types of dusty miller (*Centaurea* spp. and *Senecio* spp.), are admired only for their stunning foliage. Lavender, rosemary, santolina, and woolly thyme are aromatic herbs suited to a gray garden.

The garden pictured on page 133 is located on the sunny south side of a beachfront home, where the soil is poor and dry.

With a yellow and gray color scheme, the garden sparkles in the intense light. But best of all, the skillful choice of plants means the garden never needs to be watered, even during a summer drought.

A Damp Flower Garden

As with a hot, dry site, why fight the conditions offered by heavy, wet, or boggy soil? Do you really have the time and money to install drainage tiles, as almost every gardening book ever written advises for such sites? Where too much soil moisture rots most perennials, select those whose roots seek water and they will reward you. In many cases, these will be perennials that gave you trouble in other sites—probably because you couldn't satisfy their thirst requirements. If the site has a natural body of water, such as a running stream or a small standing pond, you can create a tranquil, natural-looking water garden with moisture-loving ferns and perennials.

You may decide that your damp or boggy garden site is a blessing rather than a detriment after discovering some of the fine perennials that will flourish there and nowhere else. In damp soil, you'll be able to grow some unusual and dramatically tall perennials that aren't seen in many gardens. Plants that thrive with wet feet include the feathery, pink-flowered Japanese meadowsweet (*Filipendula purpurea*), golden yellow bigleaf goldenray (*Ligularia dentata*) with its purple-tinged stems and leaves, bold-blossomed Joe-Pye weed (*Eupatorium purpureum*), and elegant cardinal flower (*Lobelia cardinalis*), to name only a few.

Plants for Dry Gardens

The flowers and shrubs listed here tolerate hot, dry conditions and poor, infertile soil. Combine them into an easy-care mixed border and you won't have to worry about babying the garden.

Annuals

Cleome hasslerana (cleome, spiderflower)
Cosmos bipinnatus (cosmos)
Eschscholzia californica (California poppy)
Gomphrena globosa (globe amaranth)
Helianthus annuus (common sunflower)
Papaver nudicaule (Iceland poppy)
P. rhoeas (corn poppy, Shirley poppy)
Portulaca grandiflora (portulaca, rose moss)
Tropaeolum majus (garden nasturtium)

Bulbs

Crocus spp. (crocuses), Zone 5
Sternbergia lutea (winter daffodil, lily-of-the-field), Zone 7
Tulipa kaufmanniana (water lily tulip), Zone 4
T. pulchella, Zone 5
T. tarda, Zone 4

Herbs

Lavandula angustifolia subsp. *angustifolia* (English lavender), Zone 5
Rosmarinus officinalis (rosemary), Zone 7

◆ ◆ ◆ ◆ ◆ ◆ ◆ ◆ ◆ ◆ ◆ ◆ ◆ ◆ ◆ ◆ ◆ ◆

Thymus spp. (thymes), Zone 5

Perennials

Achillea filipendulina (fernleaf yarrow), Zone 3

Anthemis tinctoria (golden marguerite), Zone 3

Armeria maritima (sea pink), Zone 4

Artemisia ludoviciana 'Silver King' (Silver King artemisia), Zone 3

A. schmidtiana 'Silver Mound' (Silver Mound artemisia), Zone 3

Asclepias tuberosa (butterfly weed), Zone 3

Aubrieta deltoidea (purple rock cress), Zone 5

Aurinia saxatilis (basket-of-gold), Zone 3

Campanula carpatica (Carpathian bellflower), Zone 3

Centaurea spp. and cultivars (centaureas), Zone 4

Coreopsis lanceolata (lanceleaf coreopsis), Zone 3

C. verticillata (threadleaf coreopsis), Zone 3

Dianthus deltoides (maiden pink), Zone 3

Echinops ritro (globe thistle), Zone 3

Gaillardia × *grandiflora* (blanket-flower), Zone 3

Rudbeckia fulgida 'Goldsturm' ('Goldsturm' black-eyed Susan), Zone 3

Salvia × *superba* (violet sage), Zone 4

Santolina chamaecyparissus (lavender cotton), Zone 6

Scabiosa caucasica (pincushion flower), Zone 3

Sedum spp. (stonecrops), Zones 3–5, depending on species

Stachys byzantina (lamb's-ears), Zone 5

Shrubs

Berberis thunbergii (Japanese barberry), Zone 4

Caragana spp. (pea shrubs), Zone 2

Ceanothus spp. (California lilacs), Zone 8

Cistus spp. (rock roses), Zone 7

Coprosma repens (mirror plant, looking-glass plant), Zone 9

Cotoneaster spp. (cotoneasters), Zone 5

Cytisus spp. (brooms), Zone 6

C. racemosus (sweet broom), Zone 10

Hypericum spp. (St.-John's-worts), Zone 4

Ilex cornuta (Chinese holly), Zone 7

Juniperus spp. (junipers), Zones 2–6, depending on species

Myrica pensylvanica (bayberry), Zone 4

Myrtus communis (common myrtle), Zone 9

Nandina domestica (heavenly bamboo), Zone 7

Nerium oleander (oleander), Zone 8

Pittosporum tobira (Japanese pittosporum), Zone 8

Potentilla fruticosa (bush cinquefoil), Zone 2

Raphiolepis indica (Indian hawthorn), Zone 8

Rosa rugosa (rugosa rose, Japanese rose), Zone 3

Plants for Damp Gardens

Don't despair if heavy, wet soil seems to thwart your garden plans. Where soil is constantly wet, the flowers and shrubs listed here will thrive.

Annuals

Browallia speciosa (browallia)
Impatiens wallerana (impatiens, busy Lizzie)
Lobelia erinus (edging lobelia)
Mimulus guttatus (monkeyflower)
Myosotis sylvatica (forget-me-not)
Nierembergia hippomanica (cupflower)
Torenia fournieri (wishbone flower)
Viola cornuta (tufted pansy)

Bulbs

Leucojum aestivum (summer snowflake), Zone 4

Perennials

Aruncus dioicus (goatsbeard), Zone 3
Astilbe spp. (astilbes, false spireas), Zones 4–5, depending on species
Athyrium filix-femina (lady fern), Zone 3
Caltha palustris (marsh marigold), Zone 3
Chelone lyonii (pink turtlehead), Zone 4
Cimicifuga spp. (bugbanes), Zone 3
Eupatorium purpureum (Joe-Pye weed), Zone 4
Filipendula purpurea (Japanese meadowsweet), Zone 3

Hibiscus moscheutos (rose mallow), Zone 5
Hosta spp. and cultivars (hostas, plantain lilies), Zone 3
Iris ensata (Japanese iris), Zone 5
I. pseudacorus (yellow flag iris), Zone 5
I. sibirica (Siberian iris), Zone 4
I. versicolor (blue flag), Zone 3
Ligularia dentata (bigleaf goldenray), Zone 5
Lobelia cardinalis (cardinal flower), Zone 3
Lysimachia punctata (yellow loosestrife), Zone 5
Mertensia virginica (Virginia bluebells), Zone 3
Mimulus guttatus (monkeyflower), Zone 9
Osmunda cinnamomea (cinnamon fern), Zone 3
Physostegia virginiana (false dragonhead, obedient plant), Zone 2
Thalictrum speciosissimum (dusty meadow rue), Zone 5

Shrubs

Clethra alnifolia (sweet pepperbush), Zone 4
Cornus alba 'Siberica' (Siberian dogwood), Zone 2
Rhododendron spp. (native azaleas), Zones 4–5, depending on species
Salix 'Melanostachys' (black pussywillow), Zone 4
Viburnum opulus (European cranberrybush viburnum), Zone 3

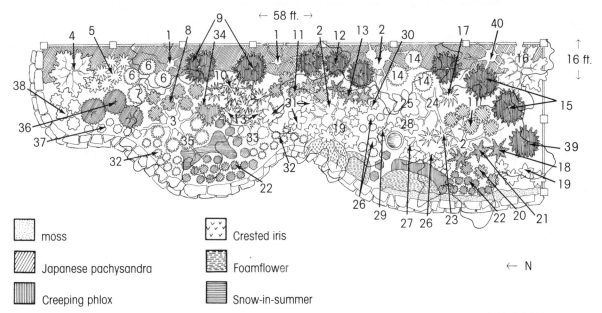

← 58 ft. →

16 ft.

← N

moss

Crested iris

Japanese pachysandra

Foamflower

Creeping phlox

Snow-in-summer

Plot Plan of Susan and Mark's Shady Perennial Border. (1) ginkgo, (2) black locust, (3) black cherry, (4) 'Palibin' Meyer lilac, (5) purple coneflower, (6) Frikart's aster, (7) white-flowered bleeding-heart, (8) 'Peach Blossom' rose astilbe, (9) 'PJM' rhododendron, (10) rubrum lilies, (11) 'Deutschland' astilbe, (12) Korean rhododendron, (13) common woodfern, (14) 'White Pearl' Kamchatka bugbane, (15) 'Pink PJM' rhododendron, (16) common lilac, (17) 'Majestic' big blue lilyturf, (18) maidenhair fern, (19) 'Gold Edger' hosta, (20) 'Sprite' star astilbe, (21) Japanese painted fern, (22) pink impatiens, (23) 'Silver Dragon' creeping lilyturf, (24) 'Aurea' Japanese maple, (25) 'Elegans' Siebold hosta, (26) wild blue phlox, (27) great white trillium, (28) Jack-in-the-pulpit, (29) round-lobed hepatica, (30) *Phlox pilosa,* (31) 'Frances Williams' Siebold hosta, (32) white impatiens, (33) 'Mrs. Moon' Bethlehem sage, (34) 'Snow Queen' Siberian iris, (35) 'Avalanche' Japanese anemone, (36) 'Alba Meidiland' rose, (37) 'Blue Clips' Carpathian bellflower, (38) 'Autumn Joy' sedum, (39) 'Windbeam' azalea, (40) sugar maple

Our shady perennial border offers varying degrees of shade and a few areas of bright sun. Shade-loving wildflowers, ferns, and compact rhododendrons grow near the fenced corner in the deepest shade, while some sun-loving perennials and even roses take advantage of the sunny spots at the other end.

Special Styles of Flower Gardening

An Old-Fashioned Cottage Garden

Cottage gardens probably originated in Europe among peasant farmers during the Middle Ages. Outside the doorsteps of their thatched stone and wood cottages, the tenants cultivated a patchwork of herbs—medicinal herbs to cure what ailed them, culinary herbs to improve the flavor of their food, and strewing herbs to fight odors and evil spirits—as well as vegetables and perhaps a fruit tree or two to round out their meals. Gradually, a few stray flowers that had no purpose other than ornament found their way into the hodgepodge.

These village gardens served purely utilitarian purposes and had no particular design—in fact, their lack of design was what made them charming. A garden usually sprang up along the path leading through a fenced or walled yard from the lane to the door. The rustic fence or tumbledown stone wall, which kept animals—both domestic and wild—out of the yard, gave the garden structure.

Over the ages, these rural cottage gardens became more picturesque. More and more ornamental flowers appeared, perhaps started from a sprig or seeds brought home by the gardener of the lord and lady of the manor. And as people became less poor and more sophisticated, the edibles were often relegated to a separate garden in the rear of the cottage, and flowers stood in the lime-light along the front path. Since there were no nurseries available where the peasant folk could shop, annual flowers that self-sowed and perennials that propagated themselves were the mainstay of these simple gardens. Today, we still find these joyful cottage gardens along the lanes of English villages.

Designing the Cottage Garden

Even if you don't live in a thatched cottage, you might consider creating a low-maintenance English cottage garden to adorn your yard. A cottage garden might be best suited to a farmhouse in the country, but a suburban setting ought not to deter you from this style of gardening. In fact, it might make you feel more bucolic.

To be authentic, locate your garden in a sunny plot surrounding your front door. If your house lends itself to the style, you can practically do away with foundation plantings and front lawn, though this may leave your house looking naked in winter. If this concerns you, blend in shrubbery with your cottage flowers to provide some winter relief. Install the garden to meander along the length of the front or back walk, and enclose the entire yard, or part of it, in a rustic fence. If this look is too informal to suit your house or neighborhood, or if the front of your house is too shady, try situating a cottage garden along the walk leading to the kitchen door or in the backyard around an informal patio.

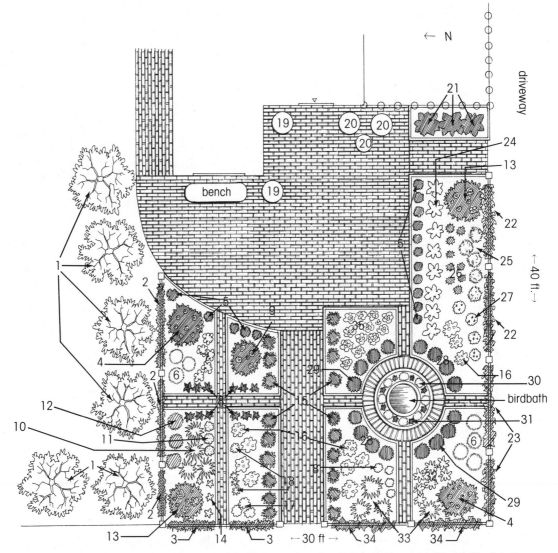

Plot Plan of a Cottage Garden. (1) Manchurian lilac, (2) Jackman clematis, (3) trumpet honeysuckle, (4) 'The Fairy' rose, (5) parsley, (6) cosmos, (7) nasturtium, (8) sorrel, (9) 'White Meidiland' rose, (10) daylily, (11) sweet alyssum, (12) cleome, (13) 'Bonica' rose, (14) farewell-to-spring, (15) 'Munstead Dwarf' lavender, (16) pot marigold, (17) Egyptian onion, (18) sage, (19) rosemary, (20) zonal geranium, (21) rhubarb, (22) pole bean, (23) cucumber, (24) Swiss chard, (25) dill, (26) bachelor's button, (27) borage, (28) silver mound artemisia, (29) 'Dark Opal' basil, (30) chives, (31) Johnny-jump-up, (32) lamb's-ears, (33) tiger lily, (34) winter squash, (35) lettuce followed by zucchini

A cottage-style garden could also work well embellishing a strip of land along the side of the house, or against the side of a freestanding garage, barn, or tool shed.

Using the house as the fourth side of the garden, you might erect a fence to form the garden's other three boundaries. A split-rail, picket, or other informal or rustic fence will look best. If you have an existing rock wall, all the better. Ambitious do-it-yourselfers can build a wall from fieldstone, which can be purchased from a masonry supplier if you don't happen to have a handy field to dig from. But this is an art and takes practice

I transformed the small lawn that bordered the sunny brick patio and walkway off my friend Edith Friedman's kitchen into a cottage garden. A fence and additional narrow brick paths define the space and give year-round structure to the garden while providing access to the plants. Planted with a selection of herbs, vegetables, perennials, and vines, the colorful garden enhances the house.

to perfect. If you lack stone, time, or ambition, but want a stone wall and have cash on hand, you can hire a mason to build a dry wall—*if* you can find one who's able. A decorative gate or arbor at the garden's entrance would add a charming finishing touch.

Traditionally, the path leading through a cottage garden proceeded in a straight line from the lane to the door—its purpose was functional, not decorative. But no one will mind if you err in favor of beauty. Carve out a meandering path through the garden, if you wish, or give it a few unexpected jogs or kinks. As for the surface of the path, almost any informal material will do: Bark chips, old bricks (be sure they are paving types,

though), or cobblestones would look right at home. Stepping stones laid in a bed of mulch or nestled among scented "path plants" such as chamomile, woolly thyme, or Corsican mint (see "Groundcovers between Pavers" on page 56) would create a pretty and fragrant greeting.

You might want to include a small tree or two along the fence for year-round structure—perhaps a crabapple (*Malus* spp.), a redbud (*Cercis canadensis*), or a fringetree (*Chionanthus virginicus*). If there is room, include a few old-fashioned shrubs, such as lilac (*Syringa vulgaris*), mock-orange (*Philadelphus coronaria*), and shrub roses (*Rosa* spp.), in the garden's corners. These

Annuals That Self-Sow

Whether you consider the tendency of these annuals to return to your garden year after year from self-sown seeds a blessing or a curse depends on your garden style. The following annuals make a perfect cottage garden that can perpetuate itself with minimal attention—just thinning or rearranging the tiny seedlings when they appear.

Antirrhinum majus (snapdragon)
Browallia speciosa (browallia)
Calendula officinalis (calendula, pot marigold)
Centaurea cyanus (cornflower, bachelor's button)
Clarkia amoena (satin flower)
C. unguiculata (rose clarkia)
Cleome hasslerana (cleome, spider flower)
Consolida ambigua (rocket larkspur)

Cosmos bipinnatus (cosmos)
Delphinium spp. (larkspur)
Eschscholzia californica (California poppy)
Euphorbia marginata (snow-on-the-mountain)
Impatiens wallerana (impatiens, busy Lizzie)
Ipomoea spp. (morning-glories)
Linaria maroccana (toadflax)
Lobularia maritima (sweet alyssum)
Lunaria annua (honesty)
Mirabilis jalapa (four-o'clock)
Moluccella laevis (bells-of-Ireland)
Myosotis sylvatica (forget-me-not)
Nemophila menziesii (baby-blue-eyes)
Nigella damascena (love-in-a-mist)
Papaver rhoeas (Shirley poppy, corn poppy)
Portulaca grandiflora (portulaca, rose moss)
Torenia fournieri (wishbone-flower)
Tropaeolum majus (garden nasturtium)
Viola tricolor (Johnny-jump-up)

will look pretty and provide further interest during the winter.

The personality of the flowers you choose should blend with the personality of the cottage garden. Mix flowers right in with your favorite herbs. Dill, parsley, and coriander will self-sow and look pretty combined with the flowers. The lists of self-sowing annuals and spreading perennials in this chapter include plants appropriate for cottage gardening—select ones that please you and are compatible with your soil and light conditions. Flowers that have a light, airy look such as daisies, cleome, and coreopsis, rather than bold, attention-getting plants such as double peonies and Japanese iris, will look best when planted this informally. But be sure to plant a mixture of flower and plant shapes to add contrast.

Plant the flowers in informal patches if you want a little order in the garden, or arrange them randomly, perhaps even mixing the seeds all together and scattering them over prepared soil so the flowers can play

Exuberantly Spreading Perennials

These perennials tend to spread—either by roots or self-sowing—once established in a suitable garden spot. Whether their spreadability is desirable or not is debatable. Depending on the personality of your garden, you may welcome their tendency to advance or curse it. In an informal cottage-type garden, these perennials might be just the ticket to gleefully cover a lot of ground, creating a joyfully haphazard scene. Where neatness is valued, perennials that cannot sit still may be a nuisance, requiring frequent division or yanking.

Achillea millefolium (yarrow), Zone 3
A. ptarmica (sneezeweed), Zone 4
Alchemilla vulgaris (lady's-mantle), Zone 4
Anchusa azurea (Italian bugloss), Zone 3
Artemisia ludoviciana 'Silver King' (Silver King artemisia), Zone 3
Cerastium tomentosum (snow-in-summer), Zone 3

Chrysanthemum parthenium (fever-few), Zone 4
Coreopsis verticillata (threadleaf coreopsis), Zone 3
Iris cristata (crested iris), Zone 4
Lathyrus latifolius (perennial pea), Zone 4
Lychnis coronaria (rose campion), Zone 4
Lysimachia punctata (yellow loosestrife), Zone 5
Lythrum salicaria (purple loosestrife), Zone 3
Macleaya spp. (plume poppies), Zone 4
Monarda didyma (beebalm), Zone 4
Oenothera pilosella (sundrops), Zone 5
Phlox stolonifera (creeping phlox), Zone 3
P. subulata (moss pink), Zone 3
Physalis alkekengi (Chinese lantern), Zone 4
Physostegia virginiana (false dragonhead, obedient plant), Zone 2
Viola sororia (butterfly violet, woolly blue violet), Zone 5

hide-and-seek with each other. However, if you don't think you'll be able to tell the flower seedlings from the weedlings, sow your flowers in large patches of a single type, so you'll know by their concentration which are the seedlings you're after. Just be sure to select an assortment of flowers (including spring-flowering bulbs such as narcissus and crocus) that bloom at different seasons, so the garden will burst with cheerful blossoms from spring through fall.

Julie Johnson, who has gardened in many states but who is presently creating a new garden in Georgia, has developed her own tried-and-true style of cottage gardening. "My method of cottage gardening—I get many compliments from our English neighbors—is to haphazardly plant perennials, regardless of size and color, in loosely shaped borders," says Julie. "Perennials transplant easily, especially in the spring, so I can change the look of the garden each year if I want. I like to visit other people's gardens and collect seeds from their flowers. Several years ago, I 'stole' a number of seeds from outside the church where my sister-in-law was getting married. This year, I presented her with plants grown from those very seeds."

To add even more to the cottage-garden effect, you can drape vines along the fence and arbor. Climbing roses might be too much work to maintain, but Jackman clematis (*Clematis jackmanii*) and climbing hydrangea (*Hydrangea anomala* subsp. *petiolaris*) are less trouble and are both beautiful. If you enjoy growing edibles, train grape vines, raspberries, or squash or gourd vines along the fence. Pop in any vegetable plants you desire wherever you find a spot, or organize low vegetables such as flowering kale, cabbages, or lettuces, or herbs such as lavender and parsley, as edging plants along the walk.

A cottage garden wouldn't be complete without a garden ornament, often the more whimsical the better. Include a birdbath, a stone statue of a frog or rabbit, a real or imitation beehive, or St. Francis among the flowers. An ornament is an important feature in a cottage garden, acting as a focal point that draws the eye, and taming the tumultuous chaos of flowers. But use restraint and don't overdo the whimsy or the number of ornaments. Keep in mind that when it comes to garden ornaments, less is more. If you go overboard with the painted dwarves, flamingos, "fat fannies," and little wishing wells, you'll end up with a yard full of kitsch, not a cottage garden!

Caring for the Cottage Garden

Because part of its charm comes from its casual design, a cottage garden requires less work to maintain than more manicured flower gardens, though weeding can be a chore in spring, when the self-sown annuals show up and perhaps need thinning or moving. Don't be overly concerned about deadheading, because in a cottage garden the flowers should be encouraged to self-sow. Even if you want a bit of neatness, don't deadhead them all, especially late in the season. You might want to pick off faded flowers early in the season to prolong the bloom of annuals that would otherwise stop blooming. Later in the season, allow seedpods to mature and disperse the beginnings of next year's garden.

In fall, after frost has killed back the flowers and herbs, cut off their brown stalks and shake them over the garden to scatter the seed. You can wait until late winter or early spring to do this if you like to look at the dried stalks and seedheads over winter. The garden in winter can resemble a huge dried flower arrangement or look like a mess, depending on the plants you include in the garden and on your own particular vision. Perennials with attractive seedheads that may last well into winter include: 'Goldsturm' black-eyed Susan (*Rudbeckia fulgida* 'Goldsturm'), purple coneflower (*Echinacea purpurea*), Autumn Joy sedum (*Sedum* 'Autumn Joy'), wild oats (*Chasmanthium latifolium*), fernleaf yarrow (*Achillea filipendulina*), and threadleaf coreopsis (*Coreopsis verticillata*). Many shrub roses, especially *Rosa rugosa* and its cultivars, feature showy rose hips in fall and winter.

Don't mulch the cottage garden heavily, or the flower and herb seeds won't be able to germinate. Unfortunately, since a heavy mulch will deter weeds as well as volunteer flowers, cottage gardens tend to need extra weeding. In a garden that returns year after year from self-sown seeds, lay down no more than an inch of mulch. I found that an inch of pine bark mini-chips (which was all I could afford when purchasing mulch to cover a new flower bed) was sufficient to dress up the garden and prevent rain from splattering dirt on the flowers, and the mulch did not deter self-sown plants from germinating.

You'll have to hand-weed cautiously in spring, but with careful observation and a good seedling identification guide like *Park's Success with Seeds,* you'll be able to distinguish weed from garden flower. Since you won't be turning over the bed every year, weeds will become less of a problem with each growing season because as those near the surface of the soil germinate, the supply of surface seeds will be exhausted. After the cottage flowers are up and growing each spring, you can renew the mulch by spreading an inch of weed-free, well-rotted compost or manure around the plants. These topdressings will decay enough to allow the self-sown seeds to come up the following year. If you want to dress up the ground a bit more, apply a thin layer of pine needles or wood chips on top of the compost.

While you're weeding, take time to transfer flower seedlings that have popped up in the wrong places to more favorable locations. When they're small, you can practically do it with your fingers. You can group similar plants together, and also thin out seedlings that are too close together. After the initial work

in spring, the garden shouldn't need much more than watering and keeping an eagle eye out for weeds.

A Traditional Perennial Garden

When I'm admiring flower gardens in books and in other people's yards, it's a sure bet that many of my favorites are traditional perennial gardens. There's just something soul-satisfying in those architecturally ordered combinations of form and color. Perennial gardens can be as formal or informal as you like, but they usually follow the bed or border format. Traditionally, a perennial **border** is backed up against a wall or hedge and is viewed from only one side. A **bed** is open on all sides and has no background. Beds are much more difficult to design than borders because they lack any structure to begin with. The background of the border, along with its outlines, gives it immediate structure. For best effect, locate your garden along the side of the yard, with a fence, the wall of a house, shrubbery, or a hedge behind it.

Perennials aren't totally care-free, so the size of your garden will determine how much maintenance time it requires. A perennial garden has to be larger than an annual garden to make a visual impact, because not all the plants in it bloom together. The minimum size for a perennial garden is 12 feet long by 3 or more feet deep. Start with this size and make it longer in following years if you wish, but don't make it wider! Making a border wider often messes up the arrangement of plants if you've put taller perennials

Especially Well-Behaved Perennials

Often deep-rooted but noninvasive, the following perennials stay put, perhaps growing larger and sturdier year after year, but rarely invading their neighbors or requiring division.

Achillea filipendulina (fernleaf yarrow), Zone 3

Aconitum napellus (common monkshood), Zone 3

Amsonia tabernaemontana (blue star), Zone 3

A. × hybrida (Japanese anemone), Zone 4

Anemone sylvestris (snowdrop anemone), Zone 4

Aruncus dioicus (goatsbeard), Zone 3

Asclepias tuberosa (butterfly weed), Zone 3

Astilbe spp. (astilbe, false spirea), Zones 4–5, depending on species

Baptisia australis (baptisia, wild blue indigo), Zone 3

Campanula carpatica (Carpathian bellflower), Zone 3

Chrysogonum virginianum (green-and-gold, golden star), Zone 5

Cimicifuga racemosa (black snakeroot), Zone 3

C. simplex (Kamchatka bugbane), Zone 4

Dicentra spectabilis (bleeding-heart), Zone 2

Dictamnus albus (gas plant), Zone 3

Filipendula rubra (queen-of-the-prairie), Zone 3

Helleborus spp. (lenten rose, Christmas rose), Zone 4

Hemerocallis cultivars (daylilies), Zone 3

Hosta spp. and cultivars (hostas, plantain lilies), Zone 4

Iris hybrids (bearded iris), Zone 4

Iris sibirica (Siberian iris), Zone 4

Paeonia lactiflora (peony), Zone 2

Papaver orientale (oriental poppy), Zone 2

Platycodon grandiflorus (balloon flower), Zone 3

Rudbeckia fulgida 'Goldsturm' ('Goldsturm' black-eyed Susan), Zone 3

Sedum spectabile (showy stonecrop), Zone 3

Solidago cultivars (goldenrods), Zone 4 (the species can be real pests)

Thermopsis caroliniana (Carolina lupine), Zone 4

in the background and lower plants in front, so it's best to start out with the width you'd ultimately like to have.

It is also a good idea to leave space within and behind the border so you can easily tend it without stomping on the plants. You can probably reach most plants in a 3-foot-deep border, but where the depth is greater,

Especially Finicky Perennials

These petulant perennials must be fussed over to perform well. They may need frequent division, rot readily over the winter, attract bugs or fungi, flop or fail to grow straight without staking, or otherwise torment a gardener who's short on time. Though many of these finicky perennials are garden favorites, grow them only if you're willing to pamper them.

Plant Name	Maintenance Problems	Plant Name	Maintenance Problems
Aster spp. **Asters**	Aster wilt can be troublesome. Mildew affects most species, especially *A. novi-belgii* (New York aster) and *A. novae-angliae* (New England aster). Tall asters need staking; pinching in mid-June may reduce the need for staking, but shortens plants. Dwarf cultivars spread vigorously and can be invasive.	*Delphinium* hybrids **Delphinium**	Short-lived, usually surviving only 2 or 3 years. Performs best in cool northern climates. Tall, brittle stems need staking. Susceptible to numerous diseases, including leaf blights and mildew. May rot over the winter. Slugs feast on new growth in spring. Heavy feeder, requiring regular fertilization and rich soil.
Chrysanthemum × *morifolium* **Garden chrysanthemum**	Should be divided every other year. Can rot over winter in heavy or wet soil. Needs regular pinching in spring and summer (until August 1) to promote branching and prevent crown buds (false flower buds) from forming. Very heavy feeders, need fertile soil and regular applications of fertilizer. Aphids and spider mites can be serious.	*Helenium autumnale* **False sunflower, sneezeweed**	Tall plants need staking; pinching in early spring promotes sturdier growth. Grow in poor soil or lanky, weak growth results. May need division every year or every other year.
Chrysanthemum × *superbum* **Shasta daisy**	Short-lived, usually surviving only 2 or 3 years. Especially susceptible to rotting over the winter in rainy areas.	*Iris* hybrids **Bearded iris**	Iris borers tunnel into rhizomes. Soft rot travels through the foliage into the rhizomes, rotting them; remove yellowing leaves without delay. Remove and destroy all foliage in fall. Aphids and thrips can damage flowers. Don't bury rhizomes under soil or mulch, but expose them to bake in the sun.
		Lobelia cardinalis **Cardinal flower**	Short-lived, often surviving only 1 or 2 years unless perfectly sited. Requires rich, wet soil in a semi-shaded location.

Plant Name	Maintenance Problems	Plant Name	Maintenance Problems
Lupinus hybrids **Lupine**	Often short-lived, but if happily established can self-sow and become weedy. Finicky about climate, requiring cool nights and high humidity to perform well.	*Rosa* hybrids **Hybrid Tea and Floribunda roses**	Numerous insect and disease problems, including Japanese beetles, aphids, thrips, mildew, and black spot. Require correct pruning, regular deadheading, and frequent watering and fertilizing to perform well. Often not winter-hardy, necessitating winter protection.
Monarda didyma **Beebalm, monarda**	Susceptible to mildew. Can grow rampantly in the rich, moist soil it prefers. Clumps may die out in the centers, requiring division every few years. May be short-lived in areas with long, hot summers. Best naturalized in a wet-soil site.	*Stokesia laevis* **Stokes aster**	Rots easily over winter if soil is wet, especially where winter rains are common. Divide every 3 or 4 years.
Phlox paniculata **Garden phlox**	Highly susceptible to rot and mildew. Spider mites troublesome in hot, dry situations. Often requires staking. Must remove first flush of flowers after they fade for repeat bloom. Does not tolerate heat and humidity well, so is short-lived in the South.	*Tradescantia* × *andersoniana* **Spiderwort**	Foliage becomes floppy and messy by midsummer, requiring support; especially a problem in good soil. Cut back for neater regrowth. Flowers often close by midafternoon. Grows rapidly and needs division every 2 or 3 years.
Primula spp. **Primroses**	Usually short-lived, demanding consistently moist, humusy soil and light shade. May rot in soil that's wet over the winter. *P. vulgaris* is the easiest and most long-lived species.		

place a few inconspicuous stepping stones among the plants to make it easy to get to those at the back. Stones will also show you where to step during the off-season when plants are all below ground and it would be easy to trample them. If the border has a fence, hedge, or shrub border backing it, you'll need to be able to walk along the shrubs to prune them, or along the fence to repair or paint it. Some garden designers recommend leaving a 3-foot unplanted strip between the back of the border and a wall, fence, or hedge. This strip is "invisible" from a distance; the border still seems to back against the hedge (or whatever). This is a good idea if you have room—it allows easy access to the back of the border, encourages good air circulation, and prevents the fence from shading the garden, causing plants to lean outward.

An **island bed,** which is set in an open lawn or in a patio, is visible from all sides. No matter what its shape—round, square, rectangular, or irregular—the bed should look good when viewed from anywhere in the yard. Locate the tallest plants in the middle of the bed, with lower ones near the edges. The bed is best positioned so that shrubbery or a fence or wall located across the yard gives it a background when viewed from a distance, providing a dark backdrop to set off the bright flowers. If an island bed is deeper than 4 feet, place a few stepping stones so you can reach the center plants.

Designing a Traditional Perennial Garden

Because it is more orderly than a cottage garden, a perennial bed or border appears more formal, but it need not be stiffly formal or stuffy. The amount of order you impose on it is up to you. Its outlines, whether they are curving or straight, any prevailing color scheme, and the shapes and masses of the flowers all contribute toward the mood of the garden.

I like gardens that have gentle curving shapes. The front edge may bend inward and then flare outward, or transcribe a clean arc around the corner of the yard. Choose a

An island of flowers floating in a sea of turf works best when the tallest perennials rise from the center, allowing the bed to be viewed from all sides. Create the bed with low maintenance in mind by using a brick edging and mowing strip to keep grass from creeping into the island bed.

pleasing outline and be sure that any incurves or outcurves are balanced on the opposite side of the yard by either a straight edge or the reverse shape. Where two outcurves are opposite each other, the layout can look oddly pinched and ungraceful. Keep in mind, too, that if lawn fronts the border, the curves should be easy to mow and you should install a permanent edging to help keep the grass where it belongs.

Curved borders are more informal-looking than straight ones. Straight-sided borders are intrinsically more formal, but if the plants within them are arranged casually rather than stiffly placed in ordered rows, the border will not seem too formal for most settings.

Keys to Success

The first key to creating a successful and eye-catching perennial border is to use bold groups of color. Perennials arranged polka-dot fashion will look just like, well, polka dots. The flowers fail to make an impact, and the garden looks amorphous and spotty. Though this extreme casualness looks charming in a cottage garden, it can turn a more formal perennial border into a jumble. The only way I know to avoid this problem is to solemnly swear that you will purchase (or beg, borrow, or steal) at least three of any one kind of perennial and then plant them together. If you can manage five of a kind, all the better.

Planting in Drifts

Groups of three and five can be arranged in a **drift.** A drift is a fancy term to describe a group of plants that are arranged in an irregular mass, a mass that looks like the flowers were planted by the wind rather than the trowel. A drift might be teardrop-shaped rather than egg-shaped or square. Drifts, not rows, should be your aim when arranging the perennials in the border.

By planting the border in drifts of various sizes, and staggering the drifts so they overlap a bit, the masses of flowers meld into a bold and colorful painting. Try to create a foreground of low plants, a middle ground of medium-height plants, and a background of taller plants, so none are obscured. But don't follow this rule too rigidly—that is, avoid the row syndrome. Weave the drifts in the foreground into the middle ground, and those in the middle ground into the background. Keep in mind that you'll be cutting off flower stalks after blooming, and what was once a tall plant may become a short one; such a plant might be suitable for the middle of the border rather than the back as long as it blooms before, or after, the plants behind it. If plants of different heights drift in and out of each other, the effect is softer and more natural than if you line the plants up by height like a bunch of grammar-school kids having a class photo taken.

Planting for Continuous Bloom

The second important factor in a successful perennial garden is somehow managing to orchestrate the flowers so that the border blooms continuously from spring through fall, or during whichever season or seasons you want the primary impact. No mean feat! There are several ways to do this. The first takes planning. You can lay out the planting scheme on paper before ever purchasing a plant. Then pick and choose promising plants from garden catalogs or books and "plant" them on the paper. "Transplant" your paper garden, moving around the imaginary plants, until you have a satisfactory design. It helps to make several copies of the plan, one for each month of the growing season. You can

♦ ♦ ♦ ♦ ♦ ♦   ♦ ♦ ♦ ♦ ♦ ♦ ♦ ♦ ♦ ♦ ♦ ♦

Mail-Order Perennials Save Time

Weekend gardeners who find they would rather spend their precious weekends with their hands in the dirt instead of shopping will find that mail-ordering plants, especially perennials, makes a lot of sense. You can browse through numerous catalogs at your leisure, making selections based on your garden's needs rather than on what your local nursery has to offer. When armchair shopping, it's easy to check up on potential selections in a reference book if need be and to compare prices from one catalog to the next. You can draw a garden plan, then thoughtfully select perennials to carry out a particular color scheme and to deliver blossoms from spring through fall. Then you can order the exact plants needed to carry out the plan from the catalogs. And all this can be done on a bleak January afternoon when no other garden chores demand your time.

Perennials ordered through the mail are often smaller—and also less expensive—than those available at your nursery. They may not bloom the first year you plant them, but don't let this discourage you. Properly situated perennials will grow and spread—that's the beauty of perennials. They are here to stay with a minimum of care. And when you start with small plants, you can afford more individual plants to create large, bold drifts that will not need division for years to come. When planting large gallon-size containers, it's more difficult to create an attractive drift, and the plants will need division in a few years. Better to plant five small perennials than one or two large ones!

The first summer after planting my sunny perennial border—mostly from mail-order plants—I had what I jokingly referred to as our wood-chip garden: The thick blanket of chips we applied as a mulch was its most prominent feature. The following year, however, the garden was magnetic, drawing visitors as they rounded the bend of the front walk and approached the door. And all we had to do was watch it grow!

color in the drifts that will be in bloom each month as a check.

I'll admit that I have never done this. My gardens have usually been much more spontaneous, and some of them showed it. In fact, the bones of all of the perennial borders in each of my houses sprang from plants I purchased on sale during July. Both of my favorite nurseries host half-price sales around Independence Day. These events define many gardener's lives in these parts; we stop purchasing in early June and begin taking notes on what we hope will still be around—at half-price—in mid-July.

Needless to say, my purchases at these sales have been haphazard at best. Even if I had planned on a color scheme and bloom schedule, I took home only what I could win from the grasp of another greedy gardener. Mark and I dug our new borders in the heat and humidity characteristic of the Fourth, with sweat trickling down our brows, and then arranged the new plants in a semblance of a design. In the following years, I added what was missing to the gardens and wasn't timid about moving plants around to create a more pleasing design. In fact, if I don't like where a perennial finds itself, I dig it right up, using a large spade to secure as huge a root ball as possible, and plop it down where I think it looks better. If kept well watered, it gets over the shock rapidly. Sometimes I rearrange plants several times. That's my method of garden design. It sprang from never having time to plan anything.

If you seem to lack time to plan, try adapting my on-the-spot designing method for a new border. Prepare the soil for your new border in spring, covering it with a deep mulch of wood chips to keep out weeds. (We get a truckload of wood chips delivered from a tree-care company every year. The huge pile costs $50 and meets our needs nicely.) Then make monthly visits to a well-stocked nursery and select plants from among the perennials that are in bloom. Try to get at least three kinds of plant on each trip. Plant them in scattered groups (of three or five, remember!) in the garden according to height, leaving plenty of space between each group. Every month repeat your purchasing and planting, installing the new drifts in between the previous ones. By fall your wood-chip garden will be a filled-in border that will bloom from spring through fall. And you didn't plan a thing!

Color Schemes

If you are creative enough and have the time to carefully plan it, a perennial border can feature a stunning color scheme that is carried through all the bloom cycles from spring through fall. Or the colors can change with the seasons.

Whenever I have attempted a strong color scheme, I've been sorry, usually because of all the plants I have to exclude. The shady border at the side of my house blooms in blue, purple, white, and pink. I like it very much, but I lamented having no place to plant lemon daylilies (*Hemerocallis lilio-asphodelus*), yellow coreopsis (*Coreopsis grandiflora*), and orange butterfly weed (*Asclepias tuberosa*). And I quickly found that the wrong shade of pink—a peachy one, for instance—looked gruesome with the lavender-pinks of my asters, lilies, and mums! So this spring, Mark and I created a perennial border in the front yard bordering a spirea hedge where there was enough sun to grow roses, iris, and all the longed-for flowers that perished in the shady side yard. I decided this border would be yellow, blue, and white, softened up with gray and silver foliage plants. However, I *still* have no designated place to grow those sun-loving, wrong-colored pink and orange flowers that I crave: I find that some have crept in, seemingly of their own accord, in defiance of the color scheme.

If you don't plan a particular color scheme, that's fine, but do try to select neighboring plants whose flower colors complement each other if they bloom at the same time or their bloom times overlap. Try using masses of white flowers, such as meadow phlox (*Phlox maculata* 'Miss Lingard') or shasta daisy (*Chrysanthemum × superbum*), and silvery gray foliage plants, such as 'Silver Mound' artemesia (*Artemesia schmidti-*

ana 'Silver Mound'), to separate and soften bright or clashing color combinations. And don't be timid about moving plants around if you find that they clash next to each other. Before transplanting them, remove a flower or two and carry it over to the proposed new neighbors to see how the colors work together. You might wish to wait until spring or fall to do the transplanting, but be sure to match colors and take notes when the flowers are *in bloom.*

Setting Up the Site

The soil in a new border should be prepared very well. Since the perennials will be in residence pretty much for the duration, the beginnings of the garden are your one and only opportunity to get the soil right. Double-dig it, if you can (see "How to Double-Dig a Garden" on page 154), incorporating lots of organic matter into both sandy and clay soils. If you are blessed with good garden loam to start with, you'll need less preparation.

Outlining the border with a mowing strip or other edging (see "Choosing and Using Edgings and Mowing Strips" on page 50) will keep the lawn from invading the flower border and prevent many a weeding headache. It's also amazing how an edging can play visual tricks and make your garden look neater than it really is. Keep the lawn and flower border distinctly separate with a crisp edging, and even if the flowers are a bit floppy or a few weeds are poking up among them, the entire scene will take on a deceptively well-manicured look.

A thick mulch, about 4 inches deep, of wood chips, compost, or shredded leaves will help prevent weed seeds from germinating and keep the soil moist enough so that watering will be needed only during extended dry spells. Renew the mulch each

year after you've divided any plants that need it.

The Mixed Border

If you cross a shrub border with a herbaceous perennial border, what do you get? A mixed border, of course! This is no joke. A hybrid garden offers many advantages for a weekend gardener. It is easy to care for, provides color and interest throughout the year, and offers enough challenging gardening opportunities to be an outlet for those stricken with flower fever.

One problem with a traditional perennial border—a problem that is solved by a mixed border—is that it looks so dead in the winter. The garden becomes an untidy strip of bare ground for many months of the year. If it is readily visible from the house or front entrance, as my sunny perennial border is, the perennial garden may detract from the appearance of your property during the winter months. You can solve this, as I am doing, by mixing in woody plants to give the garden year-round structure. The mixed border makes a perfect low-maintenance flower bed for a weekend gardener because shrubs require less care than perennials but can put on an equally showy display, a display that doesn't stop at the end of the growing season.

A mixed border is not the easiest garden to design. You can't simply plant a row of shrubs with rows of perennials in front—that would be a throwback to the herbaceous border with a hedge for a background. The woody plants in a mixed border must be carefully arranged within the border to form the bones of the garden without dominating it. The herbaceous material—perennials,

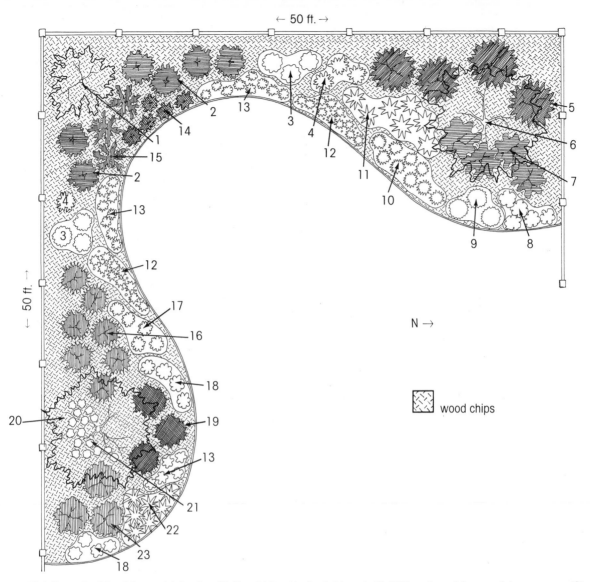

Plot Plan of a Mixed Perennial Border. (1) 'Arnold Promise' witchhazel, (2) 'Filifera Aurea' Sawara false cypress, (3) 'Avalanche' Japanese anemone, (4) 'Wonder of Staffa' Frikart's aster, (5) 'White Cascade' Japanese pieris, (6) Chinese kousa dogwood, (7) Korean rhododendron, (8) 'Vera Jameson' sedum, (9) 'Silver Mound' artemisia, (10) 'Golden Showers' threadleaf coreopsis, (11) lemon daylily, (12) 'Silver Carpet' lamb's-ears and *Tulipa pulchella,* (13) 'Blue Clips' Carpathian bellflower, (14) 'Crimson Pygmy' Japanese barberry, (15) 'Limemound' Bumald spirea, (16) dwarf fothergilla, (17) 'Citrinum' basket-of-gold, (18) perennial candytuft, (19) mugho pine, (20) paperbark maple, (21) daffodils, (22) 'Stella d'Oro' daylily, (23) 'PJM' rhododendron

bulbs, and annuals—will flesh out the garden, giving it personality.

Because the majority of shrubs bloom in spring, your mixed border might feature a scheme that offers numerous spring-flowering shrubs and bulbs for a euphoric "thank goodness it's finally spring" display. Rely on summer- and fall-flowering annuals and

A well-planned assortment of plants brings this mixed border to life every month of the year. The springtime show stars flowering shrubs, trees, and bulbs, while an assortment of perennials and colorful shrub foliage perform in the summer months. Fall brings a splashy display when the leaves of the deciduous trees and shrubs change color. Even in winter the garden captures attention—the small trees feature colorful mottled and peeling bark, the evergreen shrubs provide foliage, and the intricate branching of the deciduous shrubs adds structure.

perennials to take over the display after the shrubs and bulbs have quieted down.

Designing a Mixed Border

A mixed border can, and probably should, be much larger—both longer and wider—than a perennial border. Design it to surround the perimeter of the entire backyard, if you wish, perhaps with a fence as a background. The shrubs provide a year-round structure for the garden, creating something interesting to look at throughout the year, and act as a permanent planting that can provide privacy or delineate a garden boundary. Group the shrubs together in widely spaced drifts, being sure to leave enough growing space for them to mature.

To create a sense of balance, make sure the shrubs take up no more than half the space in the border. Tall shrubs can be in the background, medium-size shrubs in the middle ground, and low shrubs in the foreground. In the areas between the groups of shrubs, plant masses of perennials and bulbs. Do not mix the perennials and shrubs together randomly, alternating a shrub with a perennial—each should be kept in distinct masses for the best year-round effect.

The overall outlines of the garden can be straight or curved, but will look more appealing if they carve out an interesting serpentine around the yard. Shrubs are best grouped in the widest parts of the garden, where the depth of the garden can balance the weight of the shrubs. Here, too, you might situate a small tree, such as a dogwood or golden-chain, underplanted with lower shrubs and perennials. Narrow incurves look best planted with perennials and only very low, spreading shrubs.

Consider how you will gain access to the shrubs and perennials when they need tending, and work a path of stepping stones into the design. If you have room, leave a deeply mulched, unplanted strip about 3 feet wide at the back of the border. This alleyway will allow you to tend plants at the rear of the border and get in there easily to prune shrubs. The alley won't be noticeable in a fully planted border, and it will also increase air circulation, which keeps plants healthy.

Choosing Shrubs for the Mixed Border

Flowering shrubs, either evergreen or deciduous, work well in a mixed border because they provide flowers and sometimes colorful berries. Needle-leaf shrubs will provide fine-textured greenery and structure year-round. Choose shrubs that look good massed together and that have a naturally refined character. Shrubs that are well-behaved and don't send up suckers or reach out arching or cascading branches, such as bumald spirea (*Spiraea* × *bumalda*), will work better than sprawling shrubs, such as forsythia, which can crowd out the perennials and which are more difficult to combine with upright flowers.

Where the soil is acid, azaleas, rhododendrons, mountain laurels, and related plants make wonderful additions to a mixed border. Choose dwarf or compact varieties of rhododendron. There are many cultivars and hybrids that grow to about 4 or 5 feet tall and have small glossy leaves that look neat

and perky all year. Different kinds bloom from early to late spring, offering bouquets of delightful flowers ranging from lavender to pink, yellow, and white.

Many types of azalea work well in a mixed border, but my favorites are the Robin Hill, Satsuki, or Macrantha hybrids; these are low, spreading, or even ground-hugging types that bloom later than more common azaleas. They bloom in early summer in my climate (which is the warm part of Zone 6), flowering in late June and into July. How surprising to be treated to their beautiful pink, coral, or white blossoms so late in the season when few other shrubs bloom. These azaleas remain neat and compact, too, so they are suitable for the foreground.

Deciduous shrubs look fine in the mixed border, especially if they have an interesting branching pattern or colorful bark or foliage. Variegated Japanese kerria (*Kerria japonica* 'Variegata') offers pleasing single yellow flowers in early spring, delicate white-edged, grass green foliage in summer, and pea green bark on its slender stems throughout the winter months. For fragrance, my favorite is koreanspice viburnum (*Viburnum carlesii* 'Compactum')—it perfumes the entire yard with a sweet, spicy aroma. Garden designers frequently use 'Crimson Pygmy' barberry (*Berberis thunbergii* 'Crimson Pygmy'), because its rich purplish red spring and summer foliage makes such a lovely contrast to bright spring greens and blue flowers. Combine this dwarf shrub with chartreuse-foliaged 'Goldflame' spirea (*Spirea* × *bumalda* 'Goldflame') for a stunning impact that lasts throughout the growing seasons.

Needle-leaf evergreens such as mugho pine (*Pinus mugo*) can be used to create cushions of greenery among the flowers. But not all dwarf conifers look attractive when massed; many are more at home in rock gar-

Shrubs, Vines, and Groundcovers for Mixed Borders

Woody plants such as vines and shrubs, and some groundcovers, give a perennial garden structure that's attractive to look at every month of the year. As a bonus, many of the plants listed here provide seasonal flowers and berries or evergreen foliage.

Vines

Clematis spp. and hybrids (clematises), Zone 3

Gelsemium sempervirens (Carolina jasmine), Zone 7

Hydrangea anomala subsp. *petiolaris* (climbing hydrangea), Zone 4

Jasminum spp. (jasmines), Zone 6

Lonicera sempervirens (trumpet honeysuckle), Zone 4

Wisteria spp. (wisterias), Zone 4

Shrub Roses

Rosa 'Alba Meidiland', Zone 3

R. 'Bonica', Zone 4

R. 'Elmshorn', Zone 3

R. *foetida* 'Bicolor' (Austrian copper rose), Zone 4

R. *foetida* 'Persiana' (Persian yellow rose), Zone 4

R. × *harisonii* (Harison's yellow rose), Zone 3

R. *hugonis* (Father Hugo rose), Zone 5

R. 'Pearl Meidiland', Zone 3

R. 'Pink Meidiland', Zone 3

R. 'Red Meidiland', Zone 3

R. *rugosa* cultivars (rugosa rose, Japanese rose), Zone 3

R. 'Scarlet Meidiland', Zone 3

R. 'Simplicity', Zone 5

R. 'Sparrieshoop', Zone 3

R. 'Square Dancer', Zone 2

R. 'White Meidiland', Zone 3

Shrubs

Berberis thunbergii var. *atropurpurea* 'Crimson Pygmy' ('Crimson Pygmy' Japanese barberry), Zone 4

Camellia japonica (camellia), Zone 7

Caryopteris × *clandonensis* (bluebeard), Zone 4

Daphne × *burkwoodii* (Burkwood daphne), Zone 6

D. cneorum (garland flower), Zone 4

D. odora (winter daphne), Zone 7

Enkianthus campanulatus (redvein enkianthus), Zone 7

Fothergilla gardenii (dwarf fothergilla), Zone 5

Gardenia jasminoides (gardenia), Zone 8

Hydrangea macrophylla subsp. *serrata* (lacecap hydrangea), Zone 6

Hypericum spp. (St.-John's-worts), Zone 4

Ilex crenata 'Helleri' (Heller's Japanese holly), Zone 6

Kalmia latifolia (mountain laurel), Zone 5

♦ ♦ ♦ ♦ ♦ ♦ ♦ ♦ ♦ ♦ ♦

Kerria japonica (Japanese kerria), Zone 5

Nandina domestica (heavenly bamboo), Zone 7

Pieris japonica (Japanese andromeda), Zone 6

Pinus mugo (mugho pine), Zone 3

Rhododendron spp. and cultivars (rhododendrons and azaleas), Zones 4–7, depending on species

Spiraea × *bumalda* (Bumald spirea), Zone 4

S. japonica (Japanese spirea), Zone 4

Syringa × *persica* (Persian lilac), Zone 5

Taxus baccata 'Repandens' (spreading English yew), Zone 6

Viburnum carlesii (Koreanspice viburnum), Zone 4

Groundcovers

Calluna vulgaris (Scotch heather), Zone 5

Ceratostigma plumbaginoides (leadwort, blue plumbago), Zone 6

Lamium maculatum (spotted dead nettle), Zone 4

Liriope muscari 'Variegata' (variegated blue lilyturf), Zone 6

Paxistima canbyi (Canby paxistima), Zone 4

Stachys byzantina 'Silver Carpet' ('Silver Carpet' lamb's ears), Zone 5

dens than in lush, flowery settings. Dwarf weeping hemlocks (*Tsuga canadensis* 'Pendula'), spreading junipers (cultivars of *Juniperus chinensis*), spreading yew (*Taxus baccata* 'Repandens'), and any other evergreen that forms a mass will work well. Specimens that grow as upright exclamation points may look strange; avoid such plants as the overly contorted Hollywood juniper (*Juniperus chinensis* 'Torulosa') and tightly conical dwarf white spruce (*Picea glauca* 'Conica').

Mixing in Bulbs and the Like

Spring- and summer-flowering bulbs (or bulblike rhizomatous plants) look right at home in the flower border. Adding clumps of daffodils (*Narcissus* spp.), crocuses (*Crocus* spp.), glory-of-the-snow (*Chionodoxa luciliae*), and grape hyacinths (*Muscari botryoides*) to the border will bring early-spring color at the same time as spring-flowering shrubs are blooming. The foliage of these spring bloomers will disappear from view by summer, as their withering leaves are hidden by the foliage of summer perennials. To avoid digging up the dormant bulbs, plant them under shrubs or in spots where you will later add annuals.

In summer, you can have magnificent color with irises (*Iris* spp.), lilies (*Lilium* spp.), and daylilies (*Hemerocallis* hybrids) —all with dramatic foliage that adds structure to the garden because it does not die back until fall. The elegant blossoms of bearded iris (a rhizomatous plant that I enjoy planting with bulbs) make a dramatic statement for two weeks in early summer. After the blooms are gone, the sword-shaped foliage remains, its flat planes forming giant fans that set off more delicate flowers and leaves to perfection. Even if it didn't bloom, bearded iris would find a place in my garden for the sake of its wonderful foliage. From mid- to late summer, a procession of lilies can perfume the garden. If sited in the cool, rich, moist soil they prefer, lilies will increase to slowly form magnificent clumps. Tall lilies should be loosely staked to prevent toppling in thunderstorms. Daylilies, another fleshy-rooted plant often planted with bulbs, are fast becoming America's most popular garden flower, because they top the list for ease of care and disease and insect resistance. Daylilies come in such a wide variety of colors, sizes, and bloom seasons. Choose early-, mid-, and late-season bloomers, and daylilies will decorate your garden with their ruffly flowers from June through August.

For late-season color, plant magic flowers (*Lycoris squamigera*). The naked flower stems shoot from the ground, seemingly overnight, producing clusters of large, trumpet-shaped, rose pink flowers in August. The foliage emerges in spring, then dies to the ground before the plants flower. Fall-flowering bulbs include the lovely golden yellow sternbergia (*Sternbergia lutea*) and the lilac- or rose-flowered autumn crocus (*Colchicum autumnale*).

Annuals in the Mixed Border

A few splashes of annuals mingled in with the perennials help to create a stable base of unchanging color for most of the growing season. The annuals act as a foil for the changing show of perennial flowers. Include easy-care annuals, using a different color or variety each year to provide some excitement to the garden, perhaps dramatically affecting the border's color scheme from year to year.

I always include repeating masses of impatiens (*Impatiens wallerana*) in my flower borders because they form such pleasing mounds of flowers and require absolutely no care. Another winner is white sweet alyssum (*Lobularia maritima*), which graces the front of a border, unifying the flower garden and softening clashing colors. Use it also as a constantly flowering groundcover and let it reseed itself. Pansies (*Viola × wittrockiana*) provide a delightful display. (Though they're technically biennial, they're sold as annual bedding plants at garden centers.) I like to plant them in masses of a single color near bulbs and let them cover up the dying foliage. Choose heat-resistant cultivars for a display that lasts throughout the summer.

An Easy Bulb Border

A garden composed of nothing but bulbs? Sound a bit wacky? Not really. An all-bulb border practically takes care of itself and if properly planted will bloom for months on end. Spring-, summer-, and fall-blooming bulbs (including corms, rhizomes, and tubers, as well as true bulbs) can be combined in perfect harmony to provide months of color in a small garden, because the "bulbs" can grow practically on top of each other. With an all-bulb border, you can pack a lot of bloom into a small space; as the earlier-maturing foliage of the spring bulbs begins to look unsightly, the foliage of the summer bulbs grows up around it, camouflaging the yellowing leaves. Plant spring and summer bulbs together in the same drifts—don't separate them as you would perennials—so there are never bare spots in the garden.

For instance, create a large drift of narcissus combined with daylilies, alternating groups of daffodil bulbs with single daylily

◆ ◆   ◆   ◆ ◆   ◆   ◆   ◆ ◆   ◆   ◆   ◆   ◆ ◆   ◆ ◆

Easy-Care Bulbs

These bulbs are vigorous plants that will increase year after year but never become weedy.

Agapanthus spp. (lily-of-the-Nile), Zone 9

Anemone blanda (windflower, Greek anemone), Zone 5

Chionodoxa spp. (glory-of-the-snow), Zone 4

Colchicum autumnale (autumn crocus, meadow saffron), Zone 5

Crocus spp. and hybrids (crocuses), Zone 5

Fritillaria meleagris (checkered lily), Zone 4

Galanthus elwesii (giant snowdrop), Zone 4

G. nivalis (common snowdrop), Zone 4

Hyacinthoides hispanicus (Endymion hispanicus, Scilla campanulata) (Spanish bluebell), Zone 4

Iris danfordiae, Zone 5

I. histrioides, Zone 5

I. reticulata, Zone 5

I. xiphioides (English iris), Zone 5

I. xiphium (Spanish iris, Dutch iris), Zone 6

Leucojum spp. (snowflakes), Zones 3–4, depending on species

Lilium spp. and hybrids (lilies), Zone 4

Lycoris squamigera (magic lily), Zone 5

Muscari spp. (grape hyacinths), Zones 2–4, depending on species

Narcissus spp. and hybrids (daffodils, jonquils, and narcissi), Zones 4–6, depending on species

Scilla siberica (Siberian squill), Zone 2

Sternbergia lutea (winter daffodil, lily-of-the-field), Zone 7

rhizomes that will increase into large clumps, in a 4-foot or longer drift. As the daylilies get larger and the daffodil clumps increase in size, the drift will fill into a beautiful mass of spring blossoms followed by a burst of summer flowers in the same garden spot. This combination is very effective together, and since there are so many delightful choices of daffodils for early, mid-, and late spring, and a rainbow of daylilies that bloom in early,

mid-, or late summer, you could even create a daylily and daffodil garden that would bloom from spring to fall.

Other bulb combinations work well, too. You might try English irises (*Iris xiphioides*), which bloom in late spring, in a drift with late-summer-blooming Asiatic lilies. Elegant Spanish bluebells (*Hyacinthoides hispanicus*) bloom in late spring and then die back, making room for rubrum lilies (*Lilium speciosum*

Bulbs to Avoid

The bulbs included here are all problematic. They may be short-lived in most gardens, flower poorly after the first season, self-sow so prolifically that they become pests in the garden or lawn, or have other undesirable traits.

Plant Name	Maintenance Problems	Plant Name	Maintenance Problems
Eranthis hyemalis **Winter aconite**	Self-sows so readily that it spreads rapidly and often invades and smothers lawns. Foliage dies down early and leaves the invaded areas bare. Plant only in a naturalistic setting where invasion isn't a concern.	*Ornithogalum* spp. **Star-of-Bethlehem**	Spreads so rapidly that it may colonize an entire garden in short order. Bulbs multiply rapidly into sizable clumps, but also self-sow prolifically, popping up as a weed all over the place, including the lawn. The tall, grassy foliage emerges and grows quickly in early spring, but begins to die back just before the white flowers bloom.
Fritillaria lanceolata **Checker lily**	Very short-lived in most gardens; rots easily over winter in damp or wet soil.		
Gladiolus × *hortulanus* **Garden gladiolus**	Produces tall flower spikes that usually need staking to grow straight. Thrips can seriously disfigure flowers, bulb mites can cause yellowed and distorted foliage, botrytis ruins flowers, and fungi can rot corms in storage. Hardy only in Zones 8–10.	*Tulipa* hybrids **Hybrid tulips**	Renowned for dying out quickly, especially in warm climates. Many never bloom a second year, and their withering foliage is particularly unsightly. Grow them as annuals in a mixed border —plant them in fall, pull them out after blooming, and plant annuals in their place.
Hyacinthus orientalis **Common garden hyacinth**	Blooms well only the first season after planting; in subsequent years, flowers line the spikes sparsely and are much less showy. Bulbs do not multiply well and die out quickly in mild-winter areas, preferring colder winters. Best treated as an annual.		

'Rubrum'). You might combine Dutch crocuses with bearded irises or lilies. Giant alliums (*Allium giganteum*) produce amazing large balls of purple-pink flowers atop tall bare stalks just about the time the foliage begins to turn a sickly yellow. This unsightly

Demanding annuals, perennials that are rampant or messy growers, plants that have lovely flowers but unattractive or disease-prone foliage, and everlastings are all at home in a cutting garden. By growing flowers in raised beds just as you would grow vegetables, you can tend the plants quickly, and you'll harvest armloads of flowers.

foliage needs disguising, and what better way to do it than with the spiky leaves of a later-blooming daylily.

A Cutting Garden

Part of the pleasure in growing flowers is in being able to cut them to enjoy indoors. But, regrettably, this all too often leaves the flower garden bare. Why rob Peter to pay Paul? Plant a cutting garden whose sole intention is to supply cut flowers for floral arrangements and you'll never feel guilty about gathering the blossoms.

The majority of flowers in a cutting garden should be annuals, because these bloom most profusely and will keep on producing more flowers as you cut off the fresh ones. Because annuals are heavy feeders and need to be replanted every year, a cutting garden can be a high-maintenance garden if you aren't careful. Keep it fairly small and design it with ease of care in mind.

Since you'll be continually harvesting its flowers, a cutting garden can look rather bare, so locate it out of sight but where the plants will get at least 6 hours of full sun a day. If the garden must be in a prominent location, enclosing it within a low picket fence, a split-rail fence, or garden wall adds to its visual appeal while masking some of the colorless plants. For ease of care, plant the cutting flowers in rows as in a tradi-

◆ ◆   ◆ ◆   ◆ ◆   ◆   ◆ ◆   ◆ ◆   ◆ ◆   ◆ ◆   ◆ ◆

Flowers for the Cutting Garden

Grow these flowers in orderly rows in a cutting garden so you can harvest armloads to use for floral arrangements. All are easy to grow, though tall plants may need staking to produce desirably straight stems. Though some of these flowers are included in the lists of high-maintenance plants, when grown for cut flowers they are no longer demanding because cutting off the flowers for arrangements substitutes for time-consuming deadheading. Cut flowers of all of these plants last well.

Annuals

Antirrhinum majus (snapdragon)
Calendula officinalis (calendula, pot marigold)
Callistephus chinensis (China aster)
Celosia cristata (cockscomb)
Centaurea cineraria (dusty miller)
Cleome hasslerana (spiderflower)
Consolida ambigua (rocket larkspur)
Cosmos bipinnatus (cosmos)
Papaver spp. (poppies)
Pelargonium × hortorum (zonal geranium)
Petunia × hybrida (petunia)
Tagetes erecta (African marigold)
Viola × wittrockiana (pansy)
Zinnia elegans (zinnia)

Bulbs

Convallaria majalis (lily-of-the-valley), Zone 3
Lilium spp. and hybrids (lilies), Zone 4
Narcissus spp. and hybrids (daffodils, jonquils, and narcissi), Zones 4–6, depending on species
Tulipa spp. and hybrids (tulips), Zones 2–4, depending on species

Perennials

Achillea filipendulina (yarrow), Zone 3
Aster hybrids (aster), Zone 4
Chrysanthemum × morifolium (garden chrysanthemum), Zone 5
C. × superbum (Shasta daisy), Zone 4
Coreopsis lanceolata (lanceleaf coreopsis), Zone 3
Delphinium hybrids (delphiniums), Zone 3
Dicentra spectabilis (common bleeding-heart), Zone 2
Digitalis hybrids (foxglove), Zone 4, actually biennial
Gypsophila paniculata (baby's-breath), Zone 3
Iris hybrids (bearded iris cultivars), Zone 4
Paeonia lactiflora (peony), Zone 2
Phlox paniculata (garden phlox), Zone 4
Rudbeckia fulgida (black-eyed Susan), Zone 3

tional vegetable garden, leaving enough space in between for easy tilling to control weeds. Plant perennials in the outer rows and locate annuals in the central rows. This way, when you turn over the soil every spring and add soil amendments, you won't disturb the perennials.

Caring for a cutting garden and a vegetable garden are similar in many ways. The time-saving techniques described in the next chapter for vegetable gardens, such as use of plastic or fabric mulch, will work well in a cutting garden. You might even wish to simply save a row or two in your vegetable garden for growing cut flowers. When you include the cut flowers with the vegetables, garden chores and harvesting can be effortlessly combined. The flowers will add beauty and color to the vegetable garden, too; you might consider planting the outer rows of the vegetable garden with flowers. Then, when viewed from the house or yard, the garden appears as an inviting vista of colorful blooms, rather than a patch of plastic and foliage.

The Key Is Care-Free

Though the public displays of flashy bedding plants we often see in parks and botanical gardens make a dramatic impression—the brighter and bolder the more memorable—it's best not to emulate these gardens at home, unless, like the public garden, you have an estate to set off the brilliant beds and a crew of gardeners to tend them. Week-end gardeners can ill afford the time it takes to care for a traditional bedded-out annual flower garden. As I've described in this chapter, it's better to learn to favor the undemanding perennials and flowering shrubs, with their ebb and flow of flowers, over the high-maintenance bedding annuals.

By designing an informal garden that relies on the less time-consuming plants, you can have your garden and your weekend, too. Designed for ease of maintenance, a flower garden composed of easy-care perennials, bulbs, shrub roses, and low-maintenance annuals can provide just enough outlet for your creativity and plant-nurturing needs. A host of beautiful, easy-care flowers awaits your discovery in the encyclopedia section near the back of the book.

The longer I garden, the more beauty I find in subtle details of my flower garden—the way sunlight passes through translucent, lacy, blue-green columbine foliage; the way the blossoms on a balloon flower first inflate into almost perfect spheres before popping open to reveal a network of navy-blue veins coursing through a sky blue background; and the rustling sounds made by the blades of fountain grass as they rub up against one another in the breeze. These details, more than the bright colors, make a flower garden a joy to the gardener. And these joys are within the reach of even the most time-pressured weekend flower gardener, as long as you remember to plant thoughtfully for a care-free garden.

THE WEEKEND GARDEN GALLERY

An Inspiring Tour of Great Gardens

Flip through these pages to enjoy a delightful visit with weekend gardeners across the country—from Maine to Colorado, New York to North Carolina. The beautiful gardens pictured here demonstrate just how successfully gardeners can transform a boring lawn or backyard into a glorious display. Whether they've created a traditional garden or a naturalistic setting, all the gardeners who share their gardens with us here rely on easy-care designs and trouble-free plants as the backbone of their labor-saving strategy. As a result, they spend less time fussing over their gardens and more time enjoying them.

All the beautiful plants featured in portraits here can shine in your garden with minimal care. These outstanding easy-care plants—including perennials, annuals, shrubs, trees, groundcovers, and wildflowers—defy insects and diseases and put on a dependable display year after year without any coddling. In fact, they practically thrive on neglect.

A successful weekend garden looks as if you've spent all week tending it, when in fact it only takes a few relaxing hours a week to keep it flourishing. Gardeners everywhere are getting into the weekend garden act—learning to conserve their valuable time and energy for the activities they enjoy most by adopting labor-saving techniques that practically do away with drudgery. So sit back, take a "tour" of the beautiful weekend gardens pictured here, and find out how to put the fun back into *your* gardening!

Because he has time to garden only on the weekends, Louis Edmonds designed a garden that can practically fend for itself. He counts on a collection of reliable, easy-care perennials and shrubs to create his long-blooming flower border. The featured flowers in this late spring photograph include rhododendrons, oriental poppies (*Papaver orientale*), bearded irises, garden pinks (*Dianthus* spp.), and peonies. Garden Design: Louis Edmonds

▼

▲

Bounded by a picket fence, this cottage garden of herbs, vegetables, and perennial flowers looks right at home in the peaceful New Hampshire countryside. The owners created a low-maintenance garden oasis within the fence, featuring a geometric arrangement of planting beds, tidy gravel pathways, and a patio conveniently located off the dining room and kitchen. Horses graze in the field outside the fence, which needs only an annual mowing. Garden Design: Pam and Dick Dalhaus

No boring high-maintenance lawn in this yard! Instead, a tumultuous collection of groundcovers, perennials, bulbs, shrubs, and vines creates a charming setting around the home's side entrance. Paths formed of native rock steps and a thick carpet of wood chips fit in with the naturalistic character of the garden. In bloom are cranesbills (*Geranium* spp.), fringed bleeding-heart (*Dicentra eximia*), snow-in-summer (*Cerastium tomentosum*), daylilies (*Hemerocallis* × *hybrida*), Siberian irises (*Iris sibirica*), coralbells (*Heuchera* × *brizoides*), peonies (*Paeonia lactiflora*), and spiderworts (*Tradescantia virginiana*). Garden Design: Conni Cross ▶

▲

This naturalistic border features white- and blue-flowered cranesbills (*Geranium* spp.), silver-leaved lamb's-ears (*Stachys byzantina*), cinnamon ferns (*Osmunda cinnamomea*), and kousa dogwood (*Cornus kousa*). Garden Design: Conni Cross

In this densely planted garden, the airy flowers and foliage of wild sweet william (*Phlox divaricata*) contrast with the heavier, prominently veined leaves of fragrant plantain lily (*Hosta plantaginea*). ▶

This yard relies on easy-care dwarf azaleas and evergreen shrubs for year-round color. Featured are disease-resistant 'Whitespire' birch (*Betula platyphylla* var. *japonica* 'Whitespire') and kousa dogwood (*Cornus kousa*). Garden Design: ◄Conni Cross

This suburban front yard features shrubs planted in a bed of ground-covers, including evergreen *Pachysandra japonica*. In bloom in early spring are yellow-flowered Japanese kerria (*Kerria japonica*) and flowering quince (*Chaenomeles speciosa*). Garden Design: Mitsuko and Andrew Collver ▼

▲
Chamomile (*Chamaemelum nobile*) rambles along this garden path, releasing a pleasant fragrance when brushed against or stepped on. A tough plant that can withstand light foot traffic, chamomile can be mowed to keep it at lawn height.

No plant can brighten up a shady spot better than 'White Nancy', a cultivar of spotted deadnettle (*Lamium maculatum* 'White Nancy'). The silvery gray foliage reflects light like a mirror, while candles of white flowers top the plants from early summer into fall. ▶

▲

Notice the low-maintenance character of this walk and patio. To eliminate the need for hand-trimming lawn edges, a bed of pebbles borders the raised patio. An edging sunk around the bed stops invading grass roots and keeps the stones out of the lawn. Flagstones set in pebbles, rather than in lawn, won't disappear beneath encroaching grass and require frequent rescue. Garden Design: Ireland-Gannon Associates, Inc.

Sweet woodruff (*Galium odoratum*) makes a delightful low groundcover, especially when its starry white blossoms dot the whorled foliage in May. Here, it romps merrily between the wood rounds that create a path through ◀this shady woodland garden.

▲
The owners of this garden turned the area beneath a large tree into a colorful garden bed. In bloom in mid-spring are daffodils, moss pinks (*Phlox subulata*), basket-of-gold (*Aurinia saxatilis*), and Confederate violets (*Viola sororia*).

A golden cultivar of English ivy ▶ (*Hedera helix* 'Buttercup') contrasts strikingly with its green-foliaged companions, delicate-looking but drought-resistant barrenwort (*Epimedium* spp.) on the right and the native vine Virginia creeper (*Parthenocissus quinquefolia*), which turns a rich red in autumn, on the left.

Parking areas don't have to be asphalt jungles, as Barbara Emerson's landscape design for the front of her North Carolina condominium demonstrates. She defined the entrance and created privacy with a low-maintenance arrangement of flowering dogwoods (*Cornus florida*) and pink azaleas. In the deeper shade near the building, grape holly (*Mahonia* spp.) provides evergreen foliage, with yellow flowers and blue berries in season. Every year, Barbara plants impatiens in the foreground for a welcoming display of carefree blossoms from summer through fall.

▼

▲

A shady shrub border beneath mature oak trees fills this Virginia yard with easy-care color year after year. The bright pink azalea in the foreground is the cultivar 'Dream'.

Native to the Eastern woodlands, ▶ mountain laurel (*Kalmia latifolia*) blooms for a month in late May and June, when most spring-flowering shrubs have finished for the year. Cultivars offer rich colors and more compact growth habits than the species, making them perfect low-maintenance shrubs for a shady garden.

▲

The rugosa rose (*Rosa rugosa*) and its cultivars top the list of low-maintenance shrub roses. Flowers appear lavishly in June and then sporadically through fall, followed by clusters of gleaming red rose hips.

◄Shrub roses bloom nonstop from early summer right up until frost. Shown here beginning its third season in Claudia and John Sholtz's New York garden, a hedge of 'Simplicity' above a sparkling green-and-white-striped groundcover of gardener's-garters (*Phalaris arundinacea* var. *picta*), an ornamental grass.

The periwinkle (*Vinca minor*) on this steep slope discourages weeds but allows bulbs and perennials to grow through it. Polyanthus narcissi (*Narcissus tazetta*) complement Japanese maple (*Acer palmatum* 'Bloodgood').

▼

▲

Unlike most hybrid tulips, which are short-lived, water-lily tulips (*Tulipa kaufmanniana*) multiply readily and return year after year if you plant them in a sunny spot with good drainage.

◀Magic lily (*Lycoris squamigera*) gives a surprise performance every year in late summer. The bulb produces magnificent pink blossoms on leafless stalks that pop from the ground seemingly overnight, long after its daffodil-like spring foliage has died back.

▲

A traditional perennial border backed up by evergreens becomes a low-maintenance garden when composed of dependable perennials, such as these pinks (*Dianthus* spp.), oriental
poppies (*Papaver orientale*), and bearded iris. Weekend gardeners short on time and patience should pass up modern
hybrid roses, like those shown here, in favor of more durable
and disease-resistant shrub roses. Garden Design: Louis Edmonds

◀ Daylilies (*Hemerocallis* × *hybrida*) are perfect weekend garden plants: They're long-lived and remarkably insect- and disease-free; thrive in any type of soil; and enjoy both full sun and partial shade. Shown here is 'Christmas Story'.

In mid-August, this Maine cottage garden features orange tiger lilies (*Lilium lancifolium*), orange and gold pot marigolds (*Calendula officinalis*), 'Silver King' artemisia (*Artemisia ludoviciana* 'Silver King'), and yellow-flowered shrubby cinquefoil (*Potentilla fruticosa*). Garden Design: Amy Melenbacher ▼

▲
Cascading herbs and perennials soften the edges of this raised patio with their fine foliage textures and tranquil flower colors. The garden is easy to maintain because it's located close at hand, so faded flowers can be easily snipped and offending weeds pulled. An inconspicuous brick mowing strip edges the bottom of the retaining wall, making lawn mowing a simple matter. Featured here are woolly thyme (*Thymus pseudolanuginosus*), chives (*Allium schoenoprasum*), lavender (*Lavandula officinalis*), and pinks (*Dianthus* spp.). Garden Design: Ngaere Macray

◀ Another old-fashioned perennial, wild blue indigo (*Baptisia australis*), forms deep-rooted, long-lived clumps that never need division. Blooming throughout spring, baptisia's deep blue flowers look splendid with bearded irises, and the lovely blue-green foliage remains attractive throughout the summer.

Bleeding-heart (*Dicentra spectabilis*) charms gardeners with its strings of heart-shaped flowers throughout the month of May. This classic perennial lives almost indefinitely and rarely needs dividing. Bleeding-heart usually goes dormant, dying back to the ground, when summer heat and drought arrive. Plant ferns, hostas, or impatiens around bleeding-heart to camouflage the vacancy.

▼

Most annuals need replanting every year, but not cleome (*Cleome hasslerana*), which re-seeds. You don't have to dead-head, either, because as flowers toward the base of the stem fade, new flowers open toward the top, continuing the display until autumn. Cleome is ideal to mass-plant at the back of the border.

Impatiens (*Impatiens wallerana*) is America's most popular flowering annual, with good reason. It flourishes in shade, never needs deadheading, is pest- and disease-free, is available in a wide range of colors, and blooms until frost. Shown here is 'Shady Lady Venus' impatiens with another low-maintenance annual, 'Crystal Palace' edging lobelia (*Lobelia erinus* 'Crystal Palace'). ▶

Easy-care annual vines, morning-glories (*Ipomoea tricolor* and *I. purpurea*) grow quickly when given full sun and bloom profusely from midsummer until frost. Shown here is *Ipomoea tricolor* 'Heavenly Blue'.
▼

▲
Not a speck of grass finds its way into Angela Garguilo's back and side yards—she's discovered easier and more beautiful landscape solutions. Seen here is a corner of the mixed border that outlines the backyard brick patio and runs along the back of the house. The side yard features a flagstone patio, built-in barbecue, walkway leading from the front gate, and more garden beds. Planted in front of the fence are the disease-resistant 'Whitespire' birch (*Betula platyphylla* var. *japonica* 'Whitespire'), everblooming shrub rose 'The Fairy', and a collection of dependable perennials and annuals. The white phlox is the mildew-resistant meadow phlox, *Phlox maculata* 'Miss Lingard'. Garden Design: Conni Cross

▲
This island bed includes purple loosestrife (*Lythrum salicaria*), astilbes (*Astilbe × arendsii*), ornamental onions (*Allium* spp.), European bistort (*Polygonum bistorta* 'Superbum'), daylilies, and 'Gold Plate' yarrow (*Achillea filipendulina* 'Gold Plate').

Planted with roof irises (*Iris tectorum*), fernleaf yarrow (*Achillea filipendulina*), stonecrop (*Sedum* spp.), thyme (*Thymus vulgaris*), daylilies, and coreopsis (*Coreopsis grandiflora* and *C. verticillata*), this flower garden survives on rainfall alone. Garden Design: Conni Cross

▲

Suzanne Helburn's colorful cottage-style garden borders her Colorado home. Dill, lettuce, spinach, and cabbages nestle among the flowers. The cheerful bright red, yellow, and orange flowers of 'Red Wings' avens (*Geum quellyon* 'Red Wings'), daylilies (*Hemerocallis × hybrida*), and coreopsis (*Coreopsis grandiflora*) hold their own in the strong Rocky Mountain sunshine, which tends to leave paler flowers powerless.

◄ 'Victoria' mealycup sage (*Salvia farinacea* 'Victoria') grows only 1½ feet tall, rather than the 3 feet typical of the species, and produces slender stalks of beautiful violet-blue flowers above its gray-green foliage from summer through fall. Most gardeners treat this fast-growing perennial, hardy only in Zones 8–10, as an annual.

◀Clematis thrives with its feet in the shade and its foliage and flowers in the sun. Here it has found a perfect situation climbing the trunk of a pine, its flowers set off by a stand of ferns.

Shown in early October, a well-planned assortment of perennials and annuals brings easy-care color late in the season. Perennials in bloom include Michaelmas daisies (*Aster novae-angliae* and *A. novi-belgi*) and 'Autumn Joy' sedum; low annuals in the foreground include ageratum (*Ageratum houstonianum*) and sweet alyssum (*Lobularia maritima*); while daylily and iris foliage provide effective contrast to the flowering plants. The stunning violet and purple color scheme stands out against the privet hedge. Garden Design: Barbara Damrosch

▼

▲
In this Long Island garden, an 8-foot-tall cage built of hardware cloth and lattice keeps deer from raised vegetable beds. Serving to both beautify the garden and to ward off rabbits, foxglove (*Digitalis purpurea*) forms a striking flower border around the fence. Garden Design: Joe Elmer

Growing vegetables in raised ▶ beds lets you reach into the center of each bed from any side, and the soil will stay loose because it isn't trampled and doesn't need repeated tilling. Garden Design: Old Westbury Gardens

A wood-chip path leads through this enticing shade garden composed of beautiful foliage plants and flowers, disproving the common complaint that nothing will grow in the shade. Along the fence, an assortment of hostas displays a range of leaf shapes, sizes, and colors. On the other side of the path, flowering perennials put on a colorful show. Blooming in the shade are fringed bleeding-heart (*Dicentra eximia*), which blooms in spring and summer, and a white-flowered astilbe cultivar (*Astilbe* × *arendsii*), an elegant, feathery-flowered plant. Sun-drops (*Oenothera fruticosa*) bloom in the sun at the edge of the shade garden. Garden Design: Conni Cross

▼

▲

Imitating a clearing in the woods, this picturesque retreat beneath high-pruned trees is a study in pink and white. Shown in late May, wildflowers—pale pink fringed bleeding-heart (*Dicentra eximia*) and false Solomon's-seal (*Smilacina racemosa*) —cluster around a pink-flowered azalea just beginning to open its buds. Shrubs on the right side of the clearing include pink-flowered beautybush (*Kolkwitzia amabilis*) in full bloom and a dwarf white-variegated cultivar of weigela (*Weigela florida* 'Variegata Nana') with rose-pink blossoms. Garden Design: Conni Cross

◀ Pale pink impatiens (*Impatiens wallerana* 'Elfin Blush') light up the edge of a shady garden path at the author's home. Maidenhair ferns (*Adiantum pedatum*) provide a graceful contrast to the impatiens and flourish in the moist, humusy soil.

Spring wildflowers provide a delightful display in a shady spot. In the foreground, foamflowers (*Tiarella cordifolia*) display creamy white flowers against a background of Virginia bluebells (*Mertensia virginica*). ▼

◀ Chinese astilbes (*Astilbe chinensis* 'Pumila') blanket the ground here along a shady trail through a naturalistic display of perennials, ferns, and other foliage plants. Garden Design: Conni Cross

Bordering a Maryland estuary, a meadow garden featuring blue cornflowers (*Centaurea cyanus*) and red and pink corn poppies (*Papaver rhoeas*) creates a stunning display that lasts from late spring into fall. Although both plants are annuals, they may not reseed reliably in all climates. Yearly sowing produces the most dependable display. Garden Design: Ken Bryan Landscaping
▼

▲
Native perennials and grasses blend the property surrounding this mountain home outside of Denver beautifully into its natural setting. In this climate, where poor soil and low summer rainfall make lawn-growing an expensive, time-consuming, and unecological proposition, a meadow like this makes low-maintenance sense. Shown here in mid-July are yellow-and-red blanketflower (*Gaillardia* × *grandiflora*), white-flowered yarrow (*Achillea millefolium*), and ox eye daisy (*Chrysanthemum leucanthemum*). Garden Design: Applewood Seed Company

◀Brightly colored wildflowers add interest to midwestern meadows when planted in groups among the grasses. Bottle gentians (*Gentiana andrewsii*) like the one shown here highlight moist prairies in autumn.

▲

A stylized meadow of ornamental grasses comes into its full glory in late summer when the warm-season grasses begin to bloom. The bleached foliage and seedheads remain standing throughout winter, resembling a giant dried flower arrangement. Deep-rooted, drought-resistant, and pest- and disease-free, ornamental grasses make an unusual low-maintenance alternative to traditional lawns and gardens. The only routine care they need is to be cut close to the ground each year in late winter. Garden Design: Carole Johnson, Planting Fields Arboretum

A tool shed located conveniently close to the garden helps weekend gardeners save steps and time, so chores get done more easily without procrastination. This attractive little gray-and-white shed becomes a garden focal point because it stands out against the dark green foliage surrounding it and reflects the white blossoms of the roses and clematis. Garden Design: Howard Purcell

▼

▲

By following the labor-saving techniques in this book, you should have plenty of time to relax outdoors and soak up the peaceful beauty you've created. Shown in bloom here is a successful combination of long-blooming, low-maintenance plants: White-flowered impatiens pop out of the shadows, forming a pretty border in front of a sweep of orange and yellow daylilies and tall tiger lilies (*Lilium lancifolium*). All these plants require very little care, leaving the gardener with plenty of time for a Sunday afternoon snooze in the hammock.

VEGETABLES FOR WEEKEND GARDENERS

Prolific Produce the Easy Way

My first vegetable garden was about as far from a weekend garden as you can get—a 1,000-square-foot, high-yield row garden. What a lot of work! I could have grown twice as much in the same space if I had gardened intensively in a series of small beds with permanent walks between them. But since I was already growing more food than we needed for eating fresh and preserving, it would have been better still to grow only the amount of produce we actually needed in half the space. This would have translated into half the energy spent turning over the soil, half the amount of time spent weeding (or time and money spent on black plastic mulch), half the amount of manure, half the length of hose needed, and half the number of steps taken.

If you're a weekend gardener, you don't have time to waste growing produce you won't eat in more space than you can comfortably tend. Think of gardening as recreation, and grow what you really enjoy—not every vegetable in the catalog. A few cages of red-ripe tomatoes, a bed of tender lettuces and salad herbs, and a stand of sweet corn, all raised to perfection, may give you more satisfaction than a big production garden that gets away from you in spite of all the time you spend on hands and knees tending it. Besides growing a careful selection of favorites, you should consider the perfect weekend crops—perennial vegetables. Once you've prepared the soil and planted, you'll have asparagus, rhubarb, and other perennial vegetables coming up year after year with a minimum of care.

If you're short on time but are determined to grow a whole range of vegetables, there are ways to have a productive garden without spending every spare moment in it. The best way to have a full-scale weekend vegetable garden—or any vegetable garden, when you get down to it—is to cultivate raised-bed gardens using intensive gardening techniques, which can produce large yields in small spaces. The basics of intensive gardening can be boiled down to two practices: creating a rich, fertile soil, and spacing plants closely in beds rather than rows. More innovations you can use to increase yields include growing vines on vertical structures, rotating crops, and using season-extending cloches, row covers, or coldframes.

Much of the work and time involved in food gardening can be reduced through intensive gardening simply because you've got a smaller piece of ground to tend. Tending a small garden—even if it contains more plants —means you'll have less ground to weed, water, fertilize, mulch, and even walk around, saving you minutes with every chore— minutes that quickly add up to hours. And growing plants close to each other means that they shade the ground, reducing moisture evaporation from the soil and discouraging weeds. Closely spaced plants also require less time to care for and harvest because they are within easy reach.

Intensive Gardening Begins with the Soil

All forms of intensive gardening rely on fluffy, nutrient-rich soil. (Soil that has lots of added organic matter and isn't compacted by footsteps and heavy equipment has a springy, fluffy texture and excellent water-holding capacity.) Without great soil—which readily supplies nutrients and water to hungry, growing plants—vegetables planted closely together compete with each other for the meager provisions, and all lose.

If you're beginning a new food garden, it's important to realize that the effort put into preparing the soil *now* will pay off in years to come. Dig and loosen the garden soil as deeply as possible, and turn in quantities of organic matter.

The favored method of soil preparation for intensive gardening is called double digging, and it's an arduous task. But the result is a loose, deep, fertile soil that water and roots penetrate easily. If your soil isn't very good to begin with—say it's light and sandy, heavy and high in clay, or compacted from being walked or driven on—then double digging is truly worth the effort. If you're gardening in a decent loam soil, however, studies have shown that the strenuous effort of double digging produces no better results than other methods of loosening the soil. Whatever method you use, you should incorporate nutrients and organic matter each year before planting.

Yearly Renewal and Other Digging Chores

Some gardeners—and I hope they're not weekend gardeners—double-dig the vegetable plot every year. This really isn't necessary, especially with raised-bed gardening, where the soil won't be compacted from walking or machinery. If the soil is sandy or high in clay, you might want to double-dig it, adding quantities of organic matter, for several years in a row until the texture of the soil is to your liking. Thereafter, all you need do is work nutrients and perhaps finely ground dolomitic limestone into the topsoil, as recommended by a soil analysis, loosen the bed with a garden fork, and then smooth out the surface with a garden rake before planting.

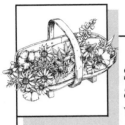

Save Time and Energy with Raised-Bed Gardening

The main advantages of intensive gardening in raised beds are:

• Soil warms up more quickly in spring so you are able to plant and harvest sooner, extending the growing season.

• A compact growing area has less space for weeds to grow in, eliminating their competition for nutrients, light, and water, and reducing time spent fighting them.

• A compact growing area means fewer square feet to water, saving labor and money spent on water and watering devices.

• Research has shown that plants grown closely together can perform better than those spaced far apart.

• Plants spaced closely together shade the soil, keeping the area cooler in summer, which reduces moisture evaporation and results in less need for watering.

• Once soil is specially prepared, it can be worked by hand and doesn't require a rotary tiller.

• Improved soil is not wasted for paths or rows between plants.

• Since the improved soil is never walked on, it doesn't become compacted and plants grow better.

• The yield per square foot of growing space is higher than in traditional row gardens.

• Gardening in a small space saves you steps with every chore performed.

• You can truck in topsoil, manure, and so forth and use it to fill raised beds with constructed walls where the native soil is too rocky, alkaline, sandy, or heavy to support a productive garden.

• Less agile folks can use the sides of constructed raised beds as seats, easing the physical strain of gardening.

• A raised-bed garden looks neat and attractive.

• Raised beds with constructed sides prevent aggressive perennial crops from growing where they aren't wanted.

Making the Bed

Double digging produces a fluffy soil which, after you've incorporated what seems like a couple of tons of organic matter into it, has increased significantly in volume. The dug soil will rise up above ground level to form a noticeable mound, which is why it is called a **raised bed,** whether it has sides constructed to hold the soil in place or not. By creating a garden of raised beds with double-dug soil, separated by permanent walks, none of that

◆ ◆   ◆ ◆   ◆ ◆   ◆ ◆   ◆ ◆   ◆ ◆   ◆ ◆   ◆ ◆

How to Double-Dig a Garden

Traditionally, garden soil is dug and loosened to one spade's depth. A double-dug garden is prepared to the depth of at least two spades without mixing up the two layers. This loosening of the subsoil allows roots to penetrate deeper in search of water and nutrients.

If you're starting a new garden, begin by stripping off the sod. You can use the sod to patch worn or generally ratty-looking areas of lawn, or to make wonderful compost. Once you're down to soil level, you're ready to begin digging. With a garden spade, dig a trench one spade (about 12 inches) deep and two spades wide, removing the soil and shoveling it into a wheelbarrow for later use. Next, with a garden fork, loosen the subsoil in the trench as deeply as you can (another 12 inches will do) by working the fork back and forth and side to side. Avoid disturbing the soil layering, and don't walk on soil once you've loosened it.

At this stage of double digging, my friend Kathy Zar-Peppler dumps in loads of leaves, which is a convenient no-work way to compost fallen autumn tree leaves. She prepares the bed in fall, and by spring-planting time in her Ohio garden the leaves are completely decomposed and the bed has settled down

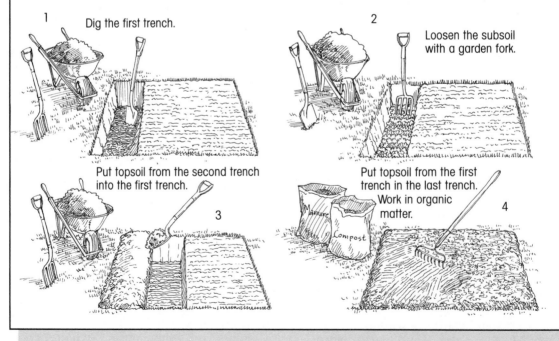

1 Dig the first trench.

2 Loosen the subsoil with a garden fork.

Put topsoil from the second trench into the first trench. 3

Put topsoil from the first trench in the last trench. Work in organic matter. 4

considerably. If the subsoil is really terrible stuff—heavy clay or practically pure sand—any organic matter you can work into it when you're double-digging will reward you no end. You can mix peat, manure, or compost into the subsoil the first time you double-dig and in subsequent years only need loosen it.

After loosening the subsoil in the first trench and adding any amendments, fill in the first trench with the topsoil removed from the next trench as you dig it. Lift off the topsoil from the neighboring trench and slide the soil gently into the first trench so it rests on top of the loosened subsoil with its sod or leaf topdressing. Do not walk on the filled trench. Continue the process, trench by trench, until you reach the end of the bed, then use the topsoil removed from the first trench to fill the last trench.

Once you've finished the initial digging, go back over the bed, spreading 2 to 4 inches of organic matter, such as compost, manure, or peat, over the top of the soil. Work this into the top several inches of soil with a garden rake, hoe, or rotary tiller.

The double-dug bed will be fluffed up several inches higher than the surrounding ground. It will settle some, but remain raised above the surrounding ground. Shape the edges of the mounded soil into a gentle slope so the bed won't erode, or use pressure-treated wood or railroad ties to build a raised edge.

precious soil created from the sweat of your brow will be trod upon and squandered as rows between the crops. And, if you never walk on that double-dug soil, it will remain light and spongy, a hospitable growing medium able to encourage high yields of vitamin- and mineral-rich produce.

The easiest way to begin bed gardening is with mounded beds with sloping earth sides. However, raised beds that are "boxed" with boards, railroad ties, or other construction materials have many advantages over mounded beds. An obvious benefit is erosion-proofing: Constructed sides ensure that soil won't wash or wear away. Raised beds with constructed sides are often higher than mounded beds, so they warm up even sooner and drain even better. This is an important advantage where the soil is heavy and wet, a condition that often delays spring planting. Raised-bed gardeners claim they are usually harvesting cool-season spring crops just about the time the neighbors are planting theirs! But in arid climates, raised beds may be a disadvantage because they can dry out rapidly. Dry-climate gardeners get better results with sunken beds, which stay cooler and retain moisture longer than ground-level gardens.

If you now have a row garden, you can transform it fairly easily into a raised-bed garden. Lay out a pattern of beds and walks within the existing plot. Mark the corners of the new beds with stakes, then string cord along the outlines of the beds. Shovel out some of the soil from the paths and toss it into the beds. Double-dig if desired. Next, work rotted manure, compost, grass clippings, or peat into the soil in the beds. Cover the paths with wood chips, shredded leaves, gravel, or a more permanent paving to keep out weeds and mud.

This easy-care vegetable garden features raised beds efficiently designed so that you can reach the plants growing in the middle of the beds. Aisles 3 feet wide give you room to kneel or maneuver a wheelbarrow and are covered with wood chips to cut down on weeds and mud.

Designing an Efficient Bed Garden

Gardening intensively in beds can save weekend gardeners time and energy as long as the layout of the garden is designed with some forethought. Don't make the all too common mistake of assuming that if small beds are good, huge beds must be even better. Huge beds may use every inch of the soil to the maximum, but tending and harvesting large beds wastes many unnecessary steps—you'll find yourself constantly walking down one side, then down the other side and back around again to simply retrieve a hoe, pick a pepper, or pull a weed. All that walking uses up a lot of time and energy. Keep in mind that you always will be walking around—never through—the beds, so make them a manageable size.

Think like an efficiency expert when designing the layout of the garden. Most seasoned raised-bed gardeners recommend beds no wider than 3½ to 4 feet, though if you have long arms, 5 feet may not be too wide. You can usually reach into the middle of these beds from either side without trampling on the soil. The best length for the main beds is usually between 20 and 30 feet, though shorter lengths will do fine. If you are constructing wooden sides for the beds, consider the length of the lumber when designing the beds and you'll avoid a lot of time and effort spent cutting wood. Landscape timbers often come in standard lengths of 4 and 8 feet. You could easily build an efficient raised bed approximately 4 feet wide by 16 feet long using two 4-foot and four 8-foot timbers.

Vegetables require full sun—no less than 6 hours of direct light a day—to produce well. Locate the garden in a sunny spot, and be sure to arrange the plants so they don't shade each other. This means locating the tallest crops, such as corn, pole beans, and tomatoes on the north side of the garden, where their shadows will fall outside the garden beds. It's also best to position the beds containing shorter crops so the length of the beds runs from north to south; this way, the plants will shade each other less as the sun moves from east to west during the day.

The width of the paths between the beds can vary, but they should be as wide as possible so you will have plenty of room to maneuver. You'll need to be able to kneel, carry tools and watering equipment, haul in compost and other organic matter (and don't forget mulch!), and harvest. I'd say 2 feet is minimal; 3 feet is better. You'll probably want a broad central path—at least 4 feet wide—to allow easy access for a garden cart, wheelbarrow, or rotary tiller.

Paved paths covered with bricks, flagstones, concrete pavers, or poured concrete give the garden year-round structure and beauty, and if well-planned, they need little care. They will be weed-free and require practically no maintenance. Paved paths also keep your shoes out of the mud, which can reduce your housekeeping chores. If you want grass paths, be sure they are wide enough for your mower. Effective and low-tech alternatives to paved or grass paths include wood chips, gravel, aged sawdust, even shredded leaves—anything that will keep down weeds and mud. (For more on paths, see "Ways with Walks" on page 55.)

Crop Tactics

No one ever said vegetable gardening was easy and spoke the truth! The vagaries of weather and insects may inflict severe damage on a garden, and fuzzy or feathered creatures may devour the remaining produce before you do. But weekend gardeners can fight back by gardening smart. Gardening smart—whether intensively or not—includes selecting the crops and their cultivars that will perform best in *your* garden, and then maximizing your garden space. Garden smart by following these tips:

- Select disease-resistant cultivars.
- Select short-season crops and cultivars, especially in northern climates.
- Rotate crops from year to year to avoid perpetuating disease and insect problems.
- Maximize garden space and increase productivity by growing vining crops on vertical supports.
- Grow no more than your family can eat fresh and/or you have time to process.
- Interplant short-season with long-season crops.
- Stagger plantings of the same vegetable so the crop doesn't ripen all at once.
- Install appropriate bird, insect, and animal deterrents and repellents.

◆ ◆ ◆ ◆ ◆ ◆ ◆ ◆ ◆ ◆ ◆ ◆ ◆ ◆ ◆ ◆ ◆ ◆

Create an (Almost) No-Work Instant Garden

It's possible to create a productive new vegetable garden in a patch of lawn without stripping off the sod or even turning over the soil! If you're planning to make a garden where lawn is presently growing, and the soil in your lawn is reasonably good, here's how to save yourself an enormous amount of work *and* create an intensive garden.

Mark out the outlines of the beds on the lawn, using a clothesline, garden hose, or sprinkling of horticultural lime, then cover the bed areas with a smothering mulch to kill the sod. Black plastic mulch is a good choice, but a 6-inch-deep layer of grass clippings, wood chips, or straw will also work. The result will be a garden of several beds with grass paths between them. After three or four weeks, depending on the temperature, the buried lawn grass should be dying and beginning to decompose, enriching the soil.

Check from time to time under the covering, and when the grass has yellowed—it needn't be totally dead or decomposed—punch holes in the plastic or clear spaces in the mulch and pop in transplants or seeds, using traditional, rather than intensive, spacing. This mulched, no-till garden will surprise you with its productivity. One reason it's so productive is that the soil strata is not disturbed by tilling, and the rotting grass contributes further to the tilth and nitrogen content of the topsoil.

You can't get away without improving the soil forever, though, or the nutrients will eventually be depleted. In fall, if you've laid down plastic, take it up and dig in the rotted grass along with additional organic matter—double-digging if you're up to it. If you've mulched with straw, it will be beginning to decompose; dig it in. In spring, plant the beds, spacing the vegetables closer together, and cover the soil with an organic mulch to continue the cycle.

You'll be creating an intensive garden in stages, avoiding the arduous task of stripping off sod, and will be able to harvest during the first growing season, though the garden may not reach its maximum productivity for several years. But for weekend gardeners with a dearth of time, this is small sacrifice to pay.

• Use a mulch to retain soil moisture and deter weeds.
• Apply 1 inch of water a week if rainfall isn't sufficient.

• When you harvest a crop, fill the bare spot with a quick-maturing transplant, an annual flower, or mulch—don't let weeds colonize exposed soil.

Selecting the Best Vegetables

As every vegetable gardener knows, all tomatoes are not created equal—and neither are all peppers, cabbages, or onions. Cultivars of each vegetable can be so distinctive that it's sometimes hard to believe they're related. Some vegetable cultivars bear more heavily than others, or bear earlier or later, or taste better, or keep better, or are more disease-resistant. When you're a weekend gardener, it makes sense to choose your favorite vegetables by name. Don't settle for a giant red 'Beefsteak' tomato if what you really want's a tangy little 'Yellow Pear', or vice versa.

It's true that if you armchair-shop through a number of seed catalogs, the choices can seem overwhelming. It may be simplest to plant whatever seeds or transplants the local garden center is offering in the spring and be done with it. But then again, "shopping" for that perfect vegetable cultivar is a winter pastime that brings tasty rewards come harvest. The nursery seed and transplant offerings are often limited to the most popular or easiest (for the nurseryman) to grow, rather than those that will do best in your area. If you want an unusual cultivar, you'll have better luck in the catalogs, too. Because growing transplants from seed takes more time and organization than some weekend gardeners want to invest, a compromise would be to order direct-seeded vegetables from the catalogs and to buy your transplants from the garden center.

If a particular disease or insect has been a problem in your garden in the past, then by all means search for a resistant cultivar. Seed catalogs, plant tags, and seed packets indicate disease resistance, often by a special code. Examples include:

A (anthracnose-resistant)
B (blight-resistant)
BM (blue mold-resistant)
BW (bacterial wilt-resistant)
DW (downy mildew-resistant)
F (fusarium-resistant)
HB (halo-blight-resistant)
M (mosaic virus-resistant)
N (nematode-resistant)
PM (powdery mildew-resistant)
RR (root-rot-resistant)
S (scab-resistant)
V (verticillium-resistant)
Y (yellows virus-resistant)

Grow crops that are known to do well where you live and you'll avoid disappointment. Though magazines are often full of stories of people boasting of how they were able to succeed with a vegetable everyone knew simply wouldn't grow in Kansas, the success was probably due to the gardener's devoting a great deal of time, attention, and coddling to the plants. Weekend gardeners are better off growing fuss-free vegetables.

Bringing Plants to Harvest

To have produce ready for harvest when *you* are ready for it, you need to know two important dates: the average last frost date in spring and the average first frost date in fall for your area. The number of days between these two dates is the length of your growing season. This basically determines which crops you can and cannot grow.

Seed catalogs and plant tags list the number of days to maturity of most cultivars. This number is an average: In reality, it varies, depending on local weather and climate conditions. However, it can be confusing if you're growing transplants as to whether the number of days to maturity indicates the days from sowing seed indoors or from transplanting seedlings into the garden. Most catalogs indicate whether their maturity dates are from sowing or setting out. Look for the catalog's introductory sections to each vegetable for this and other useful information. To find the approximate time to sow seeds in summer for fall harvesting, count back the number of days to maturity from the average first frost date or best harvest date.

Where the growing season is short, go for quick-to-mature cultivars of vegetables that normally take a longer time to ripen; avoid those that need a long, hot growing season if you want a harvest. Though melons, for instance, can and do grow in northern climates, their production is limited because of the short growing season and their sweetness may be reduced by cool or cloudy weather.

I tried to grow cantaloupes and watermelons in my first garden in upstate New York, where the growing season was on the short side. Though the vines covered a lot of ground (actually, a lot of black plastic), the harvest was almost nonexistent. One day in late August, when I began to wonder where all the melons were, I went on a scouting expedition. To my horror, while investigating I stepped directly on the one and only watermelon—it was the size of a baseball! I should have chosen an early-maturing cultivar, a watermelon that ripened in 65, 70, or 75 days, rather than the more standard 100-day cultivar I planted.

Selecting seeds from a catalog that specializes in vegetables for your part of the country is the best idea yet. If you live in the far North, for instance, a catalog aimed at northern gardeners will offer cultivars that mature early and produce the most reliable harvest for your climate. A catalog for southern gardeners will offer the best heat-resistant and slow-to-bolt cultivars, as well as cultivars that resist local diseases and insects.

Heirloom vegetables, offered in many specialty seed catalogs, are old-fashioned cultivars passed down by home gardeners over the years. These cultivars are open-pollinated rather than hybrids, so their seeds come true to type and can be saved from year to year. In many cases, heirloom vegetables are perfect plants for the weekend gardener because they're often more flavorful and may ripen over a prolonged period rather than all at once. All too often, modern hybrids are bred for the needs of large-scale farmers, for whom a one-time harvest of bruise-resistant (translate: tough) fruits is best. However, heirloom vegetables may lack the hybrid vigor and disease resistance offered by modern cultivars.

Gardeners may be lured into thinking they will get bigger yields in less space by planting "bush," "compact," or "miniature" vegetable cultivars, but this is not necessarily the case. Most compact cultivars are comparatively poor bearers. For instance, bush cultivars of vining plants such as cucumbers, melons, and winter squash are all available. But unless a fruit or two is enough, resist these cultivars, even though it's tempting to think you might be able to produce a crop of luscious melons in a fraction of the space normally required by the sprawling plants. When researchers compared a bush cultivar of cucumber to a regular vining type, the bush type was found to produce only a third as many cukes as the vine.

Bush cultivars have been dwarfed by changing their vining habit, which dramatically reduces the amount of foliage on each plant. Bush melons and winter squash (which, by the way, aren't always as dwarf as expected) don't produce as many or as large fruits as full-size plants, and the fruits they do produce often lack flavor and sweetness. Since a plant's foliage absorbs the sun's energy and transforms it into sugars and starches to fuel plant growth, a pint-size plant simply won't have the strength to produce fruit that's as sweet and abundant as its full-size relatives'. As a general rule of thumb, you can expect that the smaller the plant, the smaller its yield.

If your intended crop is a mature vine-ripened fruit, such as watermelon or winter squash, forget the bush, compact, or mini-cultivars unless you have a postage-stamp garden and have your heart set on home-grown. If, however, you'll harvest an immature fruit, such as a summer squash or snap bean, where small size and tenderness count, compact cultivars hold more promise. And, after all, reducing the yield of zucchini is an achievement some gardeners would cheer.

Vertical Gardening

A standard watermelon vine takes up about 100 square feet of garden space—an entire 4 × 25-foot bed. No wonder breeders have tried to develop compact cultivars! But if the compact melons aren't worth growing, what's a gardener to do? You could grow up. If you encourage vining crops such as cucumbers, beans, squash, and melons to grow on trellises, fences, or poles, they'll take up minimal ground space. Besides saving space, when grown vertically rather than horizontally, these crops yield better.

Because vertically grown plants bask in the sun all day, high above neighboring plants, they have plenty of energy for producing the biggest and best crop possible. The foliage dries quickly in the sun and breeze, discouraging fungal diseases, and the fruits are off the ground, leaving them clean and free from rot.

A string trellis will do for lightweight crops such as peas, but you'll have to make a sturdier structure for heavy plants such as melons. There are about as many types of trellises and vertical structures used to hold up crops as there are gardeners who use them. You can make a tepee of bamboo stakes, 2 × 2s, or wire mesh. Impressive-looking folding A-frames faced with wire mesh can be used for years, while twiggy brush usually lasts a single season. Strings suspended from a permanent overhead structure are ideal for pea-growing—once the peas are harvested, the withering vines can be cut down, strings and all, and relegated to the compost heap. You'll have to remove the dried-up vines from more permanent structures, which can be an annoying (and time-consuming) task if they're faced with small mesh.

If your garden is fenced in, the fence can double as a vertical growing space. For instance, a chain-link or split-rail fence faced with hardware cloth or chicken wire keeps out small animals and serves as a trellis for twining crops to climb. The fence provides good support for crops of heavy melons. To prevent the weight of the ripening fruits from pulling down the vines, suspend each melon with a sling tied to the fence, adding the slings when the melons are about half-grown. You can construct slings from old stockings or mesh bags, but be sure to make them large enough to accommodate the expanding girth of the melons. Unlike melons and cucumbers, peas and beans grow best on strictly vertical structures like sticks or strings. The horizontal honeycomb of a length of chicken wire just seems to confuse them.

Tomatoes may be easier to grow if they're simply left to sprawl on the ground, but the harvest will suffer. Fruits are too susceptible to rotting and attack by slugs and other

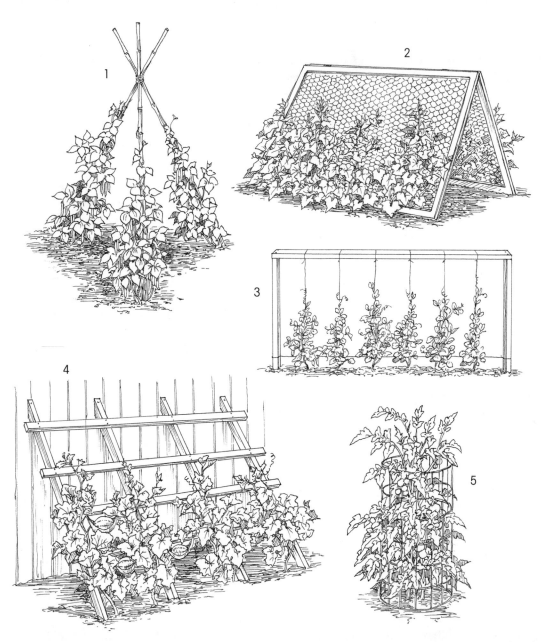

Vining crops take up less room, produce better, and require less care when grown on trellises. Here are an assortment of effective trellis styles. (1) Beans climb vigorously up a tepee made of bamboo stakes. (2) Cucumbers scale an A-frame made of chicken wire. (3) Peas prefer to climb up twine or string, which can be easily suspended from an overhead structure. (4) Melon plants, with their heavy fruit suspended in slings, will scramble up a sturdy trellis propped against a sunny wall. (5) Wire cages confine tomato plants without any bothersome tying, so the plants don't sprawl and their fruit doesn't rot on the ground.

pests when grown on the ground. You can tie tomatoes to strong wooden stakes or grow them in cages. I recommend tomato cages over stakes because they are practically work-free. Staked tomatoes require weekly tying to keep the new growth controlled, but once cages are settled around a young tomato plant, it will stay in bounds for the season! Ready-made cages are easily installed, removed, and stacked for storing over winter. Just be sure you purchase the largest ones possible, because healthy indeterminate tomato plants—the ones that keep on growing as long as they live—can grow almost as tall as a person. If a tomato begins to outgrow its cage, stack another one on top, securing the two firmly together, or just allow the tomato plant to sprawl and cascade over the top.

Keep in mind that upwardly mobile crops will cast a long shadow, so don't put them on the south side of the garden—the north side is usually best. However, in hot climates, the shade cast by a trellis can be a boon to heat-sensitive crops. A trellis located on the west side of the garden will cast shade to the east in the afternoon, providing a cool retreat for crops such as lettuce and spinach.

Spacing Crops

Space individual plants grown in garden beds much closer than you would in a conventional garden. You aren't growing them in rows, but in a mass planting within the bed. A good rule of thumb is to check the instructions on the seed packet or plant tag. It will usually say something like "space plants 6 inches apart in rows 18 inches apart." Ignore the row part of the instructions and note only the spacing within the row. Use that spacing for that crop in the bed; in this case,

by locating a plant so it is 6 inches away from each neighboring plant. If you remember your geometry, you'll recall that this means that the plants won't end up in rows within the bed, but will create a hexagonal pattern—equidistant from all neighboring plants.

Not only does this hexagonal spacing make maximum use of garden space, it minimizes hoeing chores. No matter where you're standing alongside the bed, you can easily run the hoe up or down the soil between young plants, because the hexagonal spacing creates diagonal lines through the bed. The entire bed is practically within hoe's reach. You need take only a step or two and several quick swipes with the hoe to chop off all the weeds that sprout up around the young vegetable plants. Once the closely spaced vegetables get larger, of course, they'll shade out most later-sprouting weeds.

Interplanting

Certain crops make excellent roommates—not because they are alike, but because they are so very different. They cohabit successfully because each has different needs or because they keep different hours. For instance, you can plant vegetables that are quick to germinate and early to mature alongside types that are slower to start and finish. Root vegetables share space well with leafy vegetables—one takes up the soil space while the other occupies the air space—rather like maximizing living space in a small dorm room by sleeping in bunk beds. Examples are lettuce with carrots and spinach with onions.

There are plenty of other examples. Leafy greens, which can tolerate and sometimes even need a bit of shade, may be nestled

Think like an efficiency expert and interplant your vegetables, harvesting short-season plants like radishes as later-maturing crops like lettuce and peppers begin to crowd them. By making the most of your garden space, you'll save time and energy in soil preparation, watering, and fertilizing. The diverse plantings will confuse pests and keep diseases from rampaging through a crop, and the crowded beds will discourage weeds.

under taller crops such as tomatoes or peppers. Vegetables with tall, skinny tops, such as onions, can be coupled with vegetables with low, spreading foliage, such as cucumbers, for efficient use of space. Interplanting radish and carrots is a time-honored practice. Sown together in the same row, radishes break the ground, making it easy for the slower, more fragile carrot seedlings to follow. The radishes are ready for pulling and munching in a few weeks, making space for the later-maturing carrots.

Pole beans will twine around the stalks of sweet corn without strangling or shading the corn too much—all the while enriching the soil with nitrogen while they borrow a bit of support. An organic market farmer I know grows corn, squash, and pole beans in the same space, following Native American practices. These "three sisters" make excellent roommates—the beans enrich the soil and wind their way up the corn stalks, while the squash vines sprawl out over the ground beneath the vertical crops.

Crop Rotation

When planning your vegetable garden, it's always a good idea to rotate crops within the beds. This means that you shouldn't grow the same crop or its relatives in the same place year after year. Rotating crops helps prevent a buildup of insects and disease organisms—a particular concern when you're gardening in permanent raised beds. Cole crops, such as cabbage and its relatives, and plants in the nightshade family, such as tomato, eggplant, pepper, and potato, are especially vulnerable to pest and disease buildup.

Rotating crops also helps you avoid depleting the soil of nutrients. A general rotation rule says to begin with fruiting plants (which need lots of phosphorus), replace with leafy plants (which use up nitrogen), follow these with root crops (which need more potassium), and finally enrich the soil with a legume. It's also a good idea to follow heavy feeders (like cole crops, cucurbits, corn, and tomatoes) with light feeders (like peppers, onions, potatoes, and carrots), and follow these two with legumes (peas, beans, and peanuts) that fix atmospheric nitrogen and can thus help improve soil fertility. If this level of planning is simply too much to bother with, simply alternate root crops with leafy or fruiting crops—it's better for the soil than not rotating at all.

If your garden space is small to begin with, you will find that all this rotating and interplanting can drive you berserk. It makes garden planning seem like playing Rubik's Cube—you solve one part of the puzzle only to discover that you've messed up the rest. When you add in tall and vertically grown crops that should be located where their shade won't be a problem, you may not sleep for days because you're worrying about juggling the pieces of your garden plot.

Don't drive yourself distracted. After all, you are gardening for pleasure, so do the best you can. Get your hands in the dirt and enjoy, even if you plant the carrots where the beets were just growing. You might help solve your planning puzzle by prioritizing your garden's needs—if a disease struck the cabbage, then be sure not to plant cabbage or its relatives in that spot the next season, but if the cabbages were healthy, you *might* take a risk and chance it. Bear in mind, though, that some diseases can persist in the soil for years—sometimes, for decades. It's a lot easier to plan a rotation schedule now than to have to dismantle all your raised beds in a few years and start all over again on unimproved soil.

If a disease does strike your crops, try to identify it in a book like *Rodale's Garden Insect, Disease, and Weed Identification Guide* by Miranda Smith and Anna Carr and follow the control recommendations. Remove stricken plants and their debris quickly and thoroughly. Dispose of these plants—do *not* compost them. In future, plant only resistant cultivars. If worse comes to worst, simply skip certain crops for a year or two to encourage the disease organisms to die off.

Staggered Plantings

One dilemma facing many exasperated gardeners is that some crops ripen or reach their peak during a very short period. They must be picked all at once, or the vegetables deteriorate. Beets and carrots are best when young and tender—they become woody if left in the ground too long. Cabbage and lettuce *bolt*, or go to seed, when mature, losing their taste and appearance. This is a real problem for many weekend gardeners who are primarily interested in growing produce to savor fresh from the garden. How many bibb lettuces, beets, or broccolis can you eat in a weekend, after all? Ideally, you'd like to harvest a bit every day or two over an extended time frame—unless you enjoy canning and freezing, when handling one giant harvest makes more sense.

One way to avoid a sudden deluge of vegetables (causing your family to moan that green beans are coming out of their ears) is to stagger plantings. This means sowing some lettuce every weekend rather than all at once, so it matures at about 1-week intervals—if you're lucky. Another way to stagger your harvest is to plant cultivars of a given vegetable that have different maturity dates. With several cultivars, you can extend your pea harvest to three weeks, your cabbage harvest two months, and so on. And it's fun to compare flavor and appearance.

Crops that have a built-in maturity date are the right candidates for staggered plantings. These include: beets, cabbage, lettuce, mustard, spinach, determinate tomatoes (the ones that stop growing at a certain

Calculating Cool- and Warm-Season Crop Harvests

Cool-Season Crops

Grow these crops in spring or fall; most can tolerate a bit of frost. Sow or set out transplants in spring as soon as the ground can be worked. Time late-season plantings so that the crops will mature during cool fall weather. The number of days until harvest can begin indicates a range among commonly available cultivars.

Warm-Season Crops

Grow these crops during the middle of the growing season, when warm temperatures will speed their growth. Do not set out until danger of frost has passed and the soil has warmed. The number of days until harvest can begin indicates a range among commonly available cultivars.

Cool-Season Crop	Days until Harvest	Warm-Season Crop	Days until Harvest
Arugula	40–60	Cantaloupe	65–90
Beet	34–70	Corn	53–100
Broccoli	60–89	Cucumber	48–75
Brussels sprouts	80–112*	Eggplant	60–80*
Cabbage	50–110	Lima bean, bush	65–81
Carrot	49–80	Lima bean, pole	85–90
Cauliflower	60–94*	Okra	48–52
Chicory	65–110	Parsnip	95–120
Chinese cabbage	35–85	Pepper	45–80
Collards	75–80	Potato	80–140†
Corn salad	45–60	Pumpkin	90–120
Escarole	40–90	Rutabaga	90
Kale	55–65	Snap bean, bush	43–60
Kohlrabi	50–60	Snap bean, pole	55–70
Lettuce, head	72–94	Spinach, New Zealand	70
Lettuce, leaf	45–50	Summer squash	40–60
Lettuce, loose-head	48–77	Sweet potato	90–150
Mustard	45–55	Tomato	50–90
Onion, bulbing	95–100†	Watermelon	68–95
Onion, bunching	20–40	Winter squash	71–100
Pea	55–74		
Radish	20–55		
Spinach	42–50		
Swiss chard	55–60		
Turnip	30–70		

*After transplanting.
†From sets.

*After transplanting.
†From seed potatoes.

height and concentrate on fruit set), radishes, carrots, and broccoli. Crops that need good cross-pollination, such as corn, should not be staggered or you might not get good fruit set. And crops that begin bearing and continue to produce right up until frost, such as squash, indeterminate tomatoes, peppers, pole beans, cucumbers, and melons, ought to be set out all at once—there is no point in staggering the planting.

Cut and Come Again

Some crops like to be harvested. The more they are picked, the more they'll produce. Or, to put it differently, if they're allowed to mature, they'll quit. Snap bean, lima bean, and pea plants produce more pods if picked regularly while pods are young. Summer squash will keep on bearing mightily, right up until frost, as long as the young fruits are picked. But the most surprising results come from cole crops, such as cabbage and broccoli. Don't pull cabbage from the ground when it's time to harvest—cut it just above ground level, leaving the stub of the stem and the roots right in the ground. Cutting an *X* into the stub of a cabbage encourages it to produce several small heads. After you cut off the main central head of broccoli, don't uproot the plant. Side shoots will sprout, and each will produce a small head.

Harvest the outer leaves—but don't take the small inner leaves and growing point—of a clump of spinach, chard, collards, kale, or looseleaf lettuce, and they'll keep producing more leaves. The pods of tall okra plants are difficult to harvest, so don't let them get out of reach. Cut the plants back to 3 feet to encourage the emergence of side branches. This creates a bushy plant that will continue to flower and reward the gardener with a second crop of pods. But perform this sur-gery only on tall plants with sturdy stems that show evidence of young side branches, or the result will disappoint you.

"Immortal" Perennial Crops

My gardening neighbors, Bea and Frank, had a patch of ruby-stemmed rhubarb, which was probably 50 years old, growing alongside their garage. It thrived on the warm south side of the building, and they generously shared the harvests that were there just for the picking early in spring. What a treat to cook up something fresh from the garden before the weather had really warmed up enough to do any real gardening! An extra-early harvest, beginning when the ground is usually too muddy to work, is just part of the appeal of growing perennial vegetables such as rhubarb and asparagus—the rest of their appeal lies in their low-care requirements once they get established. Perennial vegetables make perfect crops for weekend gardeners (or anyone who's short on time), though some types may take several years to get well enough established to produce high yields.

Other perennial vegetables that provide easy crops for smart gardeners are perennial onions, Jerusalem artichoke, good-King-Henry (a perennial spinach substitute), and sorrel. Once established, all of these will produce for years with very little care, and unlike asparagus and rhubarb, they'll provide fair harvests the first year you grow them. Because most of these perennial vegetables are either little known or require special techniques to get them started, I'm going to provide detailed growing instructions for each.

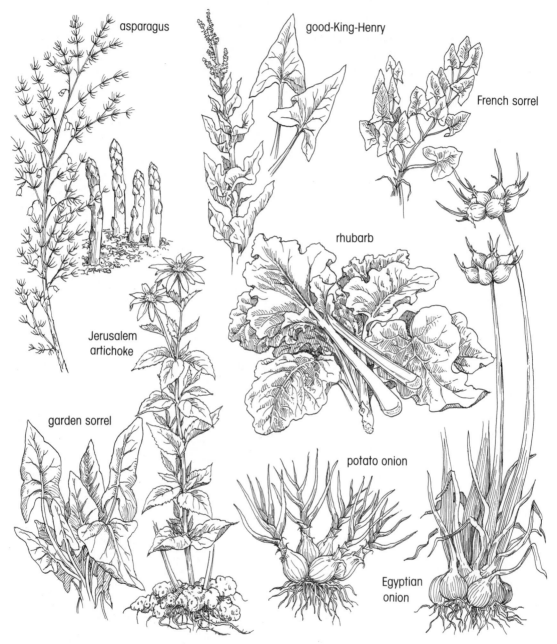

asparagus

good-King-Henry

French sorrel

rhubarb

Jerusalem
artichoke

garden sorrel

potato onion

Egyptian
onion

Perennial Vegetables.

It's best to give perennial vegetables their own area in the garden, because they might be injured by working the soil each time you plant or remove annual crops. You might combine them in a bed just for perennial vegetables—rhubarb and asparagus are traditionally planted together, with the tall asparagus lined up behind the lower-growing rhubarb plants. Jerusalem artichoke can be very invasive, so grow it where you can keep its spread under control. Perennial onions will grow anywhere there's full sun and humus-rich soil. The other perennials are used for greens and will grow happily together side by side, making salad picking a quick stop. Replenish the soil in fall or spring by carefully working a couple of inches of rotted manure or compost into the top layer of the soil.

Asparagus (*Asparagus officinalis*)

The tall, feathery tops of mature asparagus make a pretty picture in the summer garden, but the delectable green shoots that precede them in early spring are what all the fuss is about. These tender, tasty asparagus spears emerge from the ground beginning in early spring. You can harvest mature plants for 6 to 8 weeks, but no longer, or the plant will exhaust itself. After harvest stops, subsequent spears grow into feathery tops that will produce enough food to sustain the plant for the following year.

Your asparagus bed will need very little attention after the first season and will produce for decades. Prepare the soil well, double-digging if you can, and remove every last bit of root from perennial weeds. Asparagus does best in sandy loam with a pH of 6.0 to 7.0, so add heaps of organic matter to

heavy soil. Asparagus will grow well anywhere the ground freezes in winter—roughly anywhere in Canada and in the United States outside the Deep South, Southwest, and mild areas of the West Coast. It's hardy in USDA Plant Hardiness Zones 2 to 8.

Fortunately for weekend gardeners, there's been a revolution in asparagus growing that promises higher yields and a lot less work. Previously, a gardener was advised to dig a deep trench, plant out asparagus on mounds in the trench, and fertilize them to a fare-thee-well. Because about half the plants were females, the patch produced numerous seedlings, which had to be rigorously weeded out each spring—otherwise, they'd not only crowd the mature plants, but also provide breeding grounds for the number one pest of asparagus, the asparagus beetle.

The asparagus breakthrough occurred with the introduction of all-male cultivars, including 'Greenwich' and 'Jersey Giant'. These male cultivars yield up to four times as much as the older cultivars (for instance, 'Mary Washington' and 'Martha Washington'), and because the plants are all male, they don't produce troublesome seedlings. These all-male asparagus cultivars are also resistant to the most serious disease of the crop, asparagus rust. Though you can grow the new all-male asparagus from seed, it is faster to begin with roots or crowns purchased locally or by mail-order. The roots should be fresh and firm, not wrinkled or limp.

There's more good news following in the wake of the male cultivars. Researchers found that asparagus grows and produces better and sooner if it isn't trench-planted. Instead, set the roots 5 to 6 inches deep in soil that's been enriched with rock phosphate or bonemeal. Asparagus doesn't really need tons of nitrogen as was once thought—an annual sidedressing of compost or manure provides all that's needed. Because of its shallow roots, asparagus resents cultivation after planting, so you should carefully remove all perennial weeds when preparing the soil. The first season, the plants need lots of water (about an inch a week). An organic mulch retains soil moisture and helps cut down weeds, too.

The final finding about the new asparagus cultivars may be the best news of all to weekend gardeners hankering for a harvest of tender spears. In the past, gardeners were admonished to never, *ever* harvest a spear before the third year. Even then, you could only harvest for 2 weeks. The fourth year, you could extend the harvest to 4 weeks, and by the fifth year, to the full 8 weeks (or even 12 weeks in long-season areas like California). Luckily for us, the new cultivars have changed this waiting game. Researchers discovered that harvesting these all-male cultivars lightly for 3 weeks the *first* season actually resulted in heavier overall yields! Now there's really no excuse for not planting these delicious perennial vegetables.

Count on planting at least 10 asparagus crowns for each family member. Set the crowns 18 inches apart in the bed, spreading the roots out as you plant them. For an asparagus patch containing 50 plants, you'll need to prepare an extensive bed of about 250 square feet, not including space for paths. If you have room, plant two 3-foot-wide rows with a 2- to 3-foot-wide path down the middle. This makes harvesting easier, and you won't need to walk on the bed, possibly stepping on the spears and certainly compacting the soil. When the crowns are set in the bed, fill in with 2 or 3 inches of soil. Gradually add more soil as the plants grow until the bed is level.

Since asparagus grows quite tall (up to 5 feet), locate the bed where the foliage won't cast shade on sun-loving plants. The roots can be invasive, too, so keep asparagus separate from most other plants. You can interplant lettuce, spinach, or other early-spring crops in the asparagus bed while it is getting established.

To harvest asparagus spears, snap or cut them off below ground. It's usually better to snap off the spears, because when cutting you may accidentally injure a nearby spear that hasn't yet emerged from the ground. The spears will break off at a transition point where the stem changes from being tender to being tough. Choose thick spears about 8 inches long and pick them before the scales at the tips begin to open. Stop harvesting when the new spears come up thin and spindly. After the harvest, allow the foliage to grow, and don't cut it down until late winter. When you do cut the foliage, destroy it to get rid of overwintering asparagus beetles. During the growing season, handpick asparagus beetles (¼-inch long, blackish insects with three yellow or orange squares on their wings), or keep them off your plants with a floating row cover. Make sure you bury the edges of the cover so the beetles can't crawl under.

Rhubarb (*Rheum rhabarbarum*)

Patience is required when growing rhubarb, because it can't be harvested at all during its first year in your garden and can only be harvested lightly the second year. But thereafter, rhubarb will provide decades of work-free spring harvests for making beautiful cobblers, pies, and sauces, with plenty left for freezing. The only edible part of this otherwise poisonous plant is the leaf stalk. Discard the green blade of the leaf.

Many cultivars of rhubarb are available. Some are tarter and tangier than others, so be sure you know your taste preference when selecting a cultivar. Red-stalked cultivars certainly look prettiest, both in the garden and when cooked up. Sweet red rhubarb cultivars include 'Chipman's Canada Red', bright red and juicy, 'MacDonald' (also sold as 'McDonald's Canadian Red'), the darkest red, and 'Valentine'. However, green-stalked cultivars, such as 'Victoria', may taste better to you if you enjoy the classic rhubarb tang. One cultivar that's very juicy and tart is 'Cherry Red', which has stalks colored cherry red outside and green inside. There are also cultivars that vary from red to green, like 'Flare', with a sweet-tart taste.

Mark and I once participated in a rhubarb pie taste-testing in the famous Mantanuska Valley of Alaska—one of life's truly remarkable experiences! Surrounded by snow-capped peaks and distant glaciers, our group devoured pies baked from four different cultivars of rhubarb. Each slice came nestled under a golden scoop of vanilla ice cream made locally from Mantanuska Valley cream. We were in heaven! But not all the pies were equal. In fact, the prettiest red one was almost bland. We voted the green pie, which had the most tang, the winner.

Rhubarb prefers a cool climate where summer days aren't too hot and where the ground is frozen in winter, but will survive where winter temperatures fall below 40°F. It will grow in Zones 2 to 7. Coolness and a sunny site promote better red coloring in the stalks. Rhubarb also needs good drainage.

Plant roots 2 or 3 inches deep in early spring in well-prepared rich soil, separating plants by 2 or 3 feet. Four or five plants should be sufficient, since each plant will produce 2 to 3 pounds of rhubarb. Since rhubarb is a heavy feeder, supply additional compost or manure every spring as a side-dressing, and again in summer once you've finished harvesting.

Harvest rhubarb when the stalks are full-grown and the leaf blade has lost most of its crinkly appearance. Do not cut the stalks, but pull them away with a twisting motion. Harvest only a few stalks from the plants during the second growing season. In subsequent years, you can harvest stalks for 2 months, but then stop harvesting so the plants remain vigorous. Make sure you leave at least half the foliage on each plant as you harvest.

Cut off flower stalks as soon as they form, since seed formation robs the roots of stored energy. When the rhubarb patch gets too crowded—probably after it is 6 or 7 years old—it's time to divide the crowns. Dig up the plants and split them into sections, take the opportunity to enrich the soil, and then replant the best divisions, discarding or sharing the rest. Crowded beds also seem most eager to flower—another good reason not to put off dividing them.

Egyptian Onion (*Allium cepa,* Proliferum Group)

An odd member of the onion family, Egyptian onions form clusters of bulbils complete with tiny curly leaves right on top of their 3-foot-tall flower stalks. It's an amusing sight in the middle of summer to see these curious stalks waving about in the garden. Eventually the stalks fall over, sending the bulbils to their destiny in the dirt. If not harvested, the bulbils will take root and make an ever-widening clump. The mother plant is perennial, however, and multiplies underground.

You can use the strong-flavored bulbils, which mature in midsummer, as you would onions or shallots, and they are favorites for pickling. All parts of this perennial onion, which doesn't form an underground bulb, are edible and useful. The young green shoots make excellent scallions, and the slender leaf tips can be chopped like chives. You can slice the tender, elongated white bases of the plant and use them like onions. They grow to about 1 inch wide and 6 inches long, and can be harvested from early spring to fall frost.

Plant bulbils 1 inch deep in well-drained soil that's been enriched with plenty of compost or well-rotted manure. Give them a sunny spot, and make sure they're well watered throughout the season (ample water makes the flavor milder). Thin to 12 inches apart, using the thinnings as scallions. In cold climates, you may need to bury the bulbils as much as 5 inches deep to protect them through the winter. Mulching will help to keep the soil moist and to deter weeds in summer. Mulch will also bring the plants through even a harsh winter. Egyptian onions can be grown in Zones 4 to 10, and in Zone 3 with winter protection.

Potato Onion (*Allium cepa,* Aggregatum Group)

Potato onions, an heirloom variety, taste delicious and are great fun to grow. Their flavor is considerably milder than that of the pungent Egyptian onions. These multiplier onions form large bulbs and small bulblets from each bulb. Plant them in fall in well-drained soil with plenty of organic matter, setting the bulbs 5 or 6 inches apart in the beds, with about half the bulb emerging from the soil. Potato onions produce green bunching onions in spring and a crop of large (3 inches or more in diameter) bulbs, which are excellent keepers, in fall. Harvest the mature bulbs when the tops dry down. Just make sure you leave some bulbs *and* some bulblets in the ground for next year's crop. (Full-size bulbs left in the ground will each produce about 20 sets the next season, while the bulblets will mature into the season's harvest).

Potato onions will withstand winter temperatures of −40°F if they're mulched, so they're hardy in Zones 3 to 9. Unlike the other perennial vegetables listed here, only two companies carry the tasty potato onion: Kalmia Farm (P.O. Box 3881, Charlottesville, VA 22903) and Southern Exposure Seed Exchange (P.O. Box 158, North Garden, VA 22959).

Jerusalem Artichoke (*Helianthus tuberosus*)

Jerusalem artichoke, also called sunchoke, hails from North America, not the Middle East, and is a close cousin to the sunflower rather than the artichoke. Its yellow daisylike flowers are borne in late summer on stems 6 to 12 feet tall and can be used for cut flowers. About a month after the flowers fade in fall, the plants turn brown and die back to the ground; you can dig up the edible knobby tubers at that time, but they'll be their tastiest —crunchy, nutty, and sweet—if dug after a frost. You can leave tubers in the ground all autumn and winter, if protected by mulch, and dig as needed—a boon to weekend gardeners with plenty of other fall garden chores to occupy their time. In fact, tubers taste best when freshly dug, so harvesting as needed is the best method. Brush off loose dirt, but store them unwashed until ready to use.

Plant pieces of sunchoke tuber 4 inches deep and 12 inches apart in early spring. A light soil is best, though they really aren't fussy. Sunchokes grow and spread exuberantly and can turn into a persistent pest if you aren't careful. Plant them in a large bed at the back of the garden or yard, where the shade they cast won't be a problem. Surround the bed with an edging 12 inches deep to keep them from invading other areas, grow them in a raised bed with constructed sides, or plant them in a patch in a meadow garden. You can grow Jerusalem artichokes in Zones 3 to 9, and in Zone 2 with winter protection. But bear in mind that their flavor is inferior in frost-free areas.

When digging up the tubers, first cut the dead stalks down to about 12 inches tall, then loosen the root system with a garden fork, using the stem as a handle to yank out the roots and tubers. You'll certainly miss a few tubers, and these will be plenty to produce a crop the following year.

Sorrel (*Rumex acetosa* and *R. scutatus*)

Sorrel—a piquant green with a pleasantly sour, faint lemon taste—is such a favorite of my husband Mark's that I always refer to the row in our garden as "your sorrel"—as in, "Go pick some of your sorrel to put in the salad." When we moved to our present home, Mark dug up two of his sorrel plants to bring along with us.

A hardy perennial, sorrel is a care-free plant that will return to your garden year after year, perking up the salad bowl and soup pot with its zippy flavor. Long appreciated in Europe, sorrel is little known here, probably because it is perishable and doesn't hold up as a market green. There are two species and several cultivars available. Garden sorrel (*Rumex acetosa*) has lance-shaped leaves and grows 18 to 36 inches tall. It is most commonly available in the U.S. The most popular cultivar is 'Large Belleville'. French sorrel (*R. scutatus*), used in Europe to make cream of sorrel soup, is a prostrate plant with arrow-shaped leaves. Though it tastes the most piquant of the two, it is seldom found in our catalogs.

Grow sorrel, starting from fall- or spring-sown seeds or purchased plants, in manure-rich, moist soil in full sun or part shade. Space the plants about a foot apart. If sorrel dries out, the foliage becomes tough. Divide the plants, which will slowly increase in size, every three or four years, improving the soil with lots of manure. Sorrel can be annoyingly weedy if you let the flower stalks go to seed. Flower stalks will also cut down on leaf production. Simply cutting off these flower stalks when they form in midsummer is the only routine maintenance the plant needs. You can grow both French and garden sorrel in Zones 3 to 9.

Harvest leaves of sorrel just before preparing a salad because they wilt quickly. Pick the outer leaves from the rosette while they are still tender, leaving the small central leaves in the plant's center so it will keep on growing. Sorrel is reported to be pest-free, but leafminers invaded Mark's. We simply picked off the disfigured leaves—there were plenty of others to meet our needs. If leafminers are a serious problem for you, floating row covers will keep them off if you bury the edges.

Good-King-Henry (*Chenopodium bonus-henricus*)

Good-King-Henry, a versatile edible plant with dark green leaves marked with purple, has young shoots in early spring that can be cooked and eaten like asparagus. They even taste like asparagus. Later in spring, young leaves can be picked and prepared like spinach. Once the rangy-looking plant starts flowering, it loses its culinary appeal for the rest of the season because the leaves become bitter.

Start good-King-Henry from purchased plants or seed. Sow the small seeds only ⅛-inch deep, and thin mature plants to 12 inches apart. The best harvests come from plants grown in rich, moist soil, where the plants remain productive for many years. To prevent self-sowing and weediness, cut off the flower stalks before seeds are dispersed. To renew a patch, rather than dividing plants, dig up old ones and scatter seeds on the ground. But you probably won't need to do this any more often than once in 10 years! You can grow good-King-Henry in Zones 3 to 9.

Overwintering Crops and Otherwise Defying Jack Frost

I remember getting off the train one Friday night in early autumn, after my usual workweek in the city, and finding Mark all in a frazzle over the imminent demise of the vegetable garden. A forecast for the first fall frost had sent him into a frenzy. Caught unprepared, panic set in—the produce had to be harvested or it would be mush by morning. He had stripped the garden down to spindly stalks and piled great heaps of vegetables in the kitchen! It looked like a fall harvest festival gone out of control. Mounds of red and green tomatoes, red and green peppers, yellow and green summer squash, cucumbers in assorted shapes and sizes, and baskets of broccoli and butternut squash gave the kitchen the look of a well-stocked farm stand.

Then it was my turn to panic. What would we do with all those vegetables? Guess. Sure enough, we spent the entire weekend chopping, slicing, blanching, boiling, pickling, and canning it all.

I tell this story to make several points, all vital to weekend gardening success—and sanity. First, don't plant more than you can eat or have time to preserve—harvesting can be even more time-consuming than planting and tending the garden! Second, tender crops *can* be protected from frost damage if you know how. And third, not all vegetables are harmed by frost—some, like parsnips, kale, and brussels sprouts, even taste better after a cold snap—so don't overload the garden with warm-season crops that will leave you cold come frost.

Smart weekend gardeners know that a light frost needn't spell disaster in fall if they are prepared. Jack Frost won't torment tender crops if you cover them up overnight to keep in enough heat to prevent frost damage. In my upstate New York garden, I successfully blanketed my vegetable garden with old curtains. It took just a few minutes to drape the large sheets over staked tomatoes and spread them out over the sprawling vining crops to ward off several frosts in early fall. Old blankets work well, too, if you give them some support such as stakes to hold them off the crops. Remove them in the morning.

Season-Extending Tricks

One way to extend your pleasure in the garden is to outwit Mother Nature by artificially extending the growing season. This can be accomplished on both ends—both hurrying things up in spring and stretching them out in fall—with a number of ingenious devices that trap solar energy and therefore heat. Relying on the greenhouse effect, clear covers such as coldframes heat up in the sun during the day and retain enough heat during the night to create an environment many degrees warmer than the actual temperature. Growing plants this way can extend your season a month or more at each end.

One type of row cover is especially well suited to weekend gardening, because it provides multiple benefits and is trouble-free. It is a floating row cover made from spunbonded polyester fabric. The best-known brand is Reemay, but several others and generics are also available. This extremely lightweight cloth can be laid directly over crops, rather than supports—thus its name "floating". It provides up to 4°F of frost protection. A floating row cover will also keep out insect pests if you seal the edges by burying them. Part of the appeal of spunbonded fabric is that—unlike plastic and glass—it lets in water and air. And about 80 percent of the available sunlight gets through the cloth.

Lay the cloth, which is available through mail-order catalogs and in nurseries, right over the beds. Anchor the ends by burying them under 3 inches of soil or weighting them with rocks or bricks. Be sure to leave enough slack for plant growth. The floating row cover can, and should, be left in place at least until your crops' normal growing season. Spunbonded polyester is sensitive to ultraviolet light and will begin to break down after about three months, but if used only in spring it will be good for two seasons.

The only other season-extender of value to weekend gardeners is a coldframe. This low, unheated miniature greenhouse is remarkably effective if you use it properly. A coldframe can lengthen your growing season by two months on either end, and perhaps even be used to overwinter frost-tolerant crops and seedlings, depending on your climate. Situate a coldframe so it faces south, absorbing maximum sunlight. Coldframes are more work than floating row covers, however. You'll have to open the glass top during sunny days to keep the plants from overheating, close it at night, and—if your climate is very cold—also cover it with insulation at night to keep your crop from freezing.

Manually opening and closing a coldframe can be a true nuisance. If you rush off to work one morning and leave it shut, you may have vegetable stew when you return. Or if one frosty evening you work late, get caught in traffic, or stop at the grocery on the way home . . . it's frozen vegetables for sure. Forget about going away for the weekend! I purchased a prefabricated coldframe that has a solar-powered thermostat to automatically open and close the top. It's wonderful—I can practically forget about the seedlings and plants inside it except for a quick watering check a couple times a week. This invaluable device makes up for a lot of human error. Automatic devices are available for use on home-built coldframes too. Just be sure they are powerful enough to lift the weight of the lid.

Growing vegetables in cold frames or under row covers can extend the growing season from a couple of weeks to more than a month. (1) A built-in cold frame provides a permanent place for growing cold-season crops like lettuce and spinach at the far ends of spring and fall. (2) You can make a simple portable cold frame or buy one from a garden catalog. You can add an automatic opener so you don't have to remember to open and close the frame. (3) A floating row cover, made of spunbonded polyester fabric, can raise the temperature under it as much as 4°F, allowing many vegetables to get a head start on spring. Mound soil over the edges for a good seal.

Hurrying Up Spring

Raised garden beds warm up faster in spring than level ground, but if you want to hurry up spring and get on with planting, here are some more warm-up tricks. Most organic mulches laid on top of the bed will help keep the garden soil cooler and more moist in midsummer, and add nutrients as they break down. But if organic mulch still lies on the ground in spring, it will prevent the soil from warming up as fast as it would without

mulch. So pull back the organic mulch in spring to let the soil warm up and dry out.

Plastic sheeting spread over the soil will heat it up, too, allowing earlier planting of warm-season crops. Clear plastic can raise the soil temperature as much as 12°F on a mid-spring afternoon compared to bare soil, but it has a drawback for weekend gardeners —it allows weeds to germinate and grow vigorously right under it. For the weekend vegetable gardener, black plastic is the mulch of choice. It raises the soil temperature (though not as much as clear plastic) and suppresses weeds. And you can leave black plastic down as a season-long mulch.

Use the plastic mulch to allow earlier planting of both cool-season and warm-season crops. With cool-season vegetables, remove the plastic or cover it with a cooling straw mulch as the weather warms to avoid overheating the plants. In northern or cool-summer climates, leave the plastic mulch uncovered all summer for vegetables that like it hot, such as cantaloupes, watermelons, tomatoes, and peppers.

Handling Weekend Chores with Ease

Believe it or not, once the garden is planted your biggest chore is going to be keeping it harvested! That may sound funny, but it's not. When many crops are just ripe for picking, they aren't going to wait for you. If you don't get them, the critters might, or the crops will just keep on maturing, becoming tough, messy, stringy, seedy, bitter, or some other unpalatable state. Some vegetables, notably snap beans, need to be harvested regularly to keep them bearing. So check your garden often, every other day at least if you can, and pick what's ripe and delicious. Plan to deal with the harvest that you collected and stored during the week—if you haven't eaten it all up—by cooking, canning, and freezing it on the weekends. If you've miscalculated and planted too much, giving your surplus produce away is a good timesaving idea, too!

The garden will need to be weeded regularly, especially early in the season and whenever new crops are put in. Springtime through early summer is when most annual weeds come up, so be diligent at that time. Early fall is another weed-sprouting season; cool-season weeds make an appearance then and may grow right up until freezing weather, ready to grow again and flower in spring. Several specialized pronged or tined tools will help you get at individual weeds or small weedy patches. These are called **claws, forks, or cultivators.** When scratched across the soil, they're useful for snagging or digging out weeds that are more mature than a hoe can effectively deal with. Many come in short- or long-handled versions for use while kneeling or standing. A weed-blocking mulch is also effective. Black plastic mulch is especially useful in vegetable gardens.

Use a rain gauge in the garden to monitor rainfall and overhead sprinkling. If Mother Nature doesn't provide at least an inch of rainfall during the week, it is advisable to help out the thirsty vegetable garden by irrigating enough to bring the week's total up to an inch a week. Check the forecast before doing so—why waste water and your time, or flood the garden? It's best to water in the morning so foliage can dry during the day—this helps to avoid fungal diseases.

Soil Fertility

Whether you're gardening intensively with annual crops or growing only a patch or two of perennial vegetables, don't take the soil for granted. You'll need to replenish soil nutrients each year for the best yields. You can add a load of well-rotted manure (or compost) each year in spring, or prepare the beds in late fall.

Fall soil preparation has an advantage in that the garden is ready to be planted in spring as soon as the ground warms up, without further work from you. Organic matter added in fall doesn't have to be as well-rotted as materials incorporated in spring, because they'll decompose further over the winter if worked in well enough. You can add fresh manure or partially decomposed compost, and even dig in freshly shredded leaves, during fall. If you've mulched the garden with straw or a similar organic material, fall is a good time to dig it into the soil—it will be partially decomposed by then.

Each year, apply at least an inch or two of animal manure or compost over the bed, and 1 pound of bonemeal for each 100 square feet of bed surface to replenish the nitrogen, potassium, and phosphorus. Most vegetables grow best in a pH range of 6.0 to 6.8. Add ground limestone, if necessary, to raise the pH, if your soil is naturally acid. Five pounds of ground limestone per 100 square feet will raise soil pH ½ to 1 unit. Add elemental sulfur to lower the pH if your soil is too alkaline—½ pound of ground sulfur per 100 square feet will lower pH ½ to 1 unit.

During the growing season, if crops appear in need of an extra boost, water them with fish emulsion or with compost- or manure-tea made by soaking a cheesecloth bag full of compost or manure in a bucket of water, or apply a sidedressing of compost or well-rotted manure. Heavy feeders, such as tomatoes, will need regular sidedressing during the growing season. Don't wait until the crop looks pinched—find the time to apply fertilizer according to the crop's needs.

Weekend vegetable gardening is not only possible, it's fun! If you use raised beds and sound organic gardening techniques—including soil building and mulching—add a few extras like vertical gardening and perennial vegetables, grow only what you really like, and remember moderation, your garden will be a resounding success. In fact, weekend vegetable gardening can become a fine art, as *Jeff Ball's 60-Minute Garden* demonstrates. Using Jeff's systems and techniques of specially designed modular raised beds, trellises, supports, row covers, and watering systems, you can reap optimal harvests in 60 minutes a week. If vegetable gardening is your favorite form of weekend gardening, the 60-minute garden is well worth the initial investment in time and equipment for setup. But whether you follow the advice in this chapter, or go all-out with a 60-minute setup, get ready to plant, harvest, and enjoy!

THE FRUITS OF YOUR LABOR

How to Grow More Fruit with Less Work

Future weekend fruit growers, heed the moral of this story of my friends John and Claudia, who moved to Long Island from California about ten years ago. Their newly acquired 1½-acre property featured a cozy farmhouse and a lot of gardening potential. Used to the cramped quarters so often found in California developments, they were thrilled at the size of the property. The first thing John and Claudia planted was a home orchard of eight fruit trees—three apples, two plums, two peaches, and an apricot. A quince and a pear already grew on the property. They followed up their fruit trees with a strawberry bed, a raspberry patch, and six blueberry bushes.

John and Claudia's berry plants were a great success. All began bearing soon after planting. The strawberries, grown by the matted-row technique, did well for several years with very little attention. And as long as the bed is periodically replanted, they harvest scrumptious amounts of ripe berries. Their blueberries have grown into large, handsome bushes that are still producing an abundant crop of rich blue, flavorful berries without much attention. The birds get their share, but there's plenty to go around, Claudia declares.

Over the years, lack of time meant that the raspberry patch, located in an out-of-the-way spot behind the toolshed, wasn't pruned properly. Allowed to grow without pruning, the raspberries sent up suckers that quickly transformed the berry patch into an impenetrable thicket that became more junglelike with each passing year. Reaching the ripe raspberries dangling tantalizingly out of arm's reach required donning a virtual suit of armor as protection from the lethal thorns. John and Claudia were able to save their raspberry patch, however, by severe rejuvenation pruning. Equipped with loppers, leather gloves, and two sweatshirts, John fought back the brambles and tamed the patch, creating a path into the thicket and removing dead canes. Now they prune the plants each year, and huge crops of berries—enough to share with friends and neighbors—reward their minimal efforts.

Their fruit trees, however, are a different —and more discouraging—story. It took four or five years for John and Claudia's fruit trees to even begin to bear, and the bushel baskets Claudia has stockpiled to carry the harvest have yet to be filled to capacity. The pear, apricot, and quince were totalled by fireblight five years ago. Every year more peaches rotted on the branches or were ruined by squirrels and yellow-jackets than ripened, and any apples that weren't spoiled by worms had holes pecked in them by birds. Claudia doesn't let a guest leave her house in summer without loading them with produce from the vegetable garden, but she has yet to give away any extras from the orchard.

John and Claudia are what I would call super-dedicated weekend gardeners. They spend the entire weekend, every week, working in their garden, tending flowers, herbs, vegetables, lawn, evergreens—and fruit trees and berry plants. What I learned from watching these enthusiastic and experienced gardeners, coupled with my own early experiences with the perils and rewards of growing fruits and berries, has convinced me that the best advice I can give any weekend gardeners who love homegrown fruit but are short on time and easily frustrated is: Don't grow fruit trees. Stick with berries.

Mark and I have also grown crops of beautiful berries, including blueberries, strawberries, currants, gooseberries, and fall raspberries, without expending much effort. But all my attempts at fruit tree cultivation failed miserably. It's possible, of course, for serious home gardeners to successfully cultivate an orchard, but to do so requires a time investment in both work and education that few of us have. No one will dispute the fact that homegrown, tree-ripened fruit tastes better than anything you can buy. However, growing small fruits is much easier and more satisfying for weekend gardeners. Because fruit trees usually require more skilled and time-consuming care than berry plants—and are also much more expensive to purchase—I strongly advise weekend gardeners (especially beginners) to start with the small fruits.

Top-Ranked Fruits for Weekend Gardeners

I asked Marcia Eames-Sheavly, a fruit specialist at Cornell University, if she could give weekend gardeners the benefit of her experience and rank the fruits by their ease of growing. Blueberries and fall raspberries top her list of low-maintenance fruits, provided the soil is properly prepared at planting time. In order of ease of culture, Ms. Eames-Sheavly ranks homegrown fruits:

Easy maintenance: blueberries, fall raspberries, bush cherries, currants, gooseberries

Moderate maintenance: summer raspberries, strawberries, blackberries

High maintenance: citrus, grapes, cherries, pears, apples, peaches, plums, quince

Ms. Eames-Sheavly's advice also bears out the wisdom of my decision to grow only small fruits. She strongly advises beginners and any gardeners looking for low-maintenance alternatives to forgo planting fruit trees, all of which fall into the high-maintenance category.

In accordance with Ms. Eames-Sheavly's list, I'm going to describe in detail the best ways to grow the easy- and moderate-care fruits. I'll tell you how to select the right cultivars for your climate and warn you about the most notable pitfalls in growing each type of fruit. My methods won't always be the most productive, but they will produce a satisfying harvest with the least amount of effort.

One other note before you plant. Whether you're growing berries or tree fruit, look for disease- and insect-resistant cultivars, if available, and be sure to choose plants adapted to your climate. Consult your local cooperative Extension service for information on cultivars best adapted to your area.

Blueberries— The Easiest Crop of All

Practically foolproof, blueberries can't be beat as a homegrown fruit. They make a perfect crop for weekend gardeners because the bushes need very little pruning, and that pruning requires minimal skill. Blueberry bushes don't need to be trained or trellised, and they aren't troubled much by insects and diseases. Furthermore, the ripe fruits keep well on the bush, an extremely important attribute for gardeners who may not be able to check their plants except on the weekends. Ripe strawberries and bramble fruits wouldn't last from one weekend to the next—ripe blueberries do, unless the birds gobble them.

Selecting Blueberries

There are three main types of cultivated blueberries—highbush, rabbiteye, and the so-called half-high blueberries, which are hybrids between the wild lowbush blueberries (*Vaccinium angustifolium*) and the highbush blueberry (*V. corymbosum*). Each performs best in different areas of the country. At least one type or another will flourish from USDA Plant Hardiness Zones 3 to 10 in any garden where their strict soil requirements can be met. As an added bonus, all are attractive shrubs that can double as landscape plants in hedges, borders, and foundation plantings. Blueberry flowers are white, bell-shaped, and resemble lily-of-the-valley; foliage gleams glossy dark green in summer and dark red in fall. In winter, stems often take on a handsome reddish cast.

Bumper blueberry crops keep well in the refrigerator if stored unwashed, but also freeze easily—just pop them unwashed into jars or Ziploc storage bags and place in the freezer. Use them in muffins, pancakes, cobblers, and pies when winter has you longing for fresh-tasting fruit.

Highbush Blueberries

Most commercially grown blueberries hail from the highbush blueberry (*V. corymbosum*), which is native to the Atlantic Coast from Maine to the Carolinas. Bushes can grow 6 to 10 feet tall and are recommended for Zones 4 to 8. There are a number of cultivars available, and if you plant a selection of early, mid-, and late-season cultivars, you'll be picking fresh blueberries from early

July to mid-August. Although highbush blueberries are self-fertile, another good reason to plant several cultivars is that the berries will be larger if they can cross-pollinate.

A new, very late fruiting cultivar called 'Elliott' fruits from mid-August into September. Mark and I intend to add this one to our blueberry planting, so we can enjoy home-grown blueberries for breakfast for almost three months. He loves them piled on top of a mound of cottage cheese nestled in half a cantaloupe.

Rabbiteye Blueberries

In the South, where highbush blueberries succumb to the heat and humidity, rabbiteye blueberries (*Vaccinium ashei*) are the plants to grow. (Both highbush and rabbiteye blueberries will grow well in the high elevations of North Carolina and Arkansas.) Rabbiteyes withstand heat and drought better than highbush blueberries, and tolerate a wider range of soil types, although they perform best in an organically rich, acid soil. Rabbiteyes are only hardy to about 0°F and grow well in Zones 7 to 10. In borderline areas, a late spring frost can nip the flowers, leaving you without a crop. These blueberries grow vigorously, reaching 15 feet tall if not pruned.

Rabbiteye blueberries have been given a bad rap because the wild ones, native to the southeastern coastal areas, produce small, tough, seedy berries. Modern cultivars yield great-tasting berries that almost equal those of their northern highbush cousins. Ripening begins in April in Florida but not until August in North Carolina. Plant more than one cultivar to ensure fruit set.

Half-High Blueberries

The new half-high blueberries, which are hybrids of the wild lowbush blueberry (*Vac-cinium angustifolium*) of Maine-blueberry fame and the highbush blueberry, make it possible for gardeners in some of the coldest parts of the country to grow blueberries. Three half-high cultivars developed at the University of Minnesota—'Northsky', 'Northblue', and 'Northcountry'—survive winter temperatures of −30 to −40°F, especially in areas with heavy snowfall, which will cover the low plants and protect them from severe weather. Grow half-highs in Zones 3 to 7, but during snowless winters, cover the plants with straw or leaves in Zones 3 and 4.

Half-high blueberries form compact plants that grow only several feet high, and for this reason they make fine additions to landscape plantings. Their low height also accounts for part of their hardiness, because in northern climes the shrubs can spend the winter tucked safely under a comforter of snow. These northern cultivars fruit best if cross-pollinated, so plant more than one for best yields.

Blueberries 101— Basic Care

Blueberries are remarkably trouble-free plants. As long as they are grown in the proper soil, you'll be able to harvest bumper crops year after year with only a minimum of care.

Soil Sense

Blueberries require soil that is quite acid—between pH 4.5 and 5.5—and highly organic. Clay soil or alkaline soil spells death for these plants. A pH higher than 5.8 may cause nutrient deficiencies, resulting in reduced growth and yellow foliage. An even higher pH may kill the blueberry plants. Rabbiteye blueberries can tolerate slightly less acid soil—up to pH 6.0 if the soil is improved with peat.

Soil Doctoring

I've never really paid very much attention to soil pH in any of my gardens, just assumed that it was on the acid side and gone about my gardening. Because most plants do well in soils with a pH between 6.0 and 7.0, and that's the range throughout much of the country, I got away with it. However, extremes do exist, and some plants are finicky, so my motto here is "Do as I say, not as I do," especially when it comes to blueberries. They are one of those plants that are finicky about pH and must have acid soil.

You needn't waste money on an expensive soil-testing apparatus, but can purchase a roll of pH paper from a scientific supply house to test your soil. Mix a soil sample with enough distilled water to get a thick suspension and dip in the paper. The paper turns colors according to the soil's pH. If the soil isn't in the proper range for blueberries (pH 4.5 to 4.8), you can lower it by adding wettable ground sulfur (available

at garden centers) to the soil, or by incorporating acid organic material such as acid peat or oak-leaf mold. To effect a large change, organic matter alone may not be effective enough, so add sulfur, too. Yearly applications may be necessary to prevent the soil from returning to its natural pH, so pull out the pH paper every year.

The following table gives the appropriate amounts of sulfur needed to change the pH the desired amount. Remember that the pH scale is logarithmic, so the rates aren't obviously proportional.

	Pounds of Sulfur per 100 Sq. Ft.	
Change	**Loam Soil**	**Sandy Soil**
7.0 to 4.5	12	3½
6.5 to 4.5	9½	3
6.0 to 4.5	6¾	2½
5.5 to 4.5	4¾	1½
5.0 to 4.5	2½	¾

For this reason, it's a wise idea to perform a soil test *before* you plant (or purchase!) blueberries to see if the proposed site falls within the necessary pH range. If soil is not acid enough, you can often lower the pH sufficiently by working in copious amounts of acid peat. Dig a large, wide planting hole and refill with a mixture of half native soil and half *sphagnum* peat moss, which is very acid. You can also lower pH by adding elemental sulfur to the soil.

These methods work where the soil is pH 7.0 or less, but you'll be fighting a losing battle where the soil is naturally more alkaline or where irrigation water is alkaline. One reference I checked described how to lower the pH of your irrigation water with vinegar! Well, it can be done, but is it really worth the trouble? If your soil is alkaline and water is not, then you might try growing blueberries in tubs of peaty soil to get around your local soil conditions.

Planting and Feeding

If the soil passes muster, plant the blueberries where they will receive at least 6 hours of full sun a day. Space highbush types 4 to 6 feet apart in rows 10 feet apart, rabbiteyes 10 feet apart in rows 15 feet apart, and half-highs 2 to 3 feet apart in rows 5 feet apart. Cover the soil surface with a 6-inch layer of organic mulch or compost. This last step is important because blueberry roots grow shallowly and don't have root hairs. They must be kept moist and undisturbed.

Don't overdo it when deciding how many blueberries to plant. Contented plants are highly productive, although it may take eight years before they reach peak productivity. A mature highbush blueberry can produce from 4 to 10 quarts of berries over its 4-week-long season. When cross-pollinated with another cultivar, highbush plants produce larger berries, so be sure to include several cultivars in the blueberry patch. To ensure a summer-long harvest, plant cultivars that ripen at different times. Because ripening periods may overlap, I suggest choosing two early-season, one mid-season, one late-season, and two very-late-season cultivars to assure a summer-long harvest. The blueberries with the best eating qualities are the mid-season cultivars, however. Keep in mind that in Zones 4 and 5 the growing season is too short to grow the very late blueberries,

which won't ripen there before frost.

A mature rabbiteye blueberry, which may be 10 to 15 feet tall, can yield 15 to 20 pints of ripe berries over the course of a month. Since you need two cultivars for cross-pollenization, I'd guess most folks would have more than enough berries from only two happy, healthy plants.

It's always discouraging to have to tell a potential fruit grower to remove flower buds and forgo a crop for one or two years, but even with blueberries it's a good idea. Remove all the flowers for the first two years after planting to encourage strong vegetative growth. Simply run your fingers along the branches and rub off the flower buds when they begin to open. You can begin harvesting the third year.

The nutritional needs of mature blueberries are low. All they need is a yearly application of 3 ounces of usable nitrogen in the form of cottonseed meal, blood meal, or soybean meal each spring. Be sure the blueberries receive at least an inch of water a week, especially during flowering and fruiting, and renew the mulch annually.

Pruning Basics

Blueberries require only a minimum of pruning. In fact, with highbush and half-highs, you won't need to prune anything more than wayward or dead branches during the first six or eight years, depending upon the plant's vigor. Thereafter, in late winter, saw off the oldest stems at ground level—these will be the twiggiest stems, which by now are unproductive and produce only small berries. From then on, each year cut out most or all of the eight-year-old canes, along with any weak or skinny canes, leaving behind the productive three- through

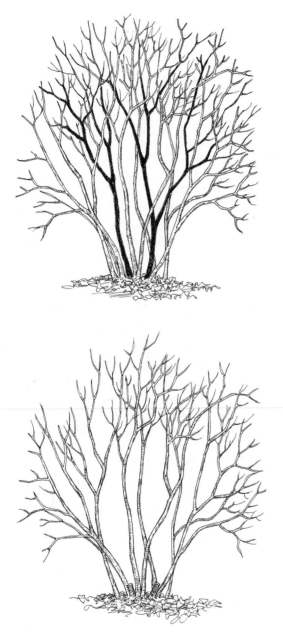

Blueberries require only a minimum of pruning. For the first six to eight years, remove only dead or wayward branches. Each year thereafter, saw off the eight-year-old stems at ground level, along with any weak or skinny branches. Leave behind the productive three- through seven-year-old stems and strong one- and two-year-old branches.

seven-year-olds, along with the strong one- and two-year-old canes. If necessary, remove branches from the center to allow light and air into the bush.

Rabbiteye blueberries need a bit more pruning so the berries don't ripen out of reach. Prune lightly each year during the dormant season. All you need to do is remove the tops of tall canes, thin out older interior growth, and remove low twiggy branches that are shaded and unproductive.

Harvest How-To

Don't be fooled into picking blueberries too soon. They turn blue a few days to a week before they're fully ripe; the central berries of a cluster ripen first. Ripe berries fall right off into your hand when brushed lightly with your fingers. Unripe blueberries have a red ring around the bud scar. The dusty blue color of many blueberries comes from a waxy coating. Be grateful for that wax—it is responsible for blueberries' long-keeping qualities. Handle the berries as little as possible, and only when dry, to preserve the protective coating.

Out-Maneuvering Birds and Other Pests

Birds are your greatest enemy when it comes to blueberry growing—or I should more accurately say blueberry harvesting, for they will be more than happy to do it for you if given the chance. Robins in particular love to supplement their earthworm diet with blueberries. Birds seem to favor very ripe blueberries more than any other home fruit crop, so be forewarned and plan to outmaneuver them if you want a large harvest all to yourself.

Bird netting is the usual recommendation, but it is not a joy to use. Netting can be a pain in the neck, to put it mildly. The stuff gets tangled in branches and must be removed and replaced each time you pick berries— it's best to hang it over a frame constructed over the plants rather than to drape it directly on the bushes. Birds will peck through it otherwise to get at any berries within a beak-length. If the net is not secured tightly at the bottom, birds often get underneath it and become hopelessly entangled.

My friends John and Claudia eschew bird netting altogether as too much trouble. They don't seem perturbed by sharing their berries with bird marauders—"There are plenty of berries to go around," Claudia says. However, Andrew and Mitsuko Collver, whose suburban acre is a showplace that includes a stunning Japanese garden, vegetables, fruits, and berries, feel more possessive about the fruits of their labor. Andrew built a walk-in cage to protect his six blueberry plants.

Although building a cage represents a significant initial investment of time, it pays off in time and frustration spared later on. Simply open the door, walk in and harvest the blues. Since rabbits and deer also browse on blueberry bark and limbs, the cage proves useful against these pests, too.

Blueberries have very few ailments, but occasionally a fungus disease called mummy berry invades the ripening crop. This is usually easily controlled by vigilantly picking out infected fruit. In addition, three types of canker sometimes attack the stems, causing the top growth to wilt and die. Cut out and burn afflicted stems as soon as you notice them. Finally, iron chlorosis, which is a nutrient deficiency, shows up where the soil is not acid enough. Chlorotic leaves become yellow between the veins. Cure iron chlorosis by treating the soil yearly with wettable sulfur.

Strawberry Growing Made Simple

Strawberry growing may seem complex, but only if you let all those different types of berries, as well as the systems for growing them, intimidate you. Actually, strawberries are relatively simple to grow and make a good choice for the weekend gardener. For beginning fruit growers, the problem arises because you must make a lot of choices before you really get started. Not only do you need to decide which of the three major types of strawberries to grow—Junebearing, everbearing, and day-neutral—you also need to settle on which of the three major management or growing methods you'll use—hill, matted row, or spaced row. And then, of course, there are countless cultivars to choose from, all of which sound too good to be true if you can believe the catalog descriptions.

Once these basic decisions have been made, strawberries have a lot to offer the weekend gardener. Depending upon the climate and the type of berry chosen, you can harvest strawberries four months to a year after planting them. And strawberry plants are inexpensive, especially when compared to fruit trees. Strawberry growing has one major drawback—the productive life of most plants is fairly short, only three to five years. But because the plants costs so little and establish easily, it's neither expensive nor difficult to till under unproductive plants and purchase new ones to start a new bed. And if you've let weeds get out of hand, tilling the bed under and starting again is easy.

Selecting Strawberries

Strawberry plants have an internal biological clock that measures the length of the

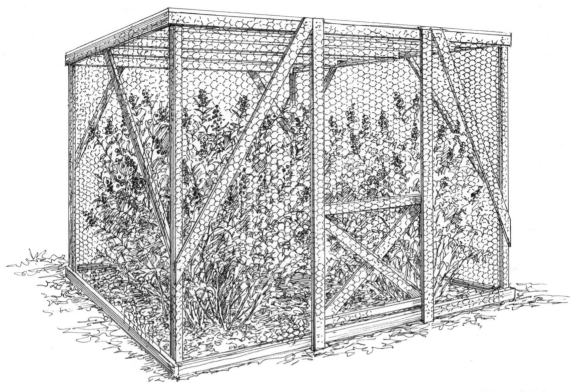

To keep birds from harvesting your ripe blueberries, build a permanent cage to enclose the bushes. With a walk-in frame and chicken wire cage to protect the berries, you won't have to tangle with bird netting.

day as the seasons change. They set flowers and fruit in response to daylength, and the three major types of strawberries are divided accordingly.

Junebearing Strawberries

Junebearing strawberries begin flowering in late spring in the North, and fruits ripen about four weeks later—in June or July. (They may begin bearing as early as April in Florida and California.) These are single-crop plants that produce fruit for about three or four weeks; there are early-, mid-, and late-season cultivars from which to choose. The shortening days of fall trigger the plants to set flower buds, which remain dormant over

the winter and provide the following season's crop.

Everbearing Strawberries

Modern research has brought us so-called everbearing strawberries, which produce a large crop in June, scattered berries in summer, and a smaller crop in late August. Before they will begin to flower and fruit, everbearers must have days that are slightly longer than those that trigger Junebearers. Although the early summer crop arises from flower buds formed the preceding fall, as days shorten after the summer solstice additional flower buds form. These produce that welcome crop of fruit in late summer or early fall. Everbearers are especially productive in northern areas where summer days are long. The total harvest for everbearers is much less than the total harvest for Junebearers, but the harvest is spread out over a longer period.

Day-Neutral Strawberries

Recently, researchers at the University of California and the USDA made the designation everbearing something of a misnomer—at least for the older everbearing cultivars. They introduced several strawberry cultivars that actually do bear fruit practically nonstop. These day-neutral berries produce flowers and berries on continuous six-week cycles, unaffected by day length, making them pretty close to being truly everbearing. Day-neutral strawberries are unusually productive and will bear fruit from June through October in northern areas; January through August in mild climates. Day-neutrals have become so popular and are so productive that the old everbearing types are quickly losing favor with both home gardeners and market growers.

Fruit expert Marcia Eames-Sheavly cautions that the day-neutral strawberries, as wonderful as they sound, require a lot of pampering. These plants are small and fragile—weeds can quickly destroy a planting, and they are more sensitive to heat and drought. Furthermore, they must be picked regularly throughout the entire season to prevent spoiled berries from stimulating a disease invasion.

Although day-neutrals are currently edging out the old everbearers in popularity, I think everbearers may make the most sense for weekend gardeners. The two fair-size harvests everbearers provide are probably easier to deal with than one huge Junebearing crop or the day-neutral's season-long picking requirement.

Strawberry Management

Strawberries have an exponential growth pattern that leads to most of the work involved in strawberry growing. Most kinds reproduce aggressively by sending out runners from the main crown. The runners root at their tips, forming daughter plants. Each daughter plant can, in turn, send out its own runners, often in the same season it was formed. It's not hard to see how this exuberant growth can get out of hand, quickly leading to a strawberry patch that is crowded, disease-ridden, and unproductive.

As it does with flowering, daylength triggers runner formation in strawberries. Long

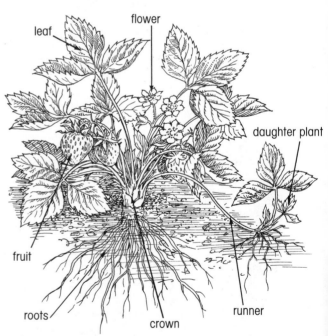

Planting a strawberry plant at just the right level is critical to its good health. Spread out the roots in the planting hole, situating the plant so the place where the roots and crown meet is right at the soil line. Make sure the crown is not too far out of the ground and is not buried by soil.

days stimulate Junebearers to produce runners, and they do so prolifically. Everbearers produce fewer runners, because some of their energy goes into producing the late-season harvest rather than into runners. Day-neutral strawberries produce even fewer runners.

I made the mistake once of edging my perennial flower border with Junebearing strawberries. Seemingly every time I turned my back, strawberry plants had sprung forth among the iris, astilbe, or peonies. It required constant grubbing to keep the flower border from turning into a strawberry patch. I had intended to use alpine strawberries, which don't form runners, but when I couldn't find them locally I impulsively purchased the Junebearers, intending to grow them as single plants and remove all the runners. After one season I realized the seriousness of my mistake and removed the plants, planting the daughter plants in a segregated bed.

Choosing a Management Method

There are three traditional methods for managing strawberries—the hill, matted row, and spaced row systems. All are based on the way the runners are handled. Although it may seem like a toss-up which way to go since each method has its pros and cons, the different kinds of strawberries perform better with different systems. In the hill system, plants are spaced fairly close and all runners are removed. The matted row system is just the opposite: For this method, the plants are spaced generously and runners are left to grow willy-nilly, with daughter plants filling in between the mother plants. The spaced row system involves a sort of compromise between the hill and matted row methods: A few runners are left on each plant and allowed to form daughter plants. These are then physically moved about and pinned down so the plantlets are spaced evenly around the mother plant. Subsequent runners are pinched off.

Of these three management methods, none is without a certain amount of labor. The hill system requires vigilant attention several times a week to remove runners, especially during the long days of summer. The matted row method is easy, and produces berries for two or maybe three years, depending upon the vigor of the strawberry cultivar you're growing, but plantings can become so crowded that mold and mildew easily invade. Half the bed in a matted row system should really be renewed every year for maximum productivity. The spaced row system might seem to involve less work than the hill system, but it probably takes just as much work: Making decisions as to which plantlets to keep and which to remove, and then deciding where to pin them down, can frustrate a harried gardener. Better to leave 'em all or get rid of 'em all, I think.

Best bet for Junebearers: Junebearing strawberries are easiest to grow if managed by the matted row system. Begin by spacing 25 plants about 18 to 24 inches apart in four or five 10-foot-long rows. The rows should be 4 feet apart.

The second summer after planting, immediately after the harvest is finished, set your lawn mower blade at 2½ inches and mow the bed. Rake out all the debris to reveal the unshorn crowns of the strawberry plants. Then, narrow the width of the rows to 12 inches by tilling under the plants on the edges. This is easy to do if you have one of the smaller rotary tillers. It's also a good opportunity to work in several inches of manure as a nitrogen source. After applying manure, water the bed and mulch the plants. The remaining plants will vigorously send out runners throughout the rest of the summer and will produce a great crop the following year.

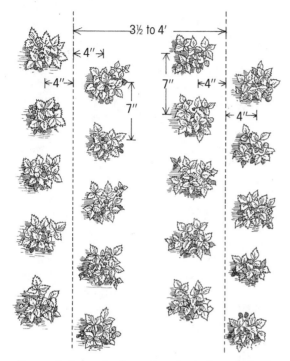

Day-neutral strawberries perform best when planted by a special method developed at Cornell University. Start by planting double rows of strawberries spaced 3½ to 4 feet apart. Four inches on each side of the centerline of the double rows, space strawberry plants 7 inches apart, staggering them so they don't line up side-by-side. Remove runners the first year, then allow the runners to fill in during the following growing season. Renovate the bed the third or fourth season.

Every year, renovate the bed this way. Keep renovating until the productivity of the bed seems to have declined, then start a new patch elsewhere with new plants.

Best bet for everbearing strawberries: Everbearers are best grown by the hill method, since midsummer renovation of the bed (as required for the matted row system) would destroy the fall crop. Everbearers produce fewer runners than Junebearers, anyhow, so it isn't a lot of work to keep up with the runner removal. Ten minutes every week-end should do it for 25 plants. Grown this way, you'll get luscious, large berries, which will have fewer disease problems because the crop will get good air circulation.

Set plants 1 foot apart in rows 2 feet apart. Remove all runners for the first two years. The third year, allow enough runners to root in the row to replace the mother plants, which will be overgrown because they have formed multiple crowns. Then remove the original plants after they have borne fruit in the fall. Apply fertilizer each year as soon as the spring harvest is finished.

Best bet for day-neutral strawberries: The best bet for day-neutral strawberries is a modification of the hill system that promises greater yields than traditional growing methods. For this system, which was developed by Dr. Marvin Pritts and his coworkers at Cornell University, start by planting double rows of strawberries spaced 3½ to 4 feet apart. Four inches on each side of the centerline of the double rows, space strawberry plants 7 inches apart, staggering them so they do not line up side by side.

Remove all flower buds for the first 6 weeks after planting and all the runners for the first season. Day-neutrals produce fewer runners than other strawberries so this won't be as much work as it sounds. Side-dress day-neutral strawberries with rotted manure once a month during the growing season.

Strawberries 101— Basic Care

Once you've settled on the plants you want to grow, and the method you're going to use to manage their growth, the rest is easy. All that's left is to select a spot for your strawberry patch, get the plants in the ground and growing, and wait for your first delicious harvest.

Planting and Feeding

Strawberries want full sun, sandy loam, and a pH of about 6.2, although they'll tolerate less than ideal conditions. Prepare the bed by tilling in 3 to 4 inches of well-rotted manure before planting time. Plant strawberries, which are almost always sold bare-root, in spring as soon as the ground has warmed. For most families, 25 strawberry plants is all you need to begin with. If you want a larger patch, you can increase the size using the plantlets formed by the runners.

Although it's best to get them into the ground as soon as they arrive, you can keep bare-root plants in the refrigerator for a few days until planting if weather or time don't cooperate. Be sure the packing material is moist but not soggy. When planting time comes, place the plants in a bucket of water and carry the bucket right out to the garden. This gives the plants a chance to rehydrate and protects them from drying out while you're planting.

Strawberry plants must be planted at just the right depth, with the crown just at the soil line. Make a deep planting hole with a cone of soil in the center to support the crown at the soil line and drape the roots down into the hole around the cone. Fill in the hole and surround with mulch. Double-check to make sure the crown isn't protruding too far above the soil or buried too deep.

Regrettably, you'll need to remove the flower buds of spring-planted strawberries so the plants can use all their energy in getting established. This means that June-bearers won't provide a harvest until a year after planting. For everbearers and day-neutral types, remove all the flower buds that form up until July 1. First-year everbearers will produce a sizable late-summer crop, and day-neutrals will produce from midsummer through fall. In the South, you can plant any kind of strawberry in fall and expect a full harvest the next growing season without having to remove any buds.

Care through the Seasons

Vigilant weed control is essential to success, or aggressive perennial weeds will outcompete shallow-rooted strawberry plants. It helps to lay down a thick mulch of straw around the plants during summer.

After the ground has frozen in winter, cover the strawberries with fresh straw, pine boughs, or spunbonded fabric to protect them from alternate freezing and thawing that can heave plants from the soil. (In climates where a snow cover remains through the winter, strawberries need no special winter mulch.) Pull the mulch away in early spring so the ground can warm up, but reapply the mulch close to the plants in time to smother weeds. Leave spunbonded fabric on over winter and into spring, but remove it when flowers form so bees will be able to pollinate the blossoms.

Because old strawberry plants become unproductive after from three to five years, strawberry plants must be replaced entirely from time to time. It's usually best to begin a new plot in a different part of the garden to avoid any disease buildup that might have occurred in the previous spot. Because certain strawberry cultivars are extremely susceptible to verticillium wilt, a prime enemy of vegetables such as potatoes, eggplants, and tomatoes, grow only resistant cultivars where these vegetables have grown in the last three years and vice versa. Even if the plants seem healthy, they may be harboring the soilborne fungus without showing any symptoms. The fungus may be lurking in the soil, just waiting to pounce on a susceptible victim, so beware!

Care-Free Alpine Strawberries

Scrumptious, tiny, intensely flavored fruits of the alpine strawberry, an ever-bearing form of the *fraise-des-boise* or wild wood-strawberry (*Fragaria vesca*) can be yours for the picking. And that's probably the only way you'll ever get them because these delectable fruits are too perishable and too sparsely produced to make it as a market crop. These gourmet fruits are easy to grow and manage because they do not form runners. Ideal for naturalizing along the sunny edge of a woods or a shrub border, alpines also make a tidy evergreen edging along a flower bed.

Begin a planting of alpine strawberries from seed started indoors—the seeds are slow to germinate and require coddling—or from crown divisions or purchased plants. Rich, moist soil is best. Fruits form the first summer after planting. Established plants bear from spring through fall, but never produce a large harvest at one time. Picking every other day or so will yield enough gourmet fruit to top your cereal or ice cream. Be sure the berries are soft and fully ripe—you'll be able to smell their aroma as you kneel near the bed—or they will be tasteless.

Because they produce no runners, alpine strawberries are easy to manage. However, seeds from fallen fruits germinate readily and can overcrowd a planting. Thin out the oldest plants each year.

Marjorie Harris, a gardener in San Francisco, has naturalized alpine strawberries in her garden, letting them grow wherever they like. She claims the birds don't eat the fruit, though occasionally her dog takes a nibble! She doesn't pay much attention to the plants, but they bear for months on end and are pretty and neat. Hers started with a packet of 'Baron Solemacher' seed some years ago and have been adorning the garden ever since. Because Marjorie found growing regular strawberries was too much trouble when she could purchase inexpensive, good-tasting strawberries at the market, she opted to instead grow the easy-care alpines for their special taste, wine-red color, and ease of care, which make up for the low yields.

Alpine strawberries are hardy from Zones 3 through 10 and will probably naturalize anywhere soil and sun conditions are favorable.

Strawberry Ailments

The worst things that can go wrong with your strawberries are fungal diseases: verticillium wilt and red stele, which infect the roots, and gray mold, which will rot the berries. Verticillium wilt and red stele are often carried in on new plants and are exacerbated by heavy, wet soil. Once plants are infected, the only recourse is to remove and destroy afflicted plants. Fortunately, there are cultivars that are resistant to both diseases. In addition to looking for resistant cultivars, it's a good idea to buy certified virus-free plants as well. They are definitely worth the extra cost because the plants are more vigorous and productive. (See the list of recommended cultivars in the encyclopedia section near the end of the book.)

Wet, humid weather and overcrowded beds with poor air circulation are the perfect invitation for gray mold. During wet or humid weather, pick out diseased berries every day to prevent the mold from spreading to ripening berries. It's best to cull the moldy berries, wash your hands, and then pick the ripe berries, to avoid spreading the mold spores to ripening fruits with your fingers.

By far the worst insect pest plaguing strawberries is the tarnished plant bug. The nymphs of this bug puncture developing fruits and suck out their juices, injecting a toxic substance in the process. The injured berries don't grow or ripen properly, but remain small and woody or form hard, seedy tips. This pest is worst in beds where nearby weeds can harbor the insect. For serious infestations, apply ryania or sabadilla dust (make sure sabadilla dust is approved for use on strawberries in your state before using).

Birds can also take a toll on strawberries. To keep birds from pecking at the berries, cover plants with netting.

Bountiful Brambles

If I could grow only one fruit, it would, without a doubt, be red raspberries. Or maybe blackberries. If I lived in southern California,

Strawberry Growing Tips

Strawberries are one of the easiest fruits to grow, and these tips will make them even more foolproof.

- Perennial weeds, especially grass, can ruin a strawberry planting. Keep them out by careful bed preparation and mulching.
- Overcrowded beds are susceptible to mildew and other fungal diseases.
- Strawberries need an inch of water a week throughout the growing season. Drip irrigation is the best method.
- Excessive overhead watering and rain during fruit ripening result in flabby, tasteless fruits.
- Spunbonded row covers make an excellent year-round protection, warding off winter cold, encouraging large early harvests, and keeping out pests such as aphids.
- Nitrogen applied during fruiting results in overly soft berries that are susceptible to mold.
- Pick ripe berries every other day to keep mold from invading and sweeping through the entire bed. Always remove all ripe berries and any infected or malformed ones to prevent disease invasion and spread.

I know it would be boysenberries. Because bramble fruits ship and store poorly and are labor-intensive to harvest, these fragile and highly perishable fruits practically cost their weight in gold at the market—and even then are usually half-spoiled by the time I get them home. I buy raspberries only for special treats and then mourn every soggy, moldy berry I find stashed at the bottom of the container. Homegrown ones taste even more luscious than anything you can buy and are less likely to go soft before you eat them. Although a little more demanding than blueberries, raspberries and blackberries are basically easy to grow and trouble-free in the home garden.

Selecting Brambles

The brambles are a prickly group of berry plants, all of which belong to the genus *Rubus*. They fall into two main groups, raspberries and blackberries, which are divided according to characteristics of the fruit. Both bear berries that actually consist of a cluster of small, jewel-like fruits with seeds in them, called drupelets. The drupelets are clustered on a thimble-shaped receptacle. When you pick raspberries, the receptacle remains on the plant, leaving a hollow-centered cluster of drupelets, or fruits. When you pick blackberries, the fruits and receptacle remain attached, so the berry has a solid center and you eat the receptacle as part of the berry.

Raspberries

The raspberries include red raspberries and yellow raspberries, which grow similarly. Black raspberries and purple raspberries also fall within this group. Purple raspberries are a hybrid between red and black raspberries.

Blackberries

Blackberries are stiff, upright plants, for the most part, but there are thornless black-berries that have trailing canes. This group also includes dewberries, boysenberries, and loganberries, all of which are trailing types.

Bramble Management

Raspberries and blackberries have many characteristics in common, but grow differently enough to make sorting out their individual cultural needs seem difficult at first. One reason for the confusion is that some raspberry types are grown more like blackberries and vice versa. If you ignore their names and pay attention to their growth habits instead, it becomes apparent how to best train and control their growth.

All cultivated brambles find a common denominator in the biennial growth pattern of their canes, or shoots, and in the plant's tendency to form great thickets if left uncontrolled.

Although the roots of each plant live indefinitely, each bramble cane lives for only two years. In the first year, a new cane sprouts from the crown and grows through the summer. It forms flower buds in the fall that will bear the following year's fruit. First year canes are called primocanes. The next year, the cane, now termed a floricane, flowers and bears fruit. It then dies by the end of the season.

I've never known any rule not to have an exception, and so it is with raspberries. Everbearing red and yellow raspberries produce two crops of berries, one in summer and one in fall. The fall berry crop develops at the tips of the primocanes, which then overwinter and fruit again the following summer before dying back. The summer crop is borne lower down on the stems.

To make up for their short-lived canes, brambles employ several ingenious ways to increase in size and invade new territory. Some, notably red raspberries, send up nu-

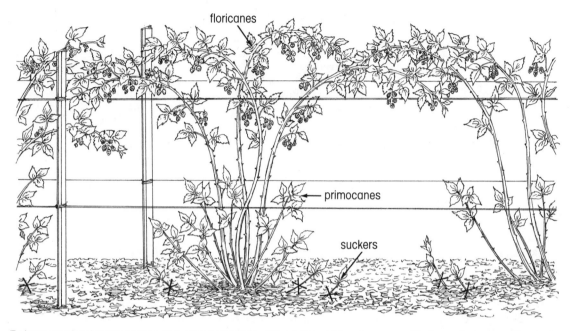

To keep raspberries productive and easy to harvest, cut out the old bearing canes (floricanes) at ground level after harvest to make way for the new growth (primocanes) that will bear next year. Routinely remove suckers that sprout outside the confines of the trellis to discourage junglelike growth.

merous suckers from the roots. The flexible canes of other brambles also bend over to the ground where they root and form new plantlets. Thus, brambles can march along, covering territory at a rapid pace.

Two Training Rules

Regardless of the type of bramble you're growing, if you let two cardinal rules govern your methods, the berries will be easy to care for and highly productive.

1. Always cut off floricanes at ground level soon after you've finished harvesting the fruit. This allows the new primocanes to receive abundant light and air, which encourages a bumper harvest the following year.
2. Ruthlessly rogue out stray suckers and thin out primocanes to the recommended spacing. This prevents overcrowding, which causes small, inferior berries and also encourages disease.

Trellising Brambles

Tying thorny bramble canes to a trellis may seem like a pain to weekend gardeners, especially when they find out that many people

Brambles Made Easy

Type	Growth and Training	Culture
Red raspberry. Fruit is sweet and fragrant. Best eaten fresh or frozen.	Long slender canes grow 5–6 ft. tall. Numerous suckers require weekly attention. Confine within 2-wire trellis in a hedgerow. Tie floricanes to wires, allow primocanes to grow in row center. Thin to best 4 primocanes per sq. ft. each spring. Cut out floricanes after harvest.	Best in cool climates; Zones 3–7 on East Coast; Zone 9 in coastal areas of West. Needs even moisture and 6 or more hours sun. Both everbearing and summer-bearing cultivars available. Everbearers are the only raspberry that can be grown for fall crop in Zone 8 in East.
Yellow raspberry. Fruit is very sweet. Golden color less attractive to birds than red fruit.	Plants grow and are trained like red raspberries.	Same as red raspberry.
Black raspberry (black-caps). Fruit more tart and flavorful than red raspberries; bears twice as much. Harvest before berries turn dull black. Good jam and fresh eating.	Plants have arching or trailing stems with numerous side branches that bear fruit. No suckers. New plants form where side branch tips meet soil. Plant 3–4 ft. apart. Cut off tips of primocanes when they reach 2 ft. tall to encourage more fruiting side branches. Cut side branches to 1 ft. in late winter.	More heat-tolerant than red raspberries. More disease-susceptible than reds. Tolerates some shade in hot climates. Zones 5 and 6–8, depending on cultivar.
Purple raspberry. Large, strong tasting, sweet berries are dark reddish purple. Good fresh or preserved.	Similar to red raspberry. A cross between red and black raspberries.	Similar to red raspberry. More cold-hardy than black raspberries. Zones 4 and 5–8, depending on cultivar.
Blackberry. Large, glossy black fruits a bit less sweet and stronger tasting than raspberries. Ripen after raspberries. Great fresh, frozen, or for jams and jellies.	Stiff, upright stems with numerous side branches. Forms fewer suckers than raspberries; plantlets grow where branch tips touch the soil. Vicious thorns. No trellis needed for upright types. Trellis trailing types as for dewberries. Cut primocanes back to 3 ft. in midsummer to induce branching and more fruit. Cut side branches back to 1 ft. in spring. Remove canes at soil level after fruiting. Thin canes in spring to 6 in. apart.	More heat- and drought-tolerant than raspberries. Zones 5–8. Thornless cultivars are available, but need trellising and are susceptible to animal damage.

Type	Growth and Training	Culture
Dewberry. Fruit is glossy black, sweet-tart, and larger than fruit of bush black-berries. Delicious fresh or preserved.	Long, trailing stems. Does not sucker. Plant 8–12 ft. apart. Tie floricanes to a 2-wire trellis in late winter. Allow primocanes to grow along the ground in summer; prune to 10 ft. long in late winter and loop over trellis.	Less hardy than upright black-berries; grow in Zones 6–9 in the South and West. Prefers some shade during hottest part of day.
Boysenberry. Large, luscious- tasting, wine-colored berries. Large seeds. Good fresh or in pies or jam.	Similar to dewberry.	Similar to dewberry. Grow in West only; Zones 8–9. Disease-susceptible on East Coast. Thornless cultivars available.
Loganberry. Long, wine-colored berries with strong, slightly tart flavor.	Similar to dewberry.	Similar to dewberry. Grow in West only; Zones 8–9. Disease-susceptible on East Coast.
Tayberry. Hybrid between raspberry and blackberry. Fruit is dark purple with fruity, sweet-tart taste.	Similar to dewberry. Plant 6 ft. apart.	Similar to dewberry. Very productive. Zones 5–8.

take a more casual attitude toward growing these berries. Although brambles can be left to grow anyway they please, these unruly plants do much better when disciplined. All brambles, with the exception of bush (upright or erect) blackberries, produce better and are easier to manage in the long run if supported by a wire trellis. Trellising simplifies pruning and harvesting, which saves you time later on. It also exposes the plants' foliage to more sunlight and air, which encourages vigorous growth and higher yields and also reduces fungal diseases. Because trel-lised canes are up off the ground, berries are within easy reach and there's no need to stoop and stretch to get at the harvest.

Most brambles need a sturdy, perma-nent trellis that will last for many years.

Fall-cropped raspberries need only a tem-porary trellis to keep the weight of the rip-ening crop from bending the canes to the ground.

Fortunately, once the permanent trellis is installed, most of your work is done. The yearly pruning and training actually takes little time and fits into a Saturday morning's schedule with no noticeable complaints.

Best Bet for Upright Brambles

Red and yellow raspberries, along with semi-trailing blackberry cultivars, which all have tall flexible canes, respond well to trellising. Though they may seem to be stand-ing up just fine all on their own, once the branches become laden with ripening fruit, they bend toward the ground, creating a tangle, dirtying the fruits, and offering them to slugs and other pests. To remedy this, some growers advocate pruning the tops off raspberry canes in the spring to encourage sturdier growth that will stand up by itself. Don't do this! The cane tips bear heavily, so you'll just be reducing the harvest. Better to use a simple wire trellis to keep the canes upright.

Probably half a dozen popular trellising methods exist for brambles, adding further to the confusion about cultivating these berries. Avoid methods that require you to tie the canes to an overhead wire—such methods require more work than is necessary. Bunching up canes around a single stake is also a bit too much work and doesn't produce particularly remarkable yields.

The easiest method, and one of the highest yielding, seems to be to grow the berries in a hedgerow, anchored in place by four wires suspended from posts. First, plant the raspberries 2½ feet apart in a long row. Then build the trellis, using pairs of 8-foot-long metal posts driven into the ground on either side of the row. Beginning at one end of the row, space pairs of posts every 20 to 25 feet. The pairs should be spaced about 2½ feet apart. Drive the posts into the ground about 2 feet deep, and suspend wires the length of each side of the row at about 2½ feet and 5 feet high.

The canes that grow up within the defined space will lean against the wires and be supported without needing to be tied. Although some growers tie the primocanes to one side of the trellis and the floricanes to the other to facilitate pruning and harvesting, I think this is more work

than really necessary for good harvest and ease of care.

Every week during the growing season, walk along the row and tuck in any wayward canes and yank out any suckers growing beyond the limits of the hedgerow. Each year in late winter or early spring, before growth begins, thin the brambles by removing weak or damaged canes. The remaining canes should be spaced 4 to 6 inches apart. The thickest canes will produce the most berries.

Best Bet for Trailing Brambles

Trailing blackberries, dewberries, boysenberries, and loganberries, along with purple and black raspberries, don't even make a pretense of standing upright. They must be trellised or else you'll have a mess. Erect posts at 10- to 15-foot intervals, and suspend wires at 3 feet and 5 feet. Stems of trailing blackberries can grow to 15 feet long, so they need plenty of space. Space the plants 5 to 6 feet apart down the middle of the wires. These brambles do not send up suckers so will not fill in the row like raspberries and upright blackberries.

Allow the primocanes to grow along the ground during the first year. Leave them on the ground over winter, but before growth begins, lift the canes off the ground and fan them out over the top wire, separating and spreading individual canes. Once these canes have flowered and fruited, cut them off at ground level, and lift the newly developed primocanes off the ground and loop them over the trellis. In cold-winter climates, leave primocanes on the ground all winter and

The Easiest Bramble Method of All

Everbearing raspberries—both the red and yellow types—can be grown as a single-crop fall berry without any trellising or selective pruning. This is the easiest way of all for weekend gardeners to grow raspberries. And it makes sense, too: If you're growing summer-bearing fruits such as blueberries, currants, or strawberries you can stagger your harvest—and work—through fall with a large crop of fall raspberries. When everbearing raspberries are grown as a single-crop fall berry, the yields are staggering.

Culture is as simple as can be. Space plants 2½ feet apart and allow them to fill in a 1½-foot-wide hedgerow, removing suckers sprouting outside the row. Each year, cut off all the canes at ground level in late winter while they're still dormant. That's all the maintenance they need. Gardeners short on time take note: The primocanes that develop over summer don't need any pruning, thinning, or trellising! Because older canes that might harbor diseases and insects are removed, pest problems are minimal.

The fall crop, borne at the tips of the primocanes, produces ripe berries for a month, usually in September. The yield is especially heavy because all the plant's energy goes to one crop rather than being shared with a summer harvest.

'Heritage', a much-revered everbearing red raspberry, adapts well to single-crop culture and is suitable to most raspberry-growing regions. However, more and more everbearing cultivars are being bred purposefully for fall harvesting. These do not do well if grown for the traditional two crops produced by earlier everbearing cultivars. When selecting a raspberry for a fall crop, be sure that the harvest will ripen before frost. Breeding programs for northern growers offer early-ripening fruits. In warmer climates, you might plant two cultivars—one early- and one later-fruiting plant—for a long, bountiful harvest.

cover with straw or leaf mulch. Thin out the primocanes in late winter to the strongest 10 or so per hill, cut these back to 10 feet long, and loop them around the trellis.

Brambles 101—Basic Care

All brambles grow and produce best in good soil with plenty of moisture, although blackberries, especially dewberries, will tolerate somewhat poor soil and drought. A fast-draining loamy soil is ideal; they do not like wet feet and are susceptible to root rot in soggy soil. An inch of water a week during the growing season, either from rain or irrigation, produces the best crop. Drip irrigation is ideal for supplemental watering because berries wetted by rain or overhead watering soak up the water, diluting their flavor.

Applying a deep organic mulch at the beginning of the growing season pays off by keeping the soil moist and suffocating weeds. Because their roots are shallow, cultivating to control weeds can injure brambles. Each spring before growth starts, pull back the organic mulch and spread a shovelful of rotted manure or compost over the ground around each plant. Replace and renew the mulch. This is all the fertilizing the plants need.

Bramble Ailments

Viral diseases are probably responsible for the rapid decline of many brambles. There's not much you can do to avoid viral infection, because prevalent insects carry the virus about from one plant to another. By purchasing certified virus-free plants, you will at least have a head start on viral diseases and perhaps will get a year or two extra from your planting. Resist the temptation to lift extra plants from a friend, because the most serious diseases—virus and verticillium wilt, which is caused by a fungus—can be carried to your garden this way. Certified virus-free stock will cost more, but the payoff can't be measured by mere dollars and cents. It is measured by an index of time invested and frustration experienced.

Though brambles do get their share of fungal diseases and insects, many are easily avoided by practicing good sanitation. Cut out and remove any sick-looking canes as soon as you spot them. Borers can cause stems to wilt, but removing the wilted canes as soon as you notice them checks their progress. Do not compost prunings of healthy or diseased canes; either burning them or putting them out for trash collection is the safest way to prevent disease or insect problems.

Wild brambles can spread pests to cultivated types, so eradicate any wild cousins growing on or near your property if possible. It's advisable to locate black raspberries at least 300 feet from red ones. Insects may carry virus from resistant reds to the more susceptible blacks. And a final warning to the vigilant gardener: Black raspberries are highly susceptible to verticillium wilt, so do not grow them where tomatoes, potatoes, eggplants, asparagus, strawberries, or other raspberries have grown in recent years.

Currants and Gooseberries— As Easy as Pie

Growing currants and gooseberries is as easy as pie. Practically trouble-free and needing very little care, these favorite fruits of Grandpa's garden and Grandma's kitchen will deliver plenty of makings for gooseberry pie and currant jelly. And you can practically ignore them except come harvest time—early summer for currants, mid-summer for gooseberries. Neither fruit is readily available at the market, so they make ideal fruits for home cultivation. Another plus is that some folks find that birds pass up currants and gooseberries; others, however, find their crops gobbled up if not protected by netting. Currants and gooseberries are extremely cold-hardy (to Zone 3), a decided advantage if you live in the far North.

An elderly neighbor of mine first introduced me to currants. She had an ancient patch of them growing in a shady and truly neglected corner of her yard, out by her chicken coop. (Yes, even though this was in suburbia, we had chickens and a rooster alarm clock next door.) Our neighbor had about ten 5-foot-tall plants, which she had left to fend for themselves. They were growing in a very shady spot overgrown with wild grape vines and native locust trees. Perhaps as a way of making amends for the rooster, she cheerfully offered us the pickings of the currants. "They'll be ripe on the Fourth of July, so just come on over and help yourselves." And help ourselves we did, filling container after container with fruits. Though neglected and shaded, the plants produced prolific strands of sparkling red berries, which we easily made into beautiful jelly.

In our next garden, Mark and I planted two currant bushes in a semi-shaded spot. They grew quite well, readily producing fruit, which, in keeping with tradition, I harvested each year on the Fourth of July. Like blueberries, ripe currants keep well on the bush—for as long as a week—making them good for weekend gardeners. However, they do not keep well once picked and should be used right away. I found that when I was pressed for time and couldn't make the treasured jelly right away, it was simple to freeze the unwashed berries in a plastic container. I probably shouldn't admit this, but our first year's harvest was so small that I froze the berries and forgot about them for an entire year. They seemed perfectly fine after a year of cold storage, so I added them to the second year's still-meager harvest and had enough to make several jars of jelly.

Selecting Currants and Gooseberries

Members of the *Ribes* genus, these close cousins have the same cultural requirements. Each offers fruits of varied colors. Fruits of currants and gooseberries are beautiful, translucent berries that catch the light and sparkle in the sun like jewels. They are almost too pretty to pick.

One word of warning, however: These species are alternate hosts of white pine blister rust, a serious disease of white pine and its five-needled relatives. The fungi cause bright orange spots on currant or gooseberry leaves in summer. Although it only weakens these plants, which can harbor the fungus indefinitely, the disease kills pine trees. For this reason, many states have outlawed growing currants and gooseberries in areas where white pine is an important timber tree. Check with your county agricultural Extension agent before purchasing currants or gooseberries. Even if growing currants is legal in your state, you may not wish to plant them if susceptible pines adorn your property.

Black currants are more susceptible than red currants to white pine blister rust. Rust-resistant cultivars are available, so I'd go for these to be on the safe side, or even opt for growing a different fruit if you have cherished pines in your garden. If you have white pines or their relatives on your property, and you feel you must have currants or gooseberries, plant them at least 500 feet away from the pines. This spacing should prevent the disease from hopping from the currants to the pines. It's also a good idea to rake up and destroy leaves of currants or gooseberries at the end of the season, because they can harbor the disease over the winter.

Currants

Currants may be red, black, or white. Fully ripe red currants (*Ribes sativum*) taste tart-sweet and can be eaten out-of-hand, but are more traditionally used to make jelly. They are my favorite because they look so beautiful and their generous juice makes such fine jelly. White currants, which are actually pale yellow, are a cultivated form of red currants.

Black currants (*Ribes nigrum*) are a prized European fruit that is not so well known or liked here. Black currants taste strongly of musk and are meatier and less juicy. Some people take an instant dislike to the fresh fruit, but black currant jam is a prized commodity.

Individual currant berries are comparatively small—save yourself needless frustration and pick the entire cluster. Don't bother to remove the stems when making jelly; they'll be caught in the cheesecloth when you strain it. Be sure, too, that not all berries are ripe, because underripe berries contain more pectin, which makes the jelly jell.

Gooseberries

Gooseberries are much larger than currants —about the size of a grape—and have dark-striped skin that may be yellowish green, purplish, or reddish. Although quite tart before they're ripe, fully ripe berries of modern cultivars are sweet. Green-fruited gooseberry cultivars are tarter than purple-fruited ones, which have a taste reminiscent of rhubarb. Some people prefer fruits with a bit of pucker-power and pick unripe berries for pies. Because they ripen over a period of a month or more and can be enjoyed green or ripe depending on your preference, pick gooseberries singly. Some gooseberry cultivars have thorny branches, so pick berries carefully. Gooseberries make fine pie, cobblers, and tarts.

Currants and Gooseberries 101—Basic Care

Both currants and gooseberries thrive in filtered shade, especially in areas with hot summers. Space plants 5 feet apart, in rows 7 or 8 feet apart. The plants grow best in soil that is fertile and deeply mulched, but they tolerate both heavy and sandy soil as long as it is moist but not wet. Apply rotted manure or compost each spring as a mulch and it will supply all the nutrition these plants need.

Prune out older stems at ground level every year, removing the four-year-old canes and leaving behind the more productive younger canes. Such simple pruning is supposed to be essential, but as our neighbor's neglected old red currant plants demonstrated, no harm will come if you slip up a bit on the pruning. Pruning to keep the plants open will discourage fungal diseases, however. Grow currants and gooseberries in Zones 3 to 7.

Red currants and gooseberries are self-fertile; some black currants—notably the rust-resistant cultivars—may require cross-pollination and do not always set a good crop of fruit. A mature currant plant will produce 2 to 3 quarts of berries annually;

gooseberries produce 3 to 4 quarts, so there's no need to plant but a few unless you're into the jelly and pie business in a big way.

Maintenance-Free Bush Cherries

Homemade cherry pie—the kind that is slightly tart and not too gooey, the kind only a home cook can bake—is my absolute favorite dessert. But until recently I thought home cherry growing—especially when it means standing on step ladders to grasp whatever fruit is within reach, shooing away birds, and worrying about which disease will attack first—was simply not worth it for gardeners short on time.

Fortunately, my prayers have been answered. There are two new, easy-care pie cherries just perfect for weekend gardeners. Both stay small enough to make harvesting simple, resist disease, and, amazingly enough, fail to attract birds. Developed by plant hybridizer Elwyn H. Meader, 'Jan' and 'Joy' bush cherries are hybrids of Japanese bush cherry (*Prunus japonica*) and Himalayan cherry (*P. jaquemontii*). Although they bear fruits almost indistinguishable in flavor from the beloved pie cherry (*P. cerasus*) 'Montmorency', the similarity stops there. These new bush cherries grow into 3- to 4-foot-tall shrubs rather than 25-foot-tall trees, and the fruits ripen in the fall rather than early summer.

One of Dr. Meader's breeding goals was to develop a cherry plant compact enough to be easily covered with netting (the best of the genetic dwarf tart cherry trees grow 8 to 10 feet tall), but he outdid himself with 'Jan' and 'Joy'. Ironically, although they grow to the perfect size for efficient bird-proofing, birds leave the fruits untouched, perhaps because they ripen so late. So you needn't fuss with bird-proofing when growing 'Jan' and 'Joy'.

These cherries have many other advantages to offer weekend gardeners—they are a decidedly low-maintenance version of a high-maintenance plant. 'Jan' and 'Joy' resist powdery mildew and Japanese beetles. They also don't get brown rot, which plagues tree cherries. Wormy fruit is never a problem either; due to the different ripening period, the fruits just aren't around during worm-attack season.

These attractive shrubs can double as a hedge or border in a landscape planting. Their blossoms are simply gorgeous, as are the ripening clusters of bright red fruits. Space young plants 8 to 10 feet apart in good soil. You'll need to plant 'Jan' and 'Joy' in pairs, since both are required to ensure cross-pollination, which is necessary for good fruit set. Use a thick mulch to retain moisture and deter weeds. Though drought-tolerant, bush cherries bear best if given supplemental moisture during dry spells. They are adaptable in Zones 4 to 8.

'Jan' and 'Joy' require no demanding pruning; remove wayward or broken branches during the dormant season and prune older plants as you would blueberries, by removing the least productive older canes.

When gleaming red, bush cherries are quite tart—just like pie cherries—and need to be sweetened and cooked into pies, tarts, and jam. But if you don't get around to harvesting, the cherries just hang onto the bush and begin to concentrate sugar as they shrivel. According to nurseryman Michael McConkey of Edible Landscaping Nursery, who first introduced 'Jan' and 'Joy' to the public, they may look past their prime, but the raisin-like dried cherries taste delicious and can be eaten right from the bush during fall and into winter.

Don't confuse 'Jan' and 'Joy' bush cherries with Nanking cherries (*Prunus tomentosa*) or with 'Hansen' sand cherry (*Prunus besseyi* 'Hansen'). Both are very hardy and attractive shrubs that make excellent hedges and produce tart, cherrylike fruits. But the similarity stops there. Their summer-ripening fruits are devoured by birds and are highly susceptible to brown rot. And if any cherries are left for you, you'll find them smaller and containing larger seeds than real cherries, requiring laborious picking and pitting. 'Jan' and 'Joy' are just as large as regular tart cherries. To save yourself some time, pop the cherries into a cherry pitter come picking and pie-making time.

A Final Word

Whatever fruits and berries you choose to grow, there are some simple steps you can take to reduce the maintenance and improve your results. When you select plants, make your choices carefully. Choose fruit types, cultivars, and techniques suited to your garden's site and climate. Look for disease- and insect-resistant cultivars when they're available. Weigh the care and maintenance the plants will require against the time and effort you want to devote to your garden. Keep in mind that harvesting isn't all reward—it takes time and effort—and ripe fruits simply won't wait until you have time to harvest and preserve them. Limiting the number of plants you grow helps reduce the chores, too. Finally, if you devote particular attention to preparing the soil before you plant, most berry plants will get off to a good start and reward your minimal efforts with tasty crops.

Although berry plants aren't without their care needs, they are certainly easier to grow and more forgiving of neglect than fruit trees. I asked my friend Keith recently if he was removing the runners from his strawberries as he had intended. His answer: "I would if I had time." Fortunately, the strawberries don't seem to mind.

CHAPTER

6

WOODLAND AND WILDFLOWER GARDENS

Easy-Care Natural Landscape Styles

Whenever I encounter a beautiful natural scene, I want to take it home with me so I can enjoy it over and over. Needless to say, I can't just order that gorgeous mountain scene or woodland waterfall from a catalog or garden center. What I *can* do is recreate the effect of the natural feature in my yard. So while I can't have the woods I loved as a child, I can have a woodland garden, featuring some of my favorite wildflowers, beneath the trees in a corner of my property.

Imitation is the most sincere form of flattery, and gardeners find they can imitate nature by recreating almost any type of naturalistic landscape in their gardens. Homemade versions of grassy meadows and fields of flowers, woodland wildflower walks, gurgling streams, and rough-and-tumble mountain peaks fall within the reach of the

imaginative gardener. Many of these naturalistic landscapes or gardens, especially woodland and meadow gardens, turn out to be ideal for weekend gardeners, because the sites require little maintenance. After all, whoever heard of a tidy woodland? Mother Nature doesn't sweep up, so why should you? The leaf-strewn ground, mossy stumps, and rock outcroppings of the forest floor add to its charm and its health, just as the leaf litter will add to your low-maintenance woodland garden.

If done properly—following the basic principles presented in this chapter—gardening naturalistically with well-adapted native plants offers a low-maintenance, ecologically sound alternative to pampering finicky hybrids and exotics. When naturalistic gardens replace large lawns, formal flower borders, or manicured hedges, the effect is enchanting and the result usually means less work for the gardener.

Bringing Nature Home: Natural Ideas for the Home Garden

There's a lot that we as gardeners can learn from nature, especially when it comes to low-maintenance weekend gardening. In fact, if you think about it, many of the most beautiful and memorable "gardens" are both completely natural and completely undemanding. Think of the early spring forest floor of a Tennessee woodland, where soft green light filters through emerging foliage and illuminates the blossoms of trillium and violets; picture an expanse of hundreds of thousands of lemon yellow desert dandelions stretching as far as the eye can see across the Mohave Desert; or imagine a pasture in Massachusetts where oxeye daisies dance in the wind, keeping rhythm with the bright orange and yellow hawkweed blossoms twisting on their wiry stems. Provided a housing development, new highway, or shopping center doesn't step in and spoil the site, these natural gardens will retain their beauty year after year.

A meadow, woodland, or other naturalistic landscape created by a gardener celebrates the best nature has to offer. Whether planted solely with native and naturalized plants, with exotics that are well adapted to the site, or with a combination of the two, such gardens add color and texture to the landscape and provide habitat for wildlife. Best of all, gardens that imitate nature offer a low-maintenance alternative for gardeners who would like to bring a touch of natu-

ral beauty to their landscapes.

Although these types of gardens require a minimum of care in the long run, as with any garden, naturalistic gardens demand an investment of time and energy in the early stages. To get off to a good start, a naturalistic landscape needs proper planning, planting, and care—especially in the first year or so. The payoff comes a few years down the road, once the well-adapted, long-lived plants you've installed have made themselves at home and can start taking care of themselves.

In this chapter, I'm going to describe how to create several types of easy-care natural, or naturalistic, landscapes that feature wildflowers and other native or well-adapted plants. To beautify a shaded spot under trees, you can grow a woodland garden of native shrubs and wildflowers. For open sunny areas, you'll learn how to start and maintain a flowery meadow or a garden of ornamental grasses. The most successful plants for inclusion in these sites are listed where appropriate throughout the chapter; you'll find their complete descriptions in the encyclopedia section near the end of the book.

Natural Landscaping Basics

There are a few basic principles that apply to any successful naturalistic landscape. Keep them in mind while planning and planting your garden, and you'll have a good chance of creating a garden that is both beautiful and low-maintenance.

Low-Work, Not No-Work

Everywhere you turn these days, it seems there's an article promoting some style of natural landscaping—meadow or prairie gardens, woodland wildflower walks, and even the so-called New American Garden of ornamental grasses. Many of the articles appearing in respectable horticultural publications deliver a pretty fair warning about the work involved in creating such gardens—and the problems that may arise. However, more often than not, general-interest magazines feature a collection of breathtaking photos accompanied by superficial instructions making it all seem as easy as pie. This hype can seduce you into making a great big mistake.

The most serious misconception being strewn about as freely as wildflower seed these days—both in the media and by overzealous (or unscrupulous) nursery owners—is that naturalistic plantings, especially meadow gardens, require no work. Although naturalistic gardens may—and often do—require less work than formal manicured gardens, they are decidedly not "no-work" gardening solutions. (Would that it were true!) As with many of the low-maintenance garden solutions in this book, naturalistic plantings demand a great deal of effort during their formative years. Proper soil preparation, planting, watering, and weeding are essential at the onset. Only when you've successfully nurtured the planting through the toddler years can you sit back and watch the garden fend for itself. Fortunately, most gardeners find the nurturing process satisfying in its own right.

Pick the Right Plants

The objective in a naturalistic landscape is to arrange plants in a design that's compatible with nature, matching the needs of the plants with the growing conditions the site has to offer naturally. A naturalistic garden will surely fulfill its easy-care mission if you select native plants—wildflowers, grasses, ferns, trees, shrubs, and vines—that are indigenous to your part of the country and naturally adapted to conditions similar to those your garden has to offer. In theory, such plantings are ecologically sound because native plants survive just fine in their natural habitats without applications of pesticides, chemical fertilizers, and artificial watering. Actually, native plants are no more immune to drought or outbreaks of insects and diseases than are well-adapted exotics. But they are often tougher and better able to endure extreme conditions than traditional garden plants selected more for beauty than adaptability. And, of course, native plants occur in nature only where conditions favor their growth—not where some hopeful gardener decided to put them.

Keep in mind that native plants and wildflowers will survive in your landscape only when they are planted in a situation that mimics their natural habitat. I've emphasized this over and over again but will say it one more time: Whether a so-called low-maintenance plant is a cultivated hybrid or a native species, it will live up to its "low-work" reputation only when provided with a climate and growing conditions that meet its needs. Plant a woodland wildflower in a sunny meadow and it will surely die. Plant a Texas bluebonnet in Vermont and it may not take hold.

If the growing conditions on your property duplicate a natural site in your region, you should be able to grow a naturalistic garden of wild plants on that site with little effort. Your basic task will be to select and plant the appropriate types of plants. Once they're established, they'll practically take care of themselves. Mark and I planted several woodland wildflower gardens beneath

Wildflower Vocabulary

According to Shakespeare, "A rose by any other name would smell as sweet." And to some, the same is true of wildflowers; as long as a plant looks pretty, it doesn't matter if it's technically a native plant or a naturalized species. But the following definitions should set you technically straight without taking away any of the beauty of the natural landscape.

Native plants. In technical jargon, native plants—herbaceous flowers, ferns, grasses, shrubs, trees, and vines—are those that originated in a specific geographical area and grow there naturally.

Naturalized plants. These are plants that were initially introduced to an area by man but have escaped cultivation and now grow in the wild without any further human assistance. Queen-Anne's-lace, a European native, is such a plant.

Wildflowers. No one will argue that the native showy herbaceous flowers of field and forest should be called wildflowers. Opinions differ, though, over whether naturalized flowers can properly be termed wildflowers. Usually, if naturalized flowers coexist with native ones without competing aggressively with them, most experts agree to lump them with the wildflowers.

Forbs. This term is used to describe wildflowers that are not grasses.

Warm-season grasses. Grasses that grow slowly during cool weather, put on rapid growth during the summer months, and go dormant or die to the ground during winter are called warm-season grasses.

Cool-season grasses. This term refers to grasses that go dormant during the heat of summer, sometimes even turning brown, and put on their major growth spurts during the cool spring and fall months, often remaining green during winter.

Weeds. Any plant growing where it is not wanted is technically a weed. Specifically, weeds are thought of as unsightly and aggressive plants. Plants that spread so rapidly as to displace native and naturalized plants or garden plants are called invasive weeds.

Indigenous plants. Plants that grow naturally in a particular area are said to be indigenous to that area.

Exotics. Non-native plants brought into cultivation from another geographical area—usually from another continent and/or a markedly different habitat—are called exotics. Exotics are often bred or hybridized to make them showier for the garden.

Cultivated plants. These are plants grown purposely by gardeners or farmers for their beauty or economic worth. Cultivated plants are often exotics and incapable of existing without human care.

high-branched groves of trees at two of our homes. The soil and shade conditions resembled those found in a forest, so all it took to turn the site into a wildflower garden was to introduce nursery-propagated wildflowers and ferns. In these woodlots at the corners of our property, I was able to grow the wildflowers that so delighted me from my childhood forays into the New England forests, recreating a miniature—but densely packed—version of a natural woodland.

If you want to remain a weekend gardener, don't fall into the trap of trying to create particular conditions where they don't exist naturally—an acid soil woodland where the conditions are naturally alkaline, for example. Such an approach takes a great deal more work, and the results may be disappointing. Better to enhance what you have rather than trying to create what you have not. Go with Nature, don't fight it.

Native or Naturalized?

When you're selecting plants for a naturalistic landscape, sooner or later the question of plant origin will come up. Just as the citizens of the United States represent a melting pot whose forefathers originated from the four corners of the world, so do the antecedents of some of America's most beloved wildflowers have their origins in other continents. Many common roadside wildflowers are actually European natives that immigrated with the Colonists, hitchhiking along as weed seed contained in the crop seed. Queen-Anne's-lace (*Daucus carota*), oxeye daisy (*Chrysanthemum leucanthemum*), and chicory (*Cichorium intybus*) are three such hitchhikers that have naturalized across the continent. On a farm or in a perennial border these flowers might be called weeds, but bedecking an empty lot or pasture or flourishing along a roadside, their pretty summer flowers become welcome wildflowers of the American landscape.

Some purists believe that naturalized plants have no place in a wildflower garden, preferring to include *only* those plants actually native to the region. Others think this extreme position is too rigid; after all, the immigrant plants now permanently reside here, thriving alongside the native sons. You'll need to decide for yourself if you want to include naturalized as well as native plants in your naturalistic landscape, but keep in mind that whether native or naturalized, your "wildflowers" will usually prove adaptable and easy to care for if sited properly.

Be careful what you plant, though, for other escaped plants are not as compatible with the native flora as the three mentioned above. Rampant growers let loose on the American landscape, such escapees as kudzu (*Pueraria lobata*) and Johnson grass (*Sorghum halapense*) have become pernicious weeds that are crowding out the more sedate native and naturalized plant life. Purple loosestrife (*Lythrum salicaria*) departed the confines of the flower bed for the wetlands of the East and upper Midwest and has there displaced thousands of acres of native plants. Some naturalists worry that the more widely we mass-plant seemingly well-behaved exotics in the natural landscape, such as in roadside plantings, the more potential for some other plant pest to be unleashed on the American landscape and crowd out our own beautiful native plants.

Designing with Nature

When designing any type of naturalistic garden, always keep an image of a natural landscape in your mind's eye. Let a close and careful observation of that landscape or ecosystem guide your artistic hand. Notice exactly how the various plants interact with each other: Do they grow in clumps or masses, intermingle with particular plants, weave in and out of each other, or grow up through one another? And remember, too, that the setting you create—the rocks and stones, fallen logs, paths, and groves of trees—adds as much to the natural garden as do the flowers. Keep these details in mind when planning and planting your naturalistic garden.

For a natural-looking effect, remember the simplicity of nature's gardens. You might want to arrange plants more thickly and in a more studied color combination than is found in the wild, but don't overdo it. In this sense, the gardener in you can come out, improving upon nature but never straying too far from your source of inspiration.

Wildflowers charm and delight us because their presence is so unexpected. Roadside flowers brighten our days; woodland flowers entice and surprise us as we wend our way along a trail. As you design and plant your garden, try to capture some of nature's unexpected, unplanned feeling in your own naturalistic landscape. Native plants and wildflowers add a graceful, gentle beauty to a garden, but bear in mind that their beauty is easily overshadowed by more flashy hybridized plants if the two are combined. It's usually best to keep wildflowers and garden hybrids in separate gardens of their own. Combine them only if their characters seem visually compatible.

Protecting Our Natural Heritage

Whatever type of naturalistic weekend landscape or garden you create, don't forget that digging plants in the wild and bringing them home to your garden is a sin! Our native plants, no matter how abundant they seem, belong to the wild—digging them up threatens their very existence. Leave them to prosper and delight others. Purchase wildflowers only from reputable growers who provide assurance that the wildflowers have been propagated in their nursery. It's a tragedy, but according to native plant expert Judy Glattstein, most of the wildflowers sold by so-called wildflower specialists or other mail-order nurseries were dug up from the wild. Though some wildflowers may be commercially propagated by seed, division, cuttings, or tissue culture, the propagation process takes a fairly long time, and the resulting plants may be expensive. Unscrupulous wildflower dealers often collect native plants from the wild by the hundreds and thousands. This practice ravages populations of wildflowers, which, in addition to depletion by wild collections, are also being robbed of their habitats by development.

Please be cautious and conservation-minded when purchasing native plants. It's sometimes tempting to order plants dug from the wild. While such plants may be incredibly inexpensive (sometimes selling for as little as 50 cents apiece), resist the temptation! If your conscience can't restrain you, then consider this: Wild-dug plants more often than not do not survive transplanting to your garden. They'll arrive in the mail dried out, wilted, and practically rootless. And some species, most notably pink lady's-slipper (*Cypripedium acaule*), are almost impossible to establish in a garden because they depend upon a complex relationship with a specific soil fungus to flourish. Nursery-grown plants adapt much better, and in the long run they're a better bargain, both for you and for our country's natural areas.

Sometimes it's not clear whether the

Wildflower Rescue Missions

When road construction, a housing development, or a condominium project threatens a woodland habitat, a rescue mission may be justified. Then again, it may not. Be cautious before rushing in and digging up plants. Get permission from the developer first, and then be certain that the plants you are "rescuing" will actually be destroyed during construction. Oftentimes, even though homes are built, much of the natural landscape remains, especially in environmentally conscious communities. Don't simply use the pending development as justification to collect wild plants. It is a far better conservation measure to leave native plants growing in their natural habitats than to transplant them to a garden.

If you are sure development will destroy the wild plants, the best alternative is to move them to a botanical garden or nature center where they will have a permanent home and proper nurturing. Another alternative is to give the rescued plants to a local nursery devoted to producing nursery-propagated wildflowers. The plants can become part of their permanent breeding stock. A spot in a home garden should be the last resort—families move and gardeners come and go, so a home garden site may not provide the best assurance of preserving the endangered plants. But preserving native plants in a naturalistic garden is a better choice than allowing their destruction.

If rare or endangered plants occupy the site slated for development, don't dig them up yourself, because you may only be hurrying their demise. Notify your state's Department of Conservation, a local wildflower society, or the Nature Conservancy office in your state. You may be able to stop the development, or at least get the plants properly rescued by professionals who can move them to a botanical garden or nature preserve. But preserving endangered plants in a botanical garden is akin to keeping rare animals in a zoo. Far better to allow them to roam and reproduce in their naturally wild habitat.

When rescuing native plants in the wild, keep the following practices in mind.

• Early spring is the best time to move plants. Fall is second best.

• Cut into the soil with a spade, making a circle just beneath the plant's leaf canopy to get the right size root ball. Too large a soil ball may fall apart, injuring the roots.

• Wrap the root ball tightly in several layers of wet newspapers and then wrap it in plastic, or place it directly into a pot filled with native soil.

• If plants wilt immediately after digging, water the roots and enclose the entire plant in a plastic bag. Keep plants cool and shaded until planting.

• When transplanting shrubs, trim off a comparable amount of top growth to compensate for lost roots.

• Replant as soon as possible, in soil and sun conditions similar to those where the plant was found. Keep moist until established.

wildflowers offered for sale at a garden center or through mail-order are wild-dug or nursery propagated. One way to be sure is to make purchases from a nonprofit organization or botanical garden, such as the New England Wild Flower Society, which propagate plants and often have plant sales to raise funds for their projects.

Woodland Gardens to Glorify the Shade

Along the north shore of Long Island where I garden, development has left only pockets of wooded land. Fortunately, one section of our half-acre property forms a woodland of sorts created by ten tall trees. Rather than leaving this corner in its wild state, which around here means a junglelike undergrowth of briars and exotic weeds such as Japanese honeysuckle and Oriental bittersweet, we decided to go native and turn this wooded corner into a reminder of the woodlands that I have always found so entrancing. The climate is a bit milder, but many of the species I enjoyed so much as a child in New England will thrive here.

Our woodland garden has been evolving over the three growing seasons we've been living here. The area—about 50 feet by 50 feet—is dominated by a towering double-trunked oak and includes five tall red maples, four black cherries, two dogwoods, and an undergrowth of sassafras saplings. Because the trees grow together in a grove, none have very wide-spreading branches. My neighbors' yards have other clusters of tall trees, creating a sort of borrowed landscape so the woodland effect carries across the property boundary.

The first season we did little to the area, having many worse-looking spots to deal with. At first, we cleared out the undergrowth only in the sunniest part of the woodland between the two trees closest to the house. There I began our collection of native woodland shrubs and wildflowers. I'm trying my best to keep out the exotics, though a few that I knew would grow well, such as Spanish bluebells (*Hyacinthoides hispanicus*, formerly *Scilla campanulata* or *Endymion hispanicus*) and sweet woodruff (*Galium odoratum*), which are native to European woodlands, have found a home on the edge of my woods. Along this edge, which was the first spot we cleared out, I've also planted cinnamon ferns (*Osmunda cinnamomea*) and hay-scented ferns (*Dennstaedtia punctilobula*). They are now spreading nicely into great patches. Violets (*Viola sororia*) appeared on their own and grow so thickly that I have had to thin them out. And I introduced cultivars of blue, white, and pink creeping phlox (*Phlox stolonifera*), Virginia bluebells (*Mertensia virginica*), and fringed bleeding-heart (*Dicentra eximia*), which are naturalizing extraordinarily well.

The second season I began to clear out the underbrush—poison ivy and honeysuckle, tiny twiglike saplings of black cherries and sassafras, and spindly clumps of wild viburnum—from the main part of the woods. With the woodland floor fairly open and clean, I began next to cut out the taller saplings—those my height or a bit taller. (In places, there were several to a square foot!) I tried to leave some in strategic places to provide screening from the view of my neighbors' backyards, but most were removed to be replaced with more ornamental shrubs and small trees.

After we cleared out all the undergrowth, I studied the area from all directions, including from inside the kitchen. I wanted to create an understory of flowering trees and

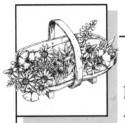

Buyer Beware: Avoiding Collected Native Plants

Digging up wild plants for use in the garden used to be common practice. Today, it's a practice to be condemned; commercial collectors have been known to dig up hundreds and thousands of plants at a time, stripping the woods and forests of their beauty and nearly eliminating some species in some areas.

When purchasing native plants, take steps to assure yourself that they have been nursery-propagated, not wild-collected. Though you can't always be certain, the following guidelines should help.

• Buy native plants only from mail-order nurseries that state clearly in the front of their catalogs that *all* species have been nursery-propagated. Nurseries that do this will be proud of the fact and won't leave you in doubt.

• Be wary of the description "nursery-grown" when it is used instead of "nursery-propagated." Nursery-grown can mean that the plants were dug up from the wild, potted, and then grown on in the nursery for a few weeks or months.

• Plants for sale at a local nursery may give no clue to their origins. Nursery-propagated plants usually have a full root system and grow in a uniform, artificial potting medium containing shredded bark, perlite, or vermiculite. Recently wild-collected plants will be growing in woodland soil and show evidence of other wildflowers sharing their pots.

• Wild-collected plants are often, though not always, incredibly inexpensive. Nursery-propagated plants will rarely be inexpensive.

• Named cultivars of native plants, such as *Cimicifuga simplex* 'The Pearl', are horticulturally improved, cultivated varieties and are therefore nursery-propagated.

• Plants that are slow to mature from seed are rarely nursery-propagated because the cost is prohibitive.

Unless you're buying from a nursery that propagates its own plants, the following popular plants are most certainly wild-collected:

Adiantum spp. (maidenhair ferns)
Arisaema triphyllum (Jack-in-the-pulpit)
Cypripedium acaule (pink lady's-slipper) and most native orchids
Dicentra cucullaria (Dutchman's-breeches)
Dryopteris spp. (wood ferns)
Epigaea repens (trailing arbutus)
Erythronium spp. (trout lilies)
Gentiana spp. (gentians)
Iris cristata (crested iris)
Osmunda cinnamomea (cinnamon fern)
O. claytonia (interrupted fern)
Polygonatum biflorum (small Solomon's seal)
Sanguinaria canadensis (bloodroot)
Trillium grandiflorum (large-flowered trillium) and most native trilliums

Once a tangled mess of weeds and saplings beneath tall trees, the shady corner of our property was easy to turn into a naturalistic woodland garden. After clearing the unattractive undergrowth, we installed a rock path studded with moss and planted shade-loving native shrubs, ferns, and wildflowers.

evergreen shrubs within the woodland. Situating these permanent large plants in just the right places so that they would block views, not each other, proved to be a challenge.

Mountain laurel (*Kalmia latifolia*), which flourishes in the woodland pockets here on Long Island's north shore, made a perfect choice for decorating the woodland. A broadleaved evergreen, it provides some much needed winter greenery and screening. It is also a favorite for extending the season, since its long-lived June blossoms appear after most of the spring flowers have passed.

I am planting only named cultivars, because the species can grow quite tall over the years and our woodland is comparatively small as far as woodlands go. Many of the cultivated forms feature a very compact habit and bear rich pink flowers. (Selecting named cultivars is also a good way to be sure you're not planting wild-collected plants.) In the back of the woodland we also included some rosebay rhododendrons (*Rhododendron maximum*), which can grow quite tall and dense. In time, they'll block the view of my neighbor's swing set in winter.

We found a place for deciduous shrubs in our woodland, too. Winterberry (*Ilex verticillata*), a holly that is adorned with gorgeous red berries from fall into winter, provides needed winter color. Summersweet (*Clethra alnifolia*) produces spires of white or pink flowers in late summer, when little else blooms at the edge of the woods. And several species of native azalea, sometimes called wild honeysuckle, provide a cloud of delicate spring blossoms. I left clumps of the native wild viburnum (*Viburnum alnifolium*) within the woods. These plants bloom for one short week in spring, turning the woodland into a haze of white. Their fall color is rusty red and purple, combined with clusters of blue berries, so I can't complain about the abundance of these gifts.

I would still like to find a spot for large fothergilla (*Fothergilla major*), a native shrub endemic to regions farther south but hardy here. This shrub captivated me years ago in a Delaware garden when I photographed its white, bottlebrush-shaped blossoms glimmering in the sun. Its fall color is probably as spectacular as it comes. The leaves turn a mixture of gold and pure orange and remain showy for a long time.

With the shrub structure in place, I began to think about creating an understory of small trees beneath the canopy of taller ones. In my mind's eye, I kept seeing an Elliot Porter photograph of a southern woodland in early spring that was displayed at the Metropolitan Museum. The woods in the photograph was a mist of unfolding purple and white blossoms from dogwoods and redbuds seen against a strong linear pattern created by the forest's dark trunks and branches. I wanted that pink and purple haze outside my kitchen window. Dogwoods are a bit risky these days, so I opted instead for shadblow (*Amelanchier canadensis*) and redbuds (*Cercis canadensis*) to create that flowering haze. And for added winter color, I planted several clumps of white-barked birches in strategic places where they can be seen from indoors in January. I chose the insect-resistant *Betula japonica* var. *platyphlla* 'Whitespire'.

After the woody plants were in place, I started planting the herbaceous wildflowers I really love in the main part of the woodland, procuring divisions from friends and purchasing plants from plant sales and nurseries selling propagated stock. Here, I planted clumps of mayapples (*Podophyllum peltatum*), with umbrella-shaped leaves that form a green carpet in the shade; white-flowered trilliums (*Trillium grandiflorum*), and trout lilies (*Erythronium americanum*), favorites from my forays into the Connecticut woodland; and cultivars of creeping phlox (*Phlox stolonifera*), wild blue phox (*Phlox divaricata*), and Virginia bluebells (*Mertensia virginica*), blue flowers that I saw for the first time during a trip to Tennessee at the height of spring. To these I've added specimens of other native wildflowers and clumps of evergreen ferns, such as Christmas fern (*Polystichum acrostichoides*). I've also planted groundcovers, such as partridgeberry (*Mitchella repens*), wintergreen (*Gaultheria procumbens*), and foamflower (*Tiarella cordifolia*), to provide greenery throughout the summer and winter.

Getting Started: Studying Woodland Sites

If you're just getting started with wildflower gardening, don't be too eager to jump in and start planting. Before taking the plunge, it's best to start by carefully evaluating the site you've selected to see just what conditions it has to offer. If you're not familiar with the natural woodlands in your area, before you begin I suggest taking some springtime hikes in local national forests, state parks, or other natural areas to learn more about the woodland habitats in your region. A forest's elevation, exposure, native soil type, and the amount of rainfall it receives influence the plants that grow in it. A particular group of tree species dominates each ecosystem, and these in turn influence the plants forming the understory and forest floor.

Feel the forest floor with your hands. Lift handfuls of soil and squeeze it. Breathe in its earthy fragrance; observe its moisture content; notice the crumbly, partially decayed leaves and twigs that are its components. This is the type of soil you'll need to have—or develop—in the site you've selected for your woodland garden.

Then look up and all around you. Take note of the different horizontal layers of the forest: the canopy of tall trees, the understory of small trees and shrubs, and the forest floor carpeted with wildflowers, ferns, groundcovers, and rotting branches and logs. Are the trees mostly evergreen or deciduous? How about the understory shrubs? Note

how the flowers are grouped. Do they occur singly or do they run rampant in an interconnected mass? This distribution results from the way the plants grow: Those with runners or stolons form expanses; those with taproots grow singly or in small clumps. Take note of the arrangement of trees, shrubs, and herbaceous plants, along with any plant combinations you find attractive, and use these to help you recreate a woodland feel in your own garden.

Only by observing the forest firsthand can you really evaluate whether your proposed garden site can offer an environment conducive to woodland plants. Only when you've felt a forest soil with your bare hands will you know if your soil has enough humus. Only by observing how the sunlight filters through the overhead foliage will you know if your site is shady enough for the delicate flowers you wish to grow. Take note of as many of these details as you can. Then go home and see how the site you've selected compares. You'll want to imitate the forest ecosystem that's most similar to the conditions that exist in your own backyard. That way, you'll create the most effortless garden. This careful study will help you create a woodland garden to be proud of, one where site and plants are carefully matched—a garden that is about as easy-care as they come.

Woodland Soil Secrets

The soil in most forest floors is layered. On top rests the litter of fallen leaves, twigs, and downed trunks. As more litter accumulates on top of this layer, the deeper parts begin to decay into a rich humus, or leaf mold. The humus layer is often 6 to 8 inches deep. Beneath the humus is the subsoil, which contains less organic matter and more mineral matter. In a forest environment, the humus and the more solid soil beneath it are usually slightly to strongly acidic. Very acid soils range from pH 4.0 to 5.0; moderately acid soils from 5.0 to 6.0; and slightly acid from 6.0 to 6.9.

The degree of soil acidity depends largely upon the types of trees growing in the forest. Oak and pine trees, for instance, produce a highly acid soil when their leaves decay; Poplar, hickory, basswood, and cedar produce only slightly acid soil. Soil acidity is also influenced by acid rainfall and the makeup of decomposing rocks.

When you start selecting plants for your garden, you'll find that there are native plants and wildflowers that tolerate a wide range of soil pH and those that are quite particular. As a weekend gardener, it pays to do your homework before planting. Test your soil's pH, and then select appropriate plants. See the encyclopedia section near the end of the book for the best pH for each plant. A range between 5.0 and 6.0 will support the widest assortment of plants.

Gardeners who claim they can't grow anything in the shade often erroneously blame the low light. But shady spots under trees can often be remarkably dry, because the trees' surface roots suck up all the available moisture and nutrients. It's the lack of moisture, not the shade, that limits these gardener's endeavors. Beneath trees with greedy surface roots, such as maples and ashes, is not the place to start a woodland garden. You'll know if dry, root-clogged soil is a problem because the ground feels hard and compacted; you'll have trouble digging a hole with a trowel.

In my own woodland garden, I was fortunately able to locate the wildflowers and most shrubs in a highly visible area that was amazingly free of tree root competition. Where roots were a problem for a few shrubs, we dug a very large planting hole, severed all tree roots smaller than an inch in diameter that got in the way, and replaced the soil with compost. The large planting hole should give the shrubs enough growing room to get established before tree roots return. It's best to grow a woodland garden only where you can scoop up the topsoil with your hands, or develop such a soil by adding humus, compost, or shredded leaves before you plant.

Studying the Shade

Rather than dealing with the many—and somewhat confusing—descriptions of shade (heavy, light, partial, diffused, filtered, or half are just a few of the descriptions I've seen), it's easier to consider first how the shade in a woodland is created. Shadows cast from overhead branches fall on the forest floor, throwing it into shadow. The density of the shadow depends upon the density of the overhead branches. In forests dominated by evergreens, such as those found along the Pacific Coast, the thickly needled branches of the trees keep the forest floor in pretty dense shade year-round—at least in the lower elevations where the trees grow thick and tall. The deciduous forests of the East allow streams of light to reach the forest floor all during winter and early spring. As the tree foliage emerges, the forest becomes shaded from late spring through fall. In the North and Southeast, forests include a mix of evergreen and deciduous, creating light conditions that vary throughout the forest.

Most woodland wildflowers do pretty well with what gardeners often call filtered light. If you take a walk in the deciduous woods on a sunny day, you'll know what kind of light this is. The sun's rays sort of sift through the foliage, creating a dappled pattern on the ground, a pattern that constantly changes so that direct light never strikes the ground in any one place for very long, thus keeping the ground cool.

The forests offering the most lush assortment of wildflowers are those where a good measure of light reaches the forest floor. This is particularly true of the eastern deciduous forest of the Appalachian and Great Smoky mountains. Flowering shrubs such as the flame azalea (*Rhododendron calendulaceum*) set the woods on fire in spring. Carpets of wildflowers color the forest floor in early spring before the tree leaves emerge. Many of these wildflowers are ephemeral—that is, they leaf out and flower in early spring, do all their growing during the bright sun of spring, and eventually die back to the ground during summer when lack of light and drier conditions stop their growth.

Selecting Your Woodland Site

If you aren't fortunate enough to have an acre or more of woods on your property, a grove of trees—such as the one on my property—will do. Trees native to your region are preferable, but exotics (perhaps once planted as lawn trees) are fine, if that's what you have. It helps if they are spaced so their canopies meet and intermingle a bit. You'll need to have deep-rooted species, with roots that go deep enough to avoid robbing the upper soil levels of moisture. If you don't have a grove of trees, woodland plants planted under the branches of a single large tree can make a pretty garden, although the limited space will frustrate any collector. (Woodland gardens can also be planted in the shade on the north or east side of a house, as long as the soil suits the plants.) It's best to use a grove of three or more trees to create the effect of a woodland and to provide enough protective shade so that the delicate woodland plants are not left to bake in the sun as the tree's shadow moves.

Refurbishing the Soil

If the grove has been neglected, as mine was, you may need to clear out undesirable undergrowth. But if it suffers from the opposite problem—too much care—you may have to try to return it to a more natural state before planting. This can take several years. By too much care, I mean that a conscientious homeowner has raked off each and every fallen leaf for years, probably leaving the ground bare, in the name of neatness. Such soil gets compacted and dry. It's also robbed of nutrients and is inhospitable to woodland plants.

You can return the soil to its natural woodsy state by layering chopped-up leaves and twigs over the soil. Chop them to the size of 50-cent pieces, and spread them several inches deep beneath the tree boughs. Sprinkle the leaves with a compost activator and keep them moist. Repeat this procedure annually until the leaves have rotted into a rich humus. By then, earthworms and their ilk will have moved in and begun to loosen up the subsoil. Only when you have a loose, friable soil can you begin installing the woodland garden.

The grove may need a bit of pruning attention to make it most conducive to growing a woodland garden. Tall, high-branched deciduous trees let in the right amount of light for most woodland residents. Prune off low-hanging branches (those below 20 feet) at the trunk and thin out upper branches so the light coming through is dappled, not dense and gloomy. If your trees are large, you may need to hire an arborist for this process. Conifers need to be pruned very carefully to retain their natural conical shapes. In a forest, many conifers lose their lower branches, but in the home landscape, most look best with a skirt of boughs sweeping the ground. Don't turn conifers into lollipops. You may need to thin the trees out every few years to maintain the proper balance of shade and light.

Selecting Plants

Unlike meadow plants—many of which nurserymen can readily propagate from seed—woodland wildflowers are not easily, or at least not inexpensively, seed-propagated. They're the species most often exploited by collectors. Hobbyists often enjoy the challenge and patience it takes to germinate seed of woodland plants, but weekend gardeners seldom have the time or patience. So you're left with the alternative of purchasing plants for your woodland garden. Before you buy, be sure that you're getting nursery-propagated plants.

You'll also need to be certain plants are adapted to the light conditions offered by your particular woodland. Plants accustomed to a coniferous forest do well in low light (and acid soil), so don't plant them under a deciduous tree. Those that call the deciduous forest their home need plenty of light at least part of the year—locate them under deciduous trees or on the edge of a shady area where they get bright, but never direct, light. Even plants native to a mixed forest may have their preferences—you may find one or another under the conifers or under the beeches, but generally not vice versa.

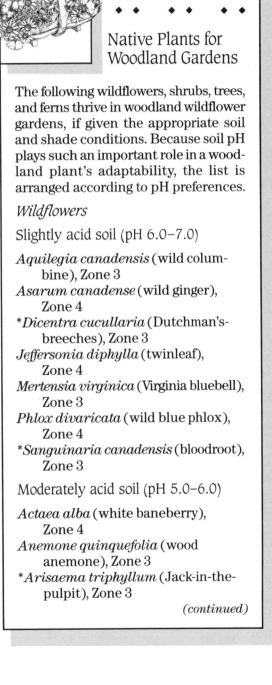

Native Plants for Woodland Gardens

The following wildflowers, shrubs, trees, and ferns thrive in woodland wildflower gardens, if given the appropriate soil and shade conditions. Because soil pH plays such an important role in a woodland plant's adaptability, the list is arranged according to pH preferences.

Wildflowers

Slightly acid soil (pH 6.0–7.0)

Aquilegia canadensis (wild columbine), Zone 3

Asarum canadense (wild ginger), Zone 4

*Dicentra cucullaria (Dutchman's-breeches), Zone 3

Jeffersonia diphylla (twinleaf), Zone 4

Mertensia virginica (Virginia bluebell), Zone 3

Phlox divaricata (wild blue phlox), Zone 4

*Sanguinaria canadensis (bloodroot), Zone 3

Moderately acid soil (pH 5.0–6.0)

Actaea alba (white baneberry), Zone 4

Anemone quinquefolia (wood anemone), Zone 3

*Arisaema triphyllum (Jack-in-the-pulpit), Zone 3

(continued)

◆ ◆   ◆ ◆   ◆ ◆   ◆ ◆   ◆ ◆   ◆ ◆   ◆ ◆   ◆ ◆   ◆ ◆   ◆ ◆

Native Plants for Woodland Gardens—*(Continued)*

Asarum canadense (wild ginger),
  Zone 4

Caltha palustris (marsh marigold),
  Zone 3

Cimicifuga racemosa (black snakeroot), Zone 3

Claytonia virginica (spring beauty),
  Zone 4

Dicentra eximia (fringed bleeding-
  heart), Zone 3

Dodecatheon jeffreyi (Sierra shooting-
  star), Zone 6

**Erythronium americanum* (trout-
  lily), Zone 4

Geranium maculatum (wild
  geranium), Zone 4

Hepatica americana (round-lobed
  hepatica), Zone 3

Jeffersonia diphylla (twinleaf),
  Zone 4

Tiarella cordifolia (foamflower),
  Zone 4

Waldsteinia fragarioides (barren
  strawberry), Zone 4

Highly acid soil (pH 4.0-5.0)

Asarum canadense (wild ginger),
  Zone 4

**Cornus canadensis* (bunchberry),
  Zone 2

*Epigaea repens (trailing arbutus),
  Zone 3

Gaultheria procumbens (wintergreen),
  Zone 4

Hepatica americana (round-lobed
  hepatica), Zone 3

Jeffersonia diphylla (twinleaf),
  Zone 4

Mitchella repens (partridgeberry),
  Zone 4

Phlox stolonifera (creeping phlox),
  Zone 3

*Be especially careful when buying these wildflowers. Plant them only if you're absolutely sure they're been nursery-propagated, or if they've been divided from a friend's planting.

Shrubs

Slightly acid soil (pH 6.0-7.0)

Hydrangea quercifolia (oakleaf
  hydrangea), Zone 5

Viburnum alnifolium (hobblebush),
  Zone 3

V. trilobum (American cranberrybush),
  Zone 2

Moderately acid soil (pH 5.0-6.0)

Clethra alnifolia (summersweet),
  Zone 4

Cyrilla racemiflora (leatherwood),
  Zone 6

Fothergilla major (large fothergilla),
  Zone 5

Hamamelis virginiana (common
  witchhazel), Zone 4

Kalmia latifolia (mountain laurel),
  Zone 5

Lindera benzoin (spicebush), Zone 5

Viburnum alnifolium (hobblebush),
  Zone 3

Highly acid soil (pH 4.0-5.0)

Fothergilla major (large fothergilla),
  Zone 5

Kalmia latifolia (mountain laurel), Zone 5

Rhododendron calendulaceum (flame azalea), Zone 5

R. maximum (rosebay), Zone 4

R. periclymenoides (pinxterbloom azalea), Zone 3

Vaccinium angustifolium (lowbush blueberry), Zone 3

Understory Trees

Amelanchier canadensis (shadblow), Zone 4

Cercis canadensis (eastern redbud), Zone 5

Chionanthus virginicus (fringetree), Zone 5

Cladrastis lutea (yellowwood), Zone 4

Cornus florida (flowering dogwood), Zone 5

C. mas (cornelian cherry), Zone 5

Halesia carolina (Carolina silverbell tree), Zone 5

Magnolia fraseri (mountain magnolia), Zone 6

Stewartia ovata (mountain stewartia), Zone 6

Ferns

Slightly acid soil (pH 6.0–7.0)

*Adiantum pedatum (maidenhair fern), Zone 4

Athyrium filix-femina (lady fern), Zone 3

*Dryopteris intermedia (common woodfern), Zone 3

Onoclea sensibilis (sensitive fern), Zone 3

Polystichum acrostichoides (Christmas fern), Zone 3

Moderately acid soil (pH 5.0–6.0)

*Adiantum pedatum (maidenhair fern), Zone 4

Athyrium filix-femina (lady fern), Zone 3

*Dryopteris austriaca var. *intermedia* (evergreen wood fern), Zone 3

Matteuccia pensylvanica (ostrich fern), Zone 3

Onoclea sensibilis (sensitive fern), Zone 3

*Osmunda cinnamomea (cinnamon fern), Zone 3

*O. claytoniana (interrupted fern), Zone 3

Polystichum acrostichoides (Christmas fern), Zone 3

Highly acid soil (pH 4.0–5.0)

Athyrium filix-femina (lady fern), Zone 3

*Dryopteris cristata (crested wood fern), Zone 3

Onoclea sensibilis (sensitive fern), Zone 3

*Osmunda cinnamomea (cinnamon fern), Zone 3

O. claytoniana (interrupted fern), Zone 3

*Be especially careful when buying these ferns. Plant them only if you're absolutely sure they've been nursery-propagated, or if they've been divided from a friend's planting.

Woodland Planting Pointers

Never, never, never do any large-scale digging or turning over of soil in a woodland site—this is not an annual flower bed or a vegetable garden. Cultivating destroys the soil layering and, more importantly, can disrupt the trees' root systems. You need those trees—they create the woodland, after all—so take care of them. Dig planting holes for shrubs and small plants, improving the backfill with humus or peat if you wish, but do not excavate large areas. And don't sever large tree roots (those over 1 inch in diameter)—plant somewhere else.

Newly installed plants, whether they're flowers, shrubs, or groundcovers, should never be left with bare ground around them the way some gardeners (but never a weekend gardener heeding the advice in this book, I'm sure!) might do in a flower bed. Forest plants always have a loose covering of humus and decaying organic matter over their roots. And taller plants often grow up through the protective cover of a carpet of groundcovers. Cuddle up some leaf mold topped with chopped-up leaves around newly installed plants.

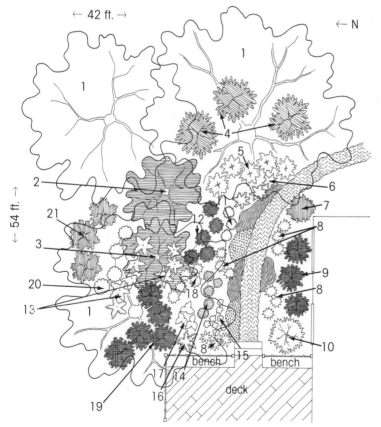
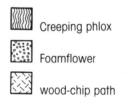

Plot Plan of a Woodland Garden. (1) red oak, (2) white pine, (3) Carolina silverbell, (4) catawba rhododendron, (5) dwarf fothergilla, (6) maidenhair fern, (7) oakleaf hydrangea, (8) fringed bleeding-heart, (9) Carolina rhododendron, (10) mountain laurel, (11) spring beauty, (12) 'White Pearl' Kamchatka bugbane, (13) common woodfern, (14) wild geranium, (15) goldenstar, (16) cinnamon fern, (17) great white trillium, (18) 'Fuller's White' wild blue phlox, (19) pinxterbloom azalea, (20) Virginia bluebell, (21) 'Dora Amateis' rhododendron

I designed this pink, blue, and white woodland wildflower garden to create an intimate setting by incorporating native shrubs along the outer edges and lower wildflowers and groundcovers toward the center. The curving wood-chip path leads the eye out of the space and, with the shrubs planted under the trees, plays down the essentially square shape of the garden.

Arranging Plants in a Woodland Garden

Place woodland plants in loose groups or masses, as you might in a traditional flower border, to create a color impact, but don't overdo it. Be sure, too, to locate plants individually or in small clumps as you would find them in nature. Allow the borders of any mass to be soft and flowing. It looks charming to encourage creeping ground-covering plants to act as "weavers," running beneath the taller plants and melding different groups together. Tall or medium-height plants naturally push right up through the groundcover plants, so be sure to add these wild weavers to the woodland garden if you are intent on duplicating nature's most artistic expressions.

It's fine, too, to have expanses of open ground covered with a natural leaf litter, and a rotting, mossy log or two between the groups of plants. These open areas will fill in naturally if the plants are well situated. And rotting wood is the favorite medium for several beautiful woodlanders. Bunchberry (*Cornus canadensis*) grows atop wet, rotting logs, and so does twinflower (*Linnaea borealis* var. *americana*); both will trail all over the fallen wood. I've read that moss can be "seeded" by grinding up a handful in a blender with buttermilk and then pouring it over the wood, rocks, or ground where you want it to grow. I have to try this soon!

Paths are a woodland's best friend. Create a meandering trail through your woodland, if it is large enough, to point the way toward viewing the flowers. A path prevents plants from getting trampled under foot and keeps the soil where they grow from getting compacted. Keep the trails simple—as if they were created by deer. Don't edge them with rocks or anything fussy or contrived, but do carpet them with a deep mulch of wood chips or shredded bark to provide a bouncy and silent cushion to walk on.

A Fern Garden

After the ephemerals of the springtime forest are gone, your woodland garden may seem bare. If this is the case in your garden, include clumps of ferns in strategic places to provide greenery and structure after the wildflowers have departed for the year. Their fronds often unfold from their curious fiddleheads just after the springtime blossoms have reached their peak.

Ferns planted alone and unaccompanied by colorful blossoms make a cool, restful garden. Colors vary from lime green through blue-green to dark green. And textures range from finely cut and lacy to coarse and bold. Some ferns, such as the cinnamon fern (*Osmunda cinnamomea*), grow strongly upright with sword-shaped fronds. Others, such as maidenhair fern (*Adiantum pedatum*), are soft and rounded, forming circular fronds of translucent foliage. Hay-scented fern (*Dennstaedtia punctilobula*) spreads to form a knee-high carpet of fragrant, quiet green beneath the trees.

To avoid buying wild-collected ferns, follow the recommendations suggested on page 213.

Exotics in the Woodland

Unless you are a purist and have a particular reason to grow only native wildflowers, you need not worry about including exotics and suitable-looking cultivated plants in the woodland garden along with the wildflowers. Many types, especially cultivars of those native to similar climates on other continents, are suitable. The delightful blue-flowered wood hyacinth (*Hyacinthoides non-scriptus*, formerly *Endymion non-scriptus* or *Scilla non-scripta*) of England will spread in a suitable American site, as will the gorgeous ground-hugging European wild ginger (*Asarum europaeum*) with its high-gloss evergreen leaves. Thriving in dry shade, the many species and cultivars of the wiry-stemmed, delicate-leaved barrenwort (*Epimedium* spp.) from Europe and Asia form an inviting groundcover along a shaded woodland path. And with most of these foreigners, you needn't worry that their presence in your garden means that a collector has stripped a pristine forest of its beauty to provide for your exclusive needs.

Many fine shade-loving garden plants will grace a woodland garden. (See "A Shady Flower Garden" on page 83 for suggestions.) Just be sure when planting them to follow a design that mimics Nature's way. Choose the delicate and graceful plants over the splashy and artificial if you want a truly naturalistic garden. Astilbes (*Astilbe* spp.) look lovely massed in the light shade on the edge of a woodland. I especially like astilbes with white and pale pink flowers because they stand out best in low light. Hostas (*Hosta* spp.) make another fine choice for a woodland. Their clumps of bold foliage last until fall, providing texture and greenery—or bright variegations—after the epehemeral wildflowers disappear. Hosta cultivars with white-variegated or yellow-green foliage draw the eye as effectively as brightly colored flowers, and their effect lasts for months!

Woodland Housekeeping Chores

A woodland garden probably requires the least amount of work of any naturalistic garden. Once you've planted and the plants have become established, there's little to do but enjoy your garden. The wildflowers certainly don't need staking, and when grown in the proper rich, water-retentive soil, they tolerate summer drought fairly well. To prolong the greenery of the spring ephemerals, it helps to water them during an early summer drought. And newly planted shrubs and flowers should be watered regularly during their first season of growth to help them get established.

As you stroll around or through the woodland, you can pull an occasional weed or tree seedling, deadhead any unsightly plants—after they have gone to seed, please —and pick up or rearrange any fallen twigs and branches. Creeping plants, such as foamflower (*Tiarella cordifolia*), that may have gotten out of control can be pulled up or divided as needed. In fall or at the close of their natural growing seasons, mark plants that are too crowded; dig and divide them in early spring just as new growth emerges.

To Rake or Not to Rake, That Is the Question

Some wildflower gardeners I know never bother about raking or removing fallen autumn leaves. They let them fall and remain where they may, just as if the woodland garden were nature's own. Others tend to the leaves a bit, or a lot. Whether you need to deal with autumn leaves or not largely depends on the type of plants you're growing and the type of trees you have.

My oak leaves certainly survive the winter completely intact. They are tough and crisp and simply refuse to rot unless helped along a bit. Come spring, the leaves have blown into great heaps against the shrubs, and their pointy edges have wedged them into stems and branches. They look unsightly, even in the wild garden. Maple leaves, on the other hand, can pack down so completely that they form a smothering mat. I usually lightly rake the fallen autumn leaves off low creeping plants such as sweet woodruff (*Galium odoratum*) and creeping phlox (*Phlox stolonifera*), leaving a thin protective coat, but never anything deep enough to smother them. A more thorough raking may be called for in spring. (Don't forget to compost those leaves or shred them for mulch!) Elsewhere, taller plants in the woodland manage to come up right through the leaf cover.

Dick Lighty, an expert on native plants and director of the Mt. Cuba Center for the Study of Piedmont Flora in Greenville, Delaware—an estate famous for its beautiful woodland gardens—takes an entirely different tactic. He and his wife care for their own eight acres—five of which are unmaintained woodlands with trails, while the remaining three contain both traditional and naturalistic gardens—and handle two tons of fallen leaves every year. They find the vigor and beauty of their woodland garden is increased by gathering and chopping up the leaves before returning them to the woodland.

In fall, Dr. Lighty uses a power vacuum-shredder on wheels to suck and chop the fallen dry leaves. The machine collects the shredded leaves in a huge canvas bag, chopping the dry leaves to the size of a 50-cent piece. He then piles the greatly reduced volume of leaves in an out-of-the-way place until early winter. Once the ground freezes, he uses a pitchfork to spread the leaf mulch over the woodland. Because they are chopped, the leaves decay more readily into a rich leafmold and look more attractive than whole leaves. The leaf pieces act as a protective mulch through the freezes and thaws of winter and spring. (Weekend gardeners with smaller properties to care for don't need the powerful machine Dr. Lighty uses.) The Lightys return about a third of the chopped leaves they gather to the woodland as mulch. They compost the remaining leaves and use them in other parts of the garden.

Dr. Lighty cautions that different wildflowers respond best to different thicknesses of the chopped mulch. Types that remain evergreen through the winter do poorly if covered with a deep mulch. Sunlight needs to get through to the foliage. A light sprinkling of very finely chopped leaves suffices for evergreen creepers such as partridgeberry (*Mitchella repens*) and wintergreen (*Gaultheria procumbens*). Evergreen plants with tufts of foliage can withstand a 3-inch-deep mulch, however, as long as the foliage is not buried completely. Trilliums (*Trillium* spp.) and other herbaceous plants that disappear during the winter can push right up through 4 or 5 inches of chopped leaves.

I have been following this leaf-shredding technique for dealing with leaves in the traditionally landscaped areas of my property. But now I'm going to apply it to the woodland area that's heavily planted with wildflowers. Though this requires a bit more work than the laissez-faire method of woodland gardening, the results promise to be worth the effort. And the late fall and early winter chores occur at a time when there's little else to do in the garden, anyway. It will be a great excuse to get outside and play in the garden during a month when few other chores beckon.

Meadow Gardening Fact and Fiction

It's a widely held misconception that all you need do to create a beautiful meadow of bright flowers and tawny grasses is to scatter handfuls of flower seeds over an established lawn and cease mowing. Let's be realistic, folks! This profligate method isn't going to result in anything more than a mess. Seeds of any kind—even of hardy wildflowers—need some assistance to grow into established plants. And typical turf grasses are the wrong kind of grass to combine with meadow flowers because their mat-forming, rhizomatous roots crowd out other plants.

I've known several people who have failed totally at meadow gardening because of this very misconception. One person who springs to mind was a fairly experienced gardener; the other, a pure novice. Both had been seduced by the stunning photos on cans of wildflower seeds. And their gardens were the victims. The experienced gardener fell victim to the propaganda that wildflowers, once seeded, needed no further care. He failed to prepare the soil properly before sowing the seeds and neglected to weed out unwanted invaders. When the novice gardener showed me her failed garden, she lamented, "I followed the instructions exactly, and nothing ever grew!" I took one look at the site where she had scattered the seed and knew why. She had tried to grow seed intended for a sunny field in the thin, compacted soil beneath a grove of tangled trees. I guess the instructions hadn't said anything about sun. And her idea of preparing the soil had been to scratch around with a weeding claw. The only saving grace was that the area was so inhospitable to plants that her new site hadn't been overrun with weeds.

But don't let these reports discourage you. I've also seen numerous successful meadow gardens. Probably the most remarkable one was reputed to be over 90 years old. This New Hampshire garden was a remnant of pasture that had been fenced off and left to beautify the property when the rest of the field was turned over to vegetable growing. The meadow bloomed thickly with a succession of perennial flowers from spring through fall. This small meadow had perpetuated itself this long with no more care from the present owners than an annual mowing.

Probably the most flamboyant meadow garden I have ever seen was growing on former farmland surrounding a newly built home in Maryland. Rather than planting an acre of lawn around the house, the owner had plowed the property and sown a field of flowers in the barren ground. The meadow was so unexpected and so colorful that motorists felt compelled to stop abruptly along the road in amazement to fully take in the sight before them. Unlike the ancient New Hampshire garden that relied on long-lived perennials for color, this newly planted field was abloom with a kaleidoscope of annuals. However, these annuals were exotics and did not reseed; they needed to be replanted

every year. Though this might sound like a lot of work and expense, you can do the sowing with the appropriate equipment on a yard tractor, or hire the work out to a farmer or landscape contractor. An acre or less of flowery meadow will certainly be easier to care for than an equal amount of lawn.

Meadow Gardening Theory: Mimicking Mother Nature

In theory, a meadow should be composed primarily of native warm-season grasses—perennial clump grasses that grow slowly in spring and fall, thrive in the heat of summer, and go dormant in winter—and flowering annuals, biennials, and perennials that will spread and seed themselves to create a self-maintaining field of flowers and foliage. In practice, as I've pointed out, many a meadow garden never achieves this target for any of a number of reasons. Understanding the dynamics of a natural meadow and the life-cycles of the plants that compose it will show you how to successfully mimic this natural site in your own garden.

A meadow is usually defined as an open sunny area of grasses and wildflowers in a normally forested region where rainfall is high. Meadows in the Northeast usually exist as transitional areas on the way to forest. Woody plants that take root in a meadow will eventually shade out the meadow natives. For this reason, a natural meadow can only exist as climax vegetation where conditions limit or prevent woody plants from invading. Alpine meadows are a good example of a climax situation—the soil is usually too wet, the growing season too short, and the winters too severe to support shrubs or trees, so the meadow lives on forever. The vast rolling meadows common along country roads or highways in the Northeast remain open because a farmer or road-worker cuts them every year; otherwise, they would fall to the cycle of natural succession and return to scrub or forest. Your meadow will require similar care.

Meadow Gardening Practice: Improving on Mother Nature

A meadow garden mimics the beauty of a natural meadow, but often attempts to improve upon it. Most natural meadows have more grass than flowers, but I'd venture to guess that most gardeners pay much more attention to the flowers than to the grass when creating a meadow. Indeed, most of those lavish packaged meadows sold in shaker cans contain no grass seed at all—a mistake, according to most experts.

"Most people are not yet sensitive to the subtle beauty of a natural meadow or prairie," according to horticulturist and native plant expert Dick Lighty. "It takes sensitivity to appreciate a grassy meadow punctuated by junipers and highlighted seasonally by goldenrod, beebalm, and butterfly weed."

Open spaces on large, sunny properties don't have to be limited to boring, high-maintenance lawns—a wildflower meadow garden makes a beautiful, low-maintenance alternative. Once established, the only maintenance a wildflower meadow requires is mowing once a year. The rest of the time, it grows and blooms without any attention from you.

The purists argue that grass is an important ingredient of any natural meadow and should therefore be included in all meadow gardens. The meadow grasses—mostly clumping, warm-season types—stabilize the soil and provide support for the flowers. The grasses add interesting color and texture in the garden, especially when they change color in fall. They also visually unify the wildflower planting, providing a neutral background for the more colorful blossoms. Because these grasses form clumps and don't spread by rhizomes, flowers find enough room to flourish between individual grass plants.

Siting Your Meadow Garden

Natural meadows occur in full sun and so should yours. The soil needn't be rich, and you need not fertilize or improve it at all—unless the soil has so much clay you could open a brickyard, or boasts so much sand that your kids build castles in the garden. Plain old ordinary soil will support the best meadow, because meadow plants are not heavy feeders.

You should be cautious, however, about where on your property you site the meadow. Your neighbors might not understand your penchant for the naturalistic if you suddenly transform your formally manicured front lawn into a flowery meadow. They may label your fledgling meadow an eyesore and a public nuisance. Neighbors have filed lawsuits over just such incidents because local ordinances often require the grass to be mown. Check local ordinances and talk to your neighbors before beginning a front-yard meadow and you'll be more likely to avoid legal action. You might select a meadow mix of low-

Meadow-Growing Essentials

The following guidelines debunk the misconceptions many people have about meadow gardening. Follow these instructions carefully and your meadow will be off to a good start.

• Clear the soil of all vegetation and then till to prepare a seedbed.

• Use a mixture of perennial and annual flowers along with native clump-forming grasses. Sow at a heavy application rate, as much as twice the rate on the package directions, and cover thinly with soil.

• Mix seed with equal portions of clean river sand to facilitate even spreading.

• Keep the seedlings moist. You may need to irrigate your meadow during the first year of growth.

• Weed diligently for at least the first year in a perennial meadow.

• To prevent invasion by woody plants and to help disperse flower and grass seed, cut or mow the meadow to 6 inches high in late fall or winter.

• For best color, sow seeds of annual flowers every year for a good show. This means some yearly soil preparation at sowing time.

growing flowers and grasses in the name of neatness as a way to avoid offending those next door.

In a suburban development, it may be best to grow a meadow only in the rear of your property. But homes located in the country or sprouting on several acres of former farmland may very well get away with growing a meadow, rather than a lawn, out front. The meadow may be more acceptable if you "landscape" the naturalistic site a bit. Confine it within a split-rail fence to give it a country look. Mow a meandering path through the flowers to provide access to a bench or old apple tree and give purpose to the field of flowers. On a large property, you might wish to grow a small lawn with well-defined contours near the house and then allow the field to spring up all around the edges, with a rough-hewn fence edging the property.

Evaluating Seed Mixes

Once you've identified the perfect site for your meadow, the next step is to choose the seed you're going to plant. Choosing a seed mix can be tricky. Don't let the pretty pictures seduce you—read the label; there you can better judge what you're actually getting. Don't purchase any meadow mix that doesn't list the species in it—all of them. And be sure the mix is a regional one that has been specially formulated for your area of the country.

If you expect the mixture to become permanently established, don't just take the company's word for it. Do some checking yourself to be certain the species are native or successfully naturalized in your area. As I've said before, you have the greatest chance of establishing a meadow garden that will perpetuate itself if you plant only species that are native or naturalized in your region.

Determining the right mix of plants may take some careful observation or research. An excellent source for this information is the National Wildflower Research Center (200 FM 973 North, Austin, TX 78725), which was founded by Lady Bird Johnson in 1982. In addition to conducting extensive research, the center provides a clearinghouse of wildflower information. Among their publications are lists of recommended wildflowers for each state, along with commercial seed sources. This is an invaluable source for gardeners short on time—the clearinghouse will quickly provide you with the information you need.

Many commercial seed mixes are formulated to include both annuals and perennials. The annuals will bloom the first year and make for a happy customer and pretty garden that first growing season. Then they're never heard from again. But no one will object if you work in some annual seed every year to provide a bit more splash. Meanwhile, that first season the perennials are sprouting, putting down sturdy roots, and just getting themselves established. The perennials will flower the second season and get even better as the years pass, particularly if they are mixed with protective grasses. They may even reseed themselves. If you're impatient for the perennials—and have the funds—you can plant container-grown or bare-root perennials in a newly seeded or established meadow.

Purchase a prepackaged mix only if it lists the proportions of each type of seed. It's best if this proportion is broken down by number of each kind rather than by weight. Some seeds are tiny and lightweight, others are large and heavy, so the individual weights won't really tell you how many of each wildflower you're getting. *The National Wildflower Research Center's Wildflower*

Handbook, edited by Annie Paulson, lists the number of seeds per pound for many recommended flowers and provides the higher math needed to figure out how to create a custom meadow mix. This handbook also lists species recommended for each region.

Winning the War on Weeds

Your greatest adversary in establishing a successful meadow garden will be weeds—the truly undesirable, unattractive, aggressive plants, such as Johnsongrass, ragweed, thistles, or bindweed. (Few object to the pretty roadside "weeds," such as butter-and-eggs, Queen-Anne's-lace, chicory, New England asters, and goldenrod, which may find their way in unasked.) Battling weeds begins when you first sow your garden and continues for at least one or more seasons. An established meadow garden, especially one that incorporates grasses, should have thick enough vegetation to shade out most incoming weeds. You might have to yank out a few offenders if you notice them in later years, but the great battles cease after the meadow becomes happily established.

The fight is most fierce at the start because not only does the newly cleared soil offer an open invitation to airborne seed, but weed seed lying dormant in the soil springs into life. Soilborne weeds prove particularly troublesome if you till the soil, because dormant seed lying too deep to germinate comes to the surface, where it takes off. One method used by organic gardeners is to till the soil (either by hand or with a power tiller), wait several weeks until weed seeds have sprouted, and then till, hoe, or disk the soil shallowly to disrupt the weed

(continued on page 234)

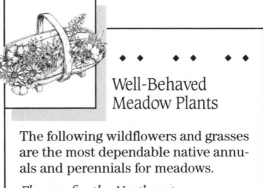

◆ ◆   ◆ ◆   ◆ ◆

Well-Behaved Meadow Plants

The following wildflowers and grasses are the most dependable native annuals and perennials for meadows.

Flowers for the Northeast

Aquilegia canadensis (wild columbine)
Asclepias tuberosa (butterfly weed)
Aster novae-angliae (New England aster)
Baptisia australis (wild blue indigo)
Chrysanthemum leucanthemum (oxeye daisy)
Coreopsis lanceolata (lance-leaved coreopsis)
Dodecatheon meadia (shooting-star)
Echinacea purpurea (purple coneflower)
Geranium maculatum (wild geranium)
Helenium autumnale (sneezeweed)
Liatris spicata (spike gayfeather)
Lilium canadense (Canada lily)
Lupinus perennis (wild lupine)
Monarda didyma (beebalm)
Penstemon digitalis (beardtongue)
Rudbeckia hirta (black-eyed Susan)
Solidago spp. (goldenrods)

Grasses for the Northeast

Andropogon virginicus (broomsedge)
Bouteloua curtipendula (sideoats grama grass)
Festuca elatior (tall fescue)

(continued)

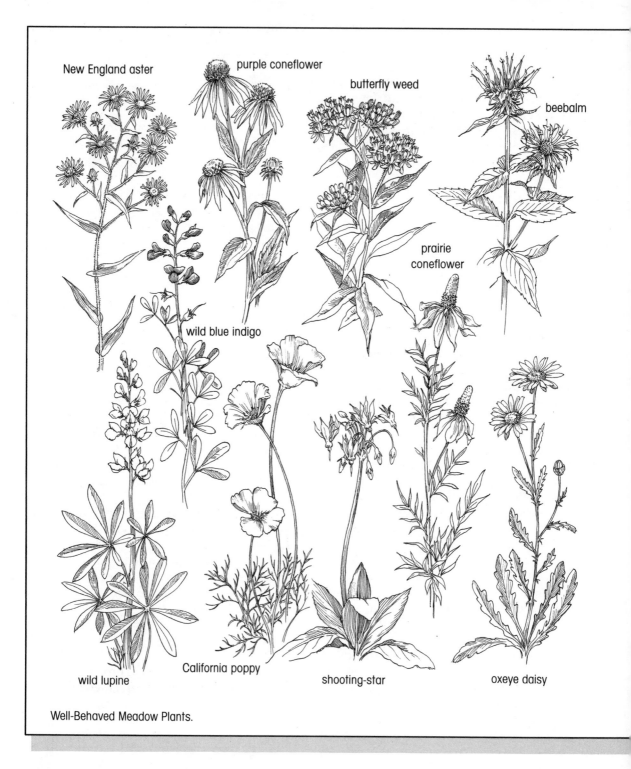

New England aster

purple coneflower

butterfly weed

beebalm

prairie coneflower

wild blue indigo

wild lupine

California poppy

shooting-star

oxeye daisy

Well-Behaved Meadow Plants.

Well-Behaved Meadow Plants—*(Continued)*

Koeleria cristata (June grass)
Panicum virgatum (switch grass)
Schizachyrium scoparium (little blue-
    stem); may also be sold as
    Andropogon scoparius

Flowers for the Southeast

*Achillea millefolium (yarrow)
Asclepias tuberosa (butterfly weed)
Baptisia australis (wild blue indigo)
*Centaurea cyanus (bachelor's-button)
Chaemaecrista fasciculata (partridge
    pea)
Coreopsis lanceolata (lance-leaved
    coreopsis)
C. tinctoria (calliopsis)
*Cosmos sulphureus (orange cosmos)
Echinacea purpurea (purple
    coneflower)
Gaillardia pulchella (Indian blanket)
Helenium autumnale (sneezeweed)
Ipomopsis rubra (Texas plume)
Liatris spicata (spike gayfeather)
Oenothera speciosa (showy evening
    primrose)
Rudbeckia hirta (black-eyed Susan)
Solidago spp. (goldenrods)
*Trifolium incarnatum (crimson
    clover)

*Indicates non-native plants that can be successfully naturalized.

Grasses for the Southeast

Andropogon virginicus (broomsedge)
Festuca caesia (blue fescue); may also
    be sold as *Festuca ovina* var.
    glauca
Miscanthus floridulus (giant
    miscanthus)
M. sinensis 'Gracillimus' (maiden
    grass)

Panicum virgatum (switch grass)
Schizachyrium scoparium (little blue-
    stem); may also be sold as
    Andropogon scoparius

Flowers for the
Midwest and Southeast

Allium cernuum (nodding pink onion)
Amorpha canescens (leadplant)
Asclepias tuberosa (butterfly weed)
Aster azureus (blue aster)
A. ericoides (heath aster)
Baptisia spp. (false indigo)
Coreopsis palmata (stiff coreopsis)
Echinacea purpurea (purple
    coneflower)
Geum triflorum (prairie smoke)
Helianthus mollis (hairy sunflower)
H. occidentalis (western sunflower)
Lespedeza capitata (round-headed
    bush clover)
Lupinus perennis (wild lupine)
Penstemon spp. (penstemons)
Rudbeckia hirta (black-eyed Susan)
Sisyrinchium campestre (prairie
    blue-eyed grass)
Solidago speciosa (showy goldenrod)
Veronicastrum virginicum (Culver's
    root)

Grasses for the
Midwest and Southwest

Andropogon gerardii (big bluestem)
Bouteloua curtipendula (sideoats
    grama grass)
B. gracilis (blue grama grass)
Carex pennsylvanica (Pennsylvania
    sedge)
Elymus canadensis (Canada wild rye)

(continued)

seedlings. Shallow disking is essential, because deeper tilling brings up additional weed seed. The process should probably be repeated one or several more times to help deplete the weed seed in the upper layer of soil. You might even water the tilled soil to encourage a really good crop of weeds, leading them on to their ultimate demise—your hoe or tiller.

Once the soil is tilled and weeded several times, then and only then should you sow the meadow garden. Do this in either spring or fall, depending on your climate; in the South and mid-Atlantic, fall sowing works best, in the North, spring sowing. It is essential to sow the seed thickly—often this means sowing seed at twice the recommended rate on the package—to further keep out weeds. Once the meadow is up and growing, hand weeding may be in order to get rid of the occasional weeds that are sure to invade despite your best efforts. It helps to be able to distinguish a weed seed from the desirable plants you're after so you can rogue them out early.

You must mow the meadow once a year to prevent brambles and tree seedlings from insidiously turning it into a woodland. This yearly mowing is the only time-consuming maintenance needed by a well-established meadow. Cut the meadow to a height of 6 inches using a small tractor or scythe because a lawn mower can't handle the tall stalks. If you enjoy the sight of the dried grasses and wildflower seedheads in winter, wait until early spring to mow; otherwise, fall mowing is fine.

The New American Garden

The so-called New American Garden is an increasingly popular landscaping style that does away with many of the elements of traditional landscapes—artificial-looking flower borders, evergreen foundation plantings, lawns, and hedges. This new style merges flower gardens with landscape plantings to create a naturalistic setting unlike any other style of garden. Weekend gardeners take note! This new style fits the new American life-style—it's naturalistic and casual, yet sophisticated, and it's decidedly low maintenance.

Supposedly inspired by America's prairies, which have increasingly delighted innovative gardeners during the last 20 years, this naturalistic style of gardening does not attempt to imitate nature. It is not a copy, even in microcosm, of any real ecosystem, as are woodland or meadow gardens. And the plants most commonly used in these gardens are not necessarily natives, but a gardener's creation of a community of natives and exotics that thrive together under the same growing conditions.

The New American Garden turns out to be rather what one might expect of an artist interpreting a prairie with bold brush strokes. In this case, the gardener's primary palette is a collection of ornamental grasses—many of them American natives, but a significant number originally hailing from Europe or Asia—and showy flowering perennials, many of them originating in the American prairie. As with any low-maintenance planting, the key to success is to carefully match plants to the conditions the site has to offer.

Although the emphasis on ornamental grasses suggests an expanse of prairie, the New American Garden hardly looks like a real prairie. Composed primarily of one or two kinds of grasses and sprinklings of bright forbs, a prairie creates a uniform swath of texture and color. The New American Garden relies on design principles more akin to

Characteristics of the New American Garden

The naturalistic style of the New American Garden relies on choosing and arranging suitable plants—mostly ornamental grasses and perennials—into a bold ground-covering tapestry. This tapestry changes throughout the year, having a distinctive appearance each season. Follow these principles for designing the new-style garden.

• Select plants that are suitable for your region's growing conditions, so they will need no special care.

• Choose perennials with an especially long period of bloom rather than those with a short burst of bloom.

• Choose plants whose foliage looks attractive even when the plant is not in bloom.

• Choose herbaceous plants that age well—even their dried stalks and seedheads should remain attractive over the winter.

• Arrange plants in masses so the garden exhibits a dynamic seasonal display and looks attractive even in winter.

• Use evergreens to form a static backdrop for the ever-changing herbaceous plants and to provide winter color.

• Allow plants to grow into their natural forms without pruning or staking.

• Allow plants to go to seed, and let dead and dried foliage, stalks, and seedpods stand over winter.

Perennials for the New American Garden

According to Carole Ottesen, author of *The New American Garden*, only plants with the "right stuff" should have a home in the new-style garden. The following flowering perennials have just the right stuff to look good all four seasons of the year.

Achillea filipendulina 'Coronation Gold' ('Coronation Gold' yarrow), Zone 3

Allium giganteum (giant onion), Zone 4

Astilbe × arendsii (astilbe), Zone 4

A. chinensis 'Pumila' (Chinese astilbe), Zone 5

A. tacquetii 'Superba' (Superba giant astilbe), Zone 4

Aster tataricus (tartarian aster), Zone 4

Boltonia asteroides (white boltonia), Zone 4

Ceratostigma plumbaginoides (leadwort), Zone 6

Coreopsis verticillata (threadleaf coreopsis), Zone 3

Echinacea purpurea (purple coneflower), Zone 3

Eupatorium purpureum (Joe-Pye weed), Zone 4

Hemerocallis hybrids (daylilies), particularly longer-blooming cultivars such as 'Stella D'Oro', Zone 3

Iris sibirica (Siberian iris), Zone 4

Liriope spp. (lilyturfs), Zones 4–6, depending on species

Papaver orientale (Oriental poppy), Zone 2

Perovskia atriplicifolia (Russian sage), Zone 5

Rudbeckia fulgida 'Goldsturm' ('Goldsturm' black-eyed Susan), Zone 3

Sedum 'Autumn Joy' (Autumn Joy sedum), Zone 3

S. 'Ruby Glow' (Ruby Glow sedum), Zone 3

S. spectabile 'Brilliant' ('Brilliant' showy stonecrop), Zone 3

Stachys byzantina (lamb's-ears), Zone 5

---

creating a traditional perennial border: The grasses and flowers are planted in large groups of a single type of plant for dramatic effect. Unlike a traditional border, however, the plantings are not confined to a bed or border but become the entire landscape, covering the ground and leaving little or no space for lawn. The result is not the uniform beauty of the prairie, but the dramatic, dynamic beauty of an all-encompassing garden. In actuality, many gardeners plant a slope or a hillside in this style, or confine the New American Garden to a large border or bed. And many garden designers find that incorporating easy-care ornamental grasses as punctuation marks among the flowers in a traditional perennial border creates a great deal of visual excitement.

Designing a New-Style Garden

Most ornamental grasses and the perennials that combine well with them need at least a half day of full sun and do well in average soil, though some need or tolerate shade, and others prefer ample soil moisture. Since the most striking ornamental grasses grow quite tall, you'll probably want to include a few clumps in the 6-foot range. They'll need plenty of growing space—most experts advise that to avoid overcrowding, you should space grasses as far apart as they will grow tall. (Mulch the bare ground between plants for the first several seasons to control weeds until the grasses fill in.) So provide your garden with generous proportions. A space at least 6 feet deep and three times as long will get you going and provide visual balance.

The garden should be enjoyed from both inside and out, if possible, so select a situation in full view of a frequently used room. Good situations include a wide border surrounding a front or backyard, if you don't dare to plant the entire yard with a new-style garden. A slope or hillside, or the strip along a driveway or walk, also makes an ideal location. (The lists in this chapter and the encyclopedia section near the end of the book will help you select grasses and perennials for the growing conditions your site has to offer.)

When a large deck or patio surrounds the garden, you'll appreciate the plants more because you can enjoy your stylized meadow close at hand. This hardscape is essential to enjoy the outdoor space if you have done away with lawn entirely, because it becomes the outdoor living area. Here is where you can relax and lounge in the sun, barbecue dinner, and play ball with the kids. Create a wide path wandering through a large-scale planting as an invitation to experience the garden close at hand. A path allows you to tend the plants—if they need it—and to explore the garden. Paths give visual depth and lure people into the garden, showing them that this is a place not just to be looked at but shared.

Plant Choices and Arrangements

Ornamental grasses—there are by now hundreds of them available to American gardeners—cover the range of sizes and heights. Some are fine-textured, others more coarse. Some feature brightly variegated foliage, and others a more subtle color scheme. Though admired for their foliage, their flower stalks —often feathery plumes that sparkle with light—command attention, usually during late summer and fall. Most ornamental grasses age well, drying in place and bleaching into wonderful almond, wheat, and rusty hues for the winter months.

The flowering perennials often found in the new-style landscape include those that Carole Otteson describes in her book, *The New American Garden*, as "perennials with the right stuff." These fine perennials bloom for long periods, look good for most of the year—even in winter—demand little care, and live for a long time. Perennials with the right stuff combine well with grasses when planted in large groups that lend unity and cohesion to the planting design.

One of Carole's favorite combinations is porcupine grass (*Miscanthus sinensis* 'Strictus') and coreopsis 'Moonbeam' (*Coreopsis verticillata* 'Moonbeam'), which complement each other in both form and color. The grass *(continued on page 240)*

Ornamental Grasses for the New American Garden

Ornamental grasses are the most dynamic part of the new-style garden. They change dramatically throughout the seasons and create billowy masses of foliage and feathery flowers that last through the winter.

Very Tall Grasses (6 Ft. Or Taller)

Cortaderia selloana (pampas grass), Zone 8

**Miscanthus floridulus* (giant miscanthus), Zone 6

M. sinensis (eulalia grass), Zone 4

M. sinensis 'Gracillimus' (maiden grass), Zone 4

Sinarundinaria nitida (clump bamboo), Zone 4

Tall Grasses (3–6 Ft.)

Calamogrostis × *acutiflora* 'Stricta' (feather reed grass), Zone 5

Miscanthus sinensis var. *purpurascens* (flame grass), Zone 4

M. sinensis 'Strictus' (porcupine grass), Zone 4

**M. sinensis* 'Variegatus' (variegated Japanese silver grass), Zone 4

Panicum virgatum (switch grass), Zone 3

P. virgatum 'Rotstrahlbusch' (red switch grass), Zone 3

Pennisetum setaceum var. *atropurpureum* (annual purple fountain grass), Zone 8

Spartina pectinata 'Aureo-Marginata' (prairie cord grass), Zone 5

Medium-Height Grasses (1–3 Ft.)

†*Carex morrowii* 'Aurea-Variegata' (variegated Japanese sedge), Zone 6

†*Chasmanthium latifolium* (sea oats), Zone 4

†*Hakonechloa macra* var. *aureola* (variegated golden hakonechloa), Zone 4

Helictotrichon sempervirens (blue oat grass), Zone 4

**Imperata cylindrica* 'Red Baron' (Japanese blood grass), Zone 5

Pennisetum alopecuroides (fountain grass), Zone 6

P. alopecuroides 'Viridescens' (black-seeded fountain grass), Zone 7

P. setaceum 'Rubrum' (purple-leaved fountain grass), Zone 8

**Phalaris arundinacea* var. *picta* (gardener's garters), Zone 4

Low Grasses (Under 1 Ft.)

Arrhenatherum elatius var. *bulbosum* (bulbous oat grass), Zone 4

†*Carex stricta* 'Bowles' Golden' (Bowles' Golden sedge), Zone 6

Festuca amethystina var. *superba* (blue sheep's fescue), Zone 4

*Liriope muscari (big blue lilyturf), Zone 6

†*Luzula* spp. (wood rushes), Zones 3–5, depending on species

**Ophiopogon japonicus* (mondo grass), Zone 7

*Indicates grasses that do well in shade or sun.
†Indicates grasses that require half or full shade.

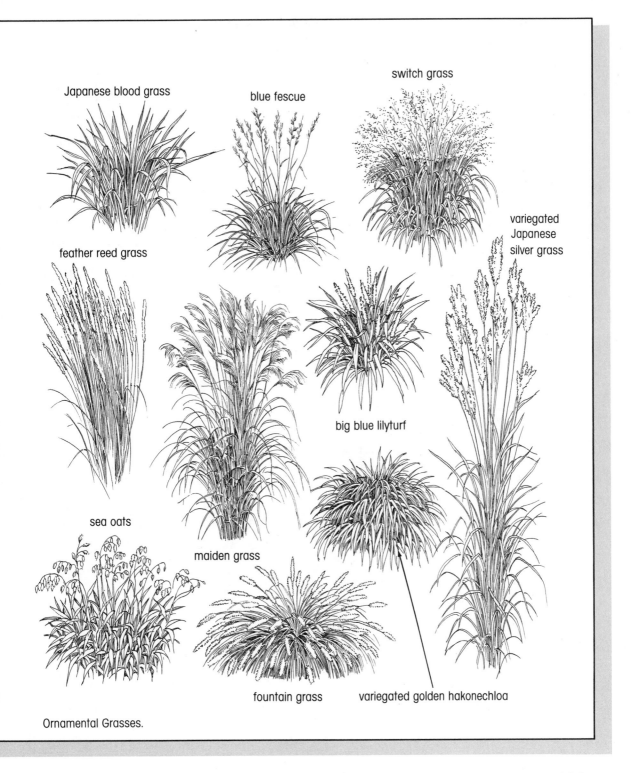

Japanese blood grass

blue fescue

switch grass

feather reed grass

variegated
Japanese
silver grass

big blue lilyturf

sea oats

maiden grass

fountain grass

variegated golden hakonechloa

Ornamental Grasses.

forms a 4-foot-tall vase of bright green foliage marked with horizontal yellow bands. The rapidly spreading coreopsis hugs the ground beneath the vase of grass blades, and its pale yellow flowers highlight the green and yellow of the foliage. Carole also creates a refreshing combination of gray, white, and pink by combining pink-flowered astilbe with silver-foliaged lamb's-ears (*Stachys byzantina*) and white-striped ribbon grass (*Phalaris arundinacea* var. *picta*). She cautions, however, that ribbon grass can be highly invasive and may need confining within a sunken edging, such as that used as a lawn

border (see "Easy-Care Edgings" on page 48).

Fountain grass (*Pennisetum alopecuroides*) works well in a variety of situations, says Carole, especially as a groundcover. Its 3-foot-long blades cascade gently and turn an eye-catching bright almond color for winter. The shimmery tails of flowers transform a groundcover planting into a miniature wheat field in summer. Fountain grass combines admirably with the golden flowers of 'Goldsturm' black-eyed Susan (*Rudbeckia fulgida* 'Goldsturm'), which begin blooming in July and continue well into fall, their seedheads drying into chocolate-colored

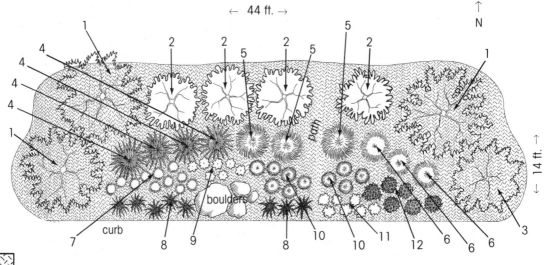

Susan and Mark's New American Garden. (1) white pine, (2) rhododendron, (3) eastern red cedar, (4) zebra grass, (5) maiden grass, (6) 'Rotstrahlbusch' switch grass, (7) 'Golden Showers' threadleaf coreopsis, (8) variegated Japanese sedge, (9) sea oats, (10) annual fountain grass, (11) Autumn Joy sedum, (12) 'Goldsturm' rudbeckia

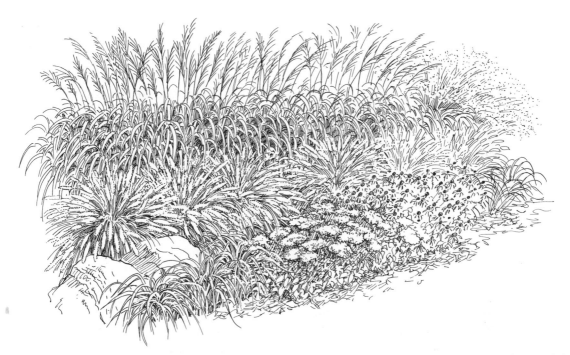

The strip of land bordering the road in front of our property was a perfect site for our New American garden. Ornamental grasses add an exciting dimension, with their bold foliage and their feathery plumes that catch the light. I combined long-blooming, yellow-flowered perennials and Autumn Joy sedum with gold-variegated grasses and placed a cluster of boulders in the foreground for a naturalistic effect.

masses that act as snow-catchers all winter.

Another favorite perennial of the new American garden set, Autumn Joy sedum (*Sedum* 'Autumn Joy'), outshines almost any other perennial when it comes to year-round interest. Starting growth with pale green mounds of succulent foliage in spring, the plant grows into a mass of tightly clustered, rounded leaves topped with green buds that open into rosy flowers in late summer. The flowers mature into rusty-colored flat disks that withstand frost and the ravages of winter. The foliage dries slowly, turning brown and dropping over winter, but the flat dried flower clusters stand stiffly on their stems to catch the snow. Mass-plant Autumn Joy sedum in the foreground or midground, where its rounded textures and seasonal color displays will add contrast and excitement to a border of linear grasses.

When you start planning your New American Garden, think of it more as a landscape style rather than simply as a garden. It requires plenty of space. Arrange the plants in your new-style garden so that they create a view from inside and out, keeping masses of the tallest material at the back and to the sides of the garden. But don't be afraid to break up the expanses of lower plants with a single tall specimen or small groups of distinctive plants. Keep in mind that ornamental grasses grow rapidly into huge clumps.

Evergreens play an essential but self-effacing role in the new-style garden. They form the backdrop to set off the seasonal changes of the herbaceous plants. Only in winter do the evergreens come into their own, adding essential color to the earth tones of the dried grasses and flowers. Plant large groups of evergreen trees, such as eastern redcedars (*Juniperus virginiana*), white pines (*Pinus strobus*), or hemlocks (*Tsuga canadensis*), at the back and sides of the garden to form a backdrop and a screen; you might also situate several specimens or small groups of evergreen shrubs, such as yews (*Taxus* spp.), junipers (*Juniperus* spp.), or mugho pines (*Pinus mugo*), among the grasses and flowers. Deciduous shrubs combine well with grasses, too. Burning bush (*Euonymus alata* 'Compactus') with its flaming red fall foliage, or rugosa rose (*Rosa rugosa*), with its coarse crinkled foliage, large, wide-open flowers, and gleaming red fall fruit accent the seasonal changes of the grasses.

Part of the naturalistic flavor of the New American Garden comes from allowing the plants to dry in place as seeds form and frost nips the foliage. Left to stand through winter, many of the grasses change from their summer hues to a bright fall color, then to an earthy hue of bleached straw, almond, or rust. The flowering perennials—chosen to keep their seedheads or change color in fall—take on deep chocolate, rusty brown, or beige hues. The garden ages into one giant dried flower arrangement that lasts all winter.

Bulbs—masses of them—also have a place in the New American Garden. Spring-flowering bulbs planted between the individual perennials and ornamental grasses will decorate the garden after the dried foliage has been removed and before the new growth becomes large enough to provide interest. The bulbs fill the bill when the garden would

otherwise be at its barest. Ornamental grasses and bulbs make a perfect combination. Just when the bulbs finish blooming and their foliage begins to wither and become unsightly, the grass blades start shooting up. The clumps of grass camouflage the withering bulb foliage to keep the garden lovely throughout every season. Crocuses, daffodils, tulips, and alliums work well, providing a sequence of bloom from the time the grass foliage is cut down in late winter until the new growth becomes tall enough to be effective.

Mark and I planted a garden of ornamental grasses and rugosa roses (*Rosa rugosa*) along a strip of ground bordering the street in front of our property. The area was a weedy spot of lawn about 10 feet deep and 25 feet long, in front of a mature screen of white pines and rhododendrons. We smothered the struggling grass with wood chips and planted the grasses and roses without any further soil improvement. Because both the grasses and the shrub roses we chose tolerate drought, we no longer have to concern ourselves with getting the hose and sprinkler down to that hard-to-reach spot. And the garden makes an unusually beautiful sight that we enjoy every time we pull in or out of our driveway.

In our garden, short, midsize, and tall grasses arranged in sweeping masses create a stunning year-round display against the evergreen foliage. I chose white-variegated and blue-green grasses to combine with the glossy dark green foliage and pale pink blossoms of the three rose bushes planted in a mass in the mid-ground. Several vase-shaped clumps of maiden grass (*Miscanthus sinensis* 'Gracillimus') form the background to the roses, their graceful arching blades with white midribs adding a delicate contrast to the substantial texture of the roses. Fan-shaped white flowers catch the sun in autumn when the rugosa roses turn yellow and red. Growing into foot-tall arching clumps of silvery-edged foliage, Japanese silver sedge (*Carex morrowii* 'Variegata') forms a foreground to the roses. A drift of 2-foot-tall, spiky mounds of blue oat grass (*Helictotrichon sempervirens*) weaves from the foreground at one end of the bed into the midground near the roses. At the other end, great white splashes from the foliage of ribbon grass (*Phalaris arundinacea* var. *picta*) form an eye-catching mass.

Why It's Low-Maintenance

The only regular gardening chore demanded by the new-style garden comes in late winter, when the dried stalks and foliage must be cut down and removed. This can be done with a hedge clipper, scythe, or power string trimmer—a regular lawn mower won't do. Cut the grasses back to 4 to 6 inches above the ground and rake away the remains. It is important to do this chore before new growth begins. Your work will be magnified enormously if you must cut out the dried foliage from among the new green sprouts.

Ornamental grasses do not need any fertilizer; they have deep roots and can pretty much seek out all the nourishment they need. Adding fertilizer only encourages them to grow to even greater heights, and some may become floppy.

After 10 or 20 years, certain grasses will have grown into huge clumps with hollow centers. They will look more attractive if they are divided. Dividing a huge clump of ornamental grass is no mean feat, because their root systems are like iron. Dig up the clumps and use an axe or chainsaw to cut them into sections for replanting—or move to a new house.

Some Like It Wild

As development encroaches on the natural beauty that once offered us peace and solace, and environmental issues make the headlines with ever more frequency, many Americans are beginning to feel an urgency about preserving the special plants and ecosystems that constitute our land. A movement toward naturalistic landscaping and wildflower gardening began in the 1920s with the work of landscape designer Jens Jensen. But only recently has the general public begun to appreciate the beauty and practicality of the naturalistic landscape.

The woodland playground of my childhood and the love of the outdoors that it taught me influenced my life profoundly and probably helped slant my taste in gardening toward the naturalistic and casual rather than toward the formal and contrived. I've been doing my part to preserve the environment by planting my own low-maintenance woodland gardens that demand little expenditure of water and energy to maintain.

Like me, many gardeners can conjure up images of natural landscapes that were special places to them as children or that impressed them while traveling as adults. Many of these natural sites can serve as inspiration for our gardening endeavors. Naturalistic gardens, whether relying upon native and naturalized plants, well-adapted exotics, or both, offer a beautiful low-maintenance choice for weekend gardeners. Celebrating the best Nature has to offer, a woodland, meadow, or new American-style garden makes itself at home on your property and requires so little care there will be plenty of time for more demanding gardening activities. All this, and your naturalistic garden will be doing something good for the environment, too!

AN ENCYCLOPEDIA OF EASY-CARE PLANTS FOR WEEKEND GARDENS

The hundreds of plants described here are proven performers in low-maintenance gardens. They are tough but attractive plants —plants that adapt to a range of growing conditions, tolerate a bit of benign neglect, and rarely suffer from diseases and insects. The encyclopedia tells you want they are, what they look like, how to grow them, and where to use them. If you don't recognize some of these plants from their names and descriptions, consult a good plant identification guide, such as the Taylor's series or a well-illustrated mail-order catalog, and choose the plants that match your taste, needs, and growing conditions.

Don't be surprised if some of the most well-known garden plants are not included here. If a common plant is left out, there's probably a reason. It may be highly pest-susceptible, require continual care to look its best, or grow unwieldy without staking or regular pruning.

The groundcovers included here are low-maintenance plants when mass-planted in place of a high-maintenance lawn or used as a living mulch beneath perennials, shrubs, and trees. The shade and ornamental trees were carefully selected to include only those species that live long lives, have strong wood, and do not litter excessively. Only evergreen and flowering shrubs that require little maintenance found their way into this encyclopedia, and you'll find recommendations for slow-growing and dwarf cultivars that work best in foundation plantings.

Though flowering annuals often require constant maintenance, only those that flourish with a minimum of attention are included here. Most of the perennials are choice types that are long-lived and rarely need division or staking; others are rampant growers that may be problems in tidy gardens, but find a perfect home in a naturalistic landscape where they will crowd out weeds. The bulbs listed don't die out or need annual digging or replanting. And the great shrub roses are beautiful, satisfying plants that require much less care than modern garden roses.

The best woodland wildflowers and hardy ferns for shade gardens are featured, as well as care-free flowers and grasses for colorful meadow gardens. Use the ornamental grasses in a "New American Garden," or as accents in a more traditional landscape.

An Encyclopedia of Plants for Weekend Gardens

Plant Name	Description	Culture and Maintenance	Landscape Use and Comments

Easy-Care Groundcovers

Aegopodium podagraria 'Variegatum' **Silveredge goutweed, silveredge bishop's weed**	Deciduous perennial. Attractive foliage toothed, three-part, green with bright white edges. Lacy white flower heads bloom in early summer. Spreads by creeping rootstalks.	Grows in any type of soil in sun or shade. Extremely aggressive in rich, moist soil, less invasive in poor soil. Cut off faded flowers for best appearance. Space 1 ft. apart. Zones 3–10.	Looks beautiful planted in a mass beneath trees or shrubs, but can become seriously invasive. Control with lawn edging or a curb. Will resprout from root pieces left in soil. The all-green form is even more weedy.
Ajuga reptans **Bugleweed, carpet bugleweed**	Semi-evergreen perennial. Shiny, ground-hugging foliage forms tight low rosettes. Spikes of blue flowers 6 in. tall in mid-spring. Spreads by above-ground runners.	Grows best in rich, moist but well-drained soil in semi-shade, but tolerates deep shade and full sun. May rot where soil is too wet or in the Deep South. Propagate by removing new plantlets at ends of runners. Space 6 to 12 in. apart. Cut back runners in spring to control spread at lawn edge. Mow off spent flowers. Zones 5–8; 5–10 on West Coast.	Makes an excellent, fast-growing cover for shady spots. Use under trees and shrubs, along walkways and paths, and in flower gardens. 'Bronze Beauty' has purplish leaves and deep blue flowers; 'Burgundy Glow' has blue flowers and light green leaves variegated with pink and silver.
Asarum canadense **Wild ginger** *A. caudatum* **British Columbia wild ginger** *A. europaeum* **European wild ginger**	*A. canadense:* deciduous perennial; *A. caudatum* and *A. europaeum:* evergreen perennial. Leaves heart-shaped; very glossy in *A. europaeum* and *A. caudatum,* matte in *A. canadense.* Flowers interesting, 3-petalled, red-brown, hidden beneath leaves. Spread by creeping rootstocks to form 8-in.-high carpets.	Grow in semi- to deep shade in moist, humusy soil. Propagate by division. Space 1 ft. apart. *A. canadense:* Zones 4–9; *A. europaeum:* Zones 5–9; *A. caudatum:* Zones 6–9.	Combine with wildflowers and ferns for a beautiful texture in a woodland setting. Use evergreen species under shrubs and in shade garden. Spread rapidly, but are not invasive.
Astilbe chinensis 'Pumila' **Chinese astilbe**	Deciduous perennial. Foliage green-bronze, fernlike; forms 6-in.-tall clumps. Flowers dusty pink, borne in 12-in.-tall plumes that bloom from bottom up in late summer. Spreads slowly by underground runners.	Grows best in partial shade in rich, moist soil. Tolerates more dryness than other astilbes. Space 1 ft. apart. Best to divide every 4 years. Zones 5–8.	The best groundcover astilbe. Use in shade gardens and along garden paths. Combine with small hostas.

(continued)

Plant Name	Description	Culture and Maintenance	Landscape Use and Comments

Easy-Care Groundcovers—(continued)

Plant Name	Description	Culture and Maintenance	Landscape Use and Comments
Bergenia cordifolia **Heartleaf bergenia**	Semi-evergreen perennial. Large, leathery, dark green, heart-shaped leaves form basal clumps. Foliage turns bronze in fall and winter. Pink or white flowers on 1-ft.-tall stalks in early spring. Increases by underground rootstalks.	Best in rich, humusy, moist soil; tolerates drought and poor soil. Best in partial shade; tolerates sun. Propagate by division. Space plants 2 ft. apart. If foliage looks battered at winter's end, cut it back. May be troubled by slugs. Zones 3–10.	Mass-plant for contrasting leaf textures with ornamental grasses, ferns, or other fine-textured plants. Use as specimen in rock or shade garden. Foliage holds up better in mild climates.
Cerastium tomentosum **Snow-in-summer**	Semi-evergreen perennial. Forms mats of narrow, silver-gray, woolly foliage. Covered with airy clusters of white flowers from late spring to early summer. Spreads by creeping stems.	Grows best in average to sandy soil in full sun; tolerates light shade. Spreads rapidly, as much as 2 ft. a year, and may get out of bounds, but easy to pull up. May self-sow. Cut off faded flowers with hedge shears. Propagate by division. Space 2 or more feet apart. Zones 3–10.	Use between paving stones; mow after blooming. Looks wonderful cascading over stone walls and in the perennial garden, where its silver foliage combines with all colors of flowers.
Ceratostigma plumbaginoides (*Plumbago larpentiae*) **Plumbago, leadwort**	Deciduous to semi-evergreen perennial. Somewhat woody stems spread across the ground, forming a dense cover about 1 ft. high. Leaves glossy green tinged red to bronze in fall. Pure blue flowers bloom over a long period in late summer and fall; faded flowers drop, leaving attractive rusty-red calyx. Spreads by underground stems.	Grow in full sun to part shade. Spreads rapidly in rich, moist soil. In colder zones, dies back completely to ground and emerges slowly in spring. Cut back to ground in late winter. Can become invasive; contain with edging if necessary. Propagate by cuttings. Zones 6–10.	Showy throughout fall and into winter. Beautiful groundcover around deciduous shrubs with fall color. Plant where lack of winter greenery poses no problem. Useful for both large- and small-scale plantings.
Chrysogonum virginianum **Goldenstar, green-and-gold**	Deciduous perennial. Triangular, hairy leaves on 4- to 10-in.-tall, spreading plants. Small, bright yellow flowers appear from spring through summer. Increases by creeping stems and seedlings.	Grow in partial to full shade in rich soil with good drainage. Tolerates full sun only in very moist soil. Propagate by division every few years. Space 1 ft. apart. Zones 5–9.	A pretty plant to use as a specimen or in masses in wildflower or shade garden, or under shrubs. Blooms in summer only in cool northern areas.

Plant Name	Description	Culture and Maintenance	Landscape Use and Comments
Convallaria majalis **Lily-of-the-valley**	Deciduous perennial. Two 8-in.-tall basal leaves clasp each flower stem. White, bell-shaped flowers on one-sided stalks bloom in late spring. Very fragrant. Increases rapidly by spreading rhizomes.	Grow in partial to full shade in moist, fertile soil. Can become invasive. Foliage looks battered and yellows by mid- to late summer and during drought. Apply compost or rotted manure annually in spring to increase flowering. Propagate by division. Zones 3–9.	Plant in masses or small groups under shrubs or in woodland or shade gardens. Locate where unsightly late summer foliage will not be a problem.
Cotoneaster spp. **Cotoneasters**	Deciduous to evergreen shrubs. Many species make useful groundcovers. Most feature neat oval leaves on twiggy stems, tiny white or pink flowers in early summer, bright red berries in late summer and fall, and good orange-red to purple-red fall leaf color.	Grow in full sun in average, well-drained soil. Susceptible to fireblight and spider mites. Fallen tree leaves catch in twiggy stems and may be time-consuming to remove by hand or leaf blower. Increases by long, spreading branches, which may root. Propagate by layering or cuttings. Space 2 to 5 ft. apart. Zones 5–9.	Useful as a groundcover on banks and in sunny areas, as a specimen in a rock garden, or as foundation plants. Where fireblight is a problem, do not mass-plant. *C. horizontalis* (rock cotoneaster), noted for its fishbone branching pattern, spreads wide and grows 2 to 3 ft high. *C. dammeri* (bearberry cotoneaster) trails along the ground; it features evergreen leaves and grows fast. *C. adpressus* var. *praecox* (creeping cotoneaster) grows slowly, creeping along the ground; it fruits heavily.
Epimedium spp. **Epimediums, barrenworts**	Sometimes woody, deciduous perennials. Compound leaves with heart-shaped leaflets on wiry stems. New foliage often light green with tinges of red. Sprays of delicate flowers in early to mid-spring. Spreads by underground runners to form dense clumps about 10 in. high.	Prefers partial shade, but grows in full sun if soil is moist. Tolerates drought if shaded. Cut back to ground in late winter. Propagate by division. Zones 3–8.	Charming in woodland or shade garden. Use as edging along trail or walk, or mass-plant under shrubs. Spreads well, but not invasive. Dried foliage may remain showy through much of the winter. *E.* × *rubrum* (red epimedium) has pink to crimson flowers and bronze-purple fall foliage. *E. grandiflorum* (bishop's hat) has pink-and-white flowers; *E.* × *versicolor* 'Youngianum' features yellow flowers and small leaves.

(continued)

Plant Name	*Description*	*Culture and Maintenance*	*Landscape Use and Comments*

Easy-Care Groundcovers—(continued)

Euonymus fortunei **Winter-creeper**	Evergreen vine. Glossy, oval foliage varies in size and coloration depending on the cultivar and may be variegated or purple-tinted. Flowers not showy. Vines trail and climb to 20 ft., rooting as they go.	Grow in sun or shade in average to moist soil. Propagate by cuttings or division. Scale insects may be very serious, apply dormant and summer oil sprays. Cut back to prevent from climbing high into trees and buildings. Zones 5–10.	Useful carpeting plant for erosion control on banks. Looks attractive cascading over a wall. Avoid mass-planting variegated cultivars because they may look too busy. Use dwarf wintercreeper between stepping stones.
Galium odoratum (*Asperula odorata*) **Sweet woodruff**	Semi-evergreen to deciduous perennial. Tiny, whorled, bright green leaves on 6- to 8-in.-high stems form extensive mats. Tiny starlike white flowers dot the plants in spring. Spreads rapidly by underground runners.	Best in partial to dense shade in rich, humusy soil. Keep moist but not wet. Prevent from invading lawn by edging. Propagate by division. Space 1 ft. apart. Zones 4–8.	Wonderful groundcover in woodland or shade garden. Combines well with tall spring bulbs and woodland plants. Mass-plant under shrubs. Fine texture looks good in small gardens. Spreads less in poor soil.
Hedera helix **English ivy**	Evergreen vine. Shiny, dark green, 3- to 5-lobed leaves with light green veins. Vines trail or climb to 20 ft., rooting as they go. Flowers form only on the bushy adult form of ivy when it climbs.	Best in moist soil in partial to full shade. Full sun in winter can cause leaf burn. Trim back two or three times a year with clippers to keep in bounds. Prevent from climbing high into trees. Clinging appendages called holdfasts can damage buildings. Propagate by cuttings or division. Space cuttings 6 in. apart. Zones 5–10.	Beautiful, fast-growing groundcover for shady spots. Good for erosion control on slopes and trailing over walls. Include spring-flowering bulbs among the ivy for seasonal color. Some people get a rash from handling the foliage; if you're susceptible, wear gloves.
Hosta spp. **Hosta, plantain lily, funkia**	Deciduous perennial. Clumps of basal foliage vary from 6 in. to 3 ft. tall. Leaves usually heavily veined, varying in color from bright green through yellow-green to blue-green. Many variegated cultivars available. Spikes of lavender, white, or purple flowers from midsummer to fall. Many species and cultivars. Increases by expanding clump size.	Does best in rich, moist soil, but tolerates drought and poor soil. Grow in partial to full shade: green hostas prefer quarter- to all-day sun; golds and variegated hostas quarter- to half-day sun; blues full shade to half-day sun. Cut off spent flower stalks, which can look unsightly; remove frost-killed foliage in late fall. Propagate by division. Slugs may be a problem. Zones 4–9.	Grown more for the fantastic foliage than for the flowers. Use yellow-green cultivars with yellow-, orange-, and purple-flowered plants; blue-green cultivars with blue, purple, and pink flowers. White-variegated hostas go well with white and pastel flowers. Use in shade garden, and along woodland paths with ferns.

Plant Name	Description	Culture and Maintenance	Landscape Use and Comments
Iberis sempervirens **Candytuft, edging candytuft**	Evergreen subshrub. Narrow green leaves on ascending branches form fine-textured, 1-ft.-tall, sprawling masses. Circular, flat-topped clusters of white flowers cover plants in spring.	Grow in fertile, well-drained soil in full sun or light shade. Shear heavily after blooming to increase plant density. Propagate by cuttings or division. Space 1 ft. apart. Zones 4–10.	Use in small-scale plantings for evergreen color and flowers. Pretty cascading over walls or on slopes. For groundcover use, avoid the lower-growing cultivars such as 'Little Gem' or 'Purity'. These work best as edgings.
Juniperus spp. **Junipers**	Evergreen shrubs. Leaves usually sharp-pointed, scalelike, varying in color from blue-green to bright green on creeping or low-spreading branches.	Grows best in full sun in average, well-drained soil. Tolerates drought and partial shade. Increases by spreading branches, which may root. Propagate by layering or cuttings. Space 2 or more ft. apart. Fallen tree leaves may be difficult to remove from branches. Shore juniper: Zones 6–9; creeping juniper: Zones 2–10; Japanese garden juniper: Zones 5–9.	Excellent for erosion control on slopes or banks. Effective cascading over walls. Use in foreground of foundation plantings or shrub borders. A few good groundcovers are: *J. conferta* (shore juniper), with fine-textured bright green foliage on feathery branches that spread 1 ft. tall and 6 to 8 ft. wide, establishes very rapidly as a groundcover. *J. horizontalis* (creeping juniper) has many attractive cultivars. *J. chinensis* var. *procumbens* (Japanese garden juniper) forms spreading mounds with ascending stem tips of dainty pale to bright green needles. Many other species and cultivars.
Lamium maculatum **Spotted deadnettle** *Lamiastrum galeobdolon* (*Lamium galeobdolon*) **Yellow archangel, golden deadnettle**	Deciduous to evergreen perennials. Toothed, heart-shaped, glossy leaves are usually variegated. Trailing to semi-trailing stems to 1 ft. tall. *Lamium maculatum* has a conspicuous white blotch in the center of each leaf and whorls of rosy-lavender flowers in spring and again in summer. *Lamiastrum* has yellow flowers.	Grow in full shade to partial sun. Both tolerate drought but perform best in moist, rich soil; need more moisture with more sun. Shear off flowers after they fade to encourage bushy growth. Both spread by rooting stems. *Lamiastrum* may become invasive; pull out as needed or trim back once or twice a year. *Lamium:* Zones 4–9; *Lamiastrum:* Zones 4–10; evergreen in Zones 7–10.	*Lamiastrum* makes the best groundcover for large-scale use because it grows more rapidly than *Lamium*. Combine *Lamium* with other groundcovers for a tapestry effect. Useful for mass-planting under trees and shrubs and under tall perennials. Plant as specimens and in patches in the shade garden.

(continued)

Plant Name	Description	Culture and Maintenance	Landscape Use and Comments
Easy-Care Groundcovers—(continued)			
Laurentia fluviatilis (*Isotoma fluviatilis*) **Blue-star creeper, isotoma**	Evergreen perennial. Leaves ¼-in. long on mat-forming creeping stems. Light blue, star-shaped flowers from spring through summer.	Grow in light shade; tolerates full sun if kept constantly moist but not soggy. Best in loose, fast-draining but moist soil. Increases by spreading stems. Space 6 in. apart. Zones 7–10.	Tolerates light foot traffic; use as a lawn substitute or between stepping stones. Makes a fine underplanting for shrubs. Popular on the West Coast, but will also grow on the East Coast.
Liriope muscari **Big blue lilyturf** *L. spicata* **Creeping lilytuft**	Semi-evergreen perennials. Grassy foliage may be dark green or variegated. Spikes of flowers in late summer. *L. muscari* grows into large clumps and produces showy flower spikes. *L. spicata* leaves are ½ in. across and form soft, 9-in.-high mounds; flowers remain close to the foliage.	Grow in rich to average, moisture-retentive soil in full sun to full shade. Somewhat drought-tolerant, but need ample water in sunny locations to look good. Cut back or mow almost to ground in late winter, especially if bedraggled. *L. muscari* spreads by expanding clumps; *L. spicata* by underground runners. Propagate by division. Space 6 to 12 in. apart. Slugs may be a problem. *L. muscari:* Zones 6–10; *L. spicata:* Zones 4–10.	Mass-plant green cultivars as a formal-looking groundcover or in place of lawn; cannot withstand foot traffic. *L. spicata* spreads faster than *L. muscari* and makes a better groundcover for large-scale plantings. Use variegated forms of *L. muscari* as specimens or small-scale groundcover in shade garden.
Mahonia repens **Creeping mahonia, creeping grape-holly**	Evergreen shrub. Dull bluish-green, holly-like leaflets form large compound leaves. Fragrant yellow flowers in spring followed by edible black berries. Grows about 1 ft. high. Spreads by underground stems.	Grow in acid, humusy soil in partial to full shade. Tolerates dry soil. Protect from winter sun. Propagate by dividing suckers. Space 2 to 3 ft. apart. Zones 5–9.	Use as a groundcover in woodland setting, beneath high-branched evergreens, or on shady sides of buildings. Native to the Northwest.
Mitchella repens **Partridgeberry, twin-berry**	Evergreen perennial. Oval, ½-in.-long leaves arranged opposite each other on thin creeping stems; leaves glossy green with white mid-veins. Pairs of white flowers bloom in midspring. Red berries persist into winter. Spreads by rooting stems.	Needs light to deep shade in moist, humusy, acid soil. Protect from winter sun. May be difficult to establish. Propagate by division or cuttings. Zones 4–8.	Use as fine-textured groundcover in woodland or rock gardens. Ideal under pines and other conifers where fallen needles form perfect mulch. Native to East Coast woodlands.

Plant Name	Description	Culture and Maintenance	Landscape Use and Comments
Nepeta × faassenii (*N. mussinii*) **Catmint**	Deciduous perennial. Gray-green, 1-in.-long, aromatic leaves. Forms loose, 1- to 2-ft.-tall mounds 2 ft. wide. Clouds of lavender-blue flowers at stem tips in late spring and early summer.	Grow in full sun to half shade in well-drained soil. Tolerates poor, dry soil. Cut off unsightly faded flowers. May rebloom if cut back. Propagate by division or cuttings. Space 1 ft. apart. Zones 4–10.	Fast-growing; forms dense growth useful for edging or cascading over a wall. Cats may be attracted to the plants and may eat or roll in them.
Ophiopogon japonicus **Mondo grass**	Evergreen to semi-evergreen perennial. Forms dense, 8- to 10-in.-tall clumps of grassy, ⅛-in.-wide, dark green leaves. Spikes of white flowers bloom in late summer and form blue berries in fall, but remain mostly hidden among the foliage. Increases by underground runners. Dwarf mondo grass (*O. japonicus* 'Nana') grows 2 to 3 in. tall.	Grow in full sun to full shade in good soil; keep moist, especially in full-sun conditions. Mow to renew growth and remove tattered foliage at winter's end. Propagate by division. Space 6 to 12 in. apart. Slugs may be a problem. Best in Zones 8–10; survives but looks tattered in Zone 7.	A mature planting forms a uniform sea with a coarse linear texture. Use instead of lawn grass in large beds in front yards and under trees; does not tolerate foot traffic.
Pachysandra terminalis **Japanese pachysandra, Japanese spurge**	Evergreen perennial. Glossy, toothed, dark-green foliage in whorls on 8- to 10-in.-tall stems. Short spikes of creamy white flowers in early spring. Spreads by underground runners.	Grow in good to average soil in partial to full shade; full shade in the South. Drought-tolerant, but performs best with adequate moisture and in fertile soil. Contain with lawn border or edging. Propagate by division or cuttings. Space 8 in. apart. Zones 5–8.	Pachysandra grows in the dense shade and terribly thin soil beneath surface-rooted trees, where little else will grow. Fills in quickly and practically defies weeds. Use 'Silveredge' to brighten shady spots under trees.
Phalaris arundinacea var. *picta* **Ribbon grass, gardener's garters**	Semi-evergreen, perennial cool-season grass. Flat, 1-ft.-long leaves, striped bright white and green, sometimes marked with pink, on stems that grow 1½ to 3 ft. tall. Inconspicuous summer flowers. Increases by underground runners.	Grows in full sun to full shade in wet to dry soil. May bleach out in too much sun or be too lanky in shade. Can be invasive, clay soil and shade may slow it down. Contain within lawn edging or border, or plant in clay drainage pipe to maintain as a specimen in perennial border. Mow to encourage new growth if it looks tattered by late summer. Propagate by division. Space 2 ft. apart. Zones 4–10.	Use as groundcover in small to large areas, in midground of ornamental grass gardens, or combined with pastel or white flowers. Useful in wet soil where other plants do poorly.

(continued)

Plant Name	Description	Culture and Maintenance	Landscape Use and Comments

Easy-Care Groundcovers—(continued)

Plant Name	Description	Culture and Maintenance	Landscape Use and Comments
Phlox subulata **Moss pink, mountain phlox**	Semi-evergreen perennial. Needlelike leaves on creeping stems form dense mosslike masses about 6 in. deep. In midspring, flowers completely cover plants, forming solid carpet of magenta, pink, white, lavender, violet, or blue. Many cultivars available.	Grow in full sun in well-drained soil. Centers may eventually die out; divide when this happens. Shear after flowering to encourage new growth. Space plants 1 ft. apart. Zones 3–8.	Use as groundcover on sunny banks, in rock gardens, between pavers, and in perennial garden. Combine with spring-flowering bulbs. Best in small-scale situations; large-scale plantings may be overwhelming when in bloom.
Potentilla cinerea **Rusty cinquefoil** *P. tabernae-montani* (*P. verna*) **Spring cinquefoil** *P. tridentata* **Wineleaf cinquefoil, three-toothed cinquefoil**	Semi-evergreen to evergreen, semi-woody perennials. *P. cinerea* and *P. tabernaemontani* leaves 5-fingered, resembling strawberry foliage; *P. tridentata* foliage 3-fingered, glossy green turning red in fall and winter. White flowers of *P. tridentata* bloom in midspring; yellow flowers of *P. cinerea* and *P. tabernaemontani* bloom in late spring. Creeping stems and runners form dense cover 4 to 6 in. high with *P. cinerea* and *P. tabernaemontani;* to 12 in. tall with *P. tridentata.*	Grow in full sun in well-drained to dry, acid soil. Increase by surface runners. Propagate by cuttings or division. Space 1 to 2 ft. apart. Zones 3–9.	Useful in small-scale plantings in difficult hot, dry sites. Plant in rock garden, along paths, or spilling over walls and ledges.
Pulmonaria angustifolia **Lungwort** *P. saccharata* **Lungwort, Bethlehem sage**	Deciduous perennials. Form spreading clumps 6 to 12 in. high. Bell-shaped flowers on nodding stalks in early spring before foliage fully emerges. Increases by creeping roots. *P. angustifolia* has narrow, dark green leaves and blue flowers.	Grow in partial to full shade in cool, moisture-retentive but not soggy soil. Provide even moisture or foliage may look tattered. Propagate by division. Space 1 to 2 ft. apart. Zones 3–8, but foliage may wilt in summer heat of Zones 7–8.	Spreads rapidly in the shade garden but is not invasive. Plant with spring-flowering bulbs, in a woodland garden, or under shrubs and trees.

Plant Name	Description	Culture and Maintenance	Landscape Use and Comments
Sedum acre **Goldmoss sedum** *S. album* *S. dashyphyllum* **Leafy stonecrop**	Evergreen perennials. Succulent foliage on upright branches and trailing stems that root as they go. *S. acre* has pointed, light green leaves and clusters of starlike yellow flowers in late spring. *S. album* has medium-green leaves tinged red, with white or pinkish flowers in summer. *S. dashyphyllum* has blue-green leaves closely packed into rosettes with white flowers in spring.	Grow in full to partial sun in well-drained soil. Water in times of drought; otherwise does well in dry soil. Propagate by division or cuttings; small stem pieces easily take root. Space 6 to 12 in. apart. *S. acre:* Zones 3–8; *S. album:* Zones 4–10; *S. dashyphyllum:* Zones 5–10.	Many species of groundcover sedums abound. All grow fairly rapidly, spreading to cover wide expanses of ground, but look best arranged in small-scale plantings. They don't withstand direct foot traffic, but can be arranged between stepping stones. Look most effective draped over walls and peeking between rocks, or in crevices of rock walls. *S. acre* grows vigorously and self-sows; can become weedy, but easy to pull up.
Stachys byzantina (S. olympica, S. lanata) **Lamb's-ears, woolly betony**	Semi-evergreen perennial. Leaves covered with a feltlike silvery gray fuzz, forming mats of 4- to 6-in.-long leaves. Flower stalks grow 18 in. tall and bear fuzzy spikes of small lavender-pink flowers. Spreads by aboveground stolons.	Grows best in full sun in well-drained soil. Tolerates some shade and drought, but may be less silvery. Remove winter-damaged leaves in spring. Remove flower stalks if they detract from garden. Rots in heavy, wet soil. Propagate by division. May self-sow. Space 1 ft. apart. Zones 5–10.	Wonderful contrast plant in the foreground of a perennial garden or sunny rock garden. Combines well with late spring bulbs, especially pastel colors. Use in a silver-gray garden with blue- and purple-flowered perennials. 'Silver Carpet' does not flower, and makes the best groundcover because it remains low.
Thymus pseudolanuginosus (T. lanuginosus) **Woolly thyme** *Thymus serpyllum (T. praecox var. arcticus)* **Creeping thyme, mother-of-thyme, wild thyme**	Evergreen perennials. *T. pseudolanuginosus* has tiny, gray, woolly leaves on creeping stems, making a ground-hugging mat; foliage takes on purplish hues in winter. Tiny, rose-pink flowers in summer. *T. serpyllum* has tiny, glossy green, aromatic leaves on creeping stems that form a 2-in.-high carpet. Purplish pink flowers cover the plant in early summer.	Grow in full sun in well-drained soil. Thrives in poor soil in hot, dry locations. May rot in heavy or soggy soil. Divide when centers die out. Increases by spreading stems, which root. Propagate by cuttings or division. Plant 6 in. apart. Zones 5–10.	Use as groundcover in small spaces, especially in rock and herb gardens. Plant between stepping stones or between pavers; both withstand light foot traffic and release pleasant herbal aroma when leaves are crushed. Flowers attract bees.

(continued)

Plant Name	Description	Culture and Maintenance	Landscape Use and Comments

Easy-Care Groundcovers—(continued)

Tiarella cordifolia **Foamflower**	Evergreen perennial. Maplelike foliage may be marked with dark brown or bronze. Forms clumps of basal leaves that send out long runners, which form new plants at their tips. Feathery spikes of white flowers bloom for a month in spring.	Grow in light to full shade in moist, humusy soil. Shear off spent flowers with hedge shears to improve appearance and avoid self-sowing. Propagate by division or layering. Space 1 ft. or more apart. Zones 4–8.	Use this native plant in woodland garden or foreground of shade garden. Combine with phlox and ferns.
Vinca major **Greater periwinkle** *V. minor* **Common periwinkle, myrtle, vinca**	Evergreen perennials. *V. minor* features glossy, dark green, oval leaves on long trailing stems that root as they go, forming a dense cover about 6 in. tall. Periwinkle blue flowers in spring. *V. major* forms dense stands 18 in. tall and has 2-in.-wide, bright blue flowers.	Grow in full sun to partial shade in moist, well-drained soil. Needs shade in hot-summer climates and protection from winter sun in cold-winter areas. May need to be hand-trimmed at lawn edges, but lawn mowing usually prevents periwinkle from creeping into lawn. Propagate by division or cuttings. *V. minor:* Zones 4–8; *V. major:* Zones 8–10; may suffer winter injury in Zone 8; variegated cultivar often used as an annual in northern climates.	Either vinca looks beautiful under shrubs and trees and draping over walls. Ideal for large- or small-scale plantings. Use *V. minor* to underplant spring-flowering bulbs or tall perennials; blooms at same time as daffodils, making a pretty combination. Useful in naturalistic settings and woodland gardens.
Waldsteinia fragarioides **Barren strawberry**	Evergreen perennial. Strawberry-like foliage deep green and lustrous on creeping stems that form 6-in.-deep carpet. Bright yellow flowers in showy clusters in late spring. Increases by stolons.	Plant in full sun to light shade in acidic soil. Fairly drought-tolerant. Propagate by division. Space 1 ft. apart. Zones 4–7.	Mass-plant under high-branched trees or shrubs. Use with ferns and wildflowers in woodland garden or shade garden.

Easy-Care Small Deciduous Trees

Acer griseum **Paperbark maple**	Slow-growing, upright, round-headed, open-branched tree that reaches 20 to 30 ft. Light green leaves toothed and divided into 3 parts. Fall color variable. Bark on trunk and branches rich cinnamon brown, peeling into beautiful curls.	Grow in full to partial sun in neutral to acid soil of average moisture. Zones 5–7.	Use this stunning tree where it can be enjoyed year-round, but especially in winter when the outstanding bark provides color and interest. Use as a patio tree, garden tree, or understory tree.

Plant Name	Description	Culture and Maintenance	Landscape Use and Comments
Cercis canadensis **Redbud**	Moderate-growing tree with spreading, flat-topped canopy, reaching 25 ft. Heart-shaped medium green leaves 3 to 5 in. wide, and turning yellow in fall. Quantities of small, reddish purple, pea-shaped flowers cluster along the branches before the foliage emerges. Pods, 3 in. long, in fall.	Grow in partial shade to full sun in moist, well-drained soil. Tolerates acid or alkaline conditions. Canker and verticillium wilt can be serious, but rarely trouble naturalized trees in a woodland garden. Zones 5–9.	Native to the mid-Atlantic and Southeast. Charming naturalized as an understory tree in a woodland. Makes a nice patio tree or specimen in a mixed border. Flowers are best displayed against a dark background.
Chionanthus virginicus **Fringetree**	Slow-growing, open, round-headed tree, to 20 ft. tall. White, fragrant, fringelike flowers, somewhat larger on male trees, bloom in late spring to early summer. Small purple berries on female trees. Large elliptical leaves turn yellow in fall.	Grow in moist but well-drained, slightly acid, rich soil in full sun. Berries usually eaten by birds and aren't messy. Plant in area with good air circulation to avoid mildew on foliage. Zones 5–9.	Native to the southern states and enchanting naturalized in a woodland. Use as specimen, garden, or patio tree. Good city tree. Leafs out late in spring. Prune while young to encourage multiple or single trunk, as desired.
Cornus florida **Flowering dogwood**	Small, spreading tree with horizontal, layered branches, reaching 20 to 25 ft. tall. Leaves glossy green with prominent veins, turning red or reddish purple in early fall. Flowers have showy white or pink bracts that last for several weeks. Red berries in fall.	Best in partial shade in fertile, moist, acid soil. Borers attack trees stressed by lawn mower injuries and drought. Fungal diseases collectively called dogwood decline have been killing trees in the Northeast; grow in areas with good air circulation. Zones 5–8.	A beautiful native tree. Quite striking when naturalized in a woodland, where it may be less susceptible to pests. Use in a mixed border or as a specimen. If your trees succumb to dogwood decline, substitute the more resistant but later-blooming *C. kousa*.
Cornus kousa **Kousa dogwood, Japanese dogwood**	Medium-sized, often vase-shaped tree with horizontal branching pattern. Oval green leaves turn brilliant dark red in fall. Long-lasting, 2- to 3-inch white blossoms may cover trees for over a month in late spring and early summer. Showy, pinkish red, raspberry-like berries in late summer. Ornamental bark a patchwork of gray and brown on older trees.	Grow in good soil in full to partial sun. Less susceptible to the insect and disease problems of *C. florida* (flowering dogwood) and more drought-tolerant. Needs another kousa dogwood nearby to produce best fruit show. Prune to encourage single trunk. Zones 5–7.	Use as patio, garden, or understory tree. Weeping forms 'Elizabeth Lustgarten' and 'Lustgarten Weeping' look especially effective planted on a hillside or above a wall. *C. kousa* var. *chinensis* and *C. kousa* 'Summer Stars' feature 5-inch flowers; flowers of 'Summer Stars' remain showy until late summer.

(continued)

Plant Name	Description	Culture and Maintenance	Landscape Use and Comments

Easy-Care Small Deciduous Trees—(continued)

Plant Name	Description	Culture and Maintenance	Landscape Use and Comments
Cornus mas **Cornelian cherry**	Moderate-growing, round-headed small tree or large shrub, often with multiple trunks. Reaches 20 to 25 ft. Glossy green, 2- to 4-in.-long, oval leaves with prominent veins. Poor fall color. Flowers a misty yellow haze in late winter or early spring. Gleaming, red, cherrylike, edible fruit in midsummer. Bark attractively mottled.	Grow in full sun to part shade in fertile, well-drained soil. Resistant to usual dogwood pests. Prune off lower branches to reveal handsome bark. Zones 5–8.	One of the earliest plants to bloom. Makes a lovely understory tree in a woodland garden. Use in a mixed border or as an informal hedge or screen. Most effective with a dark background that shows off the blossoms.
Elaeagnus angustifolia **Russian olive**	Fast-growing tree or shrub to 20 ft. with rounded, open shape. Small, oval, silvery green leaves. Flowers inconspicuous but fragrant, followed by yellow-green berries with silvery scales. Stems may be thorny with silvery scales; trunks have rich brown, shredding bark.	Grow in average soil in full sun. Performs well in dry soil, windy sites, and seashore conditions. Prune to encourage single trunk. May form root suckers. Zones 3–7.	Useful informal hedge or windbreak, or use as a specimen in a mixed border. Silvery foliage looks good with other gray-leaved plants and contrasts well with darker green foliage.
Halesia carolina **Carolina silverbell**	Slow-growing, broad-spreading, round-headed tree to 25 ft., sometimes 30 to 40 ft. Oval leaves 2 to 5 in. long turn yellow in fall. Delicate, white, bell-shaped flowers in clusters dangle along undersides of branches in midspring as foliage unfolds. Attractive striped bark on mature trunks.	Grow in moist, highly organic, acidic soil in full sun or partial shade. Zones 5–9.	Native to the Southeast. Makes an excellent understory tree in a woodland garden. Use in mixed border or as a patio tree. Looks best with a dark background that shows off the flowers, or planted on a hillside where flowering branches can be viewed from below.
Laburnum × watereri **Golden-chain tree**	Fast-growing, vase-shaped tree to about 20 ft. Bright green compound leaves with rounded leaflets. Long, dangling clusters of bright yellow flowers in late spring. Green bark on twigs and branches attractive in winter.	Grow in light shade in loamy soil. Dislikes dry, windy sites. Protect from wind and afternoon sun in hot-summer areas. Zones 6–8.	Use in a mixed border or as a patio or garden tree. 'Vossii' has especially large flower clusters. All plant parts, and especially the seeds, are poisonous if eaten.

Plant Name	Description	Culture and Maintenance	Landscape Use and Comments
Magnolia stellata **Star magnolia**	Slow-growing, often multi-trunked tree or shrub to 20 ft. Oblong leaves 2 to 4 in. long turn yellowish in fall. Fragrant, many-petaled, 3-in. flowers cover trees in early spring before leaves emerge. Attractive, smooth, silvery gray bark.	Grow in full sun in loamy soil. Prune to encourage multiple trunks. Late freezes can ruin blossoms; avoid southern exposures, which encourage early frost-susceptible flowering. Establish strong branch structure to avoid breakage from winter ice. Zones 5–9.	Use in mixed border, as a specimen, or against a house wall or dark-green background, giving it plenty of space. 'Royal Star' has very large flowers and is most cold-hardy; 'Waterlily' is a bushy plant with pink buds opening white.
Stewartia ovata **Mountain stewartia** *S. pseudo-camellia* **Japanese stewartia**	Slow-growing, pyramidal trees, often with multiple trunks, reaching 25 to 30 ft. with age. Rich green leaves of *S. pseudo-camellia* turn deep purplish red in fall; those of *S. ovata* turn orange to scarlet. White camellialike flowers bloom in mid- to late summer. Trunk bark smooth and mottled with patches of reddish brown, tan, and gray; more pronounced in *S. pseudo-camellia* than in *S. ovata*.	Grow in partial shade in moist but very well-drained acid soil with morning sun and afternoon shade. Difficult to establish all but small container-grown trees. Zones 6–8.	*Stewartia pseudocamellia* looks beautiful as specimen in the mixed border. *S. ovata* looks charming naturalized along the edges of a woodland. *S. koreana* and *S. pseudo-camellia* 'Korean Splendor' are probably the same plant; these have larger flowers and bloom longer, with brighter fall colors.
Styrax japonicus **Japanese snowbell**	Moderate-growing tree with horizontal branches, wider than tall, reaches 20 to 30 ft. Long, pointed, dark green leaves turn yellow in fall. Numerous bell-shaped flowers dangle along the undersides of the branches in late spring and early summer. Fissured bark.	Grow in moist, acid soil in full sun or partial shade. Remove low-growing branches if desired. Zones 6–8 and moderate-summer regions of Zone 9.	A graceful tree, perfect for a patio or mixed border. Plant on a hillside where blossoms can be seen from below.

(continued)

Plant Name	*Description*	*Culture and Maintenance*	*Landscape Use and Comments*

Easy-Care Medium-Height Deciduous Shade Trees

Amelanchier laevis **Allegheny serviceberry, shadblow**	Moderate-growing tall shrub or small tree with multiple trunks and an open branching pattern. Reaches 35 to 40 ft. Leaves open reddish and change to gray-green in summer, turning red and yellow in fall. Hazy white flowers in early spring as the leaves emerge. Small red berries in summer. Bark is an ornamental pinkish gray.	Grow in full sun to partial shade in moist, fertile, acid soil. Susceptible to fireblight and rose-family insects, but not usually serious in naturalized plantings. Zones 4–8.	Native to the eastern U.S., this shrubby tree works best naturalized in a woodland, where its early spring flowers brighten the forest and the summer berries feed the birds.
Carpinus betulus **European hornbeam, ironwood**	Slow-growing, round-headed tree to 30 ft.; eventually 50 ft. or more. Dark green, oblong, pointed leaves with saw-tooth edges turn yellow or orange in fall. Sinewy trunks and branches with smooth gray bark similar to beech tree's.	Grow in average soil in full sun; tolerates a wide range of conditions. Good city tree. Zones 5–7.	Excellent lawn tree for shade. Mass-plant 'Columnaris' as a wind-break or screen. 'Fastigiata' is vase-shaped, not columnar.
Cladrastis lutea **Yellowwood**	Slow-growing, round-headed tree to 25 ft. Light green compound leaves turn gold and orange in fall. Clusters of pendulous fragrant white flowers in early summer. Smooth gray bark.	Grow in full sun in acid or alkaline soils. Prune in summer, since sap will bleed profusely in late winter and spring. Zones 4–8.	Native to the southern states and effective naturalized in a woodland. Use as lawn shade tree alone or in groups. Casts a dense shade and is deep-rooted. Does not bloom well when young.
Magnolia virginiana **Sweet bay**	Reaches 10 to 20 ft. in the North and up to 60 ft. in the South. Deciduous in the North; evergreen or semi-evergreen in the South. Leaves 3 to 5 in. long, glossy bright green with white undersides. Fragrant, creamy white, 3-in. blossoms appear sparsely from late spring to autumn. Twigs green. Fall fruits with red seeds.	Grow in partial to full shade in acid, moist to wet soil. Susceptible to ice storm damage, but less so than most magnolias. Zones 5–9.	Native to coastal regions along the East and Gulf Coasts. Excellent naturalized in a woodland where evergreen foliage provides winter interest. Good tree in border along shady side of house.

Plant Name	Description	Culture and Maintenance	Landscape Use and Comments
Parrotia persica **Parrotia**	Moderate-growing, wide-spreading tree with horizontal ascending branches; reaches 20 to 40 ft. Dark green leaves open reddish purple; 3 to 5 in. long with wavy edges. Stunning bright gold and orange fall color. Red flowers appear in late winter or early spring before the leaves and are not showy. Peeling bark with gray, green, brown, and white patches.	Grow in well-drained, loamy soil in full sun to light shade. Prune lower branches to expose bark, or leave low branches for most graceful shape. Zones 6–9.	This outstanding tree should be better known. Use unpruned as a specimen, mulched or underplanted with a groundcover, or use pruned specimen in a mixed border where it can be appreciated in winter.

Easy-Care Tall Deciduous Shade Trees

Plant Name	Description	Culture and Maintenance	Landscape Use and Comments
Acer saccharum **Sugar maple**	Moderate-growing, round-headed to oval tree, to 75 ft. Leaves 5-lobed, medium green in summer, turning brilliant yellow, orange, and red in fall. Greenish yellow haze of flowers before foliage emerges in spring. Bark smooth gray-brown when young, becoming deeply furrowed with age.	Grow in good, loamy soil in full sun or light shade. Less tolerant of stress (including compacted soil, pollution, and road salt) than other maples. May suffer leaf scorch during drought years. Zones 3–7.	Excellent lawn shade tree. Use to create woodland; may be planted as an understory tree that will eventually grow tall enough to become the dominant tree.
Betula nigra 'Heritage' **'Heritage' river birch**	Moderate- to fast-growing tree, pyramidal when young, becoming round-headed with age; reaches 40 to 70 ft. Leaves toothed, arrowhead-shaped, 3 in. long, open yellow-green, changing to dark green in summer and yellow in fall. Ornamental reddish brown bark peels to reveal lighter patches of salmon and cream on young and middle-aged trees. Bark on older trees may become rough.	Grow in moist, acid soil in full sun. Tolerates wet soil. Resistant to borers, which trouble other birches. Cut out older trunks of maturing trees to encourage regrowth with attractive bark. Zones 4–9.	Stunning tree for use in lawn or garden; casts light shade. Locate where it can be appreciated in winter. Be sure to purchase the 'Heritage' cultivar; the species has variable bark characteristics.

(continued)

Plant Name	*Description*	*Culture and Maintenance*	*Landscape Use and Comments*

Easy-Care Tall Deciduous Shade Trees—(continued)

Cercidi-phyllum japonicum **Katsura tree**	Fairly fast-growing, upright to spreading tree, reaching 40 to 60 ft. Heart-shaped, blue-green leaves open purplish and change to yellow or apricot-gold in fall. Attractive, slightly shaggy bark.	Grow in full sun in moist, acid soil; water during drought. Often multi-trunked; prune when young to encourage single trunk if desired. Zones 5–9, but only in partial shade and excellent soil in Zones 8 and 9.	A wonderful tree that should be planted more frequently. Use for specimen or shade tree on lawn or along street.
Gleditsia triacanthos var. *inermis* **Thornless honeylocust**	Fast-growing, open, spreading tree; 30 to 70 ft. tall. Leaves fernlike, twice-divided into oval leaflets. Fragrant flowers in late spring are inconspicuous. Bark dark brown and deeply furrowed. The variety *inermis* is thornless; the species has dangerous thorns.	Grows best in full sun in rich, moist soil, but tolerates drought, alkalinity, and road salt. Long, leathery seedpods are a cleanup problem; choose only fruitless cultivars. Insects are an increasing problem; choose resistant cultivars. Zones 4–9.	Casts light shade, so you can garden under it. Use as a lawn or street tree or even in a mixed border. Choose only nonfruiting, webworm-resistant cultivars such as 'Shademaster' and 'Moraine'. 'Sunburst', with gold-tipped foliage, is highly webworm-susceptible and does poorly in stressful conditions.
Liquidambar styraciflua **Sweet gum**	Moderate- to fast-growing, pyramidal tree, reaching 60 to 75 ft. Star-shaped leaves emerge pale green and mature to glossy dark green, changing to purple, red, yellow, and bronze in fall. Round, knobby, woody fruits drop in late fall and winter. Bark silver-gray on young trunks, becoming deeply furrowed with age.	Grow in full sun in moist, acid soil. Fruits are slow to break down and may be a cleanup nuisance in some situations. Does not tolerate air pollution. Zones 5–9.	Excellent lawn or street tree. Plant in mixed border or woodland so fruits drop where no cleanup is needed. (Fruits are beautiful in dried wreaths and crafts.)
Zelkova serrata **Japanese zelkova**	Moderate- to fast-growing, vase-shaped tree, reaching 40 to 80 ft. Oval, toothed leaves emerge light green and mature to dark green, changing to yellow-orange in fall. Smooth gray bark.	Grow in full sun in moist, rich soil. Tolerates drought and pollution once established. This elm relative is resistant—though not immune—to Dutch elm disease. Zones 6–9.	Attractive lawn and street tree, suggested as replacement for American elm. 'Village Green' is fast growing, with a strong upright vase-shape; grows in Zones 5–9.

Plant Name	Description	Culture and Maintenance	Landscape Use and Comments

Easy-Care Evergreen Trees

Plant Name	Description	Culture and Maintenance	Landscape Use and Comments
Chamaecyparis lawsoniana **Lawson false cypress** *C. obtusa* **Hinoki false cypress**	Moderate-growing, columnar to pyramidal trees, with soft, scalelike evergreen needles; eventually reaching 100 ft. *C. obtusa* has flat, fan-shaped sprays of dark green needles. Both have attractive shredding, reddish brown bark.	Grow in full sun in moist, loamy, acid soil. Prefer a cool, humid climate; may get mites in hot climates. *C. lawsoniana:* Zones 6–8; *C. obtusa:* Zones 5–8.	Use these large-growing evergreens as lawn trees or screening. *C. lawsoniana* does best on the West Coast, where its many cultivars make popular specimens and foundation plants. *C. obtusa* 'Nana' forms a 3-ft. round mound.
Picea omorika **Serbian spruce**	Slow-growing, narrowly columnar tree with symmetrical pendulous branches. Reaches 20 to 25 ft. after 50 years, 100 ft. with great age. Glossy, dark green needles marked with white. Cones 2 in. long.	Grow in full to partial sun in deep, rich, moist soil. Tolerates both acid and alkaline conditions. Protect from winter wind. Mites may be troublesome in warm climates. Zones 4–8.	The most graceful spruce. Very useful because of its narrow shape; use as a specimen, street tree, or screen.
Pinus strobus **White pine**	Fast-growing, single-trunked tree with open, airy branching. Pyramidal when young, developing wide-spreading horizontal and somewhat pendulous branches with age. Reaches 50 to 80 ft., over 100 ft. with great age. Needles 3 to 5 in. long, bright green to bluish green. Cones 6 to 8 in. long.	Grow in well-drained, fertile, acid soil. Tolerates heavy soil and drought once established. Very susceptible to white pine blister rust, but the disease needs nearby wild or cultivated currants (*Ribes* spp.) as an alternate host to infect the pines. Does not tolerate air pollution or road salt. Zones 3–9.	One of the easiest and most beautiful pines for landscape use. Plant singly as a specimen or mass-plant as a screen. Works well in a naturalistic area because of its informal, graceful shape.
Podocarpus macrophyllus **Podocarpus, yew podocarpus**	Slow-growing, upright, oval tree; reaches 20 to 35 ft., but may be shorter in colder climates. Needles 1 to 2 in. long, glossy dark green, arranged spirally around stems. Red berrylike fruits.	Grow in full sun to partial shade in well-drained, fertile soil. Best in shade in the South; protect from winter sun in all climates. Branches may be thinned to restrict size. Zones 8–9.	Use as a specimen tree, or plant as a privacy screen or distant background. May be sheared for a formal hedge.

(continued)

Plant Name	Description	Culture and Maintenance	Landscape Use and Comments

Easy-Care Evergreen Trees—*(continued)*

Plant Name	Description	Culture and Maintenance	Landscape Use and Comments
Pseudotsuga menziesii **Douglas fir**	Moderate-growing, open, pyramidal tree with stiff branches. Reaches 40 to 80 ft. Needles dark green to bluish green, 1 to 2 in. long. Cones 2 in. long.	Grow in well-drained, moist, acid to neutral soil in full sun. Protect from wind. Does poorly in the Midwest. Zones 3–6, also 7 and 8 in moderate-summer areas.	Lovely specimen; effective mass-planted as a screen or distant background. *P. menziesii* var. *glauca*, from the Rocky Mountains, has blue-green needles, grows more compactly, and is more cold- and wind-tolerant than the species, which is from the Northwest.
Sciadopitys verticillata **Umbrella pine**	Very slow-growing, pyramidal tree with horizontal branches arranged in whorls. Reaches 20 to 30 ft., 60 to 90 ft. with great age. Needles 5 in. long, dark glossy green, also arranged in whorls.	Grow in fertile, moist, acid soil in full sun. Protect from wind and late afternoon sun in hot climates. Zones 6–7; Zone 8 where summers are mild.	A distinctive evergreen with a coarse texture and very dark foliage. Use as a specimen or in a mixed border, or foundation planting where its eventual size can be accommodated. Plants are costly because of slow growth rate.
Taxus cuspidata **Japanese yew**	Slow- to moderate-growing, pyramidal tree, eventually becoming wide-spreading; to 50 ft. tall. Needles 1 in. long, glossy dark green. Red berrylike fruits on female plants. Bark reddish brown.	Grow in full sun or shade in moist, well-drained soil. Cannot tolerate wet soil. Withstands air pollution. Can be pruned by thinning or shearing for hedges or screens. Zones 4–7.	Useful specimen, screen, or hedge. Many shrub cultivars available for foundations and hedges. Foliage and berries are poisonous if eaten in quantity.
Tsuga canadensis **Eastern hemlock**	Fast- to moderate-growing, pyramidal tree with somewhat pendulous horizontal branches and soft outline. Reaches 40 to 70 ft. Flat ½-in.-long needles, glossy dark green. Cones ½ in. long.	Grow in rich, acid soil in full sun or light shade; shade is best in hot-summer areas. Does poorly in dry, exposed sites. Mites can be troublesome in hot sites. Woolly adelgids are a growing concern in some areas; can be controlled with dormant and summer oil sprays. Zones 3–7; 8 in cool sites.	A graceful tree. Makes a lovely specimen, screen, or backdrop. Can be pruned into formal and informal hedges.

Plant Name	Description	Culture and Maintenance	Landscape Use and Comments

Easy-Care Deciduous Shrubs

Berberis thunbergii **Japanese barberry** *B. thunbergii* var. *atropurpurea* **Purple-leaf Japanese barberry**	Moderate-growing, dense, round shrubs reaching 3 to 6 ft. tall. Leaves 1 in. long, bright green in the species, deep burgundy in var. *atropurpurea*. Yellow, gold, or scarlet fall color. Yellow flowers inconspicuous, but followed by bright red, long-stemmed berries that remain showy into winter. Stems have sharp thorns.	Grow in full sun in average soil; tolerates drought once established. Zones 4–9.	Low-growing forms especially useful as foundation plants. Purple-leaved types look stunning in mixed borders. Taller-growing types make effective informal hedges and thorny barriers. 'Crimson Pygmy' grows 3 ft. tall with burgundy foliage. Many others available.
Calycanthus floridus **Carolina allspice, sweetshrub**	Slow-growing, round shrub reaching 6 to 9 ft. tall. Leaves oval, dark green, turning yellowish in fall. Reddish brown flowers with fruity fragrance in late spring and early summer followed by interesting brown capsules in fall. Foliage and stems aromatic when crushed.	Grow in sun to shade in rich, moist soil. Flowers both on current and previous season's growth; prune after flowering. If plant gets leggy, cut out stems at ground level. Zones 5–9.	Handsome shrub native to the Southeast. Performs well in a woodland garden, or in a large-scale border or foundation. Plant where its fragrance will be noticed.
Caryopteris × *clandonensis* **Bluebeard, blue spirea**	Rapid-growing, loose shrub to 2 ft. tall. Gray-green foliage turns yellowish in fall. Flat clusters of blue flowers appear in late summer and early fall.	Grow in sandy loam in full sun. Best treated as an herbaceous perennial and cut back severely or to the ground in late winter; flowers on new growth. Zones 4–8; killed to ground during winter in Zones 4–6.	Useful in midground of mixed border. 'Blue Mist' has light blue flowers; 'Azure Blue' and 'Heavenly Blue' have dark blue flowers.
Clethra alnifolia **Sweet pepperbush**	Slow- to moderate-growing, upright to oval shrub. Sharply toothed, oblong leaves 2 to 4 in. long, deep green changing to yellow or gold in fall. Spires of fragrant white or pale pink flowers in mid- to late summer.	Grow in full sun to light shade in moist to wet acid soil (pH 5.0 to 6.0). May form colonies from suckering roots; do not use in manicured landscapes. Spider mites attack in dry soil. Zones 4–9.	Native to coastal regions of the eastern U.S.; lovely naturalized along a stream or in a moist woodland. Effective in a shrub border. 'Rosea' has light pink flowers.

(continued)

Plant Name	Description	Culture and Maintenance	Landscape Use and Comments

Easy-Care Deciduous Shrubs—(continued)

Plant Name	Description	Culture and Maintenance	Landscape Use and Comments
Daphne × burkwoodii **Burkwood daphne**	Slow-growing, rounded shrub reaching 3 to 4 ft. tall. Blue-green, 2-in.-long leaves arranged in whorls around the stems; usually last well into winter before dropping. Fragrant, creamy white to pinkish flowers in dense clusters in midspring. Red berries in summer.	Grow in full sun to light shade in light, well-drained, heavily mulched soil. Zones 4–7.	Effective as a foundation plant or in a mixed border. 'Carol Mackie' has leaves with bright, creamy white leaf margins; it grows 3 ft. tall. Foliage and fruits of daphne species are poisonous.
Enkianthus campanulatus **Redvein enkianthus**	Slow-growing, upright shrub, reaching 8 to 10 ft. tall. Leaves blue-green with red stems, turning bright red or wine-red in fall. Clusters of bell-shaped, yellowish flowers with pink stripes in midspring, followed by brown seed capsules.	Grow in full sun to partial shade in moist, fertile, acid soil. Zones 7–9.	Excellent shrub for the mixed border or in naturalistic plantings where the flowers and fall color draw attention. Combines well with evergreens.
Euonymus alata **Burning bush, winged euonymus**	Fast-growing, round to spreading shrub with horizontal branches; reaches 15 to 20 ft. tall. Branches have ornamental corky wings. Elliptical leaves 1 to 2 in. long emerge yellow-green, turn dark green in summer, and change in fall to brilliant red in full sun, bright pinkish red in shade. Flowers yellowish green with new foliage.	Grow in full sun to shade in average, well-drained soil; does not tolerate soggy soil. Rarely infested with scale, which plagues other *Euonymus* species. Zones 4–8.	Makes handsome informal or formal hedge. 'Compactus' grows to 10 ft. tall, but decorative corky wings are less prominent; useful for informal hedge or screen because it won't require pruning. 'Rudy Haag' grows to 5 ft.; best for foundations.
Forsythia × intermedia **Forsythia**	Fast-growing, vase-shaped shrub, reaching 8 to 10 ft. tall. Oval, toothed leaves medium-green, turning yellowish in fall. Golden yellow blossoms in early spring line the branches.	Grow in full sun in fertile, moist soil; tolerates a range of conditions. Prune after flowering by cutting out old stems at ground level; do not shear. Zones 5–8.	Use as a specimen or mass in a shrub border or an informal hedge where there is plenty of room for the arching branches to develop.

Plant Name	Description	Culture and Maintenance	Landscape Use and Comments
Fothergilla gardenii **Dwarf fothergilla** *F. major* **Fothergilla**	Slow-growing, round shrubs. *F. gardenii* reaches 3 ft. tall; *F. major* reaches 6 to 10 ft. Rounded leaves 2 to 4 in. long, dark green on top, hairy below, changing to brilliant yellow, orange, and red in fall. Flowers short, creamy white bottlebrush spires in midspring.	Grow in full sun to partial shade in moist, well-drained, acid loam with a pH of 4.0 to 6.0. Best flowering and leaf color in sun. Zones 5–9.	Native to the Southeast. Both species look lovely mass-planted along a woodland or in a naturalistic landscape. Use *F. gardenii* in a mixed border or foundation planting where its compact size works perfectly.
Hydrangea quercifolia **Oakleaf hydrangea**	Fast-growing, upright shrub, reaching 6 to 8 ft. tall. Leaves oak-shaped, dark green on top with white fuzz on the undersides, turning deep red, orange, or purplish in fall. White flowers in upright 4- to 12-in.-tall clusters in midsummer, changing to rose-tinted cream, and ultimately drying tan. Bark reddish brown and peeling.	Grow in full to partial shade in fertile, heavily mulched, slightly acid soil (pH 6.0 to 7.0). Prune after flowering. Shoots and flower buds may be winter-killed in Zones 5 and 6. Remove winter-killed branches if necessary. Zones 5–9.	Native to the Deep South. Wonderful plant for year-round interest in the informal shrub border or woodland garden. 'Snow Queen' has large, dense, pure white flower clusters.
Hypericum prolificum **Shrubby St.-John's-wort**	Stiff, rounded shrub, reaching 4 ft. tall. Narrow bluish green leaves 1 to 3 in. long without good fall color. Yellow, 2-in., buttercup-like flowers all summer. Reddish brown, peeling bark.	Grow in full sun or partial shade in average to poor soil; tolerates drought and alkaline soil. Remove deadwood in spring if necessary after harsh winters in colder zones. Zones 4–8.	Colorful small shrub for specimen or mass planting in mixed borders and foundation plantings.
Kerria japonica **Japanese kerria**	Upright, arching plant, reaching 3 to 6 ft. Long, pointed, bright green leaves with toothed margins. Bright yellow, 1½-in., buttercup-like flowers in midspring. Stems and branches bright yellowish green in winter.	Grow in well-drained, moist soil in full to partial shade. Deadwood may need removal every year; thin every few years after flowering to keep compact. May grow rampantly in fertile soil and send up suckers. Zones 5–9.	Pretty plant in the mixed border or shady shrub border. 'Variegata' has single yellow flowers and leaves variegated with white; makes an airy mound that brightens shady spots; remove all-green sports.

(continued)

Plant Name	*Description*	*Culture and Maintenance*	*Landscape Use and Comments*

Easy-Care Deciduous Shrubs—(continued)

Myrica pensylvanica **Bayberry**	Moderate-growing, upright shrub, reaching 5 to 10 ft. Highly aromatic, leathery, oblong leaves are 2 to 4 in. long, dark green with white resin glands on the undersides; persist well into winter. Flowers inconspicuous. Blue-gray, waxy, aromatic berries borne thickly on female plants.	Grow in full sun in average to poor soil; tolerates drought, seashore conditions, and road salt. Plant male and female plants together for berries. Tends to produce new plants from suckers; do not use in tidy gardens. Zones 4–9.	Native to the East Coast. Use as an informal hedge or naturalize in a difficult site. Effective year-round. The berries are used to make bayberry candles.
Potentilla fruticosa **Shrubby cinquefoil**	Slow-growing, rounded, spreading shrub, 2 to 4 ft. tall. Dark green silky, oblong, ½- to 1-in.-long leaflets arranged on compound leaves. Yellow, 3-in. flowers borne prolifically in early summer, continuing through fall. Peeling brown bark.	Grow in full sun to partial shade. Best in fertile, moist soil, but extremely tolerant of dry, wet, and alkaline soils and road salt. Zones 2–7 or 8.	Excellent as a fine-textured mass planting in border or as a specimen in a small-scale garden. Useful in front of taller evergreen shrubs in a foundation planting. Performs well in difficult sites.
Rhododendron calendulaceum **Flame azalea** *R. periclymenoides* (*R. nudiflorum*) **Pinxterbloom azalea**	Upright, rounded shrubs. Deep green foliage with little fall color. Clusters of 2-in. yellow, golden, orange, or scarlet flowers in late spring on *R. calendulaceum*, which grows to 12 ft. tall. Clusters of white, pale pink, or deep pink fragrant flowers on *R. periclymenoides*, opening with the foliage in mid-spring; grows 3 to 6 ft. tall and forms thickets.	Grow in light shade in moist, humus-rich, acid soil. *R. calendulaceum:* Zones 5–8; *R. periclymenoides:* Zones 4–9.	Native to the open woods of the Appalachian Mountains. Naturalize in a woodland or under high-branched pines.
Rhododendron mucronulatum **Korean rhododendron**	Slow-growing, upright shrub, to 4 to 8 ft. tall. Leaves lance-shaped, 1 to 4 in. long, soft green changing to golden yellow or bronze-red in fall. Lavender-pink flowers in early spring before the foliage emerges.	Grow in partial shade in fertile, humus-rich, acid soil. Best sited with an eastern or northern exposure to avoid early flowering susceptible to late frosts. Zones 4–8.	Lovely as a specimen or massed in the shrub border, especially with a dark background. 'Cornell Pink' has bright pink flowers.

Plant Name	Description	Culture and Maintenance	Landscape Use and Comments
Spiraea × *bumalda* **Bumald spirea** *S. japonica* **Japanese spirea**	Fast-growing, rounded, spreading shrubs. *S.* × *bumalda* reaches 3 ft. tall; *S. japonica* reaches 4 to 5 ft. Oblong, dark blue-green leaves to 3 in. long, turning bronzish in fall. Flat-topped clusters of white, pale pink, or deep pink flowers for 6 weeks in midsumer.	Grow in full sun in average soil. Both do poorly in wet soil. Prune before growth starts in spring. Zones 4–9.	Fine-textured shrubs ideal for mass-planting in a shrub border or as an informal hedge. Use *S.* × *bumalda* and its cultivars in the foreground of a foundation planting or in a mixed border. 'Gold-flame' has new growth mottled red and orange, maturing to yellow-green and rosy pink flowers.
Spiraea nipponica 'Snowmound' **Snowmound spirea** *S.* × *vanhouttei* **Vanhoutte spirea**	Fast-growing, vase-shaped shrubs, reaching 4 to 5 ft. tall. *S. nipponica* 'Snowmound' denser and a bit lower than *S.* × *vanhouttei*. Leaves toothed, 1 in. long, blue-green, lacking fall color. Dense clusters of white flowers cover the branches in late spring.	Grow in full sun in average soil. Tolerates drought once established. Prune only to renew shrubs. Zones 3–8.	Excellent mass-planted as an informal hedge that will not require pruning. Use as a background planting to perennial border.
Syringa meyeri **Meyer lilac**	Slow-growing, mounded shrub, reaching 4 to 6 ft. tall. Oval leaves rich green, 1 to 2 in. long. Pale purple, fragrant flowers cover the plant in late spring after common lilacs bloom.	Grow in full sun in average soil. Rarely needs pruning. Resistant to powdery mildew that infects other lilacs. Zones 4–7.	More fine-textured and compact than common lilac. Use in mixed border or foundation planting, or mass-plant as a border or screen. May be confused with *S. patula* (Manchurian lilac), which has sparser, highly fragrant flowers; 'Miss Kim' grows 3 to 6 ft. tall with lavender-blue flowers (Zones 3–7).
Viburnum carlesii **Koreanspice viburnum**	Slow-growing, round shrub, reaching 5 to 8 ft. tall. Gray-green, roundish leaves, 2 to 4 in. long with reddish fall color. Highly fragrant white flowers in round clusters with pink buds. Fruits not showy.	Grow in full sun to partial shade in moist, fertile soil. Occasionally troubled by mildew or leaf spot, but not seriously. Zones 4–8.	Beautiful as specimen or in shrub border. 'Compactum' remains under 5 ft. *V.* × *carlcephalum* (fragrant viburnum) has similar flowers, but is less dense and larger (Zones 5–8). *V.* × *judii* (Judd viburnum) is similar to *V. carlesii*, but is more resistant to disease (Zones 5–8).

(continued)

Plant Name	Description	Culture and Maintenance	Landscape Use and Comments

Easy-Care Deciduous Shrubs—(continued)

Viburnum opulus **European cranberry-bush viburnum** *V. trilobum* **American cranberry-bush**	Moderate-growing, upright, spreading shrubs, reaching 10 to 12 ft. tall. Three-lobed, maplelike leaves, 2 to 4 in. long, dark green on top, hairy on the undersides; little fall color in *V. opulus*. Flat, pinwheel-shaped clusters of white flowers in mid- to late spring. Bright red, cranberry-size, edible berries ripen in autumn and last into winter.	Grow in full sun to partial shade in moist, fertile, acid soil. *V. opulus* flourishes in wet or boggy soil. Do not allow either to lack water. *V. opulus:* Zones 3–8; *V. trilobum:* Zones 2–8.	Mass-plant in shrub border or use in naturalistic landscape. Attractive throughout the year. *V. opulus* 'Compactum' is very dense and floriferous, reaching only 5 to 6 ft. tall. *V. trilobum* is native to the Northeast, less commonly sold than *V. opulus* but equally beautiful.
Weigela florida **Weigela**	Fast-growing, rounded or vase-shaped shrub with arching branches. Reaches 6 to 9 ft. tall. Oval, medium-green leaves with long points are 2 to 4 in. long; undistinguished fall color. Funnel-shaped, pink, rose, or white flowers in late spring and early summer.	Grow in full sun in well-drained soil. Thin out oldest stems at ground level every few years after flowering. Zones 5–9.	Makes a beautiful informal hedge or screen that will need little pruning. Use as a specimen in a large-scale shrub border. Many cultivars, some with variegated foliage.

Easy-Care Evergreen Shrubs

Buxus microphylla **Littleleaf boxwood**	Slow-growing, dense, rounded shrub, reaching 3 to 4 ft. tall. Broadleaf evergreen. Glossy, dark green, oval leaves are ½ to 1 in. long; may turn brownish green in winter. Fragrant flowers not showy.	Grow in full sun to light shade in moist, well-drained, heavily mulched soil. Shade from winter sun in North. Does not tolerate road salt. Fewer pests than *B. sempervirens* (common boxwood). Zones 6–8.	*B. sempervirens* grows to 15 or 20 ft., requiring pruning in most landscape situations, so *B. microphylla* is an easier-care choice. Useful as an informal or formal hedge. Use as a background to a perennial garden or in a foundation planting. *B. sempervirens* var. *koreana* (Korean boxwood) has even tinier leaves; Zones 5–8.

Plant Name	Description	Culture and Maintenance	Landscape Use and Comments
Camellia sasanqua **Sasanqua camellia**	Slow-growing, pyramidal shrub, reaching 6 to 10 ft. tall. Broadleaf evergreen. Glossy, dark green, oval leaves, 2 to 4 in. long with hairy undersides. Solitary flowers, 2 to 3 in. wide, are pink, white, red, or bicolored, blooming in early winter. May be single or double.	Grow in moist, humus-rich, acid soil. Needs full sun during the growing season, but provide light shade in winter in Zone 7. Remove faded flowers throughout the bloom period for best appearance. Zones 7–9.	Use in mixed border or foundation planting. Grows less tall and is more open than *C. japonica* (Japanese camellia), which grows to 15 to 20 ft. tall and will need pruning in most situations. Cultivars abound.
Daphne cneorum **Garland flower, rose daphne**	Slow-growing, rounded mound, reaching 1 ft. tall and twice as wide. Broadleaf evergreen. Leaves 1 in. long, dark green year-round. Masses of rosy pink, very fragrant flowers bloom in spring and again in late summer. Yellowish berries.	Grow in light shade in well-drained, heavily mulched, moist soil. Prune after first flowering. Protect from winter sun. Does not transplant well; plant in permanent location. Zones 4–7.	Excellent in the mixed border or a foundation planting, especially where it can be seen in winter.
Gardenia jasminoides **Common gardenia, cape jasmine**	Moderate-growing, rounded shrub, reaching 4 to 6 ft. tall. Broadleaf evergreen. Foliage is glossy dark green and 2 to 4 in. long. Solitary, creamy white flowers, 2 to 4 in. across, are highly fragrant; bloom in late spring and summer.	Remove faded flowers throughout the blooming season. Purchase plants grafted to nematode-resistant rootstocks. Whitefly and sooty mold may be problems. Zones 8–9.	Lovely in a foundation planting or mixed border. 'Radicans' (dwarf gardenia) grows 1 to 3 ft. tall and spreads; Zone 9.
Ilex crenata **Japanese holly**	Slow-growing, rounded shrub, reaching 5 to 10 ft. tall. Broadleaf evergreen. Leaves oval, ½ to 1 in. long, glossy dark green all year. Flowers and fruits inconspicuous.	Grow in full sun or shade in moist, well-drained, acid soil. Shade is best in hot-summer climates to ward off mites. Zones 6–9.	Use as an informal or formal hedge, or as a background for a perennial border. Dwarf cultivars work well in a mixed border or foundation planting. 'Helleri' has tiny leaves and grows only 1 to 3 ft. tall.

(continued)

Plant Name	Description	Culture and Maintenance	Landscape Use and Comments

Easy-Care Evergreen Shrubs—(continued)

Plant Name	Description	Culture and Maintenance	Landscape Use and Comments
Ilex glabra **Inkberry**	Slow-growing, rounded shrub; reaches 6 to 8 ft. tall. Broadleaf evergreen. Dark green, lustrous, oblong leaves to 2 in. long. Inconspicuous flowers; black berries in fall.	Grow in full sun or shade in moist, acid soil. Tolerates seashore conditions and road salt. Zones 5–9.	Native to the East Coast. Useful as an informal or formal evergreen screen or hedge. 'Compacta' is a female clone to 4 ft.; use in foundation or border plantings.
Kalmia latifolia **Mountain laurel**	Slow-growing shrub, reaching 8 to 15 ft. tall. Broadleaf evergreen. Elliptical, 2- to 5-in.-long, glossy, dark green leaves. Flowers in 4- to 6-in. clusters, with buds often dark pink opening to pale pink or white. Blooms in late spring or early summer.	Grow in full sun to deep shade in moist, humus-rich, acid soil. Blooms best in sun. Mulch well to keep soil cool, especially in hotter locations. Zones 5–9.	Native to mountainous regions of the East Coast. Naturalize in woodlands or use in naturalistic landscapes. Performs well in shrub borders, shade gardens, and mixed borders when given enough room. Named cultivars usually have more vivid flower colors.
Leucothoe axillaris **Coast leucothoe**	Moderate-growing, arching shrub, reaching 2 to 4 ft. tall. Broadleaf evergeen. Lance-shaped, glossy, dark green leaves, turning bronzish to purple in winter. Flowers white, bell-shaped, in 2- to 3-in.-long clusters; hang from leaf bases throughout spring.	Grow in partial to full shade in moist, fertile, acid soil. Will not tolerate strong, drying winds or drought. Zones 6–9.	Native to the Southeast. Useful massed in a shady border, or used as a specimen or clump in a shade garden or foundation planting in front of taller shrubs. *L. keiskei* foliage turns wine-red in winter; Zone 6.
Nandina domestica **Heavenly bamboo, nandina**	Moderate- to fast-growing, upright, open shrub of unbranched canes, reaching 6 to 10 ft. tall. Leaves divided into lance-shaped leaflets 2 to 4 in. long. Leaves blue-green, becoming reddish in winter. Long sprays of white flowers in late spring. Large clusters of bright red berries showy from fall into winter.	Grow in full sun to shade. Best in moist, fertile soil, but tolerates drought and poor soil. Remove branches at ground level to maintain a lower size. May suffer from mildew if air circulation is poor. Usually drops foliage in winter in Zone 7; best in Zones 8–9.	Attractive open habit, graceful foliage, and winter berries provide year-round interest. Use massed as a hedge or screen, or in groups in the mixed border or foundation planting. 'Harbour Dwarf' is the most popular compact form; becomes a 2- to 3-ft. mound.

Plant Name	Description	Culture and Maintenance	Landscape Use and Comments
Picea glauca 'Conica' **Dwarf Alberta spruce**	Extremely slow-growing, conical, needle-leaf evergreen shrub, reaching 10 to 12 ft. in 25 years. Fine-textured, light-green needles, densely packed and radiating around the branches.	Grow in full sun in moist, fertile soil. Mulch soil heavily to protect spruce from dehydration; protect from winter wind. Mites can be troublesome in hot, dry locations. Zones 5–7.	Use in formal landscapes as foundation plants or as accent plants in a mixed border. Rigid shape may be difficult to integrate into a landscape design.
Pieris floribunda **Mountain pieris, mountain andromeda** *P. japonica* **Japanese pieris, Japanese andromeda**	Slow-growing, upright to rounded, broadleaf evergreen shrubs. *P. floribunda* reaches 6 ft. tall; *P. japonica* reaches 9 to 12 ft. Glossy, dark green, oval leaves, 1 to 3 in. long, emerge rusty red or bronze. Bell-shaped white flowers in long clusters. *P. floribunda* flower clusters are upright, standing above the foliage in mid-spring; *P. japonica* flower clusters dangle from the branches; bloom starts in very early spring. Flower buds are attractive all winter.	Grow in light to full shade in moist, fertile, well-drained, acid soil. Protect from full sun and wind in winter. Remove dried flower clusters if desired. *P. floribunda* resists lacewing, which can trouble *P. japonica*. *P. floribunda:* Zones 5–7; *P. japonica:* Zones 6–8.	*P. floribunda* is native to the Southeast; naturalize in woodland plantings for year-round interest. Use either species in foundation plantings, shrub or mixed borders, or shade gardens.
Pinus mugo **Mugho pine**	Slow-growing, rounded or spreading shrubs, reaching 3 to 16 ft. tall and twice as wide. Needle-leaf evergreen. Tufts of medium-green needles on ascending branches. Scaly, brownish gray bark. Cones 1½ in. long.	Grow in full sun to partial shade in moist, fertile, well-drained soil. Usually trouble-free, but scale and sawfly may occasionally be serious. Zones 3–7.	Use in foundation plantings or mixed borders. Seedling-grown plants of *P. mugo* can vary in ultimate height. To be assured of dwarf habit, choose named cultivars such as 'Compactus', which forms a dense 2-ft.-tall globe in 20 years, and 'Slavinii', which is even smaller. 'Gnom' grows 15 ft. tall and twice as wide in 25 years. *P. mugo* var. *pumilio* is a shrubby, prostrate plant that can spread to 10 ft. wide. *(continued)*

Plant Name	Description	Culture and Maintenance	Landscape Use and Comments

Easy-Care Evergreen Shrubs—(continued)

Rhododendron dwarf hybrids and cultivars **Dwarf rhododendrons** | Slow-growing, small shrubs with compact habits, varying in ultimate size with species and cultivar. Broadleaf evergreens. Leathery foliage dark green on top, often with bronzy undersides or taking on burgundy tones in winter, varying from ½ in. to ⅔ in. long. Flowers in early to mid-spring in small clusters above the foliage. | Grow in full sun to partial shade in moist, humus-rich, well-drained, acid soil. Mulch heavily. Protect from winter wind. Remove faded flowers for best bloom the following year. Zones 4–8. | Dwarf rhododendrons make ideal compact evergreen plants for mixed borders, foundation plantings, rock gardens, and shade gardens. Their texture is much more refined than the large-growing rhododendrons and works well in small-space gardens. Several favorites include: 'Dora Amateis', with masses of white flowers, 3 to 5 ft. tall; 'PJM', with lavender-pink flowers and wine-colored winter foliage, 3 to 5 ft. tall.

Rhododendron indicum cultivars and hybrids **Glenn Dale azaleas, Satsuki/ Macrantha azaleas** | Fast-growing, rounded to spreading, broadleaf evergreen shrubs, 2½ to 8 ft. tall. Oval, leathery, deep green leaves are 1 to 1½ in. long and semi-evergreen; those at the stem tips remain all winter, often taking on bronzy tones. Funnel-shaped flowers in red, pink, salmon, violet, purple, or white blanket the shrubs. The Glenn Dale hybrids are upright, rounded plants that thrive in the mid-Atlantic states. The Satsuki or Macrantha hybrids are low-growing plants that bloom in early summer. | Grow in partial shade in moist, well-drained, humus-rich, acid soil. Keep moist. Mulch heavily. Do not shear, but thin branches if needed after flowering. Glenn Dale hybrids: Zones 6–9; Satsuki/Macrantha hybrids: Zones 7–9. | Use the Glenn Dale hybrids in mixed borders, or mass-plant in naturalistic settings and shade gardens. Be sure to allow plenty of growing room for larger types. Use Satsuki/Macrantha hybrids in foundation plantings and mixed borders.

Plant Name	Description	Culture and Maintenance	Landscape Use and Comments
Rhododendron maximum **Rosebay**	Fast-growing, broadleaf, evergreen shrub reaching 12 to 30 ft. tall. Leathery leaves 5 to 20 in. long. Flowers rose-pink or purple-pink, borne in small clusters in midsummer.	Grow in partial to full shade in moist, well-drained, humus-rich, acid soil. Keep moist. Mulch heavily. Deadhead to improve next year's flowering. Zones 4–8.	Native to open woodlands of the eastern U.S. Useful large-scale evergreen for background plantings and woodland gardens. 'Album' has white flowers.
Taxus baccata dwarf cultivars **Dwarf English yews** *T. cuspidata* dwarf cultivars **Dwarf Japanese yews** *T. × media* dwarf cultivars **Dwarf Anglo-Japanese yews**	Slow-growing, needle-leaf, evergreen shrubs, reaching 2 to 4 ft. tall. Needles dark, glossy green, flattened and succulent, arranged in a single plane. Red berrylike arils on female plants.	Grow in full sun to shade in moist, well-drained soil. Protect from winter sun in coldest climates and summer sun in warmest climates. Prune by thinning rather than shearing to keep shrubs compact and fluffy. *T. baccata:* Zones 6–7; *T. cuspidata:* Zones 4–7. *T. × media:* Zones 5–7.	Use dwarf cultivars in foundations, in informal and formal hedges, and in mixed borders for evergreen color. *T. baccata* 'Repandens' (spreading English yew) grows slowly to 3 ft. tall and twice as wide. *T. cuspidata* 'Densa' grows 2 to 4 ft. tall and twice as wide. *T. cuspidata* 'Prostrata' (spreading Japanese yew) is low and wide-spreading. *T. cuspidata* 'Nana' or 'Brevifolia' is blocky, growing 3 to 4 ft. tall. *T. × media* 'Hicksii' is columnar and can reach 20 ft.

Easy-Care Annuals

Plant Name	Description	Culture and Maintenance	Landscape Use and Comments
Browallia speciosa **Browallia, sapphire flower**	Fine-textured, gracefully trailing plants, 10 to 18 in. tall. Flowers 2-in. stars in lavender-blue, dark blue, violet, purple or white.	Plant out in early summer. Space 6 to 10 in. apart in fertile, well-drained soil in partial to light shade. Tolerates full sun in constantly moist or damp soil. Mulch to keep soil cool. Does not need deadheading. Will self-sow in warm climates.	Lovely mass-planted in a shady spot under trees or shrubs as long as soil remains cool and moist. 'White Bell' is compact and bushy with ice-white flowers. 'Vanja' flowers are deep blue with a white eye.

(continued)

Plant Name	Description	Culture and Maintenance	Landscape Use and Comments

Easy-Care Annuals—(continued)

Plant Name	Description	Culture and Maintenance	Landscape Use and Comments
Calendula officinalis **Calendula, pot marigold**	Upright, well-branched plants. Tall cultivars reach 24 in. tall; dwarf cultivars, 10 to 12 in. Fluffy, chrysanthemum-like flowers, 3 to 4 in. across, are gold, orange, apricot, or ivory.	Grow in full sun in rich, well-drained, moist soil. Space 12 to 16 in. apart. Prefers cool climates and tolerates frost. Will self-sow readily. Mildew can be a problem; do not wet foliage. Grow in winter in hot climates.	Tall-growing cultivars make attractive, long-lasting cut flowers. Use tall cultivars in an herb garden, cottage garden, or informal flower border. Dwarf cultivars not recommended for informal gardens or cutting.
Catharanthus roseus (*Vinca roseus*) **Madagascar periwinkle**	Upright, growing to 2 ft. tall and spreading 2 ft. wide. Glossy green, oval leaves. Flowers are pink, mauve, or white with red eyes, to 1½ in. across. They bloom lightly all summer.	Grow in full sun or partial shade in evenly moist soil after danger of frost is past. Space 1 ft. apart. Does not need deadheading. Tolerates drought. Thrives in heat and humidity. Will self-sow.	A refined plant that can be used for a summer-long groundcover. Plant in a sunny border. 'Carpet' series grows 3 in. tall. 'Little Bright Eye' flowers are white with red eye; to 12 in. tall.
Centaurea cineraria **Dusty miller**	Forms mounded or upright plants, 12 to 18 in. tall. Grown for the deeply lobed foliage, which is densely covered with feltlike, silvery white hairs. Yellow flowers not particularly showy.	Grow in full sun in sandy, well-drained soil. Space 10 to 12 in. apart. Cut off flower stalks as they form. Cut back overwintered plants or take cuttings.	Plant in masses between flowering perennials or annuals in formal or informal borders. Combines beautifully with pastel or brightly colored flowers. Foliage is long-lasting when cut for flower arrangements.
Centaurea cyanus **Cornflower, bachelor's button**	Fine-textured, upright plants, 1 to 3 ft. tall. Fringed, 1½-in. flowers of true blue, pink, or mauve bloom most prolifically during cool weather.	Grow in full sun in average to fertile soil. Tolerates poor soil. Prefers cool climates; heat reduces flowering. Space 1 ft. apart. Deadhead to prolong bloom. Tall plants may flop unless supported by other plants. Self-sows readily.	Charming flower for cottage gardens or informal flower beds. Naturalized throughout the U.S.; looks at home in a meadow garden. Flowers last well as cut flowers.

Plant Name	Description	Culture and Maintenance	Landscape Use and Comments
Cleome hasslerana **Cleome, spiderflower**	Striking plants grow rapidly to 3 to 5 ft. tall. Large, airy, pink, rose, or white flower heads with long, showy stamens bloom all summer as the stems elongate. Attractive compound leaves have 3 to 7 leaflets. Stems have short, sharp spines.	Grow in full sun in average, well-drained soil. Space 2 ft. apart. Tolerates poor soil and some drought. Thrives in heat. Self-sows readily.	Tall, graceful plant for the back of a flower border or for a cottage garden. Flowers are long-lasting when cut, but their strong scent may be objectionable to some people.
Cosmos bipinnatus **Cosmos**	Daisylike, 4-in., rose, pink, burgundy, or white flowers with yellow centers bloom from summer to frost. Lacy foliage. Tall cultivars reach 5 ft.; dwarf cultivars to 2 ft.	Grow in full sun in average soil; will not bloom in highly fertile soil. Space 1 ft. apart. Tolerates drought and heat. Remove faded flowers for best appearance. Self-sows readily.	Lovely for cut flowers. Enchanting in the cottage garden; use in the back of the garden against a fence. 'Gloria' is rose-carmine darkening toward the center, to 4 ft.; 'Purity' is white, to 4 ft.
Eschscholzia californica **California poppy**	Reaches 1 ft. tall and wide. Finely cut, blue-green foliage. Masses of cup-shaped, 3-in., gold or orange flowers blanket the plants in spring and early summer. Cultivars include pink, red, white, and yellow as well as double flowers.	Grow in full sun in sandy, alkaline soil. Space 6 to 8 in. apart. Tolerates drought. Flowers best with cool nights. Plants die back after flowering when hot weather arrives. Readily self-sows, especially in mild climates. Sow seeds outdoors in fall in the West and South, in early spring in the Northeast.	Ideal annual for difficult, poor-soil sites. Use in a cottage garden or rock garden. Naturalize in a dry meadow or naturalistic garden, especially in the Northwest. 'Orange King' has brilliant orange flowers; 'Thai Silk' is a mix of pink shades.
Helianthus annuus **Common sunflower**	Upright plants; to 12 ft. tall for tall cultivars, 3 ft. for dwarfs. Single flowers up to 1 ft. across have yellow, gold, or mahogany petals surrounding large dark centers, which contain edible seeds when they mature. Double flowers are pompon-like.	Grow in full sun in fertile, loamy soil for best flowers. Sow seed after danger of frost is past. Space 2 ft. apart. Thrives in heat; tolerates drought and alkaline soil. Tall sunflowers may need staking, but lower cultivars are carefree.	Nostalgic plants for a cottage garden or cutting garden. Line up along a fence. 'Piccolo' has numerous 4-in. golden flowers on 4-ft. stalks. 'Sunspot' has 10-in. golden flowers on 2-ft. stems. 'Luna' has numerous pale yellow, 5-in. flowers on 5-ft. stems.

(continued)

Plant Name	Description	Culture and Maintenance	Landscape Use and Comments

Easy-Care Annuals—(continued)

Plant Name	Description	Culture and Maintenance	Landscape Use and Comments
Impatiens wallerana **Impatiens, busy lizzie**	Mounded plants with neat foliage, covered with flowers from early summer until frost. Flat, 2-in., short-spurred flowers in all shades of pink, red, violet, purple, orange, salmon, and white; bicolored cultivars available. Reaches 8 to 18 in. tall and wide depending on the cultivar.	Grow in light to full shade in moist, fertile, humusy soil. Space 8 to 15 in. apart, depending on height. Tolerates full to partial sun if kept well watered. Needs no deadheading. Will self-sow, but seedlings differ from the parents. Trouble-free.	Mass-plant in groups of a single color in shade gardens or for season-long color in a mixed border. Choose pastel colors for dark, shady spots. Cultivars are too numerous to list. Select for flower color and ultimate height.
Lobelia erinus **Edging lobelia**	Upright or trailing plants, reaching 3 to 8 in. tall. Fine-textured, lance-shaped foliage. Clusters of vivid blue, purple, violet-red, pink, or white tubular flowers at stem tips all summer or during cool weather.	Grow in full sun to partial shade in fertile, loamy soil. Space 6 in. apart. Mulch to keep soil cool and moist. Cut back to induce reblooming if heat stops the bloom. No deadheading needed.	Charming flower for edging or mass-planting beneath taller flowers. Use trailing plants to cascade over walls and rocks. 'Crystal Palace' has dark blue flowers on trailing plants; 'Cambridge Blue' has sky blue flowers.
Lobularia maritima (*Alyssum maritimum*) **Sweet alyssum**	Clusters of tiny, honey-scented, white, violet, or rose flowers cover the low, fine-textured plants. Reaches 3 to 6 in. tall and spreads 12 to 15 in.	Grow in full sun or partial shade in average, well-drained soil. Flowers best during cool weather. Does not need deadheading, but shearing back once during hot summer weather will encourage more blooms. Readily self-sows. Tolerates light frost.	Beautiful mass-planted as a groundcover beneath taller flowers or between stepping stones. Use as a formal edging along flower beds. 'Carpet of Snow' has white flowers and forms neat, ground-hugging plants spreading to 15 in.
Mirabilis jalapa **Four-o'clock**	Heavily branched, shrubby plants reach 18 to 36 in. tall. Very fragrant, trumpet-shaped flowers, 1 to 2 in. long. Flowers may be pink, white, violet, or yellow, and striped, spotted, or splashed with contrasting colors; they bloom from early summer to frost. Two or more flower colors may appear on the same plant. Flowers open in the afternoon and evening and on overcast days.	Grow in full sun or partial shade in sandy loam. Sow or plant outside after danger of frost has passed. Space 1½ to 2 ft. apart. Tolerates heat and drought as well as cool weather. Self-sows readily.	Plant where the flowers and fragrance can be appreciated in the afternoon and evening. An old-fashioned flower that's perfect for a cottage garden. The substantial plants work well surrounding a deck or patio or in a naturalistic setting. 'Jingles' has striped flowers in a variety of colors.

Plant Name	Description	Culture and Maintenance	Landscape Use and Comments
Myosotis sylvatica (*M. alpestris*) **Forget-me-not**	Upright, slightly branched plant, to 2 ft. tall; stems tipped with a coiled cluster of tiny blue flowers with yellow eyes. Cultivars may be pink or white.	Grow in light shade in moist or wet soil. Sow seeds in summer for bloom the next spring. Dies after flowering and going to seed in early summer. Reseeds freely. Can be biennial.	Delicate and charming used as an underplanting for spring bulbs, or with early perennials in a mixed border or cottage garden. Naturalize along streams or ponds.
Nierembergia hippomanica var. *violacea* **Cupflower**	Small, cup-shaped, violet-blue, white, or purple flowers literally cover mounds of needlelike foliage all summer.	Grow in full sun to partial shade in fertile, well-drained soil. Space 6 to 12 in. apart after danger of frost. Keep moist. Perennial in Zones 9–11.	Colorful, neat plant for the foreground of a flower garden or used as an edging. 'Purple Robe' forms a 6-in.-high mat of 1-in. purple flowers.
Papaver nudicaule **Iceland poppy** *P. rhoeas* **Corn poppy, Shirley poppy**	*P. nudicaule* forms clumps of blue-green, feathery foliage. Flower stems rise 1½ to 2 ft. above foliage, with 2- to 3-in. silky flowers. Flowers may be orange, apricot, pink, yellow, white, or scarlet, with yellow centers. *P. rhoeas* is similar, producing scarlet flowers with white blotches near the black centers.	Grow in full sun in light, well-drained soil. May not bloom in overly fertile soil. Sow seed in fall or early spring for spring and summer bloom. Thin to 8 to 12 in. apart. Tolerates drought. Self-sows readily.	Delightful flowers for cottage gardens or informal borders. Naturalize in a meadow garden. Make excellent cut flowers if blossoms are cut when the buds just begin to split open and the cut stem end is seared in a flame.
Portulaca grandiflora **Portulaca, rose moss**	Sprawling plants with succulent foliage grow about 6 in. tall and 18 in. wide. Single or double flowers with satiny petals bloom all summer on sunny days, close on cloudy days. Colors include yellow, red, pink, orange, white, and salmon.	Grow in full sun in average to poor, well-drained soil. Do not overwater. Tolerates drought and heat. Needs no deadheading. Self-sows readily.	Colorful plant for the rock garden or tucked into cracks in a rock wall. Mass-plant in difficult hot, dry sites that defy other annuals. 'Afternoon Delight' offers mixed colors and flowers that remain open into the evening.
Torenia fournieri **Wishbone flower**	Upright plants reaching 8 to 12 in. tall with an equal spread. Profuse, dark purple, tubular, 2-lipped flowers with white centers and yellow throats bloom all summer.	Grow in partial to full shade in fertile, humusy soil. Space 8 in. apart after danger of frost is past. Tolerates damp soil. Self-sows readily.	Ideal for mass-planting in damp, shady spots. 'Clown Mix' has compact 6-in. mounds with 1-in. flowers in a mix of cool colors.

(continued)

Plant Name	Description	Culture and Maintenance	Landscape Use and Comments
Easy-Care Annuals—(continued)			
Tropaeolum majus **Garden nasturtium**	Trailing plants with lotus-shaped, blue-green foliage. Long-stemmed, spurred flowers, 2 to 3 in. wide, in gold, orange, red, or cream; flowers may hide beneath the foliage in older varieties. Dwarf, nontrailing cultivars available.	Grow in full sun in average to poor soil. Sow seeds as soon as soil can be worked in spring. Thin to 1 ft. apart. Tolerates drought and poor soil. Flowers best in cool weather. Self-sows readily.	Flowers and leaves are edible. 'Whirlybird' has dwarf flowers in mixed colors, borne well above the foliage. 'Jewel Mixed' has semi-double flowers in mixed colors held above the compact plants.
Viola cornuta **Viola, tufted pansy** *Viola × wittrockiana* **Pansy**	Plants reach 6 to 8 in. tall. Flat, 2- to 3-in. flowers with 5 overlapping petals and yellow eyes bloom during cool weather in spring and summer. Colors include blue, purple, lavender, yellow, rose, ruby, apricot, orange, and creamy white. *V. × wittrockiana* flowers are often blotched with a contrasting color in the center.	Grow in full sun or partial shade in rich, well-drained soil. Prefers cool weather. Tolerates light frost. Remove faded flowers to prolong bloom. Pull out or cut back plants when they cease blooming. May be biennial.	Delightful flowers to combine with spring bulbs in a mixed border or cut-flower garden. Use to edge a walk in a cottage garden. Combine with other plants that will fill in after the pansies succumb to the heat.
Viola tricolor **Johnny-jump-up**	Slender, 1-ft.-tall plants topped with tiny purple-yellow-and-white, pansy-like flowers in spring.	Grow in full sun or partial shade in rich, well-drained soil. Prefers cool weather. Tolerates light frost. Pull out plants when they stop blooming or, if they're in an unobtrusive spot, leave them to rebloom in fall. Self-sows readily.	Perky plant for naturalizing in a meadow or cottage garden. Allow to weave between other plants and self-sow at will. Combines well with spring-flowering bulbs.

Easy-Care Perennials

Achillea filipendulina **Fernleaf yarrow**	Summer-blooming. Flat clusters of golden, 5-in. flower heads produced for many weeks. Deeply cut green foliage. Stems reach 3 to 5 ft. tall.	Grow in full sun in average soil. Space 1½ to 2 ft. apart. Tolerates drought, heat, and poor soil. Grows leggy and may need staking in fertile, moist soil. Zones 3–9.	Beautiful in the midground or background of a perennial border, or mass-planted with ornamental grasses. 'Coronation Gold' is well-branched, bears 3- to 4-in. flat yellow flower clusters, has attractive gray-green foliage, and reaches 2 to 3 ft. tall; it doesn't need staking.

Plant Name	Description	Culture and Maintenance	Landscape Use and Comments
Aconitum napellus **Common monkshood, helmet flower**	Summer- to late-summer-blooming. Violet-blue, 1- to 2-in., helmet-shaped flowers in tall spikes. Finely divided green leaves on 3- to 4-ft.-tall stalks.	Grow in full sun to partial shade in moist, humus-rich soil. Space 1 to 1½ ft. apart. Does not perform well in heat and humidity; prefers cool nights. Remove faded flower spikes to allow flowers on sideshoots to develop. Staking may be needed in shade. Zones 3–7, cool parts of 8.	Elegant late-blooming plant for perennial border and cottage garden. Extremely poisonous. 'Bicolor' grows 3 to 4 ft. tall with blue-and-white flowers. 'Bressingham Spire', with violet-blue flowers, and 'Newry Blue', with navy blue flowers, have very strong stems.
Alchemilla mollis (*A. vulgaris*) **Lady's-mantle**	Spring-blooming. Misty clusters of tiny yellow-green blossoms held well above the foliage. Leaves velvety olive green with scalloped edges. Forms loose 1-ft.-tall clumps.	Grow in full to light shade in moist, humus-rich soil. Best if kept moist, but tolerates drought. Susceptible to leaf diseases in areas with late afternoon thundershowers that cause the foliage to stay wet during the night. Cut off faded flowers to prevent self-sowing. Zones 4–7.	Lovely in flower, but more valued for its foliage, which is delightful in a shade garden. Leaves look lovely beaded with dew-drops. Use to edge paths or weave between contrasting plants.
Amsonia tabernae-montana **Willow amsonia, blue star**	Early-summer-blooming. Star-shaped, pale blue flowers clustered at the tops of the stems. Leaves willowlike, glossy green, turning brilliant golden yellow in fall. Forms clumps of upright, un-branched stems 2 to 3 ft. tall.	Grow in full sun to light shade in moist, loamy soil. Stems may get floppy in shade; cut them back and they'll regrow. Rarely needs division. Zones 3–9.	Attractive but not splashy. Old-fashioned plant for the flower border. Locate where the fall color can be admired.
Anemone × hybrida **Japanese anemone**	Late-summer- and fall-blooming. Palmately cut green leaves form loose mounds, above which rise 2½- to 5-ft.-tall flower stalks. Loose clusters of silky flower buds and 5-petaled white or pink flowers with yellow centers bloom for almost 2 months. Spiky, silvery seedpods are ornamental.	Grow in full sun to half shade in average to fertile, well-drained soil. Taller cultivars may need staking; shorter plants do not. Double-flowered forms may droop. Zones 4–8.	Stunning plant for late summer and fall show in a perennial border. Blooms with asters and chrysanthemums. 'Alba' has white flowers, to 3 ft. tall; 'September Charm' has silvery pink flowers and is 2½ ft. tall; 'Whirlwind' has white, semidouble flowers. *A. hupehensis* and *A. viti-folia* are similar, less common species.

(continued)

Plant Name	Description	Culture and Maintenance	Landscape Use and Comments
Easy-Care Perennials—*(continued)*			
Anemone sylvestris **Snowdrop anemone**	Spring-blooming. Nodding, white, 5-petaled flowers with yellow centers borne singly. Flower stalks rise well above mounds of light green, segmented leaves, reaching 10 to 18 in. tall. White, woolly seedpods are attractive, glistening in the sun.	Grow in partial shade in light soil. May spread eagerly from underground roots if well-sited, but unwanted plants can be easily removed. Zones 4–8.	Pretty spring bloomer for the shade garden or a naturalistic setting.
Anthemis tinctoria **Golden marguerite**	Summer-blooming. Bright yellow, daisylike flowers 1½ in. wide grow on 1½- to 3-ft.-tall stems. Finely cut green leaves with white, woolly undersides.	Grow in full sun in well-drained, average to poor soil. May become lanky in fertile soil. Tolerates drought. Cut back faded flowers to prevent rampant self-sowing. Does poorly with heat and humidity. Short-lived unless well sited in lean soil. Best in Zones 3–7, but grows in 3–10.	Blooms all summer. Decorative in an informal perennial border or cottage garden.
Armeria maritima **Sea pink, common thrift**	Early-summer-blooming. Rounded, pink, red, or white flower heads, ½ in. wide, top 6- to 12-in.-tall stalks for several weeks. Grassy, blue-green leaves form tufted mounds 6 to 8 in. tall.	Grow in full sun (partial shade in the South) in average to poor, well-drained soil. Space 1 ft. apart. Tolerates drought, salty soil, and seashore conditions. Zones 4–8.	Cute little plant for the rock garden or as an edging or clump in a flower border. Makes an effective groundcover when mass-planted.
Artemisia schmidtiana 'Silver Mound' **Silver mound artemisia**	Grown for its silvery foliage rather than its flowers. Forms a lacy, silky mound of finely dissected, silvery green foliage about 2 ft. high and wide.	Grow in full sun in poor, dry soil. Lanky growth occurs in fertile, moist conditions. Space 1 to 1½ ft. apart. Best in Zones 3–6 because the mounds flop open in hot-summer climates.	Arrange in masses for foliage contrast in the perennial border. Sets off white- and blue-flowered perennials particularly well. *A. ludoviciana* 'Silver King' has undivided silvery gray leaves with woolly undersides, borne on upright stems reaching 2 ft. tall; it can run rampant in good soil, so use with caution in well-kept formal gardens (Zones 3–9).

Plant Name	Description	Culture and Maintenance	Landscape Use and Comments
Aruncus dioicus (*A. sylvester*) **Goatsbeard**	Early-summer-blooming. Feathery plumes of tiny, creamy white flowers rise above the foliage on 4- to 6-ft.-tall stalks. Large, light green leaves are deeply cut and form huge mounds.	Grow in light to partial shade in evenly moist, well-drained, fertile soil. Do not allow to dry out. Must be shaded in hot-summer climates. Best in Zones 3–6; grows but may not thrive in Zones 7–8.	Native to the moist, wooded ravines of the mid-Atlantic and Midwestern states. Use in dramatic clumps in large-scale shade gardens, or naturalize in a moist, shady site. 'Kneiffii' grows only 3 ft. tall, with leaves cut into threadlike segments.
Aster tataricus **Tartarian aster**	Late-fall-blooming. Numerous, long-lasting, small, blue to purple flowers with yellow centers top flower stalks. Leaves form coarse basal rosettes. Reaches 3 to 6 ft. tall.	Grow in full sun in well-drained, average soil. Space 2½ to 3 ft. apart. Sturdy stems rarely need staking. Resistant to mildew, which affects many asters. Zones 4–8.	Dramatic plant, especially valuable for providing perennial color in the fall when other fall-blooming plants are on their last legs. Use in masses or clumps in the perennial border, cottage garden, or combined with ornamental grasses in a New American Garden.
Astilbe × *arendsii* **Astilbe, false spirea**	Late-spring- and summer-blooming. Feathery plumes of white, pink, peach, lavender-pink, or red are 6 to 24 in. long, depending on the cultivar, with plant heights varying from 1 to 5 ft. Deeply cut, handsome, dark green foliage forms basal clumps; may be bronze in red-flowered types.	Grow in light shade in moist, fertile, humus-rich soil. Space 2 to 2½ ft. apart. Do not allow to dry out. Tolerates sun if kept constantly moist. Zones 4–9.	Premier plants for the shade garden and New American Garden. Bloom times vary from early to late summer. Cultivars too numerous to list. A few favorites include: 'Peach Blossom', dense, peach-pink plumes on 3-ft. plants in late spring; 'Deutschland', white plumes on 2-ft. plants in late spring; 'Bressingham Beauty', clear pink plumes on 3½-ft. stems in late summer.

(continued)

An Encyclopedia of Plants for Weekend Gardens—*Continued*

Plant Name	Description	Culture and Maintenance	Landscape Use and Comments

Easy-Care Perennials—(continued)

Plant Name	Description	Culture and Maintenance	Landscape Use and Comments
Astilbe tacquetii 'Superba' **Fall astilbe**	Late-summer-blooming. Huge, bright magenta-pink plumes on 3- to 4-ft. stalks rise above the foliage clumps. Leaves large, compound, glossy dark green, and deeply cut.	Grow in partial shade in moist, humus-rich soil. Tolerates heat and drought better than other astilbes. Space 2 to 3 ft. apart. Zones 4–8.	Dramatic perennial for a large-scale shade garden or New American Garden. Plant in groups.
Aurinia saxatilis **Basket-of-gold**	Early-spring-blooming; evergreen. Clusters of golden yellow flowers on 1- to 2-ft.-tall stems blanket the plants. Gray-green, softly hairy, spoon-shaped leaves borne in 1-ft.-tall mounds.	Grow in full sun in average to poor, well-drained soil. Space 1½ ft. apart. Plants sprawl in fertile, moist soil. Cut off faded flowers before seedpods form. Zones 3–7; short-lived in heat and humidity of Zones 8–10.	Classic plant for the rock garden or rock wall. Works well in a perennial border, where the foliage provides a gray contrast after blooming. Blooms with *Aubrieta, Arabis,* and spring bulbs. 'Citrinum' has light yellow blossoms; 'Compactum' grows 6 to 8 in. tall and sprawls less.
Baptisia australis **Baptisia, blue false indigo**	Early-summer-blooming. Indigo blue, two-lipped, tubular, 1-in. pealike flowers on long spikes at the tips of each stem. Blue-green, rounded leaflets, like those of pea plants, on upright stems. Attractive seedpods remain until fall. Forms dense 3- to 6-ft.-tall clumps.	Grow in full sun to partial shade in rich, moist, acid soil. Space 4 ft. apart. Plants spread slowly into sizable clumps that do not need dividing unless they take up too much room. May need staking if grown in partial shade. Zones 3–9.	An old-fashioned perennial that looks at home in a formal or informal perennial garden. Seed-grown plants vary in flower color from light to dark blue.
Boltonia asteroides 'Snowbank' **'Snowbank' white boltonia**	Late-summer- and fall-blooming. Airy clusters of small white daisylike flowers top the lanky plants. Blue-green, 5-in.-long linear leaves contribute to the plant's fine texture. The cultivar 'Snowbank' grows 3 to 4 ft. tall, rather than the 5 to 6 of the species, and is less floppy.	Grow in full sun in moist, humus-rich soil. Tolerates some drought and partial shade, though may need staking in shade. Space 2 ft. apart. Divide every 3 or 4 years. Zones 4–9.	Lacy plant for late-season color in a perennial border or naturalistic setting. Combines well with ornamental grasses in a New American Garden. *B. asteroides* var. *latisquama* 'Nana' grows 2 to 3 ft. tall with pink flowers.

Plant Name	Description	Culture and Maintenance	Landscape Use and Comments
Campanula carpatica **Carpathian bellflower, Carpathian harebell**	Summer-blooming. Cup-shaped, 2-in., blue, pink, or white flowers dance above the foliage for most of the summer. Leaves are dark green, triangular, and toothed, forming 9- to 12-in.-tall rounded mounds.	Grow in full sun to partial shade in well-drained, average soil. Tolerates dry soil. May rot in overly moist soil. Mulch to keep roots cool, especially in the South. Removing flowers as they fade will promote the longest bloom. Zones 3–8.	Spreads rapidly where well situated. Charming in the foreground of a perennial garden or in a rock garden. 'Blue Clips' has 3-in. blue flowers on compact plants; 'White Clips' has 3-in. white flowers on compact plants.
Coreopsis verticillata **Threadleaf coreopsis**	Summer-blooming. Golden yellow, 2-in., daisylike flowers bloom for several months in summer. Foliage is finely cut, very lacy, forming open, airy, upright clumps 2 to 3 ft. tall. The cultivars are preferred over the species.	Grow in full sun in average, well-drained soil. Tolerates drought. Space 1 to 1½ ft. apart. Spreads very rapidly; can be invasive in fertile soil. Cut off seedpods with hedge shears if blooming stops in late summer to encourage fall bloom. Zones 3–9.	Lovely, fine-textured plant for the perennial border. Attractive with ornamental grasses in the New American Garden, where the decorative dried plants and seedheads can be left to stand through the winter. 'Moonbeam' has pale primrose yellow flowers that bloom all summer and fall.
Dianthus deltoides **Maiden pink**	Summer-blooming. Grassy, 4- to 6-in.-tall leaves on prostrate stems form dense mats. Rose, red, pink, or white, 3- to 4-in.-wide flowers with notched petals and a contrasting band of spots at the petal bases blanket the plants for 2 or more months.	Grow in full sun to partial shade in fertile, alkaline soil. Does not need deadheading, but after the major flowering ceases, shear back the plants to promote further bloom. Zones 3–9.	Spreads rapidly and makes a good groundcover. Use in the foreground of a perennial border, in a rock garden, or between paving stones. Numerous cultivars include: 'Helen', with fragrant salmon-pink flowers; 'Tiny Rubies', with double, deep pink flowers.
Dicentra eximia **Fringed bleeding-heart**	Spring- and summer-blooming. Pink, rose, or white pantaloon-shaped flowers on long stalks that rise above the foliage bloom for months. Foliage fernlike, gray-green, forming basal clumps 1 to 1½ ft. tall.	Grow in partial or light shade in moist, slightly acid, humus-rich soil. Must have good drainage. Space 1½ ft. apart. Reseeds readily, but seedlings are easy to pull up if undesired. Performs poorly with high heat and humidity. Zones 3–9.	Lovely, long-blooming plant with attractive foliage for the shade garden. Naturalize in a woodland; native to woodlands in the eastern U.S. 'Snowdrift' has pure white flowers; 'Bountiful' has soft rosy red flowers.

(continued)

Plant Name	Description	Culture and Maintenance	Landscape Use and Comments

Easy-Care Perennials—(continued)

Dicentra spectabilis **Bleeding-heart**	Early- and mid-spring-blooming. Heart-shaped, pink-and-white flowers dangle from the undersides of long, arching stems. Foliage is blue-green and cut into lacy segments, forming large, spreading clumps 2 to 3 ft. tall.	Grow in partial shade in moist, humus-rich soil. Space 2 ft. apart. Dies back to the ground usually by midsummer; remains longer in cool, moist climates. Cut out stems after they turn completely yellow. Zones 2–9.	Emerges rapidly in spring and blooms along with spring bulbs. A beautiful specimen for the shade garden or shady perennial bed. 'Alba' has milky white flowers and light green foliage, and remains smaller than pink types. 'Pantaloons' has pure white flowers and is more vigorous than 'Alba'.
Dictamnus albus **Gas plant**	Early-summer-blooming. Flowers white, pink, or purple, in dense upright clusters at the stem tips. Lemon-scented, medium-green foliage is divided into rounded leaflets. Bushy plants reach 3 to 4 ft. tall; older stems woody.	Grow in full sun in well-drained soil. Do not disturb roots. Never needs dividing. Does not need staking. Prefers areas with cool nights. Zones 3–8.	Very long-lived plant. Ideal for an old-fashioned perennial border. Plant in its permanent location. 'Purpureus' has mauve-purple flowers with darker veins; 'Rubra' has rosy pink flowers veined purple.
Echinacea purpurea **Purple coneflower**	Summer- and fall-blooming. Large, daisylike flowers with dark brown centers surrounded by somewhat drooping, purplish pink petals; may reach 6 in. wide. Coarse, bristly, dark green, lance-shaped leaves 4 to 8 in. long. Multibranched plants reaching 2 to 3 ft. tall.	Grow in full sun in average, well-drained soil. Drought-tolerant. Space 2 ft. apart. Needs no staking unless grown in partial shade. Mildew can be troublesome. Zones 3–8.	Stunning, bold-textured plant blends well with ornamental grasses in a New American Garden. Works well in masses in an informal perennial border. 'White Luster' has white flowers with orange centers and reaches 3 ft. tall; 'Ovation' has bright rosy pink flowers.
Echinops ritro **Globe thistle**	Summer- and early-fall-blooming. Spherical, 2-in. flower heads are steely bluish purple. Thistlelike leaves green on top, gray and woolly on the undersides. Plants reach 3 to 4 ft. tall.	Grow in full sun in average to poor soil. Space 2 ft. apart. Tolerates drought. Doesn't need staking unless grown in partial shade. Rarely needs division. Zones 3–8.	Unusual, long-blooming plant for summer and fall color in the perennial border. May be confused with other similar species. 'Taplow Blue' has dark blue flowers, blooms in late summer and fall, and grows to 3 ft. tall.

Plant Name	Description	Culture and Maintenance	Landscape Use and Comments
Eupatorium purpureum **Joe-Pye weed**	Late-summer- and fall-blooming. Coarse, divided leaves are vanilla-scented. Tall, hollow green stems marked with purple reach 4 to 7 ft. tall. Huge heads of mauve flowers can be 12 to 18 in. wide.	Grow in full sun to partial shade in moist, well-drained soil. Tolerates wet soil. Space 3 ft. apart. Do not allow to dry out. Prefers cool night temperatures. Zones 4–9.	Bold, dramatic plants for planting in groups in a New American or naturalistic garden. Native to stream banks and other moist sites in the eastern U.S. 'Atropurpureum' has purple flowers and leaves.
Filipendula purpurea **Japanese meadow-sweet** *F. rubra* **Queen-of-the-prairie** *F. ulmaria* **Queen-of-the-meadow**	Summer-blooming. Spectacular, loose, feathery heads of pink or white flowers top the plants for 2 to 3 weeks. Foliage is bold-textured and deeply cut. *F. purpurea* grows 3 to 6 ft. tall, with deep pink, fragrant flowers and crimson stems; *F. rubra* grows 6 to 8 ft. tall, with peach-pink flowers; *F. ulmaria* grows 3 to 6 ft. tall, with fragrant, creamy white flowers.	Grow in full sun in evenly moist to wet, fertile, humus-rich soil. Space 2 ft. apart. Sturdy stems do not need staking. *F. purpurea:* Zones 3–8; *F. rubra* and *F. ulmaria:* Zones 3–9.	Impressive plants for large-scale gardens. Naturalize along a pond or stream. *F. rubra* 'Venusta' has deep carmine-pink flowers. *F. ulmaria* 'Flore-Pleno' has double, bright white flowers.
Gypsophila paniculata **Baby's-breath**	Summer-blooming. Clouds of tiny white or pink flowers. Stems wiry and brittle, with narrow, gray-green leaves. Forms mounds 1½ to 4 ft. tall and twice as wide.	Grow in full sun in alkaline, well-drained soil. Space 2 ft. apart. Taller cultivars need staking with metal hoops; the shorter ones do not. Plant in permanent location. Zones 3–9.	Use for a light-textured contrast to bolder plants in the perennial border. Makes fine cut flower and filler in arrangements.
Hemerocallis hybrids and cultivars **Daylilies**	Late-spring-, summer-, and early-fall-blooming. Long, arching, strap-shaped foliage forms grassy clumps ranging in height from 8 to 36 in., depending on the cultivar. Large funnel-shaped flowers, to 6 in. wide, bloom only one day each, but abundant flowers provide a long bloom period. Flowers in every shade except pure white and blue; some have ruffled petals, contrasting throats, or double petals.	Grow in full sun to partial shade in fertile, well-drained soil for best results. Space 2 ft. apart. Tough and durable, tolerant of poor soil, drought, and shade. Needs no staking. Remove faded flowers regularly for best appearance. Cut off flower stalks after bloom. Zones 3–9.	Outstanding, long-blooming plants for almost any situation: beautiful in formal and informal perennial gardens; effective as a tall groundcover for erosion control on banks; wonderful mass-planted with ornamental grasses in a New American landscape or naturalized. Dwarf cultivars are ideal in the foreground of the border. Cultivars are too numerous to name.

(continued)

Plant Name	Description	Culture and Maintenance	Landscape Use and Comments

Easy-Care Perennials—(continued)

Plant Name	Description	Culture and Maintenance	Landscape Use and Comments
Iris ensata (*I. kaempferi*) **Japanese iris**	Summer-blooming. Huge, flat, butterfly-like blossoms may be white, purple, blue, or lavender and veined with contrasting colors. Upright clumps of grassy green foliage reach 2 to 3 ft. tall.	Grow in full sun to bright shade in moist or wet, fertile, humus-rich, acid soil. Tolerates standing water. Do not allow to dry out, especially while in bloom. Divide every 4 years immediately after flowering. Performs poorly in hot, dry situations. Zones 5–10.	Elegant flower for the perennial border or for naturalizing along a pond or stream. Numerous cultivars available. *I. pseudacorus* (yellow-flag iris) grows 2½ to 5 ft. tall, with bright yellow blossoms; requires similar culture. Used as a parent for yellow-flowered hybrids of *I. ensata*. *I. versicolor* (blue flag iris), with blue, lavender, or purple flowers, is native to marshy sites on the East Coast; Zones 3–9.
Iris sibirica **Siberian iris**	Late-spring- and early-summer-blooming. Lovely, graceful, 1- to 2-in. flowers in purple, lavender, blue, or white marked with yellow bloom for several weeks. Grassy green foliage forms arching clumps 2 to 3 ft. tall.	Grow in full sun to partial shade in fertile, moist, slightly acid soil. Keep soil moist; tolerates boggy soil. Cut off seedpods after flowering. Zones 4–10.	Delicate-looking flower for a perennial border or for a light-shade garden. Will thrive in boggy conditions along a stream or pond. Many cultivars available.
Ligularia dentata **Bigleaf ligularia, bigleaf goldenray**	Mid- to late-summer-blooming, but often grown just for the foliage. Golden-orange flowers with ragged petals borne on 4-ft. stalks. Huge, leathery, kidney-shaped, green leaves are 20 in. long, with coarse teeth; often marked with purple. Forms impressive clumps 3 ft. tall.	Grow in full sun to light shade in moist to wet, fertile, humus-rich soil. Space 3 to 4 ft. apart. Mulch soil heavily to keep it cool. Do not allow to dry out. Best in Zones 5–6; 7–8 only in moist soil with afternoon shade.	An architectural plant for large-scale gardens, especially in naturalistic landscapes along ponds or streams. 'Desdemona' has foliage that emerges beet red in spring, changing to green with purple undersides; more heat-tolerant and compact than the species. Remove flower stalks to enjoy as a foliage plant.

Plant Name	Description	Culture and Maintenance	Landscape Use and Comments
Oenothera pilosella **Sundrops** *O. fruticosa* **Common sundrops**	Summer-blooming perennial. Clusters of bright yellow, upward-facing, 2-in. flowers bloom during the day, unlike many other species of *Oenothera*, which bloom in the evening. Slightly hairy leaves are oval to lance-shaped, 4 in. long, and often tinged with red. Stiff stems form upright plants reaching 1½ to 2 ft. tall. The two species are similar.	Grow in full sun in average well-drained soil. Tolerates dry soil. Space 1 to 2 ft. apart. Spreads very rapidly and may be invasive in well-tended gardens, but not difficult to remove. Zones 4–8.	Cheerful, long-blooming flower for informal gardens where its wandering ways are acceptable. Beautiful combined with blue flowers.
Paeonia lactiflora **Common garden peony, Chinese peony**	Late-spring- and early-summer-blooming. Perfumed flowers, 4-in. wide, may be single with showy yellow stamens, semi-double with large outer petals and short tufted inner petals, or fully double globes. Colors include white and shades of pink, rose, and red. Dark green, glossy foliage is cut into rounded lobes; it looks very attractive all summer and may turn red in fall. Bushy plants reach 1½ to 3 ft. tall.	Grow in full sun (partial shade in hot climates) in fertile, well-drained, humus-rich soil. Space 2 to 3 ft. apart. Plant with buds (eyes) on fleshy roots 1 to 2 in. below soil surface; planting too deep produces foliage but no flowers. Keep soil moist. Botrytis fungus may attack emerging stems in spring and flowers as they bloom. Never needs division. Double-flowered forms look neater when grown through wire rings. Zones 2–8.	Exceptionally long-lived plants make elegant specimens in the perennial border. Handsome, shrubby plants make a beautiful edging along a drive, look spectacular in front of a stone wall. Numerous cultivars. Choose early-blooming cultivars for the South so they bloom before warm weather arrives. Single-flowered cultivars are less susceptible to botrytis, which can ruin the flowers.
Papaver orientale **Oriental poppy**	Early-summer-blooming. Huge flowers with satiny crinkled petals and fluffy centers of yellow or black stamens atop 2- to 3-ft.-tall hairy stems. Notable hairy buds. The species has orange-red petals with black blotches at their bases. Cultivars include white and shades of pink, peach, orange, scarlet, and red. Leaves are thistlelike, 10 to 12 in. long, forming prickly basal clumps.	Grow in full sun in well-drained, fertile soil. Space 2 ft. apart. Best in cool-summer areas. Divide every 4 or 5 years immediately after flowering. Does not need staking. Zones 2–7.	Eye-catching plant for the perennial border; effective with ornamental grasses in the New American Garden. Foliage dies down after flowering, leaving a hole in the garden, so plant only in small groups of 3 plants and arrange so that other plants, such as *Gypsophila* or warm-season ornamental grasses, fill in the gap. Numerous cultivars.

(continued)

Plant Name	Description	Culture and Maintenance	Landscape Use and Comments

Easy-Care Perennials—(continued)

Plant Name	Description	Culture and Maintenance	Landscape Use and Comments
Perovskia atriplicifolia **Russian sage**	Mid- to late-summer-blooming woody perennial or subshrub. Lavender-blue flowers in airy, branched clusters atop the stems. Leaves silver-gray and lance-shaped. Stiff stems form bushy plants reaching 3 to 5 ft. tall.	Grow in full sun in well-drained, average to poor soil. Space 2 ft. apart. Drought-tolerant. Cut back to 1 to 1½ ft. in spring before new growth begins. Zones 5–9.	Unusual and eye-catching plant to provide fine-textured gray contrast in a large-scale mixed or perennial border. Effective combined with ornamental grasses in the New American Garden.
Phlox maculata **Wild sweet william, meadow phlox**	Early-summer-blooming. Small, notched flowers in large, fragrant, cone-shaped flower heads. The species is mauve-pink, but cultivars offer white and beautiful clear shades of pink. Glossy, dark green leaves lance-shaped, 2 to 4 in. long. Upright, hairy stems may be mottled with red and form bushy plants reaching 2 to 3 ft. tall.	Grow in full sun in moist, well-drained, humus-rich soil. Space 2 ft. apart. This species resists mildew, which seriously troubles *P. paniculata* (garden phlox). Spider mites can be troublesome in hot, dry weather. Cut back after flowering to induce a second flush of flowers. Rarely needs staking. Zones 3–9.	Similar in growth habit to *P. paniculata,* so it makes an ideal low-maintenance substitute in the perennial border or cut flower garden. 'Alpha' has rose-pink flowers with a darker eye; 'Miss Lingard' has pure white flowers; 'Omega' has white flowers with a lilac eye; 'Rosalinde' has dark pink flowers.
Physostegia virginiana **False dragonhead, obedient plant**	Late-summer- to fall-blooming. Spikes of tubular, 1-in., 2-lipped flowers bloom over a long period. Species has purplish pink flowers, but cultivars include white, pink, and crimson. Lance-shaped, glossy green leaves with sharply toothed edges on square stems. Forms 3- to 4-ft.-tall spreading clumps.	Grow in full sun to partial shade in moist, humus-rich, acid soil. Tolerates wet soil. Space 3 ft. apart. Spreads rapidly by underground roots and can be invasive, especially in fertile soil. Rogue to keep in check. Rarely needs staking in full sun. Zones 2–9.	Native to the eastern U.S. Naturalize along ponds and stream banks or in damp sites. Lovely for late-season color in an informal or naturalistic garden. 'Alba' has white flowers; 'Pink Bouquet' has bright pink flowers on 3- to 4-ft. stems; 'Summer Snow' has white flowers on 2-ft. stems and is less invasive.

Plant Name	Description	Culture and Maintenance	Landscape Use and Comments
Platycodon grandiflorus **Balloon flower**	Summer-blooming. Cup-shaped, 3-in. flowers open from intriguing inflated buds over a long period. Flowers are usually purple-blue with darker veins, but cultivars include white, pink, and pure blue flowers. Upright stems cloaked with gray-green, oval, sharply toothed leaves. Bushy plants reach 1½ to 2½ ft. tall.	Grow in full sun in the North, light shade in the South, in moist, well-drained, fertile soil. Space 1 ft. apart. Emerges late in spring. Tall cultivars may need staking with a metal ring. Rarely needs division. Zones 3–8.	Gorgeous blue-flowered plant for the perennial garden. 'Mariesii' grows 1 to 2 ft. tall, with purple-blue flowers; 'Shell Pink' has pale pink flowers on 1½- to 2-ft. stems; 'Double Blue' has bright blue double flowers on 1½- to 2-ft. stems; 'Snowflake' has white flowers.
Rudbeckia fulgida 'Goldsturm' **'Goldsturm' rudbeckia, 'Goldsturm' black-eyed susan**	Summer- and fall-blooming. Daisylike, golden yellow flowers with dark brown centers are 3 to 4 in. wide and bloom abundantly for a long period. Coarse-textured, lance-shaped leaves to 6 in. long on strong, well-branched stems. Plants form bushy clumps 2 to 3 ft. tall.	Grow in full sun to partial shade in moist to dry, average to poor soil. Space 2 ft. apart. Fast spreading though not invasive in fertile soil. Does not suffer from mildew, unlike the species. Zones 3–9.	A rugged and lively perennial for the informal flower border, cottage garden, or cut flower garden. Well-loved in combination with ornamental grasses in the New American Garden; allow the rusty brown dried seedheads to stand in place over the winter for a naturalistic effect.
Salvia × *superba* **Violet sage**	Late-spring- and summer-blooming woody perennial. Slender spikes of violet-purple flowers rise above the foliage for a long bloom period. Gray-green, lance-shaped foliage cloaks upright branched stems, forming bushy clumps 1½ to 3 ft. tall.	Grow in full sun in moist, average soil. Tolerates dry soil. Tall cultivars become floppy and need staking in hot-summer areas; use dwarf forms in the South. Space 1 to 1½ ft. apart. Zones 4–8.	Use in the perennial border or cottage garden. Very effective combined with yellow flowers. 'Blue Queen' has bright violet flowers on 1½- to 2-ft. stems and tolerates heat and drought. *S. azurea* (azure sage) grows to 3 to 4 ft. tall in Zones 5–9 and tolerates heat and humidity better than *S.* × *superba*.

(continued)

Plant Name	Description	Culture and Maintenance	Landscape Use and Comments

Easy-Care Perennials—(continued)

Sedum spectabile **Showy stonecrop**	Late-summer- and fall-blooming. Showy clusters of tiny flowers, pale green in bud and opening pink, form dense heads above the foliage. Succulent, round, light green leaves surround the stiff stems, forming upright clumps 1½ to 2 ft. tall.	Grow in full sun to partial shade in well-drained, average soil. Needs full sun in the South or the plants grow too tall and may become floppy by flowering time. Space 1½ ft. apart. Zones 3–10.	Effective plants in the perennial border or rock garden. Favorites for mass-planting in a New American Garden. 'Brilliant' has intense pink flowers. *S.* × 'Autumn Joy' has 6-in. pink flower heads that age rusty red and remain ornamental over the winter. *S.* × 'Ruby Glow' has vivid ruby red flowers and red-edged leaves; it grows to 1 ft. tall.

Easy-Care Bulbs

Allium aflatunense **Ornamental onion** *A. christophii* **Star-of-Persia** *A. giganteum* **Giant onion** *A. moly* **Lily leek**	Spring-, summer-, and fall-blooming bulbs, depending on the species. Rounded to perfectly spherical clusters of star-like flowers, one to a stem, rise above the grassy foliage. *A. aflatunense* has lilac-purple, 4-in.-wide balls of flowers on 2½-ft. stalks in late spring and broad, straplike basal leaves; *A. christophii* has lilac, 8- to 10-in.-wide flower clusters in early summer on stalks to 3 ft. tall and long, grasslike leaves; *A. giganteum* has 4- to 5-in., bright blue balls of flowers on 5-ft. stalks in early summer and straplike basal leaves; *A. moly* has 3-in. clusters of yellow flowers in early summer on 1½-ft. stalks and grasslike foliage; it self-sows, spreads rapidly, and may become weedy.	Grow in full sun in well-drained, dry soil. Plant bulbs at a depth 3 times their diameter; place tall species 18 to 24 in. apart. shorter species 6 in. apart. Must have sharp drainage; will not persist in damp or heavy soil, otherwise very easy. Remove seedheads to prevent self-sowing, especially with *A. moly,* which can be weedy. *A. aflatunense, A. christophii*, and *A. giganteum:* Zones 4–8; *A. moly:* Zones 3–9.	Use tall alliums in the mid- or background of a dry perennial border; shorter species in a rock garden or the foreground of a border. Foliage often dies soon after flowering, so place alliums behind other plants that will fill in the gap. Dried flowers are very decorative.

Plant Name	Description	Culture and Maintenance	Landscape Use and Comments
Chionodoxa luciliae **Glory-of-the-snow**	Early-spring-blooming bulb. Stalks of several 1-in.-wide, brilliant blue flowers with white eyes rise above the strap-shaped foliage. Grows about 4 to 6 in. tall.	Grow in sunny spot in well-drained soil. Plant 3 in. deep and 4 in. apart. Spreads and self-sows readily. Zones 4–9.	Plant in large groups for a dramatic display. Foliage dies down in early summer; camouflage it with other plants, such as dwarf daylilies.
Colchicum autumnale **Autumn crocus, meadow saffron**	Fall-flowering corm. Large, 4-in.-long, vase-shaped violet, lilac, pink, or white flowers emerge directly from the bare ground. Each corm produces several flowers. Coarse, bright green leaves 8 to 10 in. long emerge in spring and persist until mid-summer, when they turn an unsightly yellow.	Grow in full sun in fertile, well-drained soil. Plant corms in late summer for fall bloom, spacing them 3 to 4 in. deep and 10 to 12 in. apart. Do not remove dying foliage until it has completely withered. Divide while in bloom. Zones 5–8.	Looks best planted in a groundcover such as *Vinca minor*, which forms a backdrop for the bare-stemmed flowers. 'Water-lily' has double violet-pink flowers.
Crocus spp. **Crocuses**	Early-spring- or fall-blooming corms. Vase-shaped flowers with prominent yellow stamens bloom many to a corm. Dark green, grasslike foliage often has white central stripe. Leaves short while plants are blooming, but may elongate to 6 to 8 in. before dying back.	Grow in full sun or light shade in well-drained to dry soil. Plant corms 3 in. deep and 3 to 6 in. apart. Perform poorly in heavy or wet soil. Will spread where happily situated. Squirrels may eat the flowers, foliage, and bulbs. Zones 5–9.	Mass-plant for best effect under deciduous trees and shrubs. Plant in clusters in a rock garden. Perennial gardens may be too moist for successful growth. Species and hybrids too numerous to name. Hybrid "Dutch" crocus have the largest and showiest flowers in lavender, purple, white, and gold. Species and their cultivars are often dainty and may bloom very early in spring. Fall crocus are delicate plants for the sunny rock garden.

(continued)

Plant Name	Description	Culture and Maintenance	Landscape Use and Comments
Easy-Care Bulbs—(continued)			
Galanthus elwesii **Giant snowdrop** *G. nivalis* **Common snowdrop**	Late-winter- and early-spring-blooming bulbs. White, nodding flowers with 3 short and 3 long petals, borne one to a stem. *G. elwesii* has 1-in. flowers and grows to 12 in. tall with 4-in.-long, gray-green leaves. *G. nivalis* has ½-in. flowers and reaches 6 to 9 in. tall.	Grow in full sun or partial shade in well-drained soil. Will rot in heavy or wet soil. Does not tolerate heat well. Divide immediately after flowering, if needed. *G. elwesii* remains as a single bulb; *G. nivalis* forms large clumps; both self-sow readily. *G. elwesii:* Zones 4–7; *G. nivalis:* Zones 3–7.	Among the earliest bulbs to bloom. Beautiful naturalized in masses on the edge of a woods or in a shade garden. *G. elwesii* is endangered in its native habitat; purchase only nursery-propagated stock.
Hyacinthoides hispanicus (*Endymion hispanicus, Scilla campanulata, Scilla hispanica*) **Spanish bluebells**	Bell-shaped, 1-in., blue flowers densely packed (at least 12 to a stem) on straight spikes, reaching 12 to 15 in. tall. Glossy, dark green, strap-shaped foliage forms clusters around the flower stems.	Grow in moist, humusy soil in light to full shade. Space 1 ft. apart and 3 to 4 in. deep. Bulbs increase readily and plants self-sow freely. Leaves may become unsightly before they die back completely. Zones 4–8.	Beautiful naturalized in a woodland or shade garden. Plant in large groups for best effect. White, pink, deep blue, and purplish blue cultivars are available. *H. non-scriptus* (English bluebells) are similar, bearing less-dense spikes of blue flowers with reflexed petals.
Iris danfordiae *I. reticulata*	Late-winter- to early-spring-blooming bulbs. *I. danfordiae* has small, bright yellow, beardless blossoms with brown blotches on the petals; narrow leaves grow to 1 ft. tall after flowering. *I. reticulata* bears gold-marked, purple, beardless flowers; narrow leaves grow 1 to 1½ ft. tall.	Grow in full sun in well-drained, dry soil. Plant 4 in. deep and 3 to 6 in. apart. Thrives in hot, dry conditions; does poorly in wet soil or areas of heavy summer rainfall. Spreads readily where well-adapted. Squirrels may eat the flowers and bulbs. Divide right after flowering. Zones 5–9.	Plant in large groups along a walk or near a window where they can be enjoyed in late winter. Good in a rock garden or sandy flower bed. Leaves die back by midsummer; camouflage with annuals. Rhizomatous iris are described under Easy-Care Perennials.
Leucojum aestivum **Summer snowflake** *L. vernum* **Spring snowflake**	Spring-blooming bulbs. Clusters of nodding, bell-shaped white flowers have petals marked with green at the tips. Foliage is dark green and strap-shaped; to 1½ ft. long. *L. aestivum* blooms in mid-spring with 3 to 5 1-in. flowers per stalk. *L. vernum* has 1 or 2 ½-in. flowers per stalk and blooms in early spring.	Grow in full sun to partial shade in moist soil. Plant 3 to 5 in. deep and 4 in. apart. Bulbs increase and self-sow if well-sited. Performs better in the South than *Galanthus. L. aestivum:* Zones 4–9; *L. vernum:* Zones 3–9.	Plant along a walkway or where they can be seen from a window, so early blossoms can be appreciated. Use in the mixed border; camouflage fading foliage behind annuals or perennials.

Plant Name	Description	Culture and Maintenance	Landscape Use and Comments
Lilium spp. **Lilies**	Early-summer- to fall-blooming bulbs. Numerous species and hybrids make lilies a diverse group. Flowers are often fragrant and may be nodding or upright and trumpet-, star-, or bowl-shaped. They range in height from 1 to 7 ft. Flowers come in every color except blue.	Grow in full sun to light or partial shade in fertile, humusy, moist but well-drained soil. Plant at a depth 2 to 3 times the diameter of the bulb and 1 ft. apart. Bulbs may rot over winter in wet soil. Tall lilies need staking. Zones 4–9.	Indispensable in a perennial or mixed border. Use in the mid-ground or background, and plant in groups of at least 3 bulbs for best effect. Grow in a cut flower garden so the elegant flowers can be enjoyed indoors without robbing the garden.
Lycoris squamigera **Magic lily, naked-ladies**	Late-summer-blooming bulb. Several fragrant, trumpet-shaped, rose-pink flowers bloom atop 1½- to 2-ft. stems. Dark green, 9- to 12-in.-long leaves emerge in early spring but die down before the flowers appear.	Grow in full sun or partial shade in fertile, moist soil. Space 1 ft. apart. Spreads rapidly. Do not remove foliage until it is completely dead. Zones 5–9.	Grow in groundcover such as *Vinca minor* or among low perennials, which will help camouflage the dying foliage and provide a foil for the naked flowers.
Muscari armeniacum **Armenian grape hyacinth** *M. botryoides* **Common grape hyacinth**	Spring-flowering bulbs. Tiny, urn-shaped, dark purplish-blue flowers form dense spikes at the ends of 8- to 12-in. flower stalks. Foliage dark green and grasslike. *M. armeniacum* has pale blue flowers; the foliage, which is longer than the flower stalk, appears in the fall and dies back as the spring flowers bloom. *M. botryoides* is similar, but flowers a bit earlier and has more globe-shaped flowers with leaves shorter than the flower stalk. *M. armeniacum:* Zones 4–8; *M. botryoides:* Zones 2–8.	Grow in full sun in well-drained soil. Plant 4 in. deep and 4 in. apart. Bulbs increase and plants self-sow readily.	Mass-plant in a naturalistic garden, plant among low groundcovers, and combine with *Narcissus* for a nice yellow-and-blue color scheme. Some species are endangered in their native habitats; purchase only nursery-propagated bulbs.

(continued)

Plant Name	*Description*	*Culture and Maintenance*	*Landscape Use and Comments*

Easy-Care Bulbs—(continued)

Narcissus spp. **Daffodils, jonquils, and narcissi**	Spring-flowering bulbs. Flowers have a trumpet-shaped corolla and surrounding petal-like perianth, may be double or single, and may have single- or multiple-flowered stalks. Flower colors include white and shades of yellow, pink, orange, red-orange, and green. Straplike leaves usually 12 to 20 in. long.	Grow in full sun to partial shade in fertile, humusy, well-drained soil. Plant at a depth 3 times the diameter of the bulb and space 8 to 12 in. apart. Bulbs will increase and form clumps. Foliage dies back in mid-summer. Zones 4–9, except for species, jonquilla, and tazetta *Narcissus*, which are hardy in Zones 6–9.	Most *Narcissus* work well mass-planted in natural-istic landscapes, especially the smaller-flowered types, which look more like wildflowers than the large-flowered or trumpet daffodils. These big daffo-dils are more dramatic in a mixed border.
Scilla siberica **Siberian squill**	Early-spring-flowering bulb. Bright blue, nodding flowers bloom 2 to 3 to a stem with several stems per bulb. Strap-shaped, dark green leaves 3 to 4 in. long.	Grow in full sun to partial shade in well-drained soil. Plant 4 in. deep and 6 in. apart. Spreads rapidly by self-sowing and increasing bulbs. Zones 2–8.	Naturalize under decidu-ous trees or in the shade garden. Arrange in groups and masses for the best effect. Blooms just after *Galanthus*.
Tulipa kauf-manniana **Water lily tulip** *T. tarda*	Early-spring-blooming bulbs. *T. kaufmanniana* produces 5- to 10-in. stalks of 3½-in., spreading flow-ers in white or pale yel-low marked with red; broad leaves are often attractively mottled. *T. tarda* has graceful, bright green leaves and 6- to 9-in.-long stems bear-ing up to 5 yellow flowers with broad white edges.	Grow in full sun in fertile, well-drained soil. Plant at a depth 3 times the bulb width and space 6 in. apart. These tulips are long-lived and will increase if sited prop-erly. Do not remove foliage until it withers completely. *T. kaufmanniana* and *T. tarda:* Zones 4–8.	Plant in groups in a rock garden or in the fore-ground of a perennial border. Several cultivars are available for each of these popular species.
Tulipa spp. **Tulips**	Spring-flowering bulbs. All hybrid tulips are ele-gant and formal in bloom, featuring a single large flower at the tip of a sturdy stem and several large basal leaves. Flow-ers in every color but blue, often bicolored or streaked; can be single or double. Early-, mid-, and late-season tulips extend the bloom season over 8 weeks.	Grow in full sun in well-drained, fertile soil. Plant at a depth 3 times the bulb width and 6 in. apart. Hybrids are short-lived, espe-cially in the South. Yellowing foliage is unsightly but must not be removed until totally withered. Remove dead flow-ers before seeds develop to have bloom the following year. Zones 2–8.	Plant in the cutting gar-den and remove them after the flowers are cut for indoor use. Elegant when treated as annuals in the mixed border; plant close together in masses of a single color.

Plant Name	Description	Culture and Maintenance	Landscape Use and Comments

Easy-Care Shrub Roses

Plant Name	Description	Culture and Maintenance	Landscape Use and Comments
Rosa 'Bonica' **'Bonica' rose**	Shrub rose. Arching canes reach 5 ft. tall; plant spreads 5 ft. wide. Masses of double, pastel pink flowers from early spring until frost. Foliage is dark, glossy green, and disease-resistant. Orange-red hips develop in fall.	Grow in full sun in moist, fertile soil. Space 3 to 5 ft. apart. May need light pruning in early spring to remove deadwood in coldest areas. Keep soil moist and well-mulched. May be killed to the ground in severe winters in coldest regions but will regrow. To renew or control size, cut back to the ground every 3 or more years. Zones 4–10.	Excellent as an impenetrable hedge; beautiful as a specimen in a mixed border or cottage garden. All-America Rose Selections award winner.
Rosa 'Elmshorn' **'Elmshorn' rose**	Hybrid of *R. spinosissima;* a shrub rose. Double red flowers, 1½-in. wide, in clusters in early summer, repeating throughout the season. Slight fragrance. Upright and vigorous, 5 to 6 ft. tall. Glossy green leaves and thorny canes.	Grow in full sun in moist, fertile soil. Zones 3–9.	Charming red rose for a mixed border or cottage garden.
Rosa 'The Fairy' **'The Fairy' rose**	Polyantha hybrid rose. Clusters of tiny, pink, double blossoms from spring until frost. Leaves are small, dark glossy green, and almost evergreen. New canes emerge from the ground, then arch over to form a 5-ft. mound without pruning.	Grow in full sun to light shade in moist, fertile soil. Tolerates poor soil and drought. Highly insect- and disease-resistant; rarely troubled, even by Japanese beetles. Zones 4–9.	Use as an impenetrable hedge or screen, or as a specimen in a mixed border or cottage garden.
Rosa × harisonii **Harison's yellow rose**	Shrub rose. Fragrant, double, yellow, 1- to 2-in. flowers produced prolifically in spring. Bright green foliage. Reaches 5 ft. tall.	Grow in full sun in moist, fertile soil. Zones 3–9.	Pretty yellow rose for a mixed border, cottage garden, or specimen. Escaped cultivation and may be found naturalized across the United States.

(continued)

Plant Name	Description	Culture and Maintenance	Landscape Use and Comments

Easy-Care Shrub Roses—(continued)

Plant Name	Description	Culture and Maintenance	Landscape Use and Comments
Rosa hugonis **Father Hugo rose**	Shrub rose. Single, pale yellow blossoms with golden stamens bloom in late spring. Small, light green leaves. Arching canes reach 6 ft. tall.	Grow in full sun in poor soil. Tolerates drought. Disease-free. Zones 5–9.	Charming yellow rose for a mixed border, cottage garden, or specimen.
Rosa Meidiland hybrids **Meidiland Series roses**	Shrub roses. Members of this group of hybrid roses are cold-hardy, ever-blooming, and disease-tolerant. Bushy types grow to 5 ft. tall and include 'Pink Meidiland', with single bright pink blossoms with white centers all summer, red hips in fall; and 'Bonica'. Groundcover types include 'Alba Meidiland', with small double white blossoms, to 2 ft. tall; 'White Meidiland', with 4-in. double white flowers, horizontal branches reaching 2 ft.; 'Scarlet Meidiland', with double red blossoms, arching canes to 3 ft. tall; 'Pearl Meidiland', with light pink blossoms, forming mounds to 2½ ft. tall; and 'Red Meidiland', with single bright red blossoms with yellow centers followed by showy red hips, reaching 2 ft. tall.	Grow in full sun in fertile, moist soil. Space groundcover types 3 to 4 ft. apart; shrub types 3 ft. apart. Disease-tolerant, but susceptible to insects such as aphids and Japanese beetles. Zones 3–10.	Excellent for mass-planting as an everblooming groundcover. Use shrub types as specimens in a mixed border or cottage garden.

Plant Name	Description	Culture and Maintenance	Landscape Use and Comments
Rosa rugosa **Rugosa rose, Japanese rose**	Shrub rose. The species has 3-in.-wide, fragrant, purple-red, single flowers with prominent yellow stamens. Blooms for entire summer. Gleaming red, edible rose hips about 1½ in. around ripen in fall. Very stout, thorny stems with attractive crinkled, dark green foliage; yellow fall color. Bushy shrub reaches 3 to 5 ft. tall. Highly disease-resistant.	Grow in full sun in average to poor soil. Tolerant of sea-shore conditions. The species is highly black-spot and mildew-resistant; not all hybrids are. The following cultivars are disease-susceptible or have other cultural problems: 'F.J. Grootendorst', 'White Grootendorst', 'Pink Grootendorst', 'Grootendorst Supreme', 'Sir Thomas Lipton', 'Henry Hudson' 'Dr. Eckener', 'Sarah Van Fleet', 'Mrs. Anthony Waterer', 'Rose a Parfume de l'Hay', 'Jens Munk', 'Flamingo', and 'Agnes'. Zones 3–9.	Mass-plant as a hedge or screen, or use as a speci-men in a mixed border or a cottage garden. Mass-plant for erosion control near a beach. Naturalized in many coastal commu-nities in the Northeast. Many cultivars available, some better than others. Double forms do not pro-duce showy hips. Excel-lent disease-resistant cultivars include 'Blanc Double de Coubert', with semi-double to double white flowers but no rose hips; 'Frau Dagmar Hartopp', with prolific pale pink blossoms and good hip production; 'Hansa', with semi-double, pur-plish pink flowers and many hips.
Rosa 'Simplicity' **'Simplicity' rose**	Floribunda shrub rose. Clusters of bright, clear pink, semi-double flowers bloom from early summer until frost. Dark green, bold-textured foliage. Upright plants reach 5 ft. tall without pruning. Grown on its own roots.	Grow in full sun in moist, fertile soil. Prune out dead-wood in winter, but other-wise needs no pruning. Susceptible to black spot in some areas, but generally insect- and disease-tolerant. Zones 5–9.	Makes a beautiful flower-ing hedge or screen. Plant as a specimen in a mixed border or cottage garden.
Rosa 'Sparries-hoop' **'Sparries-hoop' rose**	A hybrid of *R. spino-sissima*. Light pink, very fragrant, 4-in.-wide, sin-gle flowers bloom in early summer and repeat sev-eral times. Upright bushy plants reach 5 ft. tall.	Grow in full sun in moist, fertile soil. Disease-resistant. Zones 3–9.	Charming rose for a mixed border or cottage garden. Mass-plant as a hedge or screen in an informal gar-den setting.

(continued)

Plant Name	Description	Culture and Maintenance	Landscape Use and Comments

Easy-Care Shade and Woodland Wildflowers*

Plant Name	Description	Culture and Maintenance	Landscape Use and Comments
Anemone quinquefolia **Wood anemone**	Deciduous perennial. Slender plant 3 to 5 in. tall. Leaves sparse, with 3 to 5 pointed lobes. Solitary, nodding, white or pinkish flowers in early to mid-spring.	Grow in light shade in moist, humus-rich soil with a pH of 5.0 to 6.0. Spreads by creeping rootstocks. Zones 3–8.	Native to open woodlands of the eastern U.S. A delicate-looking plant for a woodland or shade garden. Similar *Anemonella thalictroides* (rue anemone) has rounded, notched leaves.
Aquilegia canadensis **Wild columbine**	Deciduous perennial. Slender plant 1 to 2 ft. tall. Leaves divided into rounded, notched, blue-green leaflets. Nodding flowers 1 to 1½ in. long with yellow petals, red spurs, and red sepals bloom in mid- to late spring.	Grow in light to partial shade in humus-rich, slightly dry soil with a pH of 6.0 to 7.0. Short-lived in moist or damp soil. Will self-sow. Zones 3–9.	Native to dry, open woodlands of the eastern U.S. Lovely flower for a rocky, wooded slope or a meadow or midwestern prairie garden.
Arisaema triphyllum (*A. atropurpurea*) **Jack-in-the-pulpit**	Deciduous corm. Tuberous plants with 2 tri-part leaves with pointed lobes. Reaches 2 ft. tall. A single flowering structure has a green-and-white-striped or green-and-purple-striped chalicelike petal curling over the elongated yellow spathe containing the flowers; blooms in late spring. Bright red berries appear in fall.	Grow in partial to full shade in moist to wet, humus-rich soil with a pH of 5.0 to 6.0. Zones 3–8.	Native to woods and swamps of eastern North America.
Caltha palustris **Marsh marigold**	Deciduous perennial. Smooth, dark green, rounded, leaves to 6 in. across form clumps about 1 ft. tall. Brilliant golden yellow, buttercup-like flowers bloom in clusters on stems above the foliage in early spring. Foliage dies back in early summer.	Grow in full spring sun or light shade in wet or marshy sites with a pH of 6.0 to 7.0. Tolerates dry to moist soil when dormant in summer. Self-sows readily. Zones 3–8.	Native to wet meadows, bogs, and streamsides of eastern and northern North America. One of the earliest spring wildflowers; blooms before tree leaves fully emerge. Naturalize in wet sites. *C. leptosepala* has white flowers; native to northwestern areas.

*Woodland wildflowers are often wild-collected. Make sure you purchase only nursery-propagated plants.

Plant Name	Description	Culture and Maintenance	Landscape Use and Comments
Cimicifuga racemosa **Cimicifuga, black snakeroot** *C. simplex* **Kamchatka bugbane**	Late-summer- and fall-blooming perennials. Long, graceful, wandlike spikes of white flowers with showy stamens top the plants, remaining effective for about 2 months. Leaves finely divided, forming loose basal mounds 2 to 3 ft. tall. Flower stalks rise to 6 to 8 ft. in *C. racemosa* and 3 to 4 ft. in *C. simplex;* otherwise similar.	Grow in partial to full shade in rich, moist, humus-rich soil with pH of 5.0 to 6.0. Tolerates wet soil. Space 3 to 4 ft. apart. Zones 3–8.	Native to open, moist woods of eastern North America. Use in clumps for dramatic height and late-season interest in an open woodland, or as background planting in a shade garden. *C. simplex* has more arching flower stalks; 'The Pearl' offers dense flower spikes opening in mid- to late fall, making an enticing combination with fall foliage.
Claytonia virginica **Spring beauty**	Deciduous tuberous perennial. Basal, strap-shaped leaves 4 to 6 in. long. Flower stems to 6 in. tall bear loose clusters of delicate-looking flowers in late spring. Flowers are pale pink with deep pink veins.	Grow in full spring sun or light shade in fertile, moist, humus-rich soil with a pH of 5.0 to 6.0. Spreads readily and self-sows. Dies back after flowering. Zones 4–9.	Native to woods and moist meadows of eastern North America. Use as a charming spring groundcover in a woodland garden.
Dicentra cucullaria **Dutchman's-breeches**	Deciduous tuberous perennial. Clumps of finely cut, pale green leaves reach 10 in. tall. Clusters of fragrant, white, pantaloon-shaped flowers on upright stalks bloom in midspring.	Grow in light shade in moist, humus-rich, well-drained soil with a pH of 6.0 to 7.0. Dies back soon after flowering. Keep well mulched. Zones 3–7.	Charming, ephemeral plant for a woodland garden.
Erythronium americanum **Trout lily, dog-tooth violet**	Deciduous bulbous perennial. Elliptical, 6-in.-long basal leaves are glossy blue-green mottled with brown. Solitary, nodding, 1- to 1½-in. yellow flowers with back-swept petals and prominent rusty brown anthers; blooms early to midspring on 3- to 8-in. stalks.	Grow in full spring sun to light shade in fertile, well-drained soil with a pH of 5.0 to 6.0. Foliage dies back in midsummer. Spreads by underground runners and self-sows. Zones 4–7.	Native to northeastern woodlands. Makes a lovely groundcover; blooms best with some sun. *E. grandiflorum* (glacier fawn lily), with bright yellow flowers, several to a 1- to 2-ft. stalk, is native to mountains on the West Coast; Zones 3–6.

(continued)

Plant Name	*Description*	*Culture and Maintenance*	*Landscape Use and Comments*

Easy-Care Shade and Woodland Wildflowers—(continued)

Geranium maculatum **Wild geranium, cranesbill**	Deciduous perennial. Bright green, roughly hairy, toothed, 5-lobed leaves arise from the base of the plant, forming a bushy mound 1½ to 2 ft. tall. Lavender-pink flowers, 1½ in. wide, bloom in clusters from spring through early summer.	Grow in full sun to partial shade in fertile, moist but well-drained soil with a pH of 5.0 to 6.0. Spreads by underground roots and self-sows. Dies down in late summer. Zones 4–9.	Native to woods and thickets of eastern North America. Makes an effective groundcover in a woodland garden.
Hepatica americana **Round-lobed hepatica, liverwort**	Semi-evergreen perennial. Clumps of 3-lobed, leathery, rusty green leaves with silky-haired stems, to 6 in. tall. Charming little flowers, one to a hairy stem, may be pink, blue, lavender, or white, with a cluster of yellow stamens in the center. Blooms in late winter or early spring.	Grow in full spring sun in somewhat dry, humus-rich soil with a pH of 4.0 to 6.0. Readily self-sows. Zones 3–7.	Native to wooded slopes of eastern North America. Locate clumps where they can be appreciated during their early blooming season. *H. acutiloba* (sharp-lobed liverwort) is similar but needs neutral soil.
Mertensia virginica **Virginia bluebells**	Deciduous tuberous perennial. Waxy, gray-green stems and oval, 3- to 4-in. leaves form slender plants to 1½ ft. tall. Blue, bell-shaped flowers open from pink buds in mid- to late spring.	Grow in full spring sun to partial shade in fertile, humus-rich, moist soil with a pH of 6.0 to 7.0. Dies down soon after flowering. Self-sows readily. Zones 3–9.	Native primarily to eastern North America. Withering foliage may be unsightly, so camouflage with ferns or other permanent plants. Dramatic in the spring wildflower or shade garden.
Phlox divaricata **Wild blue phlox, wild sweet william, blue wood phlox**	Deciduous perennial. Delicate-looking plant with slender stems and narrow, 2-in.-long, lance-shaped leaves. Dense clusters of blue, pink, or white flowers with notched petals bloom for a month in midspring. Forms airy clumps 1½ ft. tall.	Grow in light shade in moist, humus-rich soil with a pH of 6.0 to 7.0. Spreads by flopping stems rooting where nodes touch the ground; self-sows readily. Susceptible to mildew. Zones 4–8.	Native to open woods in eastern North America. Entrancing blue flower for the wildflower or shade garden. Variety *laphamii* has large, blue-violet flowers. *P. pilosa* is similar but with pink flowers; it blooms several weeks later and for a longer time.

Plant Name	Description	Culture and Maintenance	Landscape Use and Comments
Phlox stolonifera **Creeping phlox**	Evergreen perennial. Creeping stems have round, dark green leaves and form dense mats. Leafy, upright flower stalks reach 6 to 8 in. tall with clusters of blue, white, or pink flowers blooming for a month in early to midspring.	Grow in light to full shade in fertile, humus-rich, moist soil with a pH of 4.0 to 5.0. Keep moist. Do not mulch heavily. Spreads rapidly by runners. Mildew-resistant. Zones 3–8.	Native to the mid-Atlantic and South. A beautiful groundcover, both in and out of flower, for the woodland and shade garden. 'Blue Ridge' has sky blue flowers; 'Bruce's White' has large white flowers with a prominent yellow eye.
Sanguinaria canadensis **Bloodroot**	Deciduous rhizomatous perennial. A single, lobed, blue-green leaf with a pale underside wraps around the flowering stem. Leaves do not fully mature until after flowering, reaching 8 to 10 in. wide. The pure white flowers with prominent yellow stamens are about 4 in. wide and bloom in midspring. Rhizomes are orange-red, inspiring the common name.	Grow in full spring sun to partial shade in moist, humus-rich, fertile soil with a pH of 6.0 to 7.0. Dies down in midsummer or earlier under dry conditions. Spreads by rhizomes and self-sows. Zones 3–8.	Native to woodlands of eastern North America. Beautiful plant for the woodland or shade garden. 'Multiplex' has stunning double flowers resembling small peonies.

Easy-Care Ferns for Shade and Woodland Gardens

Adiantum pedatum **Maidenhair fern**	Deciduous fern. Lacy, bright blue-green leaflets are so delicate they look almost translucent. Feathery fronds have wiry black stems radiating from a circular main stem that is almost parallel to the ground, creating a fanlike effect. Forms graceful, open plants 1 ft. tall.	Grow in light to partial shade in moist, fertile, humus-rich soil with a pH of 5.0 to 7.0. Sensitive to drying out; keep well mulched. Zones 4–8.	Native to woodlands of the East Coast. An entrancing fern for a woodland or shade garden. Do not crowd—give it plenty of room to show off its silhouette.

(continued)

Plant Name	Description	Culture and Maintenance	Landscape Use and Comments

Easy-Care Ferns for Shade and Woodland Gardens—(continued)

Plant Name	Description	Culture and Maintenance	Landscape Use and Comments
Athyrium filix-femina **Lady fern**	Deciduous fern. Fine-toothed leaflets in long, tapering fronds are yellow-green, maturing to dark green with a reddish cast. New fronds unfurl all season, providing color contrast. Yellow fall color. Bushy clumps reach 2 to 3 ft. tall, taller in marshy ground.	Grow in full to light shade in constantly moist, fertile, humus-rich soil with a pH of 4.0 to 7.0. Tolerates wet and dry soil. Keep well mulched. Clumps spread slowly, but may self-sow. Zones 3–8.	Native to swamps and streamsides of the East Coast. Ideal naturalized beside a water garden or in a moist woodland or shade garden.
Athyrium goeringianum 'Pictum' **Japanese painted fern**	Deciduous fern. Long, tapered fronds have red stems and colorful leaflets generously marbled with silver-gray. Edges and undersides of the leaflets are dark green. Forms 2-ft. clumps of spreading fronds.	Grow in light to full shade in moist, humus-rich soil with a pH of 5.0 to 7.0. Keep constantly moist; mulch well. Clumps spread slowly. Zones 3–8.	The silvery sheen of the fronds stands out in a shade garden or woodland site. Combines well with white-flowered wildflowers.
Dennstaedtia punctilobula **Hay-scented fern**	Deciduous fern. Delicately cut, 1½- to 2½-ft.-long fronds are light yellow-green, turning pale creamy yellow in fall. Foliage gives off the scent of new-mown hay when brushed. Forms a dense groundcover.	Grow in light to deep shade in humus-rich soil. Tolerates wet or dry soil, but best in moist conditions. Spreads very rapidly and may become invasive. Zones 3–8.	Native to the East Coast woodlands. Beautiful as groundcover in a shady spot. Effective for erosion control. Naturalize in a woodland garden. Situate where it can't overrun precious wildflowers.
Dryopteris cristata **Crested wood fern**	Semi-evergreen fern. Finely toothed, dark green, somewhat leathery fronds are 2½ ft. long and ½ ft. wide. Leaflets grow at right angles to the stem, like a ladder. Forms clumps to 3 ft. tall.	Grow in light shade in constantly moist to very wet, humus-rich soil with a pH of 4.0 to 6.0. Zones 3–8.	Native to the eastern U.S. Plant in clumps and as specimens in the woodland or shade garden.

Plant Name	Description	Culture and Maintenance	Landscape Use and Comments
Matteuccia pensylvanica (*M. struthiopteris*) **Ostrich fern**	Deciduous fern. Glossy, dark green fronds form vaselike clumps 5 to 10 ft. tall in boggy native sites, usually 3 ft. in drier soils.	Grow in partial to full shade in fertile, humus-rich soil with a pH of 5.0 to 6.0. Prefers moist to wet soil, but tolerates drier conditions. Zones 3–8.	Native to eastern North American bogs. Use as a bold accent plant in a moist woodland or shade garden; be sure to provide plenty of growing space.
Onoclea sensibilis **Sensitive fern**	Deciduous fern. Flat, light green fronds are shallowly cut, making it distinctive. Dark brown, rattlelike fruiting stalks form in the center of the clumps, often remaining after foliage dies in fall. Clumps 2 ft. tall.	Grow in partial sun to light shade in wet to moist soil with a pH of 4.0 to 7.0. Tolerates full sun in wet soil. Zones 3–8.	Native to eastern North American bogs. Spreads to forms mats, making a good groundcover in woodland or shade gardens.
Osmunda cinnamomea **Cinnamon fern** *O. claytoniana* **Interrupted fern**	Deciduous ferns. Bright green, coarse-textured fronds emerge from woolly fiddleheads in early spring, forming 2- to 3-ft.-tall, vase-shaped clumps. *O. cinnamomea* has hairy reddish-brown stems with feathery fertile stalks growing in the center of the clump. *O. claytoniana* produces its feathery brown fertile structures in the middle of the green fronds, "interrupting" them.	Grow in light to deep shade in fertile, humus-rich soil. Prefers moist to wet soil, but will tolerate drier conditions. Tolerates sun if soil is constantly wet. Zones 3–8.	Native to eastern North America. Elegant tall ferns for the background of a shade garden. Use in clumps planted in a groundcover or among wildflowers in the woodland garden.
Polystichum acrostichoides **Christmas fern**	Evergreen fern. Boldly cut, feather-shaped fronds 1½ to 2 ft. long. New foliage emerges light green, maturing to dark, leathery green. Forms attractive 2-ft.-tall clumps.	Grow in light to full shade in moist soil with a pH of 5.0 to 7.0. Tolerates drier conditions. Foliage may look battered at winter's end; remove before new growth emerges. Zones 3–8.	Native to woodlands in eastern North America. Provides welcome evergreen color in a shade or woodland garden. Situate where the greenery can be appreciated in winter.

(continued)

Plant Name	Description	Culture and Maintenance	Landscape Use and Comments

Easy-Care Meadow Wildflowers

Plant Name	Description	Culture and Maintenance	Landscape Use and Comments
Achillea millefolium **Common yarrow**	Summer-blooming perennial. White flowers in flat, 2-in.-wide clusters on 2- to 2½-ft.-tall, leafy stems; last for about 6 weeks. Finely divided, dark green leaves form mats.	Grow in full sun in average to dry soil. Spreads rapidly, may be invasive; combine with other aggressive meadow plants. Zones 3–9.	Naturalized throughout U.S. Use in naturalistic meadow gardens in any part of the country. Cultivars are preferred in garden settings, but can also be seeded in a meadow. 'Rosea' has soft pink flowers; 'Rubra' has red flowers; 'Cerise Queen' has bright rosy-pink flowers. Hybrids include 'Beacon' with rich red flowers; 'Appleblossom' with peach-pink flowers; and 'Salmon Beauty' with salmon-pink flowers.
Asclepias tuberosa **Butterfly weed**	Midsummer-blooming perennial. Gorgeous, flat-topped, orange flower clusters bloom atop 1- to 2-ft. stems. Flowers attract butterflies. Seedpods split open to release silky airborne seeds. Forms dense clumps of narrow, medium-green foliage.	Grow in full sun in well-drained to dry soil. Tolerates drought. Extremely deep-rooted and difficult to transplant. Will self-sow. Zones 3–8.	Native to eastern U.S. Plant in a meadow garden in the Midwest or in a dry meadow garden in the North or Southeast. Cultivar colors may vary from gold to deep orange-red.
Aster novae-angliae **New England aster**	Late-summer- and fall-blooming perennial. Bushy plants reaching 2 to 4 ft. tall with fine-textured leaves. Clusters of deep violet flowers with yellow centers.	Grow in full sun in average to wet soil. Plant with other aggressive species. Zones 4–8.	Beautiful for late-season color in northwestern, northeastern, and midwestern meadow gardens. Other asters for wildflower meadows are: *A. azureus* (sky blue aster), with brilliant blue flowers on 2- to 3-ft. stems and striking blue-green foliage; *A. ericoides* (heath aster), with white flowers on 2-ft. stems; and *A. laevis* (smooth aster), with pale blue flowers on 2- to 4-ft. stems. All three bloom in late summer.

Plant Name	Description	Culture and Maintenance	Landscape Use and Comments
Baptisia australis **Baptisia, false indigo, wild blue indigo** *B. leucantha* **White false indigo, white wild indigo** *B. leucophaea* **Cream false indigo, black rattlepod**	Early-summer-blooming perennials. *B. australis* has lovely indigo-blue, 2-lipped, tubular, 1-in. flowers on long spikes at the tips of each stem. It bears blue-green, rounded leaflets, like those of pea plants, on upright stems. Attractive seedpods remain until fall. Forms dense 3- to 6-ft.-tall clumps. *B. leucantha* is similar, with eye-catching white flowers on 3- to 4-ft.-tall stalks. *B. leucophaea* has creamy yellow flowers on 1- to 2-ft.-tall stalks.	Grow *B. australis* in full sun in rich, moist, acid soil. Grow *B. leucantha* and *B. leuco-phaea* in full sun in average to dry soil. All three species tolerate partial shade. Zones 3–9.	*B. australis* performs well as a meadow plant in the Northeast and Southeast. The white-flowered species are very showy native prairie plants that may take several years to bloom after seeding, but are well worth the wait.
Chrysan-themum leucan-themum **Oxeye daisy**	Summer-blooming perennial. Deeply toothed basal rosettes form nice clumps bearing 1- to 2-ft.-tall, sparsely leaved flowering stems. Showy white petals surround a large, central, bright yellow disk.	Grow in full sun in average to moist soil. Performs best in poor soil; too much fertility results in floppy plants. Self-sows readily and can become invasive. Zones 4–8.	Naturalized throughout the U.S. Charming in a meadow garden. Especially adaptable to the Northwest and Northeast.
Coreopsis lanceolata **Lance-leaved coreopsis**	Summer-blooming perennial. Bears golden yellow, daisylike blossoms with notched petals. Grows 2 ft. tall. Basal rosettes of lance-shaped leaves; leaves also sparsely cover the flowering stems.	Grow in full sun to light shade in poor, sandy, well-drained soil. Zones 3–8.	Native to the Midwest and Southeast. Pretty in a meadow garden in the eastern or midwestern U.S.
Coreopsis tinctoria **Calliopsis, annual coreopsis**	Summer-blooming annual. Numerous bright yellow, deep red-brown, or banded flowers with dark centers. Feathery foliage on bushy plants to 4 ft. tall.	Grow in full sun in moist, well-drained, fertile soil. Self-sows readily.	Native to moist, sandy spots in western and southern regions of North America. Unlike many annuals, this one is likely to reseed successfully in a meadow garden.

(continued)

Plant Name	Description	Culture and Maintenance	Landscape Use and Comments

Easy-Care Meadow Wildflowers—(continued)

Plant Name	Description	Culture and Maintenance	Landscape Use and Comments
Epilobium angustifolium **Fireweed**	Mid- to late-summer-blooming perennial. Long, tapered spikes of brilliant pink flowers bloom for a long season on 2- to 6-ft. stems. Seedpods release silky, airborne seeds. Willowlike leaves turn a beautiful reddish fall color.	Grow in full sun in light soil that's dry to moist. Grows tallest in fertile soil. Spreads rapidly by creeping rootstocks and self-sows. Zones 3–8.	Native to much of middle and northern North America; rapidly colonizes fire-swept sites. Stunning plant from summer through fall for northeastern and northwestern meadow gardens.
Gaillardia pulchella **Indian blanket**	Summer- and fall-blooming annual. Rusty red flowers with yellow fringed edges and dark centers bloom nonstop from midsummer until frost. Plants reach 1½ to 2 ft.	Grow in full sun in average to dry soil; does best in fertile sites. Thrives in heat and is drought-tolerant.	Native to much of North America. A common component of meadow garden mixes. *G. aristata*, a perennial, forms dense colonies and blooms from late spring to fall in Zones 2–10.
Gentiana andrewsii **Bottle gentian, closed gentian**	Late-summer- and early-fall-blooming perennial. Dark blue-purple, 1½-in., bottle-shaped flowers borne in upper leaf axils. Leaves 6-in., lance-shaped, borne horizontally in pairs on unbranched stems. Plants reach 1–2 ft. tall.	Grow in sun to shade in rich, moist, well-drained soil. Zones 3–9.	Native to northeastern and north central North America. Use in midwestern meadow and prairie gardens, and in moist meadows or alongside streams in northeastern meadow gardens.
Liatris aspera **Rough blazingstar** *L. pycnostachya* **Prairie blazingstar** *L. spicata* **Spike gayfeather, dense blazingstar**	Summer-blooming perennials. *Liatris spicata* has deep rosy-purple flowers in long, showy terminal spikes in midsummer; it reaches 2 to 6 ft. tall. *L. aspera* produces short spikes of magenta-purple flowers in the leaf axils in late summer and reaches 2 to 4 ft. tall. *L. pycnostachya* produces magenta-purple flowers in terminal clusters and blooms in midsummer, reaching 2 to 4 ft. tall.	Grow *L. spicata* and *L. pycnostachya* in full sun in moist, well-drained soil, *L. aspera* in dry to average conditions. Zones 3–9.	*L. spicata* native to eastern North America; it naturalizes in meadow gardens in its native area. *L. aspera* and *L. pycnostachya* are native to the midwestern prairies; naturalize them in a Midwest meadow garden for summer color.

Plant Name	Description	Culture and Maintenance	Landscape Use and Comments
Lilium canadense **Canada lily, meadow lily**	Summer-blooming bulb. Tall, slender stems can reach 6 ft. or more. Graceful flowers with backswept golden-orange or red flowers with brown spots and prominent brown anthers.	Grow in partial sun in rich, moist soil. Seedlings take 5 or 6 years to flower. Zones 4–8.	Native to northeastern North America. Plant in moist meadows in the Northeast. *L. superbum* (Turk's-cap lily), with brilliant orange flowers, is native to the Midwest and suitable for moist midwestern meadow gardens.
Linum perenne subsp. *lewisii* **Blue flax**	Late-spring- and summer-blooming perennial. Fine-textured plant with very slender stems forms 2-ft.-tall clumps. Pale blue, 5-petaled, cup-shaped flowers bloom over an extended period; only open in morning.	Grow in full sun to partial shade in average to dry soil. Will rot in winter in wet soil. Heat-tolerant. Zones 4–9.	Native to northwestern prairies. Colorful plant for meadow gardens, especially in the Northwest and Midwest.
Lupinus densiflorus var. *aureus* **Golden lupine** *L. perennis* **Wild lupine**	Early-summer-blooming perennials. *L. densiflorus* var. *aureus* produces spikes of golden yellow, pealike flowers on silky-haired plants. *L. perennis* produces spires of blue-violet, pink, or white, pea-like flowers above graceful palmately-lobed foliage. Both plants reach 2 ft. tall.	Grow in full sun in average to dry, sandy soil. Best in cool climates. Does not compete well with grass, but can spread and reseed to form great colonies. Zones 4–9.	*L. densiflorus* var. *aureus* is native to the coastal mountains in the West; naturalize in a meadow garden in the Northwest. *L. perennis* is native to eastern and midwestern North America; naturalize in a meadow garden.
Oenothera caespitosa **Tufted evening primrose** *O. speciosa* **Showy evening primrose**	Summer-blooming perennials. Flowers of *O. caespitosa* open rapidly from folded buds into 4-in.-wide white or pink blossoms late in the afternoon; they last all evening. *O. speciosa* has soft pink flowers that open in the morning and last a single day. Plants are upright to sprawling on 8- to 16-in. stems.	Grow in full sun in average soil. Both spread rapidly to form large, dramatic colonies. Zones 4–7.	*O. caespitosa* is native to western North America; it will establish itself in a meadow garden in the Northwest. *O. speciosa* is native to the southern United States and Mexico, and makes an eye-catching addition to prairie or meadow gardens in those areas and in the Plains.

(continued)

Plant Name	Description	Culture and Maintenance	Landscape Use and Comments
Easy-Care Meadow Wildflowers—(continued)			
Rudbeckia hirta **Black-eyed susan**	Summer-blooming annual or biennial. Rough stems with hairy leaves reach 2 to 3 ft. tall and bear orange-yellow flowers with dark centers.	Grow in full sun in almost any soil. May be disfigured by mildew in gardens, but the disease is not so noticeable in a naturalistic site. Self-sows where adapted.	Native to the Northeast. Especially useful in meadow gardens in the Northeast, Southeast, and Midwest, but adaptable elsewhere. *R. fulgida* (orange coneflower) is similar, but is a short-lived perennial blooming in late summer, reaching 1½ to 2 ft.
Solidago erecta **Upright goldenrod** *S. juncea* **Early goldenrod** *S. rigida* **Stiff goldenrod** *S. speciosa* **Showy goldenrod**	Late-summer- and fall-blooming perennials. Graceful arching plumes of brilliant yellow flowers bloom for an extended period. *S. erecta* blooms late summer and fall, reaching 4 ft. tall; *S. juncea* blooms mid- to late summer, reaching 2 to 4 ft. tall; *S. rigida* blooms late summer and fall, reaching 1 to 5 ft. tall; *S. speciosa* blooms late summer and fall, reaching 2 to 7 ft. tall.	Grow in full sun in average to moist soil. Spreads aggressively by stolons to form great clumps. Zones 4–8.	There are *Solidago* species native to all parts of the country. Use in meadow and prairie gardens anywhere. They combine well with asters. Erroneously blamed for causing hayfever—ragweed is really to blame.

Easy-Care Native Grasses for Meadow Gardens

Andropogon gerardii **Big bluestem**	Deciduous warm-season perennial grass. Reaches 3 to 8 ft. tall with attractive reddish turkey's-foot-shaped flowers and seedpods. Foliage changes from deep green to coppery red in fall.	Grow in full sun in average, wet or dry soil. May not flower or set seed in dry soil. Hardy to Zone 4.	Native to the midwestern tall-grass prairie; the most dominant and magnificent species. Useful for soil stabilization in sandy, hilly terrain. Use in a midwestern or northwestern meadow garden.
Bouteloua curtipendula **Sideoats grama grass** *B. gracilis* **Blue grama grass**	Deciduous warm-season perennial grasses. *B. curtipendula* grows to 12 to 36 in. tall. Ornamental purplish, oatlike seedheads are lined up along one side of the stem tops. Turns bleached buff in fall. *B. gracilis* grows to 20 in. tall and forms dense clumps.	Grow in full sun in dry soil. Extremely drought-tolerant. Moderately aggressive. Hardy to Zone 4.	Native east of the Rockies. Attractive and important additions to meadow gardens in the Northeast and Midwest.

Plant Name	Description	Culture and Maintenance	Landscape Use and Comments
Festuca ovina **Sheep fescue**	Cool-season, semi-evergreen perennial grass. Forms tussocks of spiky, blue-green foliage, reaching 1½ ft. tall. Flowers in late spring or early summer are borne on stalks 2½ ft. tall and are pale green or violet changing to tan.	Grow in full sun in sandy soil. Drought-tolerant. Does poorly in wet sites. Hardy to Zone 4.	Native to rocky, hilly sites throughout North America. Use as a meadow grass in the Northwest or Northeast. *F. caesia* (*F. ovina* var. *glauca*), blue fescue, native to the Northwest, has striking blue-gray foliage; it makes an effective color scheme in a naturalized setting. *F. elatior* (tall fescue) grows to 4 ft.; it's an escaped European forage bunchgrass useful in meadow gardens.
Koeleria cristata **June grass** *K. pyramidata* **June grass**	Cool-season perennial grasses. Form clumps 18 in. tall. Leafless flowering stems rise above the clumps in early to midsummer, bearing dense, cylindrical, silver-green flowers and seedheads resembling timothy.	Grow in full sun to partial shade in average to dry soil. Hardy to Zone 4.	Native to open woods and dry prairies of the Midwest. Attractive grass for northeastern and midwestern meadow gardens.

Easy-Care Ornamental Grasses

Plant Name	Description	Culture and Maintenance	Landscape Use and Comments
Calamogrostis × acutiflora 'Stricta' **Feather reed grass**	Cool-season perennial grass. Dull green, 2-ft.-long leaves form arching clumps bearing stiff, 5-ft.-tall flowering stems. Showy flowers white in early summer, turning pinkish, followed by tan seedheads. Foliage turns bright gold in fall and lasts through the winter.	Grow in full sun to partial shade in average soil. Tolerates heavy soil. Cut to the ground in late winter. Zones 5–9.	Very upright form; use for vertical accent in a garden. Attractive year-round; fills in early in spring. Combines well with pink flowers.

(continued)

Plant Name	Description	Culture and Maintenance	Landscape Use and Comments

Easy-Care Ornamental Grasses—(continued)

Plant Name	Description	Culture and Maintenance	Landscape Use and Comments
Carex morrowii 'Aurea-Variegata' **Variegated Japanese sedge** *C. morrowii* var. *expallida* **Silver-variegated Japanese sedge**	Evergreen perennial sedge. 'Aurea-Variegata' has arching blades with a central creamy stripe; var. *expallida* has white leaf margins. Both form low mounds 1 to 1½ ft. tall. Flowers are inconspicuous, nestled among the foliage.	Grow in light to full shade in moist soil; full sun in cool locations. Cut to the ground in late winter. Zones 6–9.	Use as specimens, or mass-plant in the foreground or midground of a border or New American Garden. Effective year-round. *C. stricta* 'Bowles' Golden' has bright yellow-green foliage and thrives in shade.
Cortaderia selloana **Pampas grass**	Warm-season perennial grass. Blue-gray, medium-textured foliage forms wide, bushy clumps 12 to 15 ft. tall. Female plants topped with 20- to 36-in. cotton-candylike white or pale pink panicles in late summer and fall.	Grow in full sun in fertile soil; tolerates drought. Does poorly where soil is wet in winter. Cut to the ground in late winter. Zones 8–10.	Huge, dramatic accent plant. Choose location carefully for best effect. Stunning silhouetted against the sky, where it is backlit. Showy through winter. 'Pumila' grows 3 to 6 ft. and is hardy to Zone 7.
Festuca amethystina var. *superba* **Blue sheep's fescue** *F. caesia* (*F. ovina* var. *glauca*) **Blue fescue**	Cool-season, evergreen perennial grasses. *F. amethystina* var. *superba* grows to 8 in. with silver-blue foliage. *F. caesia* forms 1-ft. clumps of steel-blue foliage. Lacy flowers bloom in midspring on tall stems much higher than the clumps.	Grow in full sun in average to fertile soil. Remove flowers if they become tattered in midsummer. Zones 4–8.	Both begin growth in late winter, so they're pretty in the spring garden mixed with bulbs. Use either as a groundcover or foreground planting. Attractive year-round. *F. cinerea* 'Solling' (Solling fescue) does not flower and tolerates heat better.
Hakonechloa macra var. *aureola* **Variegated golden hakonechloa**	Cool-season perennial grass. Variegated, cascading foliage forms creamy yellow, 1½-ft.-tall mounds. Clumps turn golden with frost. Flowers not showy.	Grow in full, partial, or light shade in fertile, moist soil. Does not do well in hot-summer areas. Cut to the ground in late winter. Zones 4–8.	Use in shade gardens or along a woodland path where its pale color shines in the low light.

Plant Name	Description	Culture and Maintenance	Landscape Use and Comments
Imperata cylindrica var. *rubra* 'Red Baron' **Japanese blood grass**	Warm-season perennial grass. Flat leaf blades are blood-red to green tinged with red. Grows 1 to 1½ ft. tall. Turns orange-brown with hard frost.	Grow in full sun to half shade in moist, fertile soil. Spreads by runners. Cut to the ground in late winter. Zones 5–9.	Plant in groups or masses in the foreground of a border. Stunning when backlit, which causes the red foliage to glow.
Miscanthus floridulus **Giant miscanthus**	Warm-season perennial grass. Pale green leaves with white midveins form coarse-textured, upright clumps of cascading foliage to 10 ft. tall. Plumes of white flowers bloom in fall. Foliage turns apricot to orange in fall before becoming cream-colored for the winter.	Grow in full sun to partial shade in fertile, moist soil. Cut to the ground in late winter. Zones 6–9.	Makes an effective screen or specimen plant. May not flower in coldest climates. Effective from summer through winter.
Miscanthus sinensis **Eulalia grass** *M. sinensis* 'Gracillimus' **Maiden grass** *M. sinensis* var. *purpurascens* **Flame grass** *M. sinensis* 'Strictus' **Porcupine grass** *M. sinensis* 'Variegatus' **Variegated Japanese silver grass** *M. sinensis* 'Zebrinus' **Zebra grass**	Warm-season perennial grasses. *M. sinensis* is vase-shaped, reaching 4 to 8 ft. tall with arching, pointed leaves. The green leaves have a white midrib. Showy, white, feathery flowers in fall. 'Gracillimus' is fine-textured and graceful, to 5 ft.; turns buff in fall. Var. *purpurascens* grows 3 ft. tall with pink fall flowers to 4½ ft.; turns brilliant orange-red in fall, with color lasting all winter. 'Strictus' has yellow bands across the foliage and a dense upright habit. 'Variegatus' has striking white-, cream-, and green-striped foliage 4 to 6 ft. tall. 'Zebrinus' has blades banded horizontally with gold or white; reaches 7 ft.	Grow in full sun to partial shade in fertile, moist soil. Cut to the ground in late winter. Zones 4–9.	Make lovely specimens and are effective mass-planted in a New American Garden or as the background of a perennial garden. Effective throughout the year. 'Strictus' is more upright and stiff than the floppy 'Zebrinus'.

(continued)

Plant Name	Description	Culture and Maintenance	Landscape Use and Comments

Easy-Care Ornamental Grasses—(continued)

Plant Name	Description	Culture and Maintenance	Landscape Use and Comments
Pennisetum alopecuroides **Fountain grass** / *P. alopecuroides* 'Hameln' **Dwarf fountain grass** / *P. alopecuroides* 'Viridescens' **Black-seeded fountain grass**	Warm-season perennial grasses. Cascading foliage forms rounded clumps to 3 ft. tall. Long, spiky, buff flower heads appear among the foliage in late summer. In fall, foliage changes to apricot, rose, or gold before bleaching to almond. 'Hameln' is identical, but reaches only 2 ft. tall. 'Viridescens', to 3 ft. tall, has long, cylindrical flower heads tinted black.	Grow in full sun in moist, fertile soil; partial shade in hot climates. Cut back in late winter. Zones 6–9 and warm parts of 5; 'Viridescens': Zones 7–9.	Use to create a meadow-like effect in a New American Garden, or as a specimen in a border or display. Very effective in the winter, because the plants retain their volume.
Pennisetum setaceum **Annual fountain grass** / *P. setaceum* var. *atropurpureum* **Annual purple fountain grass** / *P. setaceum* 'Rubrum' **Purple-leaved fountain grass**	Perennial grasses grown as annuals. Narrow green leaves with rolled margins form clumps 3 ft. tall. Long, nodding, bristly, rose-colored flower spikes. Foliage turns beige in fall. Variety *atropurpureum* has wine-red foliage and purple flowers; 'Rubrum' has purple-red foliage and rose-colored flowers.	Grow in full sun in moist, fertile soil. May self-sow, and can become a pest, especially in the desert Southwest. Remove plants in fall when they begin to topple. Hardy in Zones 8–9.	Eye-catching mass-planted in a border. Contrast purple-foliaged cultivars with bright green foliage or masses of pink, blue, or yellow flowers. Not effective in winter.
Schizachyrium scoparium (*Andropogon scoparius*) **Little bluestem**	Deciduous warm-season perennial grass. Fine-textured plant reaches 2 to 3 ft. tall and forms clumps 6 to 8 in. wide. Bluish-green foliage turns various shades of rust-red in fall. Fluffy seedhead is pinkish with red tinges.	Grow in full sun in average to dry soil. Moderately aggressive. Hardy to Zone 4.	Native to Midwest. Use in meadow gardens across the country. *A. virginicus* (broomsedge) is similar; it's native to open, sandy sites throughout North America, and is useful for meadow gardens in the Northeast and Southeast.
Sinarundinaria nitida **Chinese clump bamboo**	Evergreen to semi-evergreen perennial grass. Blue-green foliage may reach 20 ft. tall. Forms clumps and does not spread by aggressive runners as do many bamboos.	Grow in partial shade. Protect from wind and hot afternoon sun. Hardy in Zones 4–8.	Plant several clumps together for a screen or accent. Mass-plant to create a bamboo woodland.

APPENDIX

A

TOOLS AND TECHNIQUES FOR WEEKEND GARDENERS

Weekend gardeners can save hours of labor and frustration by knowing which tools perform best for which chores, and by using them properly. Don't take your garden tools for granted—well-made, quality tools outlast cheaper ones and make garden work a pleasure. By investing only in the hand tools and the few power tools that are necessary for your yard, you will ultimately save money, too.

Power tools exist for just about every gardening chore imaginable, and my neighbors seem to have them all. The din from these machines lasts most of Saturday, but Sunday and scattered summer weekdays aren't immune. It doesn't even seem to matter if the power version does a better job than a hand tool; if it can be powered, my neighbors will buy it. They don't hesitate to spend hundreds of dollars on fancy power equipment, burn fossil fuels to run it, and pollute the environment with noise and fumes in the process.

This power frenzy may be most homeowners' idea of weekend gardening, but, as you know by now, true weekend gardeners don't need to spend all their spare hours pushing the latest power gizmo. Having the right tools and knowing the best techniques simplifies garden work and assures success. This appendix is a guide to the best hand *and* power tools and the most effective techniques I've found for getting gardening chores done.

Digging and Planting Tools

Digging, preparing beds, planting, and lifting are strenuous tasks, but using the right tool for these activities cuts down on the amount of physical effort required. Some gardeners dig, plant, and lift with the same tool, but they shouldn't. Others know to use a different tool for each of these activities, choosing the implement designed to save the most time and energy.

Spades. The spade is the traditional English digging tool. It has a flat, rectangular blade attached at a slight angle to a fairly short handle. A 27-inch-long handle with a D-grip allows you to put your weight behind the tool while you push the blade straight into the ground with your foot. The handle is short because you aren't meant to lift the blade very high above the ground. Gardeners over 6 feet tall will find a somewhat longer handle—30 or 32 inches—easier on the back, since it won't require them to stoop as much.

There are many types of spades: Look for one with a handle length, tread, blade size, and weight comfortable for your height and strength and suited to the tasks you have to do. You may find you need more than one type.

Spades are subject to a lot of levering strain, so they need to be very well built. Choose one with heavy gauge steel, solid-socket or solid-strap construction, and a heavy tread. Typically, English-made spades are considered superior to American-made, which are usually of hollow-back construction and therefore much heavier and less strong.

Shovels. Designed primarily for scooping and lifting, a shovel has a rounded blade with a pointed end. It is attached at an angle to a long handle, which provides good leverage for moving piles of gravel, sand, or soil. Since Americans prefer to dig with shovels, American manufacturers have had to defend themselves by manufacturing sturdy shovels. These are often better made than English tools. Quality shovels offer a blade and shank created from a single piece of high-carbon, heat-tempered steel, which is stronger than an open socket. Closed-back shovels, in which a metal triangle is welded over the crimp in the back of the blade, are the strongest and most expensive. Choose a shovel with a weight and capacity that match your strength; nothing will tire you more than lifting an already heavy shovel bearing the addition of a hefty load.

My friend Virginia Blakelock, president of the Hobby Greenhouse Society, is both an Army brat and an Army wife. She declares that the old Army trenching shovel is her favorite all-purpose tool. Available from Army surplus stores, this folding shovel is sharp and convenient. Virginia has used it in gardens all around the world for planting shrubs and perennials, weeding, and even edging!

Crowbars. Don't use your shovel for prying up rocks and heavy root balls; save this work for a crowbar. Prying action puts excessive strain on a shovel. It may take some getting used to, but dig with a spade (look for a slightly pointed variety if you like), scoop with a shovel, and pry with a crowbar, and your tools will live long lives.

Mattocks. For severe problem soil—rocky, hard-baked clay, for example—use a long-handled mattock as a digging tool. One end of the mattock resembles a thick axe head and will cut large roots; the other is more hoelike and will chop into and pull up the soil. You swing the mattock over your head, so centrifugal force helps drive it into the soil. It takes a bit of practice to perfect a strong, accurate swing. Use this tool very carefully!

Forks. For lifting or for loosening or turning over soil, a fork is the tool of choice. Although it won't dig much of a planting hole, a fork does a first-rate job of digging up potatoes and bulbs, dividing perennials, and breaking up clods. Forks come in a confusing array of types; the number of tines, along with their shape (square or flat in cross-section) and length vary, as does the length of the handles. Each has its intended purpose.

Forks of any type need to be extremely sturdy from handle to tip, even sturdier than a spade, because the narrow tines are subjected to so much pressure when jammed into the soil or compost heap and wriggled around. Choose one of fine-quality tempered steel and solid-socket construction. The tines should spring back readily when a stone gets forced between them; one way to test for this is to squeeze the tines together and observe whether they pop back or remain squeezed.

English garden fork. This is a square-tined fork used for loosening and aerating the soil. The sturdy, sharp-pointed tines penetrate the soil more easily than a flat-tined fork. Use the garden fork for loosening double-dug soil in spring without turning it over. Push the fork into the soil with your foot, then rock it back and forth to break up the soil. Use this fork for dividing perennials; it will do less root damage than a broader-tined model. Two forks can be plunged from opposite sides into a clump of tough-rooted perennials like daylilies to pry the mass apart.

Spading fork. Use this model for turning over and lifting new soil, as opposed to simply stabbing and loosening it. Its broader tines have more surface area for lifting clods of soil. My friend Donna Bickley, a mental health professional who gardens to maintain her own mental health, swears by a spading fork for working the heavy, stony soil in her garden.

Compost fork. For hoisting wood chips, manure, or compost from pile to wheelbarrow, a compost or manure fork is ideal. It's much lighter than a shovel, so you don't waste energy hoisting the tool. This fork is ideal for turning compost; use it to move coarse material that won't fall between the tines. It has numerous curved tines that are longer, thinner, and more widely spaced than those of a spading fork. The tines are angled much like a shovel blade for better leverage and to cut down on the need to stoop. The handle should be longer than a garden fork's to provide better leverage and lifting ability.

Pitchfork. With only three or four widely spaced tines, a pitchfork weighs even less than a compost fork. If you toss around a lot of lightweight, coarse-textured materials such as straw, a pitchfork will save your strength.

Garden rakes. A garden rake provides the finishing touch when getting a bed ready for planting. These are comblike steel rakes with short, straight teeth used for making a new bed or preparing an old one for annual flowers or crops. After loosening or turning over the soil with a fork or other implement, use a rake to level it off and remove any debris. Drag the teeth through the prepared soil to snag loose weeds, roots, stones, and clods. This action is also useful for working fertilizer or lime into the soil. There are two basic types of garden rakes.

Level-headed rake. This model has a handle that meets up directly with the flat bar across the top of the tines. You can use it to pull soil and loose debris toward you, then flip it over to the flat side, and level the soil with the push stroke.

Bow rake. The handle of a bow rake

does not meet up directly with the bar holding the teeth; instead, a bow attaches them. This gives the rake more spring, which many people prefer, but makes it less useful for leveling.

Trowels. Commonly used for planting seedlings and small plants, trowels are hand tools that require you to kneel or sit while working. Trowels are so indispensable that you'll probably want several with different blade shapes. Those with very narrow blades, often called transplanting trowels, are useful for planting small seedlings or tiny bulbs; those with wider blades are multipurpose. Choose a trowel that feels well balanced and comfortable in your hand. The proper way to hold and use a trowel is the way you would use an ice pick: With your knuckles wrapped around the back of the handle, jab it into the soil to create a planting hole.

Bulb planters. These cylindrical digging tools can be handy for planting individual daffodil and tulip bulbs. (Smaller bulbs, such as crocuses, require only a trowel.) The blade punches out a cylinder of earth as you jam and twist it into the ground. You pop in the bulb and knock the soil back into the hole. But this process sometimes needs improvisation: Large, double-size daffodil bulbs are usually too wide to fit into the standard hole punched out by a bulb planter—you need to cut two overlapping holes.

Long-handled bulb planter. This professional planter is meant to be pushed into the soil with a foot as you grip the long T-handle and twist with both hands, saving your back and your palms. Several years ago, when I ordered a thousand spring-flowering bulbs for fall planting, Mark and I set up a production line of sorts: On my hands and knees, I crawled around indicating each planting spot, he drove the planter into the soil, I dropped in the bulb, and then he tapped the soil back in place while I got the next bulb ready. We sped through planting those thousand bulbs in several hours.

Bulb auger. Jane Aussicker, who runs a business out of her home in northern New Jersey and enjoys gardening as an escape from the house, uses a bulb auger to plant bulbs in her rocky soil. The auger is a soil-drilling bit that fits any standard electric drill. It can be found in many gardening catalogs.

Power Tillers

Power tillers are useful for preparing large beds, working in soil amendments, and tilling in weeds and cover crops. However, most weekend gardeners won't need to power-till their gardens. The essence of low-maintenance gardening comes from permanent plantings of shrubs, flowering perennials, groundcovers, and even perennial vegetables. So after the initial bed preparation, soil doesn't need to be turned over in most parts of the garden. Small weekend vegetable gardens can be prepared efficiently in spring with people-powered tools; once the soil of a vegetable garden is double-dug, it only needs to be loosened with a fork each spring. And because weekend gardeners will be planting vegetables close enough together to shade out weeds—and mulching to further reduce weeds and conserve water—there won't be much call for cultivating to control weeds.

Advertisements for mini-tillers—those small tiller/cultivators that run on 2-cycle engines—abound these days. The minis, which range from .9 to 2 horsepower, can supposedly break up new ground, turn over existing beds, and cultivate to control weeds between rows of vegetables, in flower beds, and even under trees and shrubs. They can churn organic matter and cover crops into the soil. Some brands even come with attachments that will edge a lawn, shear shrubs, and dethatch and aerate the lawn. They seem to be the ideal item for a weekend gardener, but think carefully before you cough up the $200 to $400 these tillers cost.

Gardeners who have tried these machines report that a mini-tiller can break up rough, uncultivated ground or lawn, but the tines only penetrate about 3 inches on the first pass. For maximum depth—about 8 inches—you'll need to go over it again. You'll have to exert a lot of control over the machine —all 25 pounds of it—gripping it while it lurches, bucks, leaps, and vibrates as it chews into the soil. Gardeners have reported that their hands, wrists, and arms quickly become exhausted holding onto these machines, even while performing simple tasks. Also, a mini-tiller runs on a noisy 2-cycle engine. Eye protection is a must, since the spinning tines can fling up stones and sticks.

Large rotary tillers are more powerful—and more expensive. Though outside the scope of most weekend gardens, they can be lifesavers on a large property, especially for preparing expanses of ground for new gardens or plantings. The smart weekend gardener will plan to do this only once per project, so it might pay to rent one of these big guys to get the job done right.

Weeding and Cultivating Tools

Gardeners cultivate soil for a number of reasons. Breaking up clods or a crusted soil surface to prepare a seedbed is one reason, and cultivating the soil to mix in amendments such as lime, peat, or other organic matter, is another. Cultivation disturbs weed seeds and seedlings in the soil and is also used for weed control. Tiny weed seedlings may die from being buried too deeply, uprooted, or severed from their roots. While this usually suffices to annihilate young annual weeds, bear in mind that perennial weeds have more staying power. Chop established perennial weeds into pieces while cultivating and they're likely to resprout into a thousand vigorous new plants—one for each piece.

Hoes. Hoes come in hundreds of variations, some ingeniously designed to fit the recommended spacing between rows of particular crops. The most common and versatile cultivating and weeding tool is the garden hoe, which has a squarish blade and a long handle. Use the sharp edge of a hoe to loosen up crusted soil while cutting through small weeds. If you hoe regularly to get rid of sprouting weeds, they'll never become established enough to be truly troublesome. You're most likely to cultivate soil in a newly planted vegetable garden, until the densely planted vegetables grow close enough to deter weeds. Smart weekend gardeners, however, won't need to be doing much hoeing, because mulched gardens naturally deter weeds.

Claws, forks, or cultivators. There are several specialized pronged or tined tools to help you get at individual weeds or small weedy patches. When scratched across the soil, they snag or dig out weeds that are more mature than a hoe can effectively deal with. Many come in short- or long-handled versions for use while kneeling or standing.

Magic Weeder. My friend Barbara Emerson, a weed specialist, sings the praises of this special hand fork, which features three long, prominently curved tines made out of carbon spring steel. The tines coil where they meet the handle, so the entire apparatus is extremely flexible. The prongs can even be squeezed together to get into small places. "The beauty of the Magic Weeder is that the curved tines go right underneath the weed, and when you pull up on it, you get the roots and all. If you don't get the roots, you'll still have the weed," says Barbara. And she ought to know; she's been using the Magic Weeder for nigh on 60 years. The Magic Weeder is made in Wiscasett, Maine, and isn't easy to come by–Gardener's Supply catalog carries it. I've seen a take-off of this tool by another manufacturer; it's called The Claw, so look around. (See "Resources for Weekend Gardeners" on page 335 for catalog details.)

Asparagus knife. This popular device goes by several aliases, including asparagus fork, dandelion weeder, and dandelion fork. It has a long probe with a forked tip; use it to get out the roots of tap-rooted weeds such as dandelions or thistles. Be sure to dig out the entire length of the root–any piece left behind in the soil will sprout again.

Pruning Tools

Which pruning tool you choose depends on the size of the branch to be cut and the type of pruning cut you're making. No one tool can do it all; you'll probably need one of each of the following tools.

Hedge shears. Hedge shears are two-handled, long-bladed tools designed to trim a hedge into flat, wall-like surfaces, and for that purpose, they're excellent. Pruning a formal hedge requires an enormous amount of work several times a year. Repeatedly clipping away with hedge shears tires the hands, arms, and shoulders. My advice is to let that formal hedge go natural, but, short of that, choose a pair of electric hedge trimmers to

ease your work. Don't use hedge shears for routine shrub pruning. The only thing I use mine for is to cut back dried stalks of perennials and ornamental grasses in late winter.

Hand-held pruning shears. Designed to cut stems less than ½-inch thick, these are the tool of choice for pruning most shrubs. Don't use them for thicker stems or you'll ruin the alignment of the blades. I prefer scissors-type pruners with sharpened blades that overlap because they cut more closely and cleanly than anvil-style pruners, which have a sharpened blade that crushes the stem against a metal anvil. Shears with steel blades stay sharp longer and are worth the extra cost.

Lopping shears. Sturdier than hand-held clippers, these feature long handles that give you extra leverage for cutting branches between 1 and 1½ inches in diameter. Because of their long handles that serve to extend your reach, lopping shears make easy work of cutting out branches at the bases of deciduous shrubs and branches just above head height. There are both scissors- and anvil-style models.

Pruning saws. For cutting through stems and branches larger than 1½ inches, use a pruning saw. Unlike a carpentry saw, a pruning saw cuts with both the push and pull strokes. Most have small, curved blades; in some models, the blade folds back into the wooden handle so it can be safely tucked into a pocket. Narrow-bladed pruning saws are best for cutting branches in confined spaces, such as among a thicket of stems or in a narrow branch crotch. A lightweight bow saw cuts quickly where you have enough room to maneuver.

Pole saws. When pruning high limbs, save yourself from climbing precariously on a ladder or scaling the tree by using a pole saw. You'll be able to remove branches 15 feet beyond your normal reach. The curved blade at the end will saw through branches about 2 inches in diameter. Some models feature a saw, a hook, and a clipper. The clipper is operated by pulling a rope to clip off small branches. The hook comes in handy for pulling down entangled branches.

Chain saws. A chain saw is invaluable for cutting down small and larger trees and turning them into firewood. Although I don't usually choose power equipment over a hand tool, a chain saw cuts larger wood than you can easily take care of with a hand saw and does a big job in minutes rather than hours. Many sizes and models, both gasoline-powered and electric, are available. Our experience is that, as with most types of power equipment, the professional-grade power tools and those made by companies that also manufacture professional models are much better designed than most of the homeowner-grade models.

Tools for Raking and Blowing Leaves

Dealing with fallen leaves is one of the biggest chores many gardeners face. Mark and I have figured out some efficient ways to handle leaves and have reduced the time we spend carting leaves around by more than half.

Leaf rakes. Also called fan or lawn rakes, these are usually lightweight, with a 48-inch-long wooden handle and long tines made of plastic, bamboo, or metal. Lawn rakes vary in size from 10 to 30 inches wide at the tips of the tines. A 24- or 30-inch-wide rake makes fast work of pulling leaves off the lawn and garden beds and into piles. You can use the rake to scoop up the pile and deposit it into a wheelbarrow or cart. Narrower rakes, 10 to 12 inches wide, fit into tight spaces, so it's easy to clean out leaves that are clogging shrubbery or tucked into nooks and crannies. I prefer bamboo rakes even though they're less durable. I've found plastic and metal types tear at the lawn, pulling up tufts of grass by the roots.

You can make short work of leaf raking if you approach the task scientifically. Try to repeat your movements and steps as little as possible and move each rakeful of leaves as few times as possible. The best way to deleaf a lawn is to first rake all the leaves into parallel rows as you walk backward across the lawn. Create the rows with a single sweep of the rake with each step you take. After you've transformed the leaf-strewn lawn into neat rows of leaves, rake each row into small piles. Use the rake to scoop up and deposit each pile into a bag or wheelbarrow or onto a tarp.

Leaf blowers. Leaf blowers are meant to clean off the lawn, walkways, driveway, and any other place you can think of. With one of these things, you can supposedly blow fallen leaves into piles fast. Then, by switching the apparatus around, you can suck up the piled leaves and shred them into coin-size pieces that gather in a zippered collection bag. Leaf blowers come in three basic versions—hand-held, backpack, or wheeled—and are gas- or electric-powered.

Electric blowers are less powerful than gasoline models, but they're somewhat quieter. They also weigh less—6 to 8 pounds, compared to 10 or 11 for a gas model. However, they just aren't powerful enough to do a good job blowing leaves once they begin to pile up, and the cord can get tangled and stuck if you must round garden beds, shrubs, or other plantings. The gasoline-powered versions do a better job, but are extremely noisy. Neither deals well with wet leaves. Both types suck up and shred leaves with pathetic slowness, although I admit that the result is a nicely chopped leaf mulch.

Hand-held leaf blower/vac/shredder. The hand-held leaf blower/vac/shredder is the most common type used by homeowners. They come in either electric- or gasoline-powered versions; gasoline versions run on 2-cycle engines fueled by a gas-oil mix. Shredded leaves get sucked up into a collection bag that hangs from the shoulder. Hand-held types cost from about $80 to well over $100.

Backpack blowers. Landscape maintenance crews often use backpack blowers, which operate with 2-cycle or 4-cycle engines. These are more powerful than the hand-held versions. Backpack blowers range from $250 to over $300.

Wheeled blowers. Both homeowners and landscapers use wheeled models, which offer high power and the convenience of not needing to be hefted around. They cost about $500. Dick Lighty, a native plant expert who gardens on eight acres in Delaware, uses a wheeled version to collect and shred the leaves on his several acres of woodland garden. This machine does an effective and speedy shredding job. He returns most of the shredded leaves to the garden as mulch but composts a portion, too. I suspect that the average home gardener doesn't have enough leaves to justify purchasing—and finding the space to store—such a powerful and expensive machine.

Each time I use a leaf blower, I come to the same conclusion: These machines can't do anything that simpler tools—tools you probably already own—don't do. I've tested four hand-held types and observed backpack and wheeled versions in action, and I find

them noisy beyond tolerance, and too awkward and too heavy to handle for any length of time without straining my back. They also vibrate painfully, and they work so slowly at shredding leaves, they try my patience. One use I've seen these gadgets put to is to blow litter—grass trimmings, leaves, dirt—off walks and driveways. It works, but I continue to marvel at the practice. I want to shout, "Get a broom!" whenever I see anyone doing this. Invariably, it takes ten minutes to get a tiny pile to the edge of the driveway—a few swift pushes of a broom would send the dirt flying much faster!

Tools for Leaf Eating and Brush Chomping

Once you've raked—or blown, if you must—the leaves into piles, you have to get rid of them. Burning or bagging them for collection are both time-honored practices that don't earn much honor these days. Burning pollutes the air, and landfills brim with more important garbage than leaves and yard debris. In response to the garbage crisis, some municipalities no longer collect grass clippings, brush, and bagged leaves. So what's a gardener to do?

Organic gardeners have always understood the value of composting leaves or using them as mulch—so should weekend gardeners. Leaves transform into compost faster and make a better mulch if they are shredded first. And shredding leaves reduces their volume to a fraction of the original, making bagging, transporting, and storing them simpler.

Power mowers. The ability to shred is part of the false allure of the blower/vac/shredder machines. There are better ways to shred leaves, however. A power mower is one of the best tools for the job. Mark and I don't usually rake leaves off the lawn. Instead, Mark uses our power mower, a model with very good suction, and simply mows them up. The clippings and chewed-up leaves collect in the grass catcher. Mark empties the bag into a pile on the driveway and runs over it again by tilting the mower back and lowering it onto the pile. This double-cuts the leaves, turning them into coin-size pieces, perfect for quick-composting or mulching. This method of getting rid of the tons of leaves that descend on our property each year makes our work easier and produces a gold mine of mulch.

The Leaf Eater. If you don't have a power mower capable of shredding leaves, this is the only other machine I can recommend for the job. Manufactured by Vornado Power Products, the Leaf Eater is a tool designed only for shredding leaves. It features a wide-mouthed leaf hopper that can sit atop a garbage can or stand on its own three legs. It's easy to fill and holds a quantity of leaves, "eating" them as fast as you can load them. A spinning nylon filament whacks at the leaves, which when chopped sift through a shutter at the bottom, providing a uniform end product. You can change the shutter setting to regulate the size of the shredded leaves. Both gasoline and electric-powered versions are available; the electric one is quieter. I'd recommend a gasoline-powered version only if you must shred leaves farther than a 100-foot extension cord can reach. The Leaf Eater may be available at your local garden center or home improvement center; mine has them. Several catalogs offer them; they're also sold at Sears under their Craftsman label.

Chipper/shredders. You may be tempted to purchase a chipper/shredder machine to get rid of leaves, brush, and clippings. These machines—there are many on the market—will chip slim tree branches and brush into wood chips and grind leaves and debris into shreds. However, most do a much better job of chipping than they do of leaf-eating. It's not that they can't chop leaves—they do, but at a rate that will try your patience. None of them have large enough hoppers to hold quantities of leaves. You have to feed them a handful of leaves at a time—which is boring and a real waste of your time! Models that have oversized leaf-holding attachments don't function as well as they promise because the leaves often get clogged on the way down the narrow chute, especially if they are wet.

Most of these chipper/shredders have a brush-eating apparatus that works quite well, turning twigs and small branches into neat-sized wood chips, perfect for mulching under shrubs. You feed the branches into the intake chute sort of the way you slice carrots with a food processor. You have to hold onto the branches, feeding them in as they're gobbled up. This isn't lots of fun; the machines make a racket and vibrate. Some models send the chips flying, others deposit them neatly. Narrow feeding tubes cannot handle side branches or crooked limbs, but wider tubes pose more hazards to hands and eyes. Eye and ear protection as well as leather gloves are a must when operating these machines.

The less powerful but quieter electric models chip branches up to 1½ inches in diameter; gasoline models, which are noisier, can handle branches as big as 3 inches. The most robust chippers list for $1,000, give or take a few hundred, and can gobble large branches. Electric versions begin at about $300. These expensive machines are not essential to good garden maintenance, although they offer a real convenience and a nifty end product. Consider how much use you will really have for one before purchasing it.

Edging Tools

If you follow the suggestions in this book, you'll have little need to waste time edging a lawn, because you'll install mowing strips and edgings to separate grass from garden beds. The mowing strips should remain low enough to accommodate the wheels of the lawn mower, so lawn edges can be neatened as you mow. And the right kind of strip or edging keeps grass from creeping into beds and borders. (See "Tree Rings, Edgings, and Mowing Strips" on page 48.) But just in case you do have some edging chores, here are the tools that will make for an easy job.

Spades. For small edging jobs where lawn grass has crept into a bed or border, a garden spade works just fine to cut it back. Hold the spade perpendicular to the ground with both hands and rest the sharp, flat blade against the grass. Then stand on the tread to drive it through the grass roots to make a neat edge. If simply standing on the tool doesn't cut the grass, hold the tool up high and jam it into the ground, then stand on the tread, using your body weight to send it home.

Half-moon lawn edger. For large edging jobs, a lighter tool will tire you less. A half-moon lawn edger with its small curved blade fits the bill. Use it as you would a spade.

Grass shears. This is the time-honored implement for edging chores around tree trunks, rock walls, and similar obstacles where a mower can't get close enough to cut. They commonly come with short handles, so you must get right down among the blades and clip away at the scraggly grass. However, there are long-handled grass shears that elim-inate the need to stoop and crawl. Both models can tire your hands very quickly. Keep the shears extra sharp and well oiled or they'll just bend the grass blades and then refuse to snap back as you squeeze the handles.

Battery-operated long-handled grass shears. Last year Mark bought me a pair of these for trimming the grass along the rock wall that borders our shady flower bed. These rechargeable shears make a pleasing buzz, require no stooping or hand-squeezing, and work like a charm. Now, instead of putting off trimming until the wall disappears behind straggly grass, I am eager to snip it away.

String trimmers. Designed for cutting the grass that your mower leaves uncut, these popular motor-driven machines operate by spinning a plastic monofilament line that whacks off the grass. Keep in mind that these trimmers, if not used carefully and cautiously, can spell disaster for your landscape. The whirling filament can injure tender bark on young trees and shrubs, visibly skinning the trunk and perhaps killing the plant. Tougher-looking tree trunks suffer less obvious injuries from repeated whacks. Although no apparent damage appears at first, eventually repeated injury causes the tree's decline by doing internal damage.

The filament can also catch a pebble, small rock, piece of wood, or other debris and send it flying like a missile. Eye injuries caused by string trimmers are keeping ophthalmologists in business. If you insist on using one of these noisy, dangerous machines, be sure to wear protective goggles. Also wear sturdy shoes and long pants; an ill-aimed string can gash a leg. Some of these trimmers make so much noise—over 90 decibels—they're a hazard to hearing, so wear protective headgear over your ears. Don't operate one with children or pets in the vicinity—they won't be wearing protective gear and could be injured by flying debris.

Heavy-duty string trimmers will cut down weeds and grass growing in neglected or unmaintained areas. However, they don't always do the job. Often, the filament cuts down grass but bounces right off some of the tougher weed stems, leaving them standing. Some models convert from a whirling filament to a whirling brush-cutter blade, which cuts through small woody stems and certainly those stiff weeds. Need I tell you how dangerous one of these can be? Also bear in mind that both string and blade trimmers send out a spray of pulverized plant parts, including poison ivy if that's what you're cutting down.

Lawn Mowers

No matter how small your lawn, you're going to need some sort of machine to mow it. A good mower can help make lawn mowing more tolerable. If you have an old mower, you might consider trading it in for a newer, more efficient one that handles better and has some very handy options for weekend gardeners. There are several types and options from which to choose.

Reel mowers. Don't be skeptical about reel mowers if all you know is an old-fashioned reel mower powered by Grandpa or some kid wearing knickers. Reel mowers have made a happy comeback. Modern versions are manufactured with heavy-duty ball bearings that reduce resistance and make pushing the mower easy enough for anyone. Often parts are made of lightweight plastic or aluminum, so the mower you're pushing around weighs only about 25 to 35 pounds—less than most push rotary gasoline mowers! Using a reel mower can be a pleasure—the mower whirrs

pleasantly and quietly, rather than emitting an ear-splitting roar the way a power mower does, and pushing a lightweight version requires only moderate strength. It also doesn't require any fussing to get it started, never runs out of gas, and doesn't need tuning.

We use our reel mower almost exclusively to cut our 3,000 square feet of lawn. Until a thunderstorm scattered tiny twigs and leaves on the lawn, we thought the mower knew no bounds, but the twigs and debris stopped it in its tracks. Whenever a twig got caught between the blades, we had to dislodge it by hand or by backing up the mower. The mower is useless on a leaf-covered lawn, so we now switch back to our power mower in fall. Stems of tough, wiry weeds weren't fazed by the reel mower, either: They just bent over, then stood right back up. I finally had to hand-trim them. The grass catcher on our reel mower doesn't hold much grass, necessitating extra trips to the compost pile. Since we're trying to return clippings to the lawn, this isn't much of a problem. Reel mowers supposedly can't cut overly-long grass, but we've never found this a problem, even when the lawn has gotten pretty ragged. The 18-inch-wide blades require several more passes around the lawn to finish the cutting job than the 22-inch-wide blades of our power mower. But we find these disadvantages minor compared to the decided advantage of using a machine that whirrs rather than roars.

Power mowers. If you're still in the market for a rotary mower, even after considering my recommendations for a reel mower, read on. Even with a small lawn, you should use a good model power mower, one that will cut well and offers enough features to take some of the annoyance out of cutting the grass. A basic, well-designed, reliable power mower costs $300 and up. The more expensive models—to as much as $800—offer desirable features such as self-propulsion, rear-bagging, optional side discharge chute, and a blade-brake-clutch. Purchase the best model you can afford.

Walk-behind power mowers can be self-propelled, which means you don't have to use your muscles to push the mower forward but need only guide it. However, this can require some force. A self-propelled mower costs more than a push power mower, which uses the engine only to spin the cutting blade; you provide the force to move the mower forward.

Mulching mowers. These mowers, which have been around for about 30 years, chop up the lawn clippings—and autumn leaves and other debris—almost to a powder and spew them back down around the grass roots. When returned to the lawn this way, the clippings disintegrate quickly and act as a natural fertilizer. And the clippings don't have to be disposed of, which saves an enormous amount of work and is ecologically sound, too.

If you are in the market for a mulching mower, be sure to purchase one that is a "dedicated" mulcher, not one that mulches by forcing clippings and leaves through an attachment. Mulching attachments clog badly and simply can't do the job. Older machines with these designs gave mulching mowers a bad name, but modern dedicated machines work well. Be sure, too, that the mulching mower can be operated in a nonmulching mode with a grass catcher. This option is essential if you want to suck up leaves from the lawn in fall and shred them to use as garden mulch or for composting.

You can operate any mower without a grass catcher to create a sort of mulching mower, but this won't have the same effect as a true mulching mower, especially if the clippings are long. If you take care to direct the clippings onto the still-to-be-mown part of the lawn, they will be cut up again when you mow that area. This is especially important for the health of the lawn when clippings are longer than ½ inch.

Although you may never use it to catch clippings, a grass catcher is a desirable feature that allows you to use your power mower as a leaf shredder. Rear-baggers cost more than side-baggers but are much better mowers. The rear bag fills to capacity because the chute is straight, so it needs emptying less often. A rear-bagger is better balanced when the bag is full; side-baggers can tilt and pull you off balance when the bag fills. Side-baggers, with the bag usually on the right side, can only mow closely on the left side, so cutting the lawn's edges around beds and borders takes extra maneuvering. If you purchase a rear-bagger, be sure the machine has a convertible side chute discharge for use when you aren't catching the grass.

All recently manufactured power mowers must meet government safety standards requiring the blade to stop spinning within three seconds of releasing the mower's handle. The best, and most costly, method for stopping the blade is called a "blade-brake-clutch." When you release the control, the blade stops spinning, but the engine doesn't stop. The less desirable alternative is called an engine-kill control; when you release the control the blade and engine stop together. This means that you have to restart the engine each time you pause.

Riding mowers. Riding mowers cost several thousand dollars, depending on their size, horsepower, and other features, and find their niche where lawns occupy at least ½ acre. For small lawns, they are actually impractical, because they're difficult to use in small spaces. Most have a large turning radius and can't maneuver in tight spaces or trim closely. It's a rare lawn where a riding mower can do all the mowing, so you'll also need a walk-behind mower for the tight spots.

Garden Hoses and Attachments

The best garden hoses are made of rubber. These surpass other types of hose in flexibility, durability, longevity, and resistance to twisting and kinking. But rubber hoses weigh and cost a lot. Second choice is a hose made of a combination of vinyl and rubber. These are less costly, lighter in weight, and, if well built with three or more ply, they should perform well. Don't waste your money on a pure vinyl hose. It will burst and tear easily. A good hose will have couplings made of brass and wide, easy-to-turn grips.

Did you know that increasing the size of the garden hose can reduce watering time? Hoses come in three standard diameters— ½ inch, ⅝ inch, and ¾ inch—and in lengths of 25, 50, 75, and 100 feet. The ½-inch-diameter hose delivers about half as much water in the same amount of time as the ⅝-inch hose, and a third as much as the ¾-inch. Friction slows down water speed, too, so using a hose that's longer than needed means a reduction in efficiency. If you want to water fast, use a ¾-inch-diameter hose that's only as long as needed. When attaching hoses together, you might step down the diameter as you get farther from the faucet. This will help maintain the water pressure, which drops with distance.

Click-in hose couplers. These nifty gadgets make using hoses and sprinklers a lot easier. We have one on the end of each faucet and on the end of each hose, nozzle, and sprinkler. Instead of twisting the gadgets to get them joined together each time you lengthen or shorten a hose or change the water delivery device, all you do is snap them apart. Both plastic and brass versions can be found in catalogs and at garden centers.

Y-connectors. We have a Y-connector with a dual shut-off valve at each faucet so we can hook up more than one hose at a time. We don't usually use them both at the same time, but having them there saves time and labor because we water our entire yard from only two faucets—one in front and one in back of the house. We actually attached a length of hose permanently to one Y of the front faucet and ran it along the house foundation so it's there to deliver water to the other end of the house whenever we need it.

Hose guides. These gadgets are essential if you tend to pull hoses carelessly around your property. These grooved caps on long spikes prevent the hose from flattening flowers and tangling with shrubs. Jam the long spike of the guide into the ground along the edges of beds and borders, especially at corners where you are likely to pull the hose.

Sprinklers. These come in several basic types, and some can be quite expensive. Check for quality by looking for models with brass nozzles or fittings where the water emerges; poor-quality sprinklers have holes punched in the tubes or arms rather than fittings.

Oscillating sprinklers have a long arm that moves back and forth in a sweeping wave of water. These are ideal for watering large lawns, but, because they send water so high, they make a poor choice for watering around low-hanging trees. They also waste a lot of water. The best types feature special gears that prevent overwatering at the end of the arc as the sprinkler changes direction.

Rotary sprinklers can send water out in squares or circles, so read the directions before purchasing. These throw water lower and less far than oscillating sprinklers, so they're well suited for small gardens and getting into corners.

Impulse sprinklers send water out in a strong on-and-off jet as they transcribe a circle or part of a circle. They can be mounted on stakes, making them ideal for sending water over a shrub bed, or set low on the ground for lawn watering. These sprinklers cover more ground than any other type: The most powerful models transcribe circles as wide as 90 feet in diameter.

My favorite sprinkler for weekend gardeners is a **traveling sprinkler.** Although you might choke on the price, a traveling sprinkler will traverse up to 250 feet of your property, watering a parcel from 5 to 50 feet wide. Simply lay out the hose in the path you want the sprinkler to follow and it slowly winds its way along. If you're likely to turn on the sprinkler, then forget it and turn your lawn into a lake, get one of these.

Wheelbarrows, Carts, and Garden Cloths

Weekend gardeners can save time and effort by using a cart or wheelbarrow. Not only are these tools terrific for moving heavy loads of compost, peat moss, grass clippings, wood chips, and what-have-you, they're also great for hauling bulky but lightweight gardening by-products such as piles of prunings, weeds, and dry leaves. You can also use a cart or wheelbarrow to save steps when moving collections of seedlings, potted plants, or tools from one place to another by rolling them all off together. A step saved here or there compounds into quite a savings over the course of a weekend.

Garden carts. A garden cart has two large wheels, a rectangular plywood body, and metal trim, handles, and legs. The cart balances the weight of its load over the axle and wheels, allowing a gardener to trundle heavy loads with only slight effort. In fact, with about 5 pounds of exertion, you can lift 400 pounds in the cart. You'll find the garden cart is the tool of choice for transporting large, heavy, or bulky loads, as long as the ground is fairly level. A heavily loaded cart will run away from you when descending a steep hill because all the weight falls forward. And the weight falls on you when trying to go up a hill. You may be able to slow the cart's progress downhill by pulling it rather than pushing it, and edge it uphill the same way. Be sure to purchase a large cart with a removable front panel so you can dump the load easily.

Wheelbarrows. Although it is less stable than a cart, a wheelbarrow traverses hilly terrain better because it divides the weight of the load between the wheel and your back, arm, and shoulder muscles. You get much better traction this way. By loading the stuff you're carting into the front of the wheelbarrow, more of the weight falls over the wheel and less on your shoulders. Because it has only one wheel, a wheelbarrow maneuvers better than a cart and can traverse a narrower path.

Garden wheelbarrow. This model is made entirely of wood, with a wooden wheel treaded in steel. Be sure you purchase one with removable side panels so you can tip it to the side to dump. But this nostalgic item costs quite a bit.

Contractor's wheelbarrow. Less expensive and easier to come by, a contractor's wheelbarrow is made with a metal or plastic tub, wooden handles, and a pneumatic tire.

The tire bumps easily along a rocky path, taking a lot of the shock away from your arms. It's easy to dump loads off the front. Whatever you do, don't try to save a few bucks by purchasing a "homeowner's" wheelbarrow. These are too small and flimsy to do a good job.

Garden cloth. A large garden cloth is handy for trundling leaves, clippings, and similar debris. A simple tarpaulin of woven polyethylene is sturdy but lightweight. Toss weeds or clippings on it as you work, then gather the four corners together and hoist it over your shoulder, or grab two corners and pull it along behind you to the compost heap. A laminated cloth will be easier to slide across the ground than a nonlaminated type.

Garden tote bag. I use a variation of the garden cloth, made of laminated polyethylene that folds up neatly and unfolds into a shallow container with handles. The reinforced corners hold the wide bag open when unfolded so it makes a good target for the weeds I toss its way. I load the bag up, then carry it by the handles from one spot to another until it's full. Then it's off to the compost pile. I consider this gadget one of the most essential time-saving tools I use; I no longer toss the weeds onto the lawn and then have to collect them.

Mulch

Without doubt, the most time-saving garden "tool" is mulch. This holds true for every garden site, from vegetable garden to flower bed. You'll save the time it takes to mulch many times over during the growing season, because mulched gardens are healthier, more weed-free, and more drought-resistant than unmulched plots. Mulch comes in two basic types: organic and inorganic. Both types discourage weeds, but organic mulches also improve the soil. Although inorganic mulches don't decompose and enrich the soil, under certain circumstances they're the type to choose. For example, black plastic warms the soil and radiates heat slowly during the night, keeping heat-loving vegetables such as eggplant and tomatoes cozy and vigorous.

Organic mulches. Organic mulches include materials such as wood chips, shredded bark, chopped leaves, straw, grass clippings, compost, sawdust, pine needles, and even paper. There are two cardinal rules for using organic mulches effectively. First, lay the mulch down on soil that is already weed-free, and second, lay down a thick enough layer to discourage new weeds from coming up through it. It can take a 4- to 6-inch-deep layer of mulch to completely discourage weeds, although I've had pretty good success with a 2- to 3-inch layer in shady spots where weeds are usually less of a problem than in the sun.

Purchased mulch. You can buy bags of decorative wood chips or shredded bark from your local garden center to mulch your garden, but while these products look beautiful, they cost a lot. Your local tree-care company is a less expensive source of wood chips. When we attacked our present half-acre property, which was badly overgrown, the tree-care folks chipped up most of the shrubs and trees they ripped out or cut down in our yard, and we got the result to spread over the ground. Then we paid $50 for another truckload to be dumped at the top of our driveway.

Other sources. There are many other sources of inexpensive mulches. Your local electric company may sell wood chips. Many communities are also chipping yard debris or composting grass clippings and fall leaves, then offering the result back to the community. If you are willing to haul the mulch, take advantage of these opportunities. If you have a lot of trees on your property, collecting and shredding the fallen leaves creates a nutrient-rich mulch for free. Grass clippings are another nitrogen-rich freebie.

Inorganic mulches. The most common inorganic mulches include gravel, stones, black plastic, and landscape fabrics.

Black plastic. Mulching a vegetable garden with sheets of black plastic film can do wonders. The plastic heats up in the sun, warming the soil and radiating heat during the night, effectively creating a microclimate about 3°F warmer than an unmulched garden. Because the plastic film remains warm and dry, it protects vegetables from rotting and keeps them clean. And the mulch prevents weed growth and retains soil moisture.

In raised-bed gardens, lay down a sheet of plastic over the entire bed. Bury the edges or weigh the plastic down with rocks. Then punch holes in it for the plants. A bulb planter makes quick work of hole cutting. Sow seeds or plant transplants in the holes. You should be able to reuse the plastic for several years if you take it up in winter and store it until the next season.

Because water can't permeate the plastic, the mulch retains soil moisture but also prevents rainwater from soaking the planting bed. A drip irrigation system is ideal for watering a garden mulched with plastic; you could also lay soaker hoses down beneath the plastic. The simplest method is to shove the end of the hose through a hole in the plastic and turn it on.

Don't use black plastic to mulch shrubs or trees. Water and air can't penetrate the plastic, so roots grow very close to the soil surface, sometimes right beneath the plastic, seeking moisture and oxygen. The shallow roots suffer from lack of oxygen and moisture and from extremes of heat and cold. Eventually the plants decline and die.

Landscape fabrics. These fabrics, made from geotextiles such as woven or spun threads of polypropylene, nylon, or polyester, were originally used for road construction and soil stabilization projects. Because both water and air permeate them, landscape fabrics originally promised to be the perfect garden mulch. They have their drawbacks, however. Although they'll last indefinitely if protected from sunlight, they break down if exposed to ultraviolet light. All look ugly and require burial under a wood-chip mulch to make them aesthetically acceptable under shrubs. Once the wood-chip layer begins to decay, weeds will germinate on top of the fabric. You'll need to pull these weeds while still small, or they'll adhere to the fabric and rip it when you give them a yank.

Now, here's the clincher: According to Dr. Bonnie Lee Appleton, a Cooperative Extension agent in Virginia who specializes in nursery problems, the original research on landscape fabrics didn't test them in situations with live landscape plants. When she and her co-researchers tested the products with plants, they found that the shrubs weren't so happy after all. When they removed the mulch and dug up the plants, they discovered the shrub roots had grown to the surface just beneath the fabric and were actually adhering to it. What this means for long-term plant health is anyone's guess. Until more research is done, Dr. Appleton advises not to use fabric mulch anywhere you think you might need to pull it up or rearrange it.

Compost

Compost is another invaluable "tool" in the weekend gardener's arsenal. Compost improves the soil, making it easier to work and encouraging plant health and vigor.

Gardeners in the know routinely transform leaves, grass clippings, garden trimmings, weeds, and kitchen waste into black gold. This black gold is merely humble compost, nothing more than organic matter that has been rotted into riches, but it can work miracles. Compost dug into the soil can transform clay or sandy soil into loose, dark brown, friable stuff.

Hot and cold composting. Making compost can be a lot of work but it doesn't have to be. By turning over your compost pile almost daily, you can transform waste into compost in a few weeks. Or you can patiently wait a year or more and harvest the riches without lifting a finger once the pile is built. The quick composting method is called hot composting, because the compost heap actually heats up to about 150°F while the alchemy takes place. The slow method is called cold composting, because the heap doesn't appreciably heat up. Weekend gardeners are best off cold composting, as Mark and I have usually done, because it saves so much time and labor. But if you're in a hurry for compost, I'll tell you the easiest ways to go about it.

If there is a secret to composting—whether hot or cold—it is in providing a nourishing diet for the microorganisms that digest the organic matter in the pile. You can create a balanced diet for your composting microbes by mixing one-third high-nitrogen to two-thirds high-carbon components in a pile large enough to retain heat and moisture. If a compost pile fails to decompose, you should suspect a nitrogen deficiency. If the pile stinks, it contains too much nitrogen.

It's easy to remember which ingredients are high-nitrogen and which are high-carbon. Think of them in terms of "green" and

"brown," "wet" and "dry," or "fresh" and "old" ingredients. Materials high in nitrogen generally appear green, wet, and/or fresh; those high in carbon generally look brown, dry, and/or old. High-nitrogen or green ingredients include grass clippings, vegetable peelings, kitchen scraps other than meats, plant trimmings, weeds (without seeds, please, if you are cold composting!), faded flowers, and manure. High carbon or brown ingredients include dry leaves, newspaper, straw, twigs, and cornstalks.

If you chop up the ingredients in your compost pile, such as by shredding leaves and newspapers, they will degrade much faster and more efficiently.

There are probably as many ways to build a compost pile as there are gardeners, but a generally recognized method is to layer the green and brown ingredients with a little garden soil thrown in to inoculate it with microbes. Create a heap at least 3 cubic feet in size. Wider and taller is okay, but remember, the bigger it gets, the harder the heap will be to work with. The heap can be left freestanding in an out-of-the-way place, or contained in a bin. Bins don't really aid the composting process, but they do keep the heaps neat-looking.

Compost tumbler. If your heart is set on hot composting, but you don't want to fork through the pile every other day, invest in a compost tumbler. Tumblers provide an easy method for making hot compost, and all they take is five minutes a day. These gadgets resemble a barrel mounted on a stand, with a handle for rotating the barrel. All you do is load the tumbler up with the recommended green and brown mix, add a sprinkling of activator or soil, and then turn the tumbler once a day. You get finished compost in several weeks.

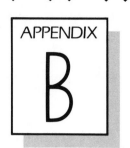

APPENDIX

B

KEY WEEKEND GARDENING ACTIVITIES CALENDAR

When you have only the weekends—or part of them—to devote to your garden, it's all too easy to turn Saturday and Sunday into what Mark and I affectionately term marathon weekends. Marathon weekends are to be avoided if at all possible, because at the end of the crush of gardening activities, we topple over with sheer exhaustion. Enthusiasm, pure and simple, spurs most of the frenzy, panic another part, and a sudden break in the weather fuels it further.

The following breakdown of key gardening activities should help you allocate your gardening chores over the weekends in a more organized way, preventing an overdose of labor that leaves you wondering—at least until your muscles stop aching—"*Why* do I do this?" And by planning your gardening activities, you'll find more time during the weekend to relax and enjoy the garden.

One chore to keep in mind throughout the summer is to make sure your plantings get their weekly inch of water.

The following list is compiled for our region, USDA Plant Hardiness Zone 7. Spring usually arrives here the first week of April when the forsythia blooms. If you live farther north or south, adjust the times accordingly.

January

First weekend: Cut off the boughs of Christmas trees and greenery and lay them over perennial beds to keep the ground frozen during the inevitable January thaw.

Second weekend: Study photographs of your garden and make plans for additions or deletions. Browse through your gardening books. Order catalogs.

Third weekend: If weather is mild enough to be outdoors, begin pruning deciduous shrubs and trees.

Fourth weekend: Order seeds for vegetable garden. Prowl around outside and pull any cool-season weeds you spot. Continue pruning if weather permits.

February

First weekend: Browse through flower catalogs and order perennials. Outdoors, be on the lookout for early bulbs; draw mulch back if necessary.

Second weekend: Lightly prune spring-flowering shrubs and bring the branches indoors for forcing.

Third weekend: Take lawn mower into the shop for sharpening and tune-up. Inspect tools; repair and sharpen them.

Fourth weekend: Inspect gardens for cool-season weeds, and eradicate them before they can set seeds. Prune berry plants.

March

First weekend: Prune needle-leaf evergreens, if needed. Remove obviously winter-damaged branches. Begin removing protective winter mulches.

Second weekend: Begin spring cleanup, raking leaves and debris left over from fall cleanup. Cut back dried stalks of perennials. Start new compost heap.

Third weekend: Continue spring cleanup. Mow the lawn short, and remove the clippings. Apply lawn nutrients and lime if necessary. Order fall-blooming bulbs.

Fourth weekend: Cut back ornamental grasses and liriope; mow winter-damaged groundcovers. Prune obviously dead or damaged branches on shrub roses. Mow the meadow garden.

April

First weekend: Loosen soil in vegetable beds (if the ground isn't saturated with water) and add compost. Begin sowing staggered plantings of cool-season vegetables.

Second weekend: Continue preparing vegetable garden. Continue sowing staggered plantings. Photograph garden, especially bulbs, for reference come bulb-planting time. Prune summer-flowering shrubs. Sow annual seeds in the meadow garden.

Third weekend: Renew mulch under shrubbery. Begin dividing perennials. Continue sowing staggered plantings. Deadhead bulbs. Mow grass, setting blades for spring height.

Fourth weekend: Continue sowing staggered plantings. Continue dividing perennials. Renew mulch in perennial beds.

May

First weekend: Begin planting perennials and shrubs. Take out hoses and inspect. Prune spring-flowering shrubs after the flowers have faded.

Second weekend: Purchase vegetable seedlings. Begin planting warm-season vegetables. Continue planting perennials and shrubs. Photograph garden for records.

Third weekend: Continue planting vegetable garden. Purchase and begin planting flowering annuals.

Fourth weekend: Finish planting flowering annuals. Finish pruning spring-flowering shrubs. Divide spring-blooming bulbs as foliage turns yellow.

June

First weekend: Mow grass; set blades for summer height. Cut back dead bulb foliage and finish dividing spring bulbs. Begin summer watering routine if necessary. Stake tomatoes, vines, and perennials.

Second weekend: Photograph gardens for records. Design new planting areas in preparation for Fourth of July plant sales; strip off sod. Compost sod.

Third weekend: Turn over the soil in new planting area, working in compost, peat moss, and other soil improvements.

Fourth weekend: Deadhead perennials. Eradicate young warm-season weeds before they get large.

July

First weekend: Attend Fourth of July plant sales; plant new garden. Harvest currants and raspberries.

Second weekend: Photograph garden for records. Finish planting new garden.

Third weekend: Deadhead perennials. Plant cool-season fall vegetable seeds. Begin harvesting blueberries, tomatoes, peppers.

Fourth weekend: Eradicate warm-season weeds.

August

First weekend: Study garden photos taken in spring and summer; order spring-flowering bulbs, dormant perennials, and dormant woody plants from catalogs.

Second weekend: Deadhead perennials. Shop for and plant cool-season vegetable transplants.

Third weekend: Plant fall-blooming bulbs.

Fourth weekend: Begin harvesting fall raspberries. Inspect gardens for weeds, especially cool-season weed seedlings; eradicate.

September

First weekend: Mow lawn, setting blades for fall height. Sow grass seed for new lawns or to repair bare patches. Apply fall nutrients to lawn.

Second weekend: Begin planting mail-order or locally purchased shrubs, trees, and perennials. Photograph garden for records. Sow seeds for meadow garden.

Third weekend: Continue planting shrubs and trees. Divide overgrown perennials, such as iris. Plant lily bulbs.

Fourth weekend: Shop for spring-blooming bulbs. Root-prune shrubs you intend to move or transplant in spring.

October

First weekend: Tidy vegetable garden.

Second weekend: Plant spring-blooming bulbs.

Third weekend: Finish bulb planting. Cut back perennials if desired, only after frost kills the tops. Remove frost-killed annuals.

Fourth weekend: Begin raking and shredding leaves. Clean up vegetable garden, composting healthy plants, discarding suspect ones in trash.

November

First weekend: If fall has been drier than usual, water shrubs and flower borders deeply to prepare plants for winter. Cut back dried perennials if desired; allow attractive seed-pods to stand over winter.

Second weekend: Continue raking and shredding leaves. Till shredded leaves into vegetable garden.

Third weekend: Continue raking and shredding leaves. Lower mower blade and perform final lawn mowing.

Fourth weekend: Final major leaf raking and shredding. Bag some shredded leaves or store under tarpaulin to be used later as mulch; compost the rest.

December

First weekend: Cut back yellow asparagus fronds. Apply lime to lawn, if needed. Water newly planted woody plants if November was dry.

Second weekend: Inspect and repair tools; put in storage.

Third weekend: Apply winter mulch of shredded leaves to frozen ground in perennial beds, shrub borders, and woodland garden.

Fourth weekend: Relax.

APPENDIX C

USDA PLANT HARDINESS ZONE MAP

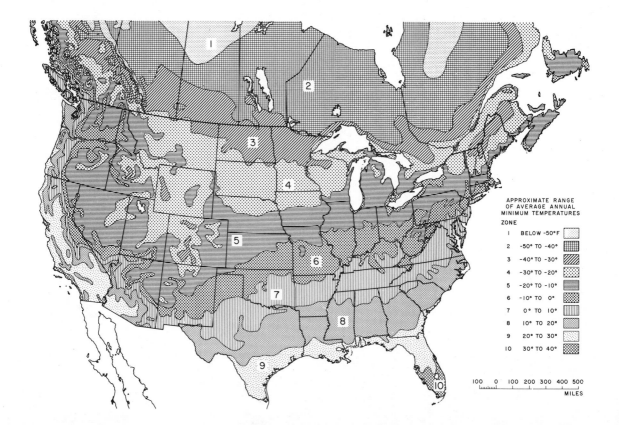

APPROXIMATE RANGE
OF AVERAGE ANNUAL
MINIMUM TEMPERATURES

ZONE	
1	BELOW -50°F
2	-50° TO -40°
3	-40° TO -30°
4	-30° TO -20°
5	-20° TO -10°
6	-10° TO 0°
7	0° TO 10°
8	10° TO 20°
9	20° TO 30°
10	30° TO 40°

100   0   100 200 300 400 500

MILES

RESOURCES FOR WEEKEND GARDENERS

Here are some of my favorite mail-order sources of plants, seeds, and tools. Many charge for their catalogs, so write for current prices.

Annuals

W. Atlee Burpee & Co.
300 Park Ave.
Warminster, PA 18974

Hastings
P.O. Box 115535
1036 White St. S.W.
Atlanta, GA 30310
  (specializes in plants for the South)

Ed Hume Seeds, Inc.
P.O. Box 1450
Kent, WA 98032
  (specializes in plants for the Pacific Northwest)

Park Seed Co.
P.O. Box 31
Greenwood, SC 29647

Porter & Son
P.O. Box 104
Stephenville, TX 76401
  (specializes in vegetables and flowers for the South)

Stokes Seeds, Inc.
P.O. Box 548
Buffalo, NY 14240

Thompson & Morgan
P.O. Box 1308
Jackson, NJ 08527

Bulbs

Bakker of Holland
U.S. Reservation Center
Louisiana, MO 63353

Peter de Jager Bulb Co.
P.O. Box 2010
South Hamilton, MA 01982

Dutch Gardens
P.O. Box 200
Adelphia, NJ 07710

Ed Hume Seeds, Inc.
P.O. Box 1450
Kent, WA 98032
  (specializes in plants for the Pacific Northwest)

McClure & Zimmerman
P.O. Box 368
108 W. Winnebago St.
Friesland, WI 53935
  (informative catalog)

Messelaar Bulb Co., Inc.
P.O. Box 269
Ipswich, MA 01938

Michigan Bulb Co.
1950 Waldorf N.W.
Grand Rapids, MI 49550

Quality Dutch Bulbs, Inc.
P.O. Box 225
Hillsdale, NJ 07642

John Scheepers, Inc.
R.D. 6
Phillipsburg Rd.
Middletown, NY 10940

Ty Ty Plantation Bulb Co.
P.O. Box 159
Ty Ty, GA 31795
    (specializes in cannas)

Wayside Gardens
1 Garden Ln.
Hodges, SC 29695

Wyatt-Quarles Seed Co.
P.O. Box 739
Garner, NC 27529
    (specializes in plants for the South)

Fruits

Ahrens Nursery
R.R. 1
Huntingburg, IN 47542
    (mainly small fruits, some fruit trees, evergreens,
    garden supplies)

The Allen Co.
P.O. Box 310
Fruitland, MD 21826
    (specializes in strawberries and other small fruits)

Vernon Barnes & Son Nursery
P.O. Box 250
McMinnville, TN 37110

Bear Creek Nursery
P.O. Box 411
Northport, WA 99157

Brittingham Plant Farms
P.O. Box 2538
Salisbury, MD 21801

Country Heritage Nursery
P.O. Box 536
Hartford, MI 49057
    (mainly small fruits, some trees)

Edible Landscaping
P.O. Box 77
Afton, VA 22920

Hastings
P.O. Box 115535
Atlanta, GA 30302
    (specializes in plants for the South)

Kelly Bros. Nurseries
Hwy. 54
Louisiana, MO 63353

Makielski Berry Nursery
7130 Platt Rd.
Ypsilanti, MI 48197
    (specializes in small fruits)

J. E. Miller Nurseries, Inc.
5060 W. Lake Rd.
Canandaigua, NY 14424

Moosebell Flower, Fruit, & Tree Co.
Rt. 1, Box 240
St. Francis, ME 04774

New York State Fruit Testing Cooperative
    Association, Inc.
P.O. Box 462
Geneva, NY 14456
    (specializes in cold-hardy small fruits and trees)

Northwoods Nursery
28696 S. Cramer Rd.
Molalla, OR 97038
    (mainly fruits and ornamental trees and shrubs)

Pacific Berry Works
P.O. Box 54
Bow, WA 98232

Raintree Nursery
391 Butts Rd.
Morton, WA 98356

Rayner Bros., Inc.
P.O. Box 1617
Salisbury, MD 21802
    (mainly small fruits, some fruit trees and evergreens)

St. Lawrence Nurseries
R.D. 5
Potsdam, NY 13676
  (mainly fruits and nuts; grown organically)

Southmeadow Fruit Gardens
15310 Red Arrow Hwy.
Lakeside, MI 49116
  (specializes in choice and unusual fruit varieties)

Stark Bro's Nurseries & Orchards Co.
Hwy. 54 West
Louisiana, MO 63353
  (specializes in fruits; ornamental trees and shrubs)

Waynesboro Nurseries, Inc.
P.O. Box 987
Waynesboro, VA 22980
  (specializes in fruits, nuts, and ornamentals)

Groundcovers

See Perennials, Groundcovers, and Ornamental Grasses on page 338

Native Plants and Wildflowers

Abundant Life Seed Foundation
P.O. Box 772
Port Townsend, WA 98368

Applewood Seed Company
5380 Vivian St.
Arvada, CO 80002

Beersheba Wildflower Gardens
P.O. Box 551
Beersheba Springs, TN 37305
  (specializes in Southeastern wildflowers)

Boehlke's Woodland Gardens
W. 140 N. 10829 Country Aire Rd.
Germantown, WI 53022
  (specializes in wildflowers for the North)

Busse Gardens
Rt. 2, Box 238
Cokato, MN 55321

Dallas Nature Center
Attn.: Randy Mock
7575 Wheatland Rd.
Dallas, TX 75249

Fancy Fronds
1911 4th Ave. W.
Seattle, WA 98119
  (specializes in spore-propagated ferns)

Green Horizons
218 Quinlan #571
Kerrville, TX 78028

High Altitude Gardens
P.O. Box 4619
Ketchum, ID 83340
  (specializes in high-altitude wildflowers)

LaFayette Home Nursery, Inc.
R.R. 1, Box 1A
Lafayette, IL 61449
  (specializes in prairie grasses and flowers for the Midwest)

Midwest Wildflowers
P.O. Box 64
Rockton, IL 61072
  (specializes in wildflower seeds for the Midwest)

Miller Grass Seed Co.
P.O. Box 886
Hereford, TX 79045
  (specializes in native grass seed)

Moon Mountain
P.O. Box 34
Morro Bay, CA 93443

Native Seed Foundation
Star Rt.
Moyie Springs, ID 83845

Native Seeds, Inc.
14590 Triadelphia Mill Rd.
Dayton, MD 21306

Oak Hill Gardens
P.O. Box 25
Dundee, IL 60118

Plants of the Southwest
930 Baca St.
Santa Fe, NM 87501

Prairie Nursery
P.O. Box 306
Westfield, WI 53964
  (specializes in seeds and plants of prairie wildflowers for the Midwest)

The Primrose Path
R.D. 2, Box 110
Scottdale, PA 15683

Clyde Robin Seed Company
P.O. Box 2366
3670 Enterprise Ave.
Castro Valley, CA 94546

Schulz Cactus Gardens
1095 Easy St.
Morgan Hill, CA 95037

Sharp Bros. Seed Co.
Rt. 4, Box 237A
Clinton, MO 64735
   (specializes in native grasses)

Southwestern Native Seeds
P.O. Box 50503
Tucson, AZ 85703

Stover Seed Co.
P.O. Box 21488
Los Angeles, CA 90021
   (specializes in drought-tolerant plants)

Sunshine Seeds
R.R. 2, Box 176
Wyoming, IL 61491
   (specializes in prairie grasses and wildflowers for
   the Midwest; woodland flowers)

Wildseed, Inc.
P.O. Box 308
1101 Campo Rosa Rd.
Eagle Lake, TX 77434
   (specializes in native grass and wildflower seed)

Windrift Prairie Shop
708 N. Daysville Rd.
Oregon, IL 61061
   (specializes in native grasses and wildflower seed)

Woodlanders, Inc.
1128 Colleton Ave.
Aiken, SC 29801
   (specializes in native trees and shrubs for
   Zones 7–9)

For more information on growing wildflowers:

National Wildflower Research Center
2600 FM 973 North
Austin, TX 78725-4201
   (Publishes wildflower books and lists of wildflowers
   for each region of the country.)

New England Wild Flower Society, Inc.
Garden in the Woods
Hemenway Rd.
Framingham, MA 01701
   (Publishes booklets and pamphlets about wildflower
   propagation. Their *Nursery Sources: Native Plants
   and Wildflowers* lists nurseries that sell only nursery-
   propagated wildflowers.)

Ornamental Grasses
   See Perennials, Groundcovers, and Ornamental
   Grasses below

**Perennials, Groundcovers,
and Ornamental Grasses**

Anderson Iris Gardens
22179 Keather Ave. N.
Forest Lake, MN 55025

B & D Lilies
330 P St.
Port Townsend, WA 98368

Kurt Bluemel, Inc.
2740 Greene Ln.
Baldwin, MD 21013
   (specializes in ornamental grasses)

Bluestone Perennials
7211 Middle Ridge Rd.
Madison, OH 44057
   (offers over 300 perennials)

Lee Bristol Nursery
P.O. Box 5
Gaylordsville, CT 06755

W. Atlee Burpee & Co.
300 Park Ave.
Warminster, PA 18974

Cal Dixie Iris Gardens
14115 Pear St.
Riverside, CA 92508
   (specializes in iris)

The Crownsville Nursery
P.O. Box 797
Crownsville, MD 21032
   (offers hundreds of perennials, many rare and
   unusual)

Daylily World
P.O. Box 1612
Sanford, FL 32772
   (specializes in daylilies)

Henry Field Seed & Nursery Co.
407 Sycamore St.
Shenandoah, IA 51602

Garden Place
P.O. Box 388
Mentor, OH 44061

Gardens in a Moment
P.O. Box 206
Lafayette, CO 80026

Greenwood Daylily Gardens
4905 Pioneer Blvd.
Whittier, CA 90601
    (specializes in daylilies)

Heritage Gardens
1 Meadow Ridge Rd.
Shenandoah, IA 51601

Ed Hume Seeds, Inc.
P.O. Box 1450
Kent, WA 98032
    (specializes in plants for the Pacific Northwest)

Inter-State Nurseries
P.O. Box 208
Hamburg, IA 51640

Kimberly Garden
R.R. 1, Box 44G
Lisle, NY 13797

Klehm Nursery
Rt. 5, Box 197
South Barrington, IL 60010
    (specializes in peonies, iris, daylilies, and hostas)

Milaeger's Gardens
4838 Douglas Ave.
Racine, WI 53402

Oak Hill Gardens
P.O. Box 25
Dundee, IL 60118

Oakes Daylilies
8204 Monday Rd.
Corryton, TN 37721
    (specializes in daylilies)

Park Seed Co. Inc.
P.O. Box 31
Greenwood, SC 29647

Porter & Son
P.O. Box 104
Stephenville, TX 76401
    (specializes in vegetables and flowers for the South)

Shady Oaks Nursery
700 19th Ave. N.E.
Waseca, MN 56093

Thompson & Morgan
P.O. Box 1308
Jackson, NJ 08527
    (seeds)

Andre Viette Farm and Nursery
Rt. 1, Box 16
Fishersville, VA 22939
    (large collections of low-maintenance perennials,
    woodland plants, and daylilies)

Wayside Gardens
1 Garden Ln.
Hodges, SC 29695

White Flower Farm
Litchfield, CT 06759
    (catalog makes good reading)

Wright Iris Nursery
6583 Pacheco Pass Hwy.
Gilroy, CA 95020
    (specializes in iris)

Wyatt-Quarles Seed Co.
P.O. Box 739
Garner, NC 27529
    (specializes in vegetables, flowers, and bulbs for the
    South)

Roses

Big Spring Nursery
940 N. College St.
Neosho, MO 64850

Emlong Nurseries Inc.
Box #ROSES
Stevensville, MI 49127

Gloria Dei Nursery
36 East Rd.
High Falls, NY 12440

Heritage Rose Gardens
16831 Mitchell Creek Dr.
Ft. Bragg, CA 95437

High Country Rosarium
1717 Downing St.
Denver, CO 80218

Historical Roses
1657 W. Jackson St.
Painesville, OH 44077

Hortico, Inc.
723 Robson Rd.
Waterdown, Ontario
Canada L0R 2H1

Inter-State Nurseries, Inc.
P.O. Box 208
Hamburg, IA 51640

Krider Nurseries, Inc.
P.O. Box 29
Middlebury, IN 46540

Lamb Nurseries
E. 101 Sharp Ave.
Spokane, WA 99202

Lyndon Lyon Greenhouses, Inc.
14 Mutchler St.
Dolgeville, NY 13329

Earl May Seed & Nursery L.P.
208 N. Elm St.
Shenandoah, IA 51603

Carl Pallek and Son Nursery
Box 137
Virgil, Ontario
Canada L0S 1T0
   (ships only in Canada)

Pickering Nurseries, Inc.
670 Kingston Rd.
Pickering, Ontario
Canada L1V 1A6

Roses by Fred Edmunds, Inc.
6235 S.W. Kahle Rd.
Wilsonville, Oregon 97070

Roses of Yesterday & Today
802 Brown's Valley Rd.
Watsonville, CA 95076
   (hundreds of old, rare, and unusual roses; some
   modern roses; catalog makes great reading)

Sequoia Nursery/Moore Miniature Roses
2519 E. Noble Ave.
Visalia, CA 93277

Stanek's Nursery
E. 2929 27th Ave.
Spokane, WA 99223

Stocking Rose Nursery
785 N. Capitol Ave.
San Jose, CA 95133

Tate Nursery
Rt. 20, Box 436
Tyler, TX 75708

Thomasville Nurseries, Inc.
P.O. Box 7
Thomasville, GA 31799

Wayside Gardens
1 Garden Ln.
Hodges, SC 29695

Tools and Garden Accessories

Amerind-MacKissic Co.
P.O. Box 111
Parker Ford, PA 19457

Bountiful Gardens
19550 Walker Rd.
Willits, CA 95490

Brookstone Co.
127 Vose Farm Rd.
Peterborough, NH 03458

The Clapper Co.
1121 Washington St.
W. Newton, MA 02165
   (tools, garden ornaments, furniture, and books)

Gardener's Eden
P.O. Box 7307
San Francisco, CA 94120
   (garden furniture and accessories)

Gardener's Supply Co.
128 Intervale Rd.
Burlington, VT 05401

Gardens Alive!
Natural Gardening Research Center
P.O. Box 149
Sunman, IN 47041
   (natural gardening supplies)

Green Earth Organics
9422 144th St. E.
Puyallup, WA 98373

Harmony Farm Supply
P.O. Box 460
Graton, CA 95444

The Kinsman Company, Inc.
River Rd.
Point Pleasant, PA 18950
(tools, rose arbors and garden arches, garden
ornaments, and fruit presses)

Lehman's Hardware & Appliances
P.O. Box 41
Kidron, OH 44636
(garden tools, kitchen and canning tools, garden
ornaments, and lawn-care equipment)

A. M. Leonard, Inc.
P.O. Box 816
Piqua, OH 45356
(extensive selection of no-nonsense gardening tools)

Kenneth Lynch & Sons
P.O. Box 488
Wilton, CT 06897
(extensive collection of garden sculptures, pools,
fountains, sundials, and furniture)

Mantis Mfg. Corp.
1458 County Line Rd.
Huntington Valley, PA 19006

The Natural Gardening Co.
217 San Anselmo Ave.
San Anselmo, CA 94960

Necessary Trading Co.
703 Salem Ave.
New Castle, VA 24127
(natural gardening supplies; informative catalog)

Walt Nicke Co.
P.O. Box 433
Topsfield, MA 01983
(catalog makes good reading)

Ohio Earth Food, Inc.
13737 Duquette Ave. N.E.
Hartville, OH 44632

Organic Pest Management
P.O. Box 55267
Seattle, WA 98155

Peaceful Valley Farm Supply Co.
P.O. Box 2209
Grass Valley, CA 95945

The Plow and Hearth
P.O. Box 830
Orange, VA 22960
(tools, garden ornaments, and furniture)

Ringer Corp.
9959 Valley View Rd.
Eden Prairie, MN 55344
(organic gardening supplies)

Smith & Hawken
25 Corte Madera
Mill Valley, CA 94941
(tools, garden ornaments and furniture, books,
seeds, and greenhouse supplies)

The Urban Farmer Store
2833 Vicente St.
San Francisco, CA 94116
(water-conserving irrigation systems and other
supplies)

Trees and Shrubs

Brooks Tree Farm
9785 Portland Rd. N.E.
Salem, OR 97305

Carino Nurseries
P.O. Box 538
Indiana, PA 15701
(over 100 selections)

Cascade Forestry Nursery
Rt. 1
Cascade, IA 52033

Forestfarm
990 Tetherow Rd.
Williams, OR 97544
(includes unusual ornamentals and conifers)

Foxborough Nursery
3611 Miller Rd.
Street, MD 21154
(extensive selection)

Girard Nurseries
P.O. Box 428
Geneva, OH 44041

Greer Gardens
1280 Goodpasture Island Rd.
Eugene, OR 97401
    (large selection of rhododendrons and azaleas; also
    offers ornamental trees and other flowering shrubs)

Lakeland Nurseries
340 Poplar St.
Hanover, PA 17331

Louisiana Nursery
Rt. 7, Box 43
Opelousas, LA 70570
    (specializes in magnolias; general plant list includes
    hundreds of ornamental trees and shrubs)

McConnell Nurseries
Port Burwell, Ontario
Canada NOJ 1TO
    (Canada only)

Mellinger's Inc.
2310 W. South Range Rd.
North Lima, OH 44452
    (large selection of trees and shrubs; gardening
    supplies)

Musser Forests, Inc.
P.O. Box 340
Rt. 119 North
Indiana, PA 15701

Northwoods Nursery
28696 S. Cramer Rd.
Molalla, OR 97038

Raintree Nursery
391 Butts Rd.
Morton, WA 98356

Wayside Gardens
1 Garden Ln.
Hodges, SC 29695

Weston Nurseries
P.O. Box 186
Rt. 135
Hopkinton, MA 01748
    (large selection)

Vegetables

Allen, Sterling, & Lothrop
191 U.S. Rt. 1
Falmouth, ME 04105
    (short-season vegetables)

W. Atlee Burpee & Co.
300 Park Ave.
Warminster, PA 18974

Butterbrooke Farm
78 Barry Rd.
Oxford, CT 06483
    (short-season vegetables)

Comstock, Ferre, & Co.
P.O. Box 125
236 Main St.
Wethersfield, CT 06109
    (disease-resistant vegetables)

The Cook's Garden
Moffitt's Bridge
P.O. Box 535
Londonderry, VT 05148

William Dam Seeds
P.O. Box 8400
Dundas, Ontario
Canada L9H 6M1
    (short-season vegetables)

Dominion Seed House
115 Guelph St.
Georgetown, Ontario
Canada L7G 4A2
    (Canada only)

Henry Field Seed & Nursery Co.
P.O. Box 700
Shenandoah, IA 51602

Good Seed Co.
St. Rt. Box 73A
Oroville, WA 98844
    (vegetables for the intermountain area of the
    Northwest)

Gurney Seed and Nursery
Gurney Bldg.
Yankton, SD 57079

Hastings
P.O. Box 115535
Atlanta, GA 30302
    (specializes in plants for the South)

High Altitude Gardens
P.O. Box 4619
Ketchum, ID 83340
    (high-altitude vegetables)

Ed Hume Seeds, Inc.
P.O. Box 1450
Kent, WA 98032
  (specializes in vegetables for the Pacific Northwest)

Johnny's Selected Seeds
Foss Hill Rd.
Albion, ME 04910
  (specializes in short-season vegetables)

J. W. Jung Seed Co.
335 S. High St.
Randolph, WI 53957

Kelly Bros. Nurseries
Hwy. 54
Louisiana, MO 63353

Lockhart Seeds
P.O. Box 1361
3 N. Wilson Way
Stockton, CA 95201
  (specializes in vegetables for central California)

Earl May Seed & Nursery, L.P.
208 N. Elm St.
Shenandoah, IA 51603

The Meyer Seed Co.
600 S. Caroline St.
Baltimore, MD 21231
  (specializes in seeds for the mid-Atlantic area)

Nichols Garden Nursery
1190 N. Pacific Hwy.
Albany, OR 97321
  (specializes in vegetables and herbs for the Pacific
  Northwest)

Park Seed Co., Inc.
P.O. Box 31
Greenwood, SC 29647

Porter & Son
P.O. Box 104
Stephenville, TX 76401
  (specializes in vegetables and flowers for the South)

Roswell Seed Company, Inc.
P.O. Box 725
Roswell, NM 88202
  (specializes in vegetables and flowers for the arid
  Southwest)

Stokes Seeds Inc.
P.O. Box 548
Buffalo, NY 14240

Territorial Seed Co.
P.O. Box 27
Lorane, OR 97451
  (specializes in vegetables for the Pacific Northwest)

Tillinghast Seed Co.
P.O. Box 738
La Connor, WA 98257
  (specializes in vegetables for the Pacific Northwest)

Tomato Growers Supply Co.
P.O. Box 2237
Fort Myers, FL 33902

The Tomato Seed Company, Inc.
P.O. Box 323
Metuchen, NJ 08840

Tsang & Ma
P.O. Box 5644
Redwood City, CA 94063
  (specializes in Asian vegetables)

Vesey's Seeds Ltd.
P.O. Box 9000
Charlottetown, PE
Canada C1A 8K6

or

P.O. Box 9000
Calais, ME 04619
  (specializes in short-season vegetables for the Northeast U.S. and Canada)

Wyatt-Quarles Seed Co.
P.O. Box 739
Garner, NC 27529
  (specializes in vegetables, flowers, and bulbs for the
  South)

FOR FURTHER READING

Chapter 1

Binetti, Marianne. *Tips for Carefree Landscapes: Over 500 Sure-Fire Ways to Beautify Your Yard and Garden*. Pownal, Vt.: Storey Communications, 1990.

Colborn, Nigel. *Leisurely Gardening: A Laissez-Faire Guide to the Low-Maintenance Garden*. London: Christopher Helm, 1989.

Duffield, Mary and Warren Jones. *Plants for Dry Climates: How to Select, Grow, & Enjoy*. Los Angeles: Price/Stern/Sloan, Inc., 1981.

Fish, Margery. *Carefree Gardening*. London: Faber and Faber, 1990.

Reilly, Ann and Susan A. Roth. *The Home Landscaper: 55 Professional Landscapes You Can Do*. Tucson, Ariz.: Home Planners, 1990.

Sinnes, A. Cort. *Easy Maintenance Gardening*. San Francisco: Ortho Books, Chevron Chemical Co., 1982.

Sunset Books and *Sunset* magazine Editors. *Easy-Care Gardening—A Low-Maintenance Handbook*. Menlo Park, Calif.: Lane Publishing Co., 1988.

Chapter 2

Bennett, Jennifer, ed. *The Harrowsmith Gardener's Guide to Groundcovers*. Camden East, Ontario: Camden House, 1987.

Cox, Jeff and Marilyn. *Flowers for All Seasons: A Guide to Colorful Trees, Shrubs, and Vines*. Emmaus, Pa.: Rodale Press, 1987.

Dirr, Michael. *All About Evergreens*. San Francisco: Ortho Books, Chevron Chemical Co., 1985.

———. *Manual of Woody Landscape Plants*. 3rd ed. Champaign, Ill.: Stipes Publishing Co., 1983.

Ferguson, Barbara, ed. *All About Trees*. San Francisco: Ortho Books, Chevron Chemical Co., 1982.

Foley, Daniel J. *Groundcover Plants for Easier Gardening*. New York: Dover Publications, 1972.

MacCaskey, Michael. *Lawns and Ground Covers: How to Select, Grow, and Enjoy*. Tucson, Ariz.: HP Books, 1982.

Millard, Scott, ed. *All About Groundcovers*. San Francisco: Ortho Books, Chevron Chemical Co., 1977.

Shultz, Warren. *The Chemical-Free Lawn: The Newest Varieties and Techniques to Grow Lush, Hardy Grass*. Emmaus, Pa.: Rodale Press, 1989.

Sinnes, A. Cort. *How to Select & Care for Shrubs & Hedges*. San Francisco: Ortho Books, Chevron Chemical Co., 1980.

Sunset Books and *Sunset* magazine Editors. *Lawns & Groundcovers*. Menlo Park, Calif.: Lane Publishing Co., 1982.

Taylor's Guide Staff. *Taylor's Guide to Ground Covers, Vines, and Grasses*. Boston: Houghton Mifflin, 1987.

———. *Taylor's Guide to Shrubs*. Boston: Houghton Mifflin, 1987.

———. *Taylor's Guide to Trees*. Boston: Houghton Mifflin, 1988.

Wyman, Donald. *Ground Cover Plants*. New York: Macmillan, 1956.

Chapter 3

Armitage, Allan M. *Herbaceous Perennial Plants*. Athens, Ga.: Varsity Press, 1989.

Ball, Jeff and Charles O. Cresson. *The 60-Minute Flower Garden*. Emmaus, Pa.: Rodale Press, 1987.

Clausen, Ruth Rogers and Nicolas H. Ekstrom. *Perennials for American Gardens*. New York: Random House, 1989.

Cox, Jeff and Marilyn. *The Perennial Garden: Color Harmonies through the Seasons*. Emmaus, Pa.: Rodale Press, 1985.

Fell, Derek. *Annuals: How to Select, Grow, and Enjoy*. Tucson, Ariz.: HP Books, 1983.

Ferguson, Barbara, ed. *Color with Annuals*. San Francisco: Ortho Books, Chevron Chemical Co., 1987.

Fish, Margery. *Cottage Garden Flowers*. London: Faber and Faber, 1961.

Genders, Roy. *The Cottage Garden—and the Old-fashioned Flowers*. London: Pelham Books, 1983.

Harper, Pamela and Frederick McGourty. *Perennials: How to Select, Grow, & Enjoy*. Tucson, Ariz.: HP Books, 1985.

Horton, Alvin and James McNair. *All About Bulbs*. San Francisco: Ortho Books, Chevron Chemical Co., 1986.

Kowalchik, Claire and William H. Hylton, eds. *Rodale's Encyclopedia of Herbs*. Emmaus, Pa.: Rodale Press, 1987.

Lathrop, Norma Jean. *Herbs: How to Grow and Enjoy*. Tucson, Ariz.: HP Books, 1981.

Rice, Graham. *Plants for Problem Places*. Portland, Ore.: Timber Press, 1988.

Scott-James, Ann. *Perfect Plant, Perfect Garden: The 200 Most Rewarding Plants for Every Garden*. New York: Summit Books, 1988.

Sinnes, A. Cort. *Shade Gardening*. San Francisco: Ortho Books, Chevron Chemical Co., 1982.

Taylor's Guide Staff. *Taylor's Guide to Annuals*. Boston: Houghton Mifflin, 1986.

———. *Taylor's Guide to Perennials*. Boston: Houghton Mifflin, 1986.

Williamson, John. *Perennial Gardens*. New York: Harper and Row, Publishers, 1988.

Chapter 4

Ball, Jeff. *Jeff Ball's 60-Minute Garden*. Emmaus, Pa.: Rodale Press, 1985.

Bartholomew, Mel. *Square Foot Gardening*. Emmaus, Pa.: Rodale Press, 1981.

Cox, Jeff and the Editors of Rodale's *Organic Gardening* magazine. *How to Grow Vegetables Organically*. Emmaus, Pa.: Rodale Press, 1988.

DeWolf, Gordon. *Taylor's Guide to Vegetables & Herbs*. Boston: Houghton Mifflin, 1988.

Hunt, Marjorie B. and Brenda Bortz. *High-Yield Gardening: How to Get More from Your Garden Space and More from Your Gardening Season*. Emmaus, Pa.: Rodale Press, 1986.

National Gardening Association. *Gardening: The Complete Guide to Growing America's Favorite Fruits & Vegetables*. Reading, Mass.: Addison-Wesley Publishing Co., 1986.

Newcomb, Duane and Karen. *The Complete Vegetable Gardener's Sourcebook*. New York: Prentice Hall Press, 1989.

Ogden, Shepherd and Ellen. *The Cook's Garden—Growing and Using the Best-Tasting Vegetable Varieties*. Emmaus, Pa.: Rodale Press, 1989.

Raymond, Dick and Jan. *Home Gardening Wisdom*. Charlotte, Vt.: Garden Way Publishing, 1982.

Rodale Press Editors. *The Organic Gardener's Complete Guide to Vegetables and Fruits*. Emmaus, Pa.: Rodale Press, 1982.

Smith, Miranda and Ana Carr. *Rodale's Garden Insect, Disease, & Weed Identification Guide*. Emmaus, Pa. Rodale Press, 1988.

Chapter 5

Bilderback, Diane E. and Dorothy Hinshaw Patent. *Backyard Fruits & Berries: How to Grow Them Better Than Ever*. Emmaus, Pa.: Rodale Press, 1984.

Ferguson, Barbara, ed. *All About Growing Fruits, Berries, & Nuts*. rev. ed. San Francisco: Ortho Books, Chevron Chemical Co., 1987.

Hendrickson, Robert. *The Berry Book*. Garden City, N.Y.: Doubleday & Company, Inc., 1981.

Hill, Lewis. *Fruits and Berries for the Home Garden*. New York: Alfred A. Knopf, 1977.

Logsdon, Gene. *Successful Berry Growing: How to Plant, Prune, Pick, and Preserve Bush and Vine Fruits*. Emmaus, Pa.: Rodale Press, 1974.

Chapter 6

Art, Henry W. *A Garden of Wildflowers: 101 Native Species and How to Grow Them.* Pownal, Vt.: Storey Communications, 1989.

Austin, Richard L. *Wild Gardening: Strategies and Procedures Using Native Plantings.* New York: Simon and Schuster, 1986.

Brown, Lauren. *Grasses: An Identification Guide.* Boston: Houghton Mifflin, 1979.

Brumback, William E. and David R. Longland. *Garden in the Woods Cultivation Guide.* Framingham, Mass.: New England Wildflower Society, 1986.

Curtis, Will C. and William E. Brumback. *Propagation of Wildflowers.* Framingham, Mass.: New England Wildflower Society, 1986.

Diekelmann, John and Robert Schuster. *Natural Landscaping: Designing with Native Plant Communities.* New York: McGraw-Hill Book Company, 1982.

Druse, Ken. *The Natural Garden.* New York: Clarkson Potter Publishers, 1989.

Martin, Laura C. *The Wildflower Meadow Book: A Gardener's Guide.* Charlotte, N.C.: East Woods Press Books, 1986.

Meyer, Mary Hockenberry. *Ornamental Grasses.* New York: Charles Scribner's Sons, 1975.

North Carolina Wildflower Preservation Society. *North Carolina Native Plant Propagation Handbook.* Chapel Hill, N.C.: North Carolina Wildflower Preservation Society, 1977.

Ottesen, Carole. *Ornamental Grasses: The Amber Wave.* New York: McGraw-Hill Publishing Co., 1989.

——. *The New American Garden: A Manifesto for Today's Gardener.* New York: Macmillan Co., 1987.

Paulson, Annie, ed. *The National Wildflower Research Center's Wildflower Handbook.* Austin, Tex.: Texas Monthly Press, 1989.

Reinhardt, Thomas A., Martina Reinhardt, and Mark Moskowitz. *Ornamental Grass Gardening.* Los Angeles: HP Books, Price Stern Sloan, 1989.

Sawyers, Claire, ed. *Gardening With Wildflowers & Native Plants.* Brooklyn, N.Y.: Brooklyn Botanic Garden, 1989.

Smith, J. Robert with Beatrice S. Smith. *The Prairie Garden: 70 Native Plants You Can Grow in Town or Country.* Madison, Wis.: University of Wisconsin Press, 1980.

Wilson, William. *Landscaping with Wildflowers & Native Plants.* San Francisco: Ortho Books, Chevron Chemical Co., 1984.

Tools for Weekend Gardeners

Crockett, James Underwood. *Crockett's Tool Shed.* Boston: Little, Brown and Company, 1979.

Damrosch, Barbara. *The Garden Primer.* New York: Workman Publishing, 1988.

Foster, Lee. *Gardening Techniques.* San Francisco: Ortho Books, Chevron Chemical Co., 1984.

Nunn, Richard V. *Repair, Maintain, & Store Lawnmowers & Garden Equipment.* Passaic, N.J.: Creative Homeowner Press, 1984.

Rodale's *Organic Gardening* magazine Editors. *The Encyclopedia of Organic Gardening.* Emmaus, Pa.: Rodale Press, 1978.

Roth, Susan A., ed. *All About Pruning.* rev. ed. San Francisco: Ortho Books, Chevron Chemical Co., 1989.

Sunset Books and *Sunset* magazine Editors. *Sunset Introduction to Basic Gardening.* Menlo Park, Calif.: Lane Publishing Co., 1981.

——. *Waterwise Gardening: Beautiful Gardens with Less Water.* Menlo Park, Calif.: Lane Publishing Co. 1989.

Williams, Jeff T. *How to Select, Use, & Maintain Garden Equipment.* San Francisco: Ortho Books, Chevron Chemical Co., 1981.

Regional Gardening Books

Doolittle, Rosalie. *Southwest Gardening*. Albuquerque, N. Mex.: University of New Mexico Press, 1967.

Duffield, Mary Rose and Warren D. Jones. *Plants for Dry Climates: How to Select, Grow, & Enjoy*. Tucson, Ariz.: HP Books, 1981.

Halfacre, Gordon R. and Anne R. Shawcroft. *Landscape Plants of the Southeast*. Raleigh, N.C.: Sparks Press, 1979.

Ladendorf, Sandra. *Successful Southern Gardening: A Practical Guide for Year-Round Beauty*. Chapel Hill, N.C.: University of North Carolina Press, 1989.

Perry, Bob. *Trees and Shrubs for Dry California Landscapes: Plants for Water Conservation*. San Dimas, Calif.: Land Design Publishing, 1987.

Phillips, Judith. *Southwestern Landscaping with Native Plants*. Santa Fe, N. Mex.: Museum of New Mexico Press, 1988.

Snyder, Leon C. *Gardening in the Upper Midwest*. Minneapolis, Minn.: University of Minnesota Press, 1985.

Sunset Books and *Sunset* magazine Editors. *Sunset Western Garden Book*. Menlo Park, Calif.: Lane Publishing Co., 1988.

INDEX

Page references in *italic* indicate tables.

Rodale Press, Inc., publishes RODALE'S ORGANIC GARDENING, the all-time favorite gardening magazine.
For information on how to order your subscription, write to RODALE'S ORGANIC GARDENING, Emmaus, PA 18098.